# Professional Spiritual & Pastoral Care

## *Other Professional Spiritual & Pastoral Care Resources from SkyLight Paths*

---

**College & University Chaplaincy in the 21st Century**
A Multifaith Look at the Practice of Ministry
on Campuses across America
*Edited by Rev. Dr. Lucy Forster-Smith*
*Foreword by Rev. Janet M. Cooper Nelson*

**Disaster Spiritual Care**
Practical Clergy Responses to Community,
Regional and National Tragedy
*Edited by Rabbi Stephen B. Roberts, BCJC and*
*Rev. Willard W. C. Ashley Sr., DMin, DH*

**How to Be a Perfect Stranger, 5th Edition**
The Essential Religious Etiquette Handbook
*Edited by Stuart M. Matlins and Arthur J. Magida*

**Jewish Pastoral Care, 2nd Edition**
A Practical Handbook from Traditional & Contemporary Sources
*Edited by Rabbi Dayle A. Friedman, MSW, MAJCS, BCC*
(A book from Jewish Lights, SkyLight Paths' sister imprint)

**Learning to Lead**
Lessons in Leadership for People of Faith
*Edited by Rev. Willard W. C. Ashley Sr., MDiv, DMin, DH*

**The Perfect Stranger's Guide to Funerals and Grieving Practices**
A Guide to Etiquette in Other People's Religious Ceremonies
*Edited by Stuart M. Matlins*

**Show Me Your Way**
The Complete Guide to Exploring Interfaith Spiritual Direction
*By Howard A. Addison*

**Spiritual Guidance across Religions**
A Sourcebook for Spiritual Directors and Other Professionals Providing
Counsel to People of Differing Faith Traditions
*Edited by Rev. John R. Mabry, PhD*

# Professional Spiritual & Pastoral Care

## A Practical Clergy and Chaplain's Handbook

Edited by
Rabbi Stephen B. Roberts, MBA, MHL, BCJC

In consultation with:
Chaplain D.W. Donovan, MA, MS, BCC
Rev. George Handzo, MDiv, BCC, CSSBB
Rev. Dr. Martha R. Jacobs, MDiv, DMin, BCC
Bishop Dr. Teresa E. Snorton, MDiv, DMin, BCC, ACPE Supervisor

*Walking Together, Finding the Way*®
SKYLIGHT PATHS®
PUBLISHING
Woodstock, Vermont

*Professional Spiritual & Pastoral Care:*
*A Practical Clergy and Chaplain's Handbook*

2014 Hardcover Edition, Fourth Printing



**Library of Congress Cataloging-in-Publication Data**
Professional spiritual & pastoral care : a practical clergy and chaplain's handbook / edited by Stephen B. Roberts in consultation with D.W. Donovan ... [et al.].
p. cm.
Includes bibliographical references and index.
ISBN 978-1-59473-312-3 (hardcover)
1. Pastoral care. I. Roberts, Stephen, 1958– II. Title: Professional spiritual and pastoral care.
BV4011.3.P76 2011
253—dc23

2011033433

ISBN 978-1-59473-403-8 (eBook)
10 9 8 7 6 5 4

Cover Design: Gloria Todt
Manufactured in the United States of America

SkyLight Paths Publishing is creating a place where people of different spiritual traditions come together for challenge and inspiration, a place where we can help each other understand the mystery that lies at the heart of our existence.

SkyLight Paths sees both believers and seekers as a community that increasingly transcends traditional boundaries of religion and denomination—people wanting to learn from each other, *walking together, finding the way.*®



*Walking Together, Finding the Way*®
Published by SkyLight Paths® Publishing
A Division of LongHill Partners, Inc.
Sunset Farm Offices, Route 4, P.O. Box 237
Woodstock, VT 05091
Tel: (802) 457-4000 Fax: (802) 457-4004
www.skylightpaths.com

This book is dedicated to mentors, teachers, and supervisors:

Sr. Theresa C. Brophy, ACPE Supervisor, and Rabbi Zahara Davidowitz-Farkas, MHL, BCJC, CPSP Diplomate Supervisor
*During my first unit of CPE, you both opened my eyes to the love of chaplaincy, and then during my year of residency, you inspired me to become the best chaplain possible.*

Rev. George Handzo, MDiv, BCC, CSSBB, and Rev. Curtis W. Hart, MDiv, BCC, CPSP Diplomate Supervisor
*You both believed in me, encouraged me, and mentored me in ways too numerous to count.*

Rabbi Ari Fridkis
*You continue to help me grow to my full potential.*
*You are a living* b'rachah.

Rabbi Dr. Richard F. Address and Dr. Leonard M. Lodish
*When I dreamed of sacred service, you both encouraged me and helped open doors. It is truly the "little things" that can make such a big difference in the world.*

R. E. Hellman, MD
*Without your continued support, love, and endless patience, none of my work in the field of chaplaincy over the past two decades would ever have been possible.*

# Contents

# Introduction

*Rabbi Stephen B. Roberts, MBA, MHL, BCJC*

## *Why This Book Now?*

Professional chaplaincy within the United States and Canada is rapidly evolving. Over the past ten years standards have been developed and published, the major chaplaincy organizations have hosted numerous joint Canadian / U.S. conferences and workshops, and the leaders of many of the organizations are now involved and work together across the United States and Canada.

The field has produced many great resources to help us move forward. This handbook / textbook developed out of numerous conversations I had at many recent chaplaincy conferences. A commonly repeated question was "Is there one place I can turn to in my desire to learn about / keep current the basic skills that I need to do effective professional chaplaincy / spiritual / pastoral care—whether as a congregational clergy member, a seminarian, or a professional chaplain?" Chaplains in particular were asking whether a single resource existed for learning and developing expertise in the newest areas of expected proficiency of a professional chaplain: quality improvement; strategic planning; research; developing and implementing tactical plans regarding who a chaplain should see; and outcome oriented chaplaincy. Educators—both CPE and seminary based—asked about a single current source for helping their students become familiar with core pastoral care skills.

The answer to all the previous questions, up until now, has been no. The field is rapidly professionalizing, and this resource is part of that development. No other current resource similar to this handbook exists. The closest is Rabbi Dayle A. Friedman's *Jewish Pastoral Care,*

*2nd Edition: A Practical Handbook from Traditional & Contemporary Sources* (Jewish Lights). This resource is a superb "201"-level text directed to a specific religious community. I strongly recommend it for all professional chaplains. However, there is no current *basic* "101"-level text. The text in your hands now fills this professional void.

## *Who Is This Book For?*

This book is not intended to be read at one sitting. Rather, it is designed with four specific groups, and their learning needs, in mind. It is intended to be used as a critical reference and learning tool, over time. *It was designed to be easily picked up, used for specific learning, and then put down again.* Each chapter is freestanding. When similar material is covered in more than one chapter, references are provided.

The first group of readers this book is designed for is current congregational clergy. Only recently have seminaries started to consistently teach professional pastoral skills to seminarians. Thus, the materials in this book may not have been available to you during your seminary studies. Further, many of you called to lead congregations have never had the opportunity to even attend seminary. This book is for both groups of current congregational clergy. This handbook will help you, leaders of faith communities, improve and / or keep your pastoral skills professional, helpful, and caring.

Seminarians (and their professors), you are the next for whom this book is intended. You will soon be serving in congregations, schools, nonprofits, chaplaincies—including health care, corrections, the military. More and more the expectations are that from the initial moment you are sent forth to serve—whether as a new priest, minister, reverend, rabbi, imam, cantor, sister, brother—you will have a strong foundation of pastoral and spiritual care skills. This resource is designed with you and your seminary coursework in mind. This book will be a resource not only while in school, but throughout the decades you serve in faith leadership positions.

Clinical pastoral education (CPE) students and educators: action, reflection, action is the model to help learn basic chaplaincy / pastoral care skills. Yet, there is a strong need to have a consistent framework for the skill sets needed to develop using action, reflection, action. This book is for you. Concepts are clearly laid out by many of the leading professionals in the field. However, only with hard work will you be able to transform the concepts covered in this book into personal proficiencies you can call upon with comfort and regularity.

Finally, professional chaplains, this is our book as well. We have taken many different paths and journeys to get the initials BCC / BCJC (board certified chaplain / board certified Jewish chaplain) after our names. As professionals helping to continue to develop our field, we have a strong mandate for continuing education to improve our skills. This handbook is designed to be a resource in this task.

## *How to Use This Book*

This book is laid out in four parts. The first part focuses on how two professionals developed their own theological grounding for doing chaplaincy / spiritual / pastoral care. The heart of part 1 is on the *how* it was developed. The goal is to allow each reader to explore, grow, and develop his or her theological grounds for doing this work. All readers should find this section helpful. I also strongly recommend that you refer to section 1 of *Jewish Pastoral Care*, published by Jewish Lights, which contains four more similar chapters. No matter what your religion, these combined six chapters will help you explore your own foundational theology for doing chaplaincy / spiritual / pastoral care.

Part 2, composed of sixteen chapters, focuses on the "core" skills one needs to be able to provide professional-level chaplaincy / spiritual / pastoral care, no matter what setting one finds oneself. This is really the foundational "101"-course-level material of chaplaincy / spiritual / pastoral care. It covers a broad range of topics, including the following: What is "reflective listening," a term used so often but often not explained, and how do I develop my ability with this needed expertise? What exactly is "life review" from a chaplaincy / spiritual / pastoral perspective, and how do I build the expertise to feel comfortable helping someone I am working with in this process? What are some of the major issues that commonly arise in chaplaincy / spiritual / pastoral care—such as hope, guilt, shame—and how do I work with these issues? Again, all readers should find spending time with the chapters of this section valuable and spiritually rewarding.

Part 3 is composed of seven shorter chapters. Each contributor was asked to answer the following question: "What are the particular chaplaincy / spiritual / pastoral / religious needs of this group, and how does a chaplain minister to them?"

The last section of eight chapters is focused on specific topics that professional chaplains, and those studying to become one, need to be aware of and to practice in their professional lives. The topics covered in part 4 are becoming "standards" and thus required for continued certification and development. We are rapidly developing as a profession. Part 4 covers many issues that as little as ten years ago were not even on our professional radars. These include outcome oriented chaplaincy, quality improvement, strategic planning, and research. Every current and future BCC / BCJC will find it valuable to spend considerable time with this section.

Most chapters in the book have either endnotes or a bibliography (or both). *The articles and books cited within the endnotes should be considered part of a chapter's bibliography.* Space limitations did not allow sources to be published twice within the same chapter.

## *Who Was Involved in Creating This Book?*

It takes collaboration among professionals to develop this type of resource. Four colleagues acted as contributing consultants in helping develop this handbook: D. W. Donovan, George Handzo, Martha R. Jacobs, and Teresa E. Snorton. They have given untold hours in helping me think through the design of this book, who should contribute, and what they should contribute. Further, each consultant was also the primary author of at least one chapter. Some consultants were coauthors on other chapters as well. Each has been responsible for helping develop this book.

The contributing consultants were invited to participate first because of their particular professional expertise, which they have shared through a chapter. Equally important in this process of consultant invitations was making sure that at least one person from the Association for Clinical Pastoral Education, Association of Professional Chaplains, National Association of Catholic Chaplains, and National Association of Jewish Chaplains, whether from a volunteer or a professional basis, had an active role in making sure the educational and training needs they were familiar with within their organization were directly addressed. *They in no way acted for their organization.* Rather, through their wisdom, knowledge, and insights, they functioned as a voice for those with whom they work closest in a professional capacity.

Chapter contributors to the book are leaders in the field of chaplaincy. Many have written and published extensively. You will find many of their names associated with a wide range of innovative projects such as *The White Paper*, *Common Standards for Professional Chaplaincy*, and *Standards of Practice for Professional Chaplains in Acute Care Settings*, which have moved the field of professional chaplaincy forward in significant ways over the past decade. Contributors include seven past presidents from the organizations just listed plus the current executive director of another. Most contributors have served in national leadership positions within at least one chaplaincy organization, some in more. Active effort was also made to reach out and include leading members of both the Canadian Association for Spiritual Care / Association Canadienne de Soins Spirituels and the College of Pastoral Supervision & Psychotherapy as contributors.

I offer gratitude to all those who participated in making this book possible.

# PART I

# *Theology of Spiritual / Pastoral Care*

# 1

## *Creating a Personal Theology to Do Spiritual / Pastoral Care*

*Rev. Dr. Martha R. Jacobs, MDiv, DMin, BCC*

An eighty-five-year-old man was dying. He seemed to be having a very difficult time with his impending death. The nursing staff asked the chaplain to talk with him, because they sensed that there was something that he needed to deal with and hoped that the chaplain could find out what that was and help him. After establishing a relationship with Sam (not his real name), the chaplain began a life review with him, which took several days, because Sam did not have the stamina for long conversations. Sam talked about his work as a philanthropist and how much pleasure he had found in helping those less fortunate than him. During those conversations, the chaplain was aware (as the staff had indicated) that Sam seemed to want to tell her something but always stopped short of doing so. After several days, and sensing that Sam had come to trust her, the chaplain told him that she thought there was something he wanted to tell her but wasn't. Sam's eyes welled up with tears. He whispered to the chaplain that he thought he was going to go to hell because he had stolen when he was six years old. The chaplain asked him to tell her about it. Sam spent the next ten minutes describing in detail how he stole a candy bar from a store. She asked him why he stole it. He told her that his siblings were very, very hungry (because of the Depression) and that he hoped the candy bar would keep them from starving. He stole the candy bar, went home, and shared it with them. Sam described how much they enjoyed it and how it seemed to make their world seem a little less hopeless. Then, in almost a whisper, he said that stealing was a sin and that he would have to pay for his sin by going to hell when he died.

The chaplain then asked Sam to tell her about who God was for him. Sam described a God who was loving and open to those who sought to do good in their lives and was always there for them. She asked if he thought that God would forgive someone if they sought that forgiveness from their heart. Sam said, "Absolutely." She asked him if he had sought forgiveness from his heart from God for stealing the candy bar. He hesitated and then said that he had. The chaplain asked if he thought that God had forgiven him. Sam paused for a few seconds and then said quietly, "Yes." She thought for a moment and then asked Sam if he had forgiven himself for stealing the candy bar. He started to cry almost uncontrollably. As she sat there with him, the chaplain thought about how Sam had carried this burden with him all his life. He was a successful businessman who generously gave to those who were most in need of food and shelter. Yet, what was foremost in his mind as he lay dying was the retribution that lay ahead for him for stealing that candy bar.

When his crying subsided, she asked Sam to pray with her. The chaplain prayed that Sam would feel God's love surrounding him, that he would be as loving and accepting of himself as God was, and that he would come to forgive himself for trying to take care of his siblings in the only way a six-year-old could manage. She also prayed that he would come to a deeper understanding of forgiveness.[1]

## *As a Chaplain—My Theology*

This story is an encounter I had with one particular patient. As a chaplain, I could have handled Sam in many different ways. I could have affirmed his belief that he was going to hell. I could have chastised him for stealing but then, since he believed that God was a forgiving God, say that God would forgive him. I could have made light of his stealing (since it was *only* a candy bar) and waived the need to seek forgiveness. I could have left Sam to wonder what would happen to him and not helped him come to "peace" with what was clearly taunting him as he was dying. I am sure that there are other possible outcomes you could suggest as well.

My decision to help him find forgiveness was based on his *own* belief of who God was for him. Since I did not know anything about his belief system, I needed to find out what his theology was before trying to help him deal with his guilt. I could not make any assumptions, even though on the hospital census it said he was "Protestant." It was important to find out what he thought about his God before moving forward with my intervention. If I had not done that, I might have gone down a path that was not in keeping with Sam's own belief system. I might have brought about more confusion and pain for him. I might not have allowed for his own set of beliefs to bring him to a place where he could accept what he had done and also accept the forgiveness he so desperately sought. Sam's theology was different from how he had been raised—since he believed that he would go to "hell" for stealing, which came from his childhood experiences in church. He also believed that God was a forgiving God but could not reconcile his youth image of God with his adult image of God. Later, when I asked Sam why he had not discussed his fear with his own minister, he said that he was afraid to have his fears confirmed. Hence, my need to understand *his* theology before trying to work with him. Affirming Sam in *his* belief system did not in any way affirm or deny *my own* theology.

My theology has to be large enough to accept the theology of those whom I serve, whether they be Christian, Buddhist, Jewish, Muslim, Sikh, Catholic, Humanist, or Atheist. If I cannot support a patient (or family member or staff person) in his or her theology, then I cannot serve as a multifaith professional chaplain. In order to be an effective multifaith chaplain, I need to be secure in my own belief system. I also need to be able to be open to understanding and interpreting Sam's theology and that of any other patient, family member, or staff person with whom I come into contact. I have to be open to other people's theology and help them through using their belief system, not my own.

## *Dual-Track Mind-Set and Heart-Set*

So, how did I get to this place—this ability to put aside my own theology so that I can support the needs of my patients? The development of my theology has taken most of my life and continues to inform how I practice chaplaincy care. I was raised Jewish and became a Christian at the age of seventeen. For many reasons, once I converted, I chose to "ignore" my Jewish roots—that is, until I was in clinical pastoral education at St. Luke's Roosevelt Hospital and, over the course of an overnight on-call assignment, realized that in order to serve *all* patients, I was going to have to reclaim my Judaic roots. Otherwise, I would not be able to be fully open to Jewish patients.

As God would have it, I was on call one night when I was paged at 10:00 p.m., for a patient who was Jewish and was dying. The patient expressed that he wanted to see his rabbi and gave me his name and the town he lived in, but couldn't tell me the name of his synagogue. Luckily, I was able to find his rabbi (this was in the days before Google). He lived about an hour from the hospital. I was concerned that he would not want to travel so far, so late in the evening, but he showed up about 11:30 p.m. I went with him to the patient's room but stayed outside, allowing private time for the rabbi with his congregant. As I listened, I heard the rabbi begin the *Sh'ma*, the Jewish prayer that every Jewish child learns at a very early age: שְׁמַע יִשְׂרָאֵל יְהוָה אֱלֹהֵינוּ יְהוָה אֶחָד (*Sh'ma Yisra'el Adonai Eloheinu Adonai Echad)*, "Hear, Israel, the Lord is our God, the Lord is One." As he recited it, I could hear the patient's respirator begin to slow down; the patient was clearly soothed by hearing this prayer. After several minutes, the rabbi came out of the room, and I commented that "the *Sh'ma* really made a difference for him." The rabbi looked at me and asked how I knew the *Sh'ma*. I was not sure how he would respond to my story but decided that it was time to face up to my own feelings around my Jewish heritage. So, I told him that I had been raised Jewish but was now a Christian. This rabbi was a real blessing for me. He could have yelled at me or dismissed me. Instead, the rabbi and I spent the night in the waiting room talking while going back and forth to his congregant's room.

At 6:30 a.m., his congregant died. The rabbi and I had spent all night talking and crying and laughing not only about my history but about his as well. As we parted ways, he said to me, "Judaism is clearly the loser. You are going to be an excellent chaplain, able to take care of all of God's people. May God bless you in your work." After he left, I cried as I began the healing of what had been two distinct and separate "lives"—first as a Jew and then as a Christian.

This "chance" encounter allowed me to begin to open the door to my Jewish heritage, which I knew inherently I needed to embrace in order to be the best chaplain I could be. As the rabbi had said to me, he believed I would "take care of all of God's people," and I knew I needed to do a lot of work in order to fulfill his words.

As I continued to process and integrate my heritage into my Christian beliefs and life, I found that I was able to be more open not only to Jewish patients, but also to patients of all different backgrounds, faiths, and traditions. Being in New York City—a true melting pot of faiths, traditions, cultures, and people—"made" me be more open to the "other."

It also made me face my own racism—of which I was unaware—when I was paged to go to the emergency room to be with a mother whose son had shot himself in the head. The child would survive, but the mother was in need of pastoral care. As I walked into the room, I had to overcome my shock when I saw that the mother was a Caucasian woman and not an African American woman, which is what I assumed I would find. Even though the hospital was located in Harlem and it was more likely that the person would be African American, the fact that I had made an assumption was clearly wrong. This was another way that I had to look at my theology and deal with any racism that was within me so that I could take care of all of God's people.

I was given a chance to do that when paged to the ER on a different overnight (while still in training) when a twenty-eight-year-old man had been killed in a gun battle; he was an innocent bystander. His family was coming in and had to be told that their loved one had died. As I sat with this family, who was African American, I wondered to myself whether I would be able to be of help to this family—our lives were as different as our skin color. As the night wore on and more and more family showed up, I found that not only was I able to be present with them, but I was also able to provide chaplaincy care to them, not because of the color of our skin, but because I had learned about who God was for them and how they lived their theology. My prayers reflected their theology and their God and enabled them to begin their grieving process. I learned that it was not about me and what I believed; it was about them and what their belief system was and who God was for them. And how did I find out? I asked them questions and listened to their conversations as they talked about how they lived their lives. I did not make any assumptions about them—except to initially think that I would not be able to help them because of my own racism. I learned that grief is grief—it doesn't matter one's skin color or culture—the pain of loss is the pain of loss, especially what seems to be "senseless" loss. Being present to them was what was important and made the difference. Equally important was my being able to be open to who their God was and to help them access their God at a time of such pain and anguish. Again, my theology had to be large enough to take their theology "into" myself for that period of time.

Oddly enough, while being open to their theology, I was silently praying to "my" God, that I would have the wisdom and the patience and the openness to serve them as they needed to be served. So, I had my own theology going in my heart, while I was also using professional chaplaincy skills such as reflective listening to allow them to affirm their theology with honesty and integrity. This dual-track mind-set and heart-set, I believe, is what enables professional chaplains to remain connected to their own theology while also supporting and enabling another's theology.

## *Prayer*

Writing about praying reminded me of the other aspect of my theology that needs to be large enough to provide appropriate chaplaincy care. Prayer is a very personal thing. It is also corporate and different for different people. Patients taught me so much about how they relate to whomever they call God. Some Protestant patients prayed only through Jesus. Many Roman Catholic patients said that they prayed to Mary or to another saint. Jewish patients prayed in their own special way. Some patients followed a pattern that they learned in church, mosque, temple, or synagogue. Some prayed silently, afraid to utter a word. Some offered prayers that flowed from their hearts.

I remember being most concerned about praying in seminary. At the start of each class, students were encouraged to lead the class in prayer. Each student prayed in his or her own way. I began to worry because at least once before leaving seminary, I would be called on to lead prayer. I went through a praying crisis because I thought I was doing it wrong.

The simple truth is that nobody ever taught me how to pray spontaneously. So I wondered if I could have been praying wrong. Was I now in seminary to learn that my praying had been misdirected or misconceived? Was God angry with me for the way I prayed? Also, I often prayed when walking down the street or traveling to work on the subway. Was this form of praying okay?

Well, my day came in class and I got up to pray. As I was walking to the front of the room, I prayed that what I was going to pray would not be offensive to anyone. When I finished leading the class in prayer, I looked up, and no one was looking at me strangely. Class went on as usual. I breathed a sigh of relief and prayed a quick "thank you" as I sat down. The crisis was over, for the moment.

Then I started training to be a chaplain. Boy, was I scared when I found out that we had to pray with patients—out loud! Again, I wasn't sure what to do. Was I praying right? Would patients feel comforted or confused by my prayers? What if I got tongue-tied or paused for a moment? Would that be okay with the patient and with God?

I was too embarrassed to ask my peers about the right way to pray. I assumed they knew better. Then I encountered the African American family I mentioned above. When paged, I went to be with them armed with the Episcopal *Book of Common Prayer*, which my peers used. I was ready to pray just the right words. I just knew that this book had the right prayers in it. Well, after the first prayer, I realized that this book didn't reflect what was going on for this family. So, I closed the book and began to pray from my heart. God's Spirit guided my words. This felt much better and much more personal.

## *Conversation as Prayer*

One of the things that surprised me when I first started working as a chaplain was the number of patients who felt like our entire conversation had been a prayer. Many patients believed that God had been listening to our conversation, so additional prayer was unnecessary. And that was a powerful lesson to learn; praying really is conversing.

I had not considered this possibility until I met a patient whom I will call Celene. Celene had been in and out of the hospital for nine months. When she had come into the hospital this time, she was frailer than she had been previously. She had advanced lung cancer. She was HIV positive, had a daughter who was HIV positive, and had a grandchild on the way. Our last visit revolved around her concerns for her daughter's and her grandchild's well-being. She was very anxious about them and how they would do without her. We talked about what it would feel like for her to give her anxieties about her daughter and grandchild over to God. As we talked, it came out that she felt guilty that she had given her daughter the HIV virus and that her grandchild might also be carrying the virus. In the midst of our conversation, it became clear that Celene was seeking forgiveness from God. She was opening her heart to God's Spirit, who was sighing deeply for Celene. Celene believed that God was a forgiving God. She said that it felt like our conversation was an open prayer to God.

I have come to believe that we each have our own idea of who God is for us and we each have a personal relationship with God. Our prayers usually reflect the individual nature of our relationship with God. Therefore, when praying with patients (or family members or staff people), I ask them what they would like me to pray for and offer them the opportunity to offer a prayer in their own words. I pray with them, allowing my own theology to expand, whether I am saying the Hail Mary or the *Sh'ma*.

## *Final Words*

Most books about a "theology of pastoral care" come from the Christian traditions and are, therefore, heavy into Christ and the tenets of Christianity. Therefore, it is difficult to give you a sense of what I mean by a "theology of pastoral care" that encompasses all that we are—and who we are—and whose we are—because theology is an individual and very personal matter. But, since we are also responsible to our faith community, we must maintain this dual-track mind-set and heart-set.

Were I to try to compare my theology with that of another United Church of Christ non-chaplain clergyperson, the other person's would look very different. I believe that to be the case for any chaplain and his or her denominational colleagues, because the work that multifaith chaplains do requires that they be open to hearing another's theology and working with *that* theology to assist the patient (or family member or staff). I have to be actively in touch with my own theology but not actively "use" it (i.e., espouse it) in order to do that. I would expect my non-chaplain colleagues to "use" their theology when counseling or providing pastoral care to one of their own congregants. That is what is expected—a house of worship clergyperson espouses the theology of the denomination of which he or she is a part. Professional chaplains must be able to move aside their own belief system(s) / theology and support the system of the person to whom they are providing chaplaincy care. We don't forget our own theology. But our theology has to be large enough to enable us to be open to the theology of the "other"—a theology that enables people to function in the situation in which they find themselves.

My job is to help them refind their theology and tap into it to sustain them through this crisis in their life. In the end, my theology has become stronger and firmer as I have come to embrace the other and welcome the other into my heart.

## Notes

1. Adapted from Martha R. Jacobs, *A Clergy Guide to End-of-Life Issues* (Cleveland: Pilgrim Press, 2010), 77–78.

## About the Contributor

**Rev. Dr. Martha R. Jacobs, MDiv, DMin, BCC,** is the author of *A Clergy Guide to End-of-Life Issues*. She provides workshops throughout the country for clergy and congregations on end-of-life issues. Martha is an adjunct professor at New York Theological Seminary, where she is the coordinator for the Doctor of Ministry in Pastoral Care and a per diem chaplain at New York Presbyterian Hospital, Columbia Campus. She is the founding managing editor of *PlainViews*.

# 2

## *Creating a Personal Theology to Do Spiritual / Pastoral Care*

*Rev. David B. Plummer, BCC, LMFT*

Why do pastoral care? What motivates a person, presumably a religious person, to care for another human being? In today's predominant culture—at least in the American marketplace / workplace—of materialism, competitiveness, amassing and utilizing wealth and power, the very act of taking the time, effort, and emotional energy to help another human being is counterintuitive. It is contrary to the culture. Yet, every year thousands positively respond to a sense of "call" and matriculate to seminaries of many faiths, rabbinical schools, and so on. They enter residencies, apprenticeships, internships, and the like. They often go into debt and suffer from inadequate material support, and their lives and schedules put a strain on both their own sensibilities and bodies and those of their friends and families. Yet they *choose* to respond affirmatively to this call. Why?

For me, the answer is a simple: "Because we are made in the image of God." I believe that God cares about and for the world that God created. Inherent in that creation is an expectation of a partnership with humanity for the maintenance of and stewardship with the creation. Some people seem to hear clearly that call to partnership. Others, it would seem, do not hear that call at all. Still others not only do not hear the voice of the One who calls, but also do not believe in the very existence of the One who calls. So, for me, creating a personal theology of doing pastoral care starts with hearing the voice of the One who calls, then choosing to respond affirmatively to the call.

What next? Now that I the author, or you the reader, has heard the call and responded with "yes" to God, what does that response entail?

A few months ago, a former graduate student counseling intern under my supervision (and presently a clinical pastoral education supervisor-in-training) asked me about my own philosophy or theology of pastoral care. My response was that I did not know, but if she asked me a specific, practical question, I could probably respond to it in a meaningful manner. Hearing my own curious response, I exclaimed, "My, isn't that odd! I have some core values and beliefs that are clear to me, but I will have to think about them, as I am not consciously aware of what they are." I have been pondering the question and response ever since.

In reflecting on the question for several months, I found that there are several core values that are key to me in my personal theology for doing pastoral care—all values that are seemingly reflected from the image of God. I suspect that the core values may also be helpful to other caregivers creating their own personal theologies: honesty, integrity, and consistency. Additionally shaping my personal theology are the human qualities of advocacy, relevancy, and understanding of the human condition and understanding God's grace, and—of course—a desire to be found pleasing to the One who calls and found faithful and attentive to that call.

In the application of these values and qualities, I have found that for myself, there is no specific methodology in creating a personal theology of pastoral care. In fact, it really seems like a dynamic swirl as these values and qualities come into implementation in different ways, at different times, and in differing emphases with each caregiver and the context(s) in which the caregivers find themselves.

## *Honesty*

Honesty involves operating in the truth regardless of circumstances and political climate or consequences of the same. And this is especially true when developing one's theology of doing pastoral care. For instance, a number of pastoral caregivers, particularly from my faith community, like to base their theology of care and their pastoral identity and practice on a number of favorite biblical passages. And to me, this is generally acceptable.

However, there is often a problem or two with this approach. The problem is that when these pastoral caregivers use scripture, they often do so independent of the historical context of the passage, independent and uninformed of the cultural context of the passage, and sometimes independent of the proper and clearly intended linguistic meaning of the passage. The caregiver is not being honest to the biblical text. And if the use of the passage is inappropriate, then the theological underpinning that the caregiver is (mis)using this passage for is equally inappropriate.

## *Personal Integrity and Pluralism*

Without integrity, ultimately one has little to say or ministry to do. If one lacking integrity does attempt to provide pastoral care, it is (or ultimately will be) rejected and disrespected—sometimes quietly and covertly and sometimes very openly. Yet, it is unfortunately common to see professional pastoral caregivers from all traditions succumb to not honoring pluralism. Although all the major professional pastoral care certifying organizations in North America (American Association of Pastoral Counselors, Association for Clinical Pastoral Education, Association of Professional Chaplains, Canadian Association for Spiritual Care / Association Canadienne de Soins Spirituels, College of Pastoral Supervision and Psychotherapy, National Association of Catholic Chaplains, National Association of Jewish Chaplains, and National Institute of Business and Industrial Chaplains) have codified and strongly worded statements of ethical practice that require the caregiver to care for all without prejudice (and to do the same when supervising subordinate pastoral caregivers), the statements are often violated. Stereotypes and presumptions continue. Integrity is also violated when the pastoral caregiver affirms a commitment to religious pluralism to gain employment and be placed in a position of trust, only to betray that trust by attempting to proselytize to the caregiver's belief system and / or cultural values.

I look forward to the day when, in the spirit of the Rev. Dr. Martin Luther King, Jr., people will be offered pastoral care or supervised by pastoral caregivers based not on the color of their skin, or on the practices of their culture, or on their ethnicity, or on the content of their faith—or lack thereof—or on their affluence, or their gender, or their sexual orientation and practices. They will be offered pastoral care because they are human beings in need of care—simply and purely.

## *Consistency*

Closely related to honesty is consistency. It is amazing how, as flawed human beings ourselves, pastoral caregivers seem to be very inconsistent (especially when political and relational circumstances seem to call for it). If a principle is truth, it is true all the time. If a practice is authentic and good and applicable to all, it should be so all the time. Hence, is there ever a time to ignore the truth or to choose to refrain from doing the right thing? Obviously the answer is "no." It is my hope that all caregivers will realize this and will seek to be consistent, always.

## *An Understanding of People, the Human Condition, and God's Grace*

All people are flawed (including the pastoral caregiver!). Yet, it is not the caregiver's place to judge or punish. Being made in the image of God, the caregiver accepts people as they are. Pastoral caregivers only want to see their clients whole and healthy—body, soul, and spirit. For those who may be enmeshed in guilt and regret, perhaps the caregiver will have the opportunity to offer them a glimpse—and maybe more—of the relief that comes with forgiveness and grace. And the caregiver may also offer an acceptance of the person that is unconditional. It grieves me greatly when I hear professional chaplaincy colleagues speak of this grace and acceptance and then, almost in the same breath, pass harsh judgment toward others who may not believe or behave as they do, or who have personal flaws that these colleagues do not understand. Sometimes it is a matter that "others" are just different in some way.

For instance, the U. S. Congress has voted to repeal the "Don't Ask, Don't Tell" policy and the president has signed this into law. Since I am an endorser, many have expressed to me deep upset by this change, in the chaplaincy community in general, and within the military chaplaincy community in particular. As I reflect upon my own personal theology as an Evangelical Christian and as an endorser for chaplains, I ask myself, "How can pastoral caregivers preach and practice grace and unconditional love and then act as though some people are unforgivable and should never receive acceptance for being who they are?" As I write, the military chaplaincy endorsing community's primary organization very recently wrestled with amending their statement of professional ethics that calls for military chaplains to minister to all. Specifically, "I will defend my colleagues and all persons in my pastoral care against discrimination that is based on gender, sexual orientation, race, religion, or national origin." While it is clear that individual chaplains will have reservations (e.g., personal, theological, denominational) with the statement, it is equally clear that, as professionals, chaplains are there to provide pastoral care to all—no exceptions. In my faith tradition there is a scripture that seems to address this inconsistency in practice: "If anyone says, 'I love God,' yet hates his brother, he is a liar. For anyone who does not love his brother, whom he has seen, cannot love God, whom he has not seen" (1 John 4:20, New International Version).

## *Orthopraxy*

Because so much of pastoral caregiving focuses on being "present" with the recipient(s) of the care, it seems appropriate to discuss doing the right things (orthopraxy). Hence, in creating a personal theology *to do* pastoral care, we must also include some activity.

Namely, *advocacy* is one act of orthopraxy—being an advocate for those unable to speak for themselves. This failure to speak up may be due to political conditions where to speak for oneself is dangerous personally and / or professionally, or perhaps due to prejudice, where any such communication will be ignored or, worse, attacked.

*Social justice* is another act of orthopraxy. From my religious tradition (Evangelical Christian), one of my favorite professors had a saying that "a personal gospel has social ramifications." We are to care for and about others and to communicate the great truth that God loves us all. No one is sinless. No one is better than another. As such, no one is to be treated with preference. It seems to me that pastoral caregivers should and often do understand this better (relatively speaking) than those in other professions. And as such, many pastoral caregivers are motivated to do what they do in order to be instruments of social justice in a world that often does not place a lot of emphasis on the same.

One last act of orthopraxy that comes to mind is *being relevant.* While the element of relevancy may seem a bit odd in developing a personal theology to do pastoral care, it perhaps can be better understood within the context of the presumed role of God in the affairs of humanity. Public Religion Institute in conjunction with Religion News Service conducted a poll the week after the March 11, 2011, earthquake and subsequent tsunami and nuclear crisis in Japan. Among the findings of this poll were that 84 percent of white Evangelical Christians and 76 percent of minority Christians believe that "God is in control of everything that happens in the world."[1] Implicit in that belief, for some, is that "God can use natural disasters to send messages."[2] Hence, in my opinion, it is important for caregivers developing their own personal theologies for caregiving that they do so with a view that they are,. perhaps, a part of God's loving response to the needs and needy of this world. Otherwise, we might turn an intentionally blind eye and deaf ear to the cries of the needy in our community or around the world—thinking that the needy and victimized were destined to be the objects of God's warning messages or, worse, wrath.

## *Final Words*

Creating a personal theology to do pastoral care starts with an understanding that humanity is indeed made in the likeness of God. The God I seek to reflect by my own life is a beneficent Being who cares about and for the needs and needy of the world. In my theology as a pastoral caregiver, I have sought to adopt the values of the One I love and worship—honesty, integrity, consistency—along with a very human desire to develop a better understanding of people and a better comprehension of the human condition and God's grace, and then apply these qualities in a very practical way with life-changing deeds. This is my approach to creating my personal theology for doing pastoral care. Now it's your, the reader's, turn!

### Notes

1. Nicole Neroulias, "Most Americans Don't Blame God for Natural Disasters," *Religious New Service*, March 24, 2011, p. 1, www.religionnews.com/index.php?/polls/americans_divided_on_whether_god_causes_disasters1.
2. Ibid.

### About the Contributor

**Rev. David B. Plummer, BCC, LMFT,** is the department head of Chaplaincy Services at Sentara CarePlex Hospital in Hampton, Virginia, in addition to being the religious endorsing body representative for his faith group, the Coalition of Spirit-filled Churches. In addition to being a board certified chaplain, he is a licensed psychotherapist and has served as a clinical supervisor for more than a decade for students from two graduate schools of counseling. Rev. Plummer is very active in the professional pastoral care community. His published works have appeared in a number of venues, but his favorites are the *Journal of Pastoral Care and Counseling* and *PlainViews*. He was recently elected chair-elect of the COMISS Network and chair-elect of the Endorsers Conference for Veterans Affairs Chaplaincy.

# PART II

# *The Process of Spiritual / Pastoral Care*

# 3

## *The Process of Spiritual / Pastoral Care*

### A General Theory for Providing Spiritual / Pastoral Care Using Palliative Care as a Paradigm

*Rev. George Handzo, MDiv, BCC, CSSBB*

The evidence for best practice in professional health care chaplaincy has been, and remains, disparate and disjointed. However, over the first decade of this century and at an increasing rate, the gaps in the "map" for how this practice should proceed are being filled in. A scan of the references in the field reveals a significant number of seminal works published in 2009 and 2010. Virtually all of the important standards for how health care chaplains should be certified and practice have been published since 2000. The first practice guidelines to officially call for board certified chaplains as part of specific health care teams appeared in 2009.[1]

The paradigm for how spiritual and religious needs are attended to in the health care process continues to shift. This shift is due to the increasing recognition of spirituality and religion as important to health, including the treatment of acute illness, coupled with the emerging recognition of what a professional, board certified chaplain can bring to this process. Increasingly, standards call for and chaplaincy training allows for the professional chaplain to be integrated into the health care team as the spiritual care professional. The model calls for the individual chaplain to focus on specific medical specialties as opposed to specific religions. This model requires a great deal more accountability and focus on outcomes than chaplains are used to. This accountability also requires a more robust skill set, including assessment, care planning, and understanding of concepts such as spiritual struggle and how it impacts patients' coping and decision making. These changes, in turn, require chaplains to be a great deal more focused and intentional in their practice than they have been previously.

Not only has chaplaincy not functioned this way in the past, but many chaplains also believe passionately that it should not function this way going forward. They believe that this form of intentional, outcome-focused practice violates some basic premises of who chaplains are—including not having an agenda and being the one person on the health care team who can simply be with the patient as a caring human being without a concern for outcomes. While this is a powerful argument and one not without merit, this chapter and this book will work from the premise that chaplains can only support imposing themselves on patients who are sick and suffering and can only support the claim that they should be financially supported as a part of the health care team to the extent that they can make the case that their presence and interventions make a difference and that difference contributes positively to the patient's and family members' coping with their situation and their healing.

## *Background*

There has been increasing awareness in health care of the relevance of understanding and treating the whole person, both body and spirit. This concept of "holistic care" has gained widespread acceptance. Studies have shown that a holistic model of care increases both patient satisfaction and cost-effectiveness.[2] Spiritual care is increasingly being promoted as an essential part of holistic care.[3] Furthermore, religious and spiritual beliefs and practices have been shown to be a major component of how patients cope with serious illness.[4]

Holistic care is a treatment philosophy that sets different and high expectations for standards of care both for health care facilities and for all the members of the health care team. Studies have shown that care that includes the spiritual dimension increases patient and family satisfaction and contributes to decreases in the extraordinary cost of excessive medical interventions at the end of life.[5]

Many people who would welcome and benefit from competent spiritual care during health crises do not receive such much-needed assistance from either religious or medical communities.[6] The spiritual needs of many patients in health care institutions are not being met.[7] All too often, health care workers do not consider the spiritual needs of their patients to be a priority. One study documented that only 42 percent of hospitalized patients could identify a spiritual counselor to whom they could turn.[8] Another study found that physicians—the central figures in treatment decisions—are less likely than all other hospital disciplines to believe it to be important to refer patients to chaplains.[9] Still other research noted that 72 percent of the cancer patients surveyed said their spiritual needs were minimally or not at all supported by the medical system.[10]

Research indicates patients' demand for spiritual care is high and increasing. A study found that 88 percent of patients in a palliative care unit with end-stage cancer expressed the desire to work with a chaplain.[11] The study also found that roughly 50 percent of patients indicated that they would like the chaplain to provide a sense of "presence," listen to them, visit with them, or accompany them on their journey.[12]

These results are particularly disturbing because religion plays an integral part in the lives of many Americans, and people are especially likely to turn to religion in response to stressful life events, including people who may not view themselves as religious.[13] According to a 1999 Gallup poll, 60 percent of American adults say religion is "very important." This figure was substantially higher (88 percent) among adults over sixty-five years of age.[14] Various studies seem to suggest that while Americans are less often affiliated with religious institutions, there is little or no decline in religious belief or practice.[15] The widespread use of religious coping has been documented in response to general emotional stress,[16] mental illness,[17] and medical illness,[18] particularly cancer.[19] Studies of older adults hospitalized for medical problems—a population that chaplains frequently assist—report that religion is their most important coping mechanism and that prayer is one of their most common religious activities.[20] Similarly, a national survey of American adults found that 35 percent of people pray about their health concerns.[21] Moreover, another study found that using religious support sources to cope with surgically related stress is associated with distinct subjective benefits beyond those contributed by nonreligious sources.[22] Lastly, there is increasing research in the field of spiritual struggle that indicates its importance and prevalence during times of stress such as illness.[23]

## Definitions

One of the major barriers to advancing the practice of spiritual care is a lack of definitional clarity among practitioners themselves. Specifically, "spiritual care," "pastoral care," and "chaplaincy care" have often been used interchangeably and without specific definitions. In writing their *Standards of Practice*, the Association of Professional Chaplains (APC) created a glossary that proposed to separate these terms. The definitions from the glossary are as follows:

> **Chaplaincy care:** Care provided by a board certified chaplain or by a student in an accredited clinical pastoral education program [e.g., Association for Clinical Pastoral Education (ACPE) in the United States; Canadian Association for Spiritual Care / Association Canadienne de Soins Spirituels (CASC / ACSS) in Canada]. Examples of such care include emotional, spiritual, religious, pastoral, ethical, and / or existential care.[24]
>
> **Pastoral care:** Coming out of the Christian tradition, "pastoral care developed within the socially contracted context of a religious or faith community wherein the 'pastor' or faith leader is the community's designated leader who oversees the faith and welfare of the community and wherein the community submits to or acknowledges the leader's overseeing. The 'faith' they share is a mutually received and agreed upon system of beliefs, actions, and values. The faith leader's care for his or her community is worked out within a dialectical relationship between the person's unique needs, on the one hand, and the established norms of the faith community, as represented by the pastor, on the other."[25] Pastoral care may form part of the care provided by a chaplain.
>
> **Spiritual care:** "Interventions, individual or communal, that facilitate the ability to express the integration of the body, mind, and spirit to achieve wholeness, health, and a sense of connection to self, others, and[/ or] a higher power."[26] Spiritual care forms part of the care provided by a chaplain.[27]

In sum, spiritual care is the overarching category representing a domain of care comparable to "emotional care" that can and should be performed to a greater or lesser degree by all health care professionals. Chaplaincy care is the part of that care performed by professional chaplains. Pastoral care is performed by chaplains and other religious professionals, usually with persons of their own faith tradition.

Another activity of many chaplains is to conduct a spiritual assessment and create a spiritual care plan. Fitchett and Canada have helpfully differentiated spiritual screening, spiritual history, and spiritual assessment.[28] Screening is defined as "a quick determination of whether a person is experiencing a serious spiritual / religious crisis and therefore needs an immediate referral to a professional chaplain. Good models of spiritual / religious screening employ a few, simple questions, which can be asked by any health care professional in the course of an overall screening." History taking is defined as "the process of interviewing patients, asking them questions about their lives in order to come to a better understanding of their needs and resources. The history questions are usually asked in the context of a comprehensive examination by the clinician who is primarily responsible for providing direct care or referrals to specialists, such as professional chaplains." Finally, assessment is defined as "a more extensive [in-depth, ongoing] process of active listening to a patient's story as it unfolds in a relationship with a professional chaplain and summarizing the needs and resources that emerge in that process. The summary includes a spiritual care plan with expected outcomes which should be communicated to the rest of the treatment team." The assessment requires the training of the professional chaplains and should only be done by someone with that training.

## *Interdisciplinary and Transdisciplinary Teams*

Chaplains increasingly function as part of teams characterized as interdisciplinary or transdisciplinary. While the definitions and understandings vary somewhat, in both cases, the members of the various disciplines caring for the patient are expected to function in a coordinated manner, sharing information and creating a synchronized plan of care aimed at agreed-upon goals. Team members are expected to be accountable to one another for their respective responsibilities. The major distinction in transdisciplinary care is that the boundaries between the practices of the various disciplines are permeable; that is, each discipline is expected to be accountable for some part of the practice of others as well as the practice of their own field. For example, chaplains doing home hospice visits are generally expected to assess the physical pain status of the patient and report back to the team. Likewise, all of the non-chaplains on the team are expected to participate in some way in the spiritual care of the patient.

## Standards

The Association of Professional Chaplains issued the first *Standards of Practice* for chaplains in acute health care, which align professional chaplaincy with other health-care disciplines.[29] These standards specify assessment of patients' spiritual needs, delivery of care, documentation of the chaplain's work, teamwork, ethical practice, confidentiality, and respect for diversity. They also cover care of staff, care for the organization, and the chaplain as leader. In sum, they suggest that chaplaincy is becoming more of a profession and that commonalities are emerging in chaplaincy practice.

It is also important to note that, in 2004, the five major chaplaincy associations in North America adopted a Common Code of Ethics to govern the professional practice of chaplains, chaplain educators, and pastoral counselors.[30] Among other provisions, this code supports respect for the patient / client / student and clearly prohibits proselytizing.

In addition to *Standards of Practice* for chaplains, many other standards are emerging that elevate the position of spiritual and chaplaincy care and require new accountability on the part of chaplains. Beginning in 2003, the Joint Commission (JC), which accredits most U.S. hospitals, required hospitals to address the spiritual needs of patients. The current standards specific to spiritual and religious services are as follows:

- **RI.01.01.01** The hospital respects patient rights.
    6. The hospital respects the patient's cultural and personal values, beliefs, and preferences.
    9. The hospital accommodates the patient's right to religious and other spiritual services.

*Note: This standard is usually interpreted by the JC to mean that institutions need a documented and workable plan for delivering chaplaincy services to patients of any faith tradition.*

- **PC.01.02.02** The hospital assesses and reassesses its patients.
    4. Based on the patient's condition, information gathered in the initial assessment includes the following: For patients who are receiving end-of-life care, the social, spiritual, and cultural variables that influence the patient's and family members' perception of grief.
- **PC.02.02.13** The patient's comfort and dignity receive priority during end-of-life care.[31]

To the extent possible, the hospital provides care and services that accommodate the patient and his or her family's comfort, dignity, psychosocial, emotional, and spiritual end-of-life needs.

In general, the JC is looking for a system that reliably assesses patients' spiritual / religious needs and then provides the necessary resources to deal with them, including chaplains with verified competence, especially at the end of life.

The JC has issued new and amended standards with regard to cultural competence. While the standards themselves will not require professional chaplains, the implementation guide makes frequent reference to the utility of professional chaplains, especially in care at the end of life.

The National Comprehensive Cancer Network (NCCN) guidelines are widely regarded as the premier source of best practice in cancer care. Their guidelines for treatment of adult cancer pain specify that spiritual and religious considerations are evaluated. The guidelines for palliative care specify chaplains as a part of the interdisciplinary team, and the guidelines for distress management require the inclusion of a certified chaplain experienced in psychosocial aspects of cancer.[32]

The National Quality Forum (NQF) is the country's most respected public-private quality forum. It has set the following guidelines for spiritual care in palliative care:

**Domain 5. Spiritual, Religious, and Existential Aspects of Care**

*Preferred Practice 20*

Develop and document a plan based on assessment of religious, spiritual, and existential concerns using a structured instrument and integrate the information obtained from the assessment into the palliative care plan.

*Preferred Practice 21*

Provide information about the availability of spiritual care services and make spiritual care available either through organizational spiritual counseling or through the patient's own clergy relationships.

*Preferred Practice 22*

Specialized palliative and hospice care teams should include spiritual care professionals appropriately trained and certified in palliative care.

*Preferred Practice 23*

Specialized palliative and hospice spiritual care professionals should build partnerships with community clergy and provide education and counseling related to end-of-life care.[33]

As a further explication of the NQF guidelines, a national consensus panel published some new working models for spiritual care in palliative care. The conclusions of the National Consensus Conference on Spiritual Care in Palliative Care (NCC) include the following:

- Spiritual care is essential to improving quality palliative care as determined by the National Consensus Project (NCP) and National Quality Forum (NQF).
- Studies have indicated the strong desire of patients with serious illness and end-of-life concerns to have spirituality included in their care.
- Interprofessional care should include board certified chaplains on the care team.
- Regular ongoing assessment of patients' spiritual issues is required.
- Patient spirituality should be integrated into the treatment plan with appropriate follow-up.
- The team should have professional education and development programs in spiritual care.
- These recommendations should be included in clinical site policies.
- Programs should engage community clergy and spiritual leaders in the care of patients and families.
- Programs should develop accountability measures to ensure that spiritual care is fully integrated into the care of patients.[34]

## *Palliative Care as a Paradigm for Chaplaincy Care*

Palliative care is a philosophy of care that is patient-centered and seeks to align treatment with the patient's wishes and values. It is often used synonymously with end-of-life care. However, this is a major misconception. Palliative care includes end-of-life care, but it is much more. It complements normal medical care by listening to the patient, incorporating the patient's beliefs and values, and attending to the patient's symptoms and quality of life, including the patient's spiritual life. Being holistic and patient-centered, chaplaincy care fits naturally as a basic component of the care team. Since it includes spiritual care and chaplaincy care as a core component of the care team, values the wishes and beliefs of the patient, and works on an interdisciplinary or transdisciplinary model, palliative care provides a paradigm for all of health care. The National Consensus Conference (NCC) provided an overall model for the inclusion of spiritual care and professional chaplaincy in all of health care.

Using the NCC model as the paradigm, the professional board certified chaplain is the spiritual care lead on the health care team. This does not mean that the chaplain is the only one to do spiritual care. It does mean that the chaplain is the spiritual care specialist who oversees the spiritual and religious component of care and is the subject-matter expert for the rest of the team.[35] This role emphasizes the importance of training and competence for the chaplain. The chaplain must be able to practice on a professional level equal to the other disciplines on the team, including medicine, nursing, social work, and mental health.

This leadership role is a new one for most chaplains. It will require chaplains to be clear about what it is that we do. Which patient issues and concerns should be referred to the chaplain? What are the interventions that the chaplain performs? And what outcomes can the team expect from the chaplain? In this new role, it is no longer acceptable for the chaplain to simply "be present" with the patient or family member without some sense of how the patient might benefit from that presence. Chaplaincy will have to make a clear contribution.

The role will also require chaplains to operate by consensus instead of isolated in a silo. Some in the chaplaincy world continue to be uncomfortable with "sharing" the provision of spiritual care. The reality is that if spiritual care continues to be only the province of chaplains, it will continue to be marginalized as a part of the holistic care process.

It is only when spiritual care is a realm of care shared by the whole team that it can truly be important. However, it does require the chaplain to be the spiritual care expert and be able to both have a body of knowledge to share and demonstrate what we add to the care process.

## *Strategic Planning*

*(Note: Strategic planning and its complete process are covered in chapter 26.)*

In my experience, most chaplaincy departments that are not able to grow their service or, worse, lose jobs for their staff, fail because neither they nor the individual chaplains within the department have aligned what they do with the mission, goals, and strategic objectives of the institution in which they work. They do what they think is right rather than engaging in a process to discover what will best serve the institution and what it is trying to do. Especially in the current context where alignment is key and every service has to support the whole, any department that thinks it can go its own way will, at best, lead a minimal and marginalized existence, if it remains at all.

Strategic planning is one of the least understood, most important, and often neglected activities involved in successful chaplaincy care in an institution. It has this status for many reasons. First, it tends not to be a lot of fun. When done correctly, strategic planning is painstaking, unexciting, and even tedious. Second, most of us imagine that we do not need this process, since we already know what we need to do. Third, the process often winds up telling us to do something we do not want to do instead of being able to do what we like and want to do.

Once we as chaplains do what the institution wants, we then have to be accountable for that performance. Because chaplaincy has been a peripheral service, we have often not had to be accountable for outcomes and our contributions. Even now, many health care administrators do not consider chaplains when planning how to carry out a strategic objective. Thus, there is no thought given to growing chaplaincy to provide this support.

The purpose of strategic planning is to make sure (1) that whatever chaplaincy does, it serves the institution, and (2) that all the service provided is done efficiently. Put in quality-assurance language, it is not just about doing things right; it is about doing the right things right.

Strategic planning should be a natural activity that professional chaplains are good at. We are taught to start where the patient is, not where we want them to be. We are taught to help the patient discover and use their resources rather than imposing our own. We are trained to start every chaplaincy encounter with an assessment to find out where patients are spiritually and emotionally so that we can maximize their strengths and minimize their needs and issues. Strategic planning is nothing more than an assessment of the institution done so we can start where the institution finds itself rather than where we would like it to be. Just as in the assessment of a patient, in strategic planning, we have to resist the temptation to rush to the bottom line. Like assessment, strategic planning is about listening and hearing what is really being said.

As in chaplaincy assessment, the great sin for chaplains and others in strategic planning is not gathering enough data. Put another way, it is not listening enough and thinking you have the answer when you do not. A good rule of thumb in this regard is to keep talking to more people and listening until you start to hear things that have already been said. First, this confirms that what you have heard is not simply one person's opinion. Second, it also confirms that you have at least the important pieces of the story.

Before a chaplain begins a strategic planning process, it is important to become familiar with some basic concepts. Two important concepts for chaplains to become familiar with are *outcomes* and *evidence*. Outcomes refer to the measurable changes in a patient's or family's experience, healing, or well-being that can be attributed to a specific intervention.[36] Evidence is the data obtained that validates the attainment of the hoped-for outcomes. Evidence involves identifying and framing a question, developing a strategy, producing and evaluating data, implementing change based on the data, and then evaluating whether the incorporated change promotes the hoped-for outcome.

It is essential that the chaplain understand how "quality" is defined in their institution. The word can have multiple meanings in the current health care lexicon, and many chief executive officers have their own idiosyncratic definitions. Knowing about quality is essential because it represents *the* central concept in modern health care. Chaplains must design their services so they deliver "quality" as their institution defines it.

It is essential for the chaplain to know what quality systems are used in their institution. Health care institutions use a variety of systems and sometimes mix elements from several. The system or systems chosen define the ways the institution strives for quality. For instance, "Lean" is a strategy used to make processes more efficient and eliminate waste. It helps institutions get the biggest "bang for the buck." An institution that embraces Lean is focused on achieving quality by reducing cost or producing more for the same cost. While many institutions use elements of Lean, they often do not identify it as a system they use. Nonetheless, it is important for chaplains to know whether their institution is focused on efficiency. This tells chaplains that they must be able to show that their services are running at peak efficiency before making any requests for expansion. Likewise, many chaplains work in institutions that use elements of the Studer method (www.studergroup.com) without having any formal Studer training. These chaplains may then not understand the importance their senior administrators put on "rounding," among other concepts. Six Sigma is another system widely used, including by the Joint Commission and the U.S. military. It focuses on effectiveness, including reduction in error. That is, does the intervention produce the same outcome every time? If not, how can the process be modified to reduce the rate of error (i.e., the times when the desired result is not delivered)? Six Sigma began in manufacturing companies like Toyota and General Electric but has now been adopted for social service settings.[37] Lean and Six Sigma are increasingly combined into a single system that can focus on effectiveness and efficiency simultaneously.

Chaplains should talk to the staff in their institution who oversee quality improvement initiatives to find out which system or systems their institution uses. Then they should study the system enough to understand the basic vocabulary. It is not necessary to learn how to run a Lean improvement project. It is essential to be able to participate in the discussion about such a project that is ongoing.

All of these systems run counter to how chaplaincy has traditionally been conducted and require significant changes in the way many chaplains think about what they do. Some chaplains will resist making this kind of change. However, the reality of the modern world of health care is that no service is going to be funded unless it can be demonstrated to be efficient (Lean) and effective (minimal error). To even reach this point, chaplains must be able to define what their processes and outcomes are and develop measures to determine whether goals are being met.

Strategic planning must be a cooperative, consensus-driven project. The chaplain should never engage in the process alone or just with other chaplains. It is always essential to have input from other stakeholders, such as institutional administration, other health care disciplines, patients, and the local religious community. Doing the planning in this way will hopefully force the chaplain to hear and incorporate how non-chaplains view and evaluate what the chaplain does.

It is important to follow a stepwise process for strategic planning. As already stated, many people doing planning, not only chaplains, either skip steps, do not give steps the attention they deserve, or put steps in the wrong order.

## *Models of Chaplaincy*

There are many models for chaplaincy practice. While there is no evidence for how prevalent any particular model is, the model used by the U.S. military seems to capture a lot of what chaplains do in the civilian health care world as well.

- **Facilitator:** The chaplain makes sure that spiritual and religious care is provided to everyone who wants to receive it. In a health care institution, this should include family and staff as well as patients. Services would normally include visits, worship and other rituals, and education to staff.
- **Provider:** The chaplain personally provides spiritual and religious services. The chaplain is not only a manager but also an active care provider. These services would normally include visitation and ritual provided to patients of the chaplain's own faith tradition who request such services.
- **Caregiver:** The chaplain provides services that would likely fall within the general category of spiritual counseling, care, or consultation. These services might include accompanying the dying, providing consultation on ethical issues, or spiritual assessment helping the team formulate a plan of care.
- **Advisor:** The chaplain advises the team or the institution on issues that might include cultural and religious sensitivity to patients and staff of various ethnic groups, relationships with local religious communities, and staff support and morale issues.

## *Best Practices*

Consensus is developing in the field of professional chaplaincy care around several best practices. The discipline is becoming a multifaith, referral service. Generally, it is no longer the case that particular chaplains visit only the patients of their faith tradition. This model does not make efficient use of scarce chaplaincy care resources and does not promote health care team integration, which is so essential to continuity of care and quality practice. In current best practice, chaplains visit patients of all faiths selected according to specific protocols and are assigned to specific locations or service lines, generally selected for their strategic importance to the institution. Even when a chaplain is assigned to a unit or service line, best practice dictates that the choice of patients to see is decided by an agreed-upon priority list.

A list of some best practices follows.

### Chaplaincy Care Services Based on a Plan with Outcomes

Chaplaincy care services are based on a plan agreed to by institutional management and other stakeholders. This plan, which is keyed to the mission and strategic plan of the organization, lays out specific objectives and goals and is consistent with institutional culture. For example, if the institution has a trauma center, the chaplaincy care plan will likely have a focus on 24/7 availability and swift response to crises.

### Targeting of Chaplaincy Care

Chaplaincy care resources are targeted to particular services or patient populations chosen for their strategic importance to the institution and / or the demonstrated impact of chaplaincy care on those patients and staff. This is preferred to having chaplains cover all parts of the hospital equally. Generally, the clinical service lines chosen reflect high volume and / or high acuity. Intensive care units often receive priority coverage along with cardiac and cancer units, where spiritual issues related to mortality and the meaning of life are common. Emerging standards of practice suggest a dedicated chaplain on palliative care teams.

### Assignment by Service Line

Given the multifaith training professional chaplains have, it is no longer best practice to assign chaplains along denominational lines; that is, it is inefficient as well as unnecessary to have the rabbi just visit all the Jewish patients, the Protestant chaplain visit all the Protestants, and so on. In most hospitals, chaplains are assigned to particular inpatient units. In this staffing pattern, the chaplain can fully integrate with the particular treatment team and be more responsive to the spiritual / religious needs of the particular group(s) of patients. As more and more outpatient practice is being brought in-house or located in physician practices proximate to the hospital itself, the natural extension of this model is to have chaplains assigned to service lines so they can see patients in all of these venues. This model greatly facilitates continuity of care, integration with the treatment team, utilization of chaplaincy care, and patient and family satisfaction. It should be noted that this practice does not obviate the need to have spiritual providers available to provide faith-specific sacraments and other kinds of ministry to patients who desire this kind of religious service.

## Protocol-Based Referrals

Except for services or units that are targeted for daily coverage because of the issues outlined above, chaplaincy care visits are generally initiated by protocol-based referrals. Chaplains should generally be included in protocols covering codes, deaths, organ donation, radical changes in prognosis, execution of advance directives, disasters, difficult families, and any adverse events. A clear protocol must be established for covering chaplaincy care needs outside of regular business hours. This protocol should spell out which situations will generate a chaplaincy care referral as well as how the chaplain on call is to be contacted.

## Screening for Spiritual and Religious Concerns

There should be a protocol for screening and diagnosing spiritual distress and need in patients and families, containing algorithms for referral to chaplaincy care. The screening should, at minimum, evaluate how important religion and spirituality are to the patient's coping, how well those coping strategies are working at the moment, and whether the patient has any immediate religious or spiritual needs that require chaplaincy care intervention. The success of the referral system depends on the ability and willingness of non-chaplaincy care clinical staff to reliably do spiritual screening. Staff need training for this task, and the protocols and infrastructure must be in place to transmit referrals reliably and efficiently. To this end, chaplains participate in the orientation of new clinical staff. We recommend a screening system developed by George Fitchett, which has been show to have a high reliability in identifying spiritual distress.[38]

## Standards of Practice for Assessment, Planning, and Outcomes

Patients referred for chaplaincy care should have an in-depth spiritual assessment by the chaplain during the initial visit and periodically thereafter, according to an agreed-upon protocol. The assessment should elicit information that will lead to a profile of the patient's spiritual and religious resources and needs, and a plan of care with interventions and expected outcomes. This author recommends a system for delivering care previously known as the discipline for pastoral caregiving, now known as outcome oriented chaplaincy.[39]

## Staff Training and Support

The impact of professional chaplains is broadened by having them provide training for staff on such topics as cultural awareness and sensitivity, listening skills, advance directives, and spiritual issues. Such training allows all staff to better serve patients' and families' emotional, spiritual, and cultural needs. While the chaplains are the spiritual care specialists on the team, all clinical staff play a role in the assessment and delivery of spiritual care. By having chaplains on units that tend to be stressful for staff, the chaplains can provide immediate support and debriefing for staff after particularly stressful incidents, thus reducing downtime and improving staff efficiency.

## Certification of Chaplaincy Care Staff

All chaplaincy care staff should be certified according to the *Common Standards for Professional Chaplaincy* and agree to abide by the *Common Code of Ethics*.[40] Basic requirements for certification include graduate theological education or equivalent, sixteen hundred hours of clinical pastoral education in an accredited program, endorsement for chaplaincy by a recognized faith group, and an appearance before a peer review committee. The *Common Code of Ethics* is significant in that it prohibits proselytizing or in any way imposing one's own beliefs and practices on a patient. This limitation is consistent with the emphasis on working with the patient's own belief system.

Volunteers and community clergy provide ministry in carefully defined roles under the supervision of the professional staff.

## Contributions to Cost Enhancement

While chaplaincy care should be primarily considered a contribution to the fulfillment of the institution's mission, it can make financial contributions as well. Intentional chaplaincy care provided to staff at times of professional and personal stress can contribute to reduction in staff downtime and turnover. These interventions can be informal or formally incorporated into an employee assistance program. In the latter case, chaplaincy staff should also have pastoral counseling training, which is different from clinical pastoral education. Chaplaincy staff often conduct memorial services where clinical staff can commemorate the deaths of a specific patient, a group of patients on a specific service, or a beloved colleague. While positioning chaplains as the primary organ requestors in the institution is controversial in that it removes chaplains from their neutral role in relationship to patients and families, many hospitals position chaplains as family advocates. Chaplains should also be included in any response protocol for medical error to help mediate between the family and the medical staff.

## Communication and Cultural Competence

Proactive involvement of professional chaplaincy care can alert the treatment team to cultural / religious issues so these can become part of the team's communication with the patient and family. Likewise, chaplains can be a bridge when staff and family function with different worldviews and ways of understanding a given situation. The contributions of chaplains to problematic situations often take the form of resolving communications issues among staff. Valuable as these contributions to individual patient situations often are, chaplaincy care's systematic contributions are an even greater contributor to long-term institutional success. According to the Joint Commission, "The emerging prominent role of clinically trained, professional board certified chaplains working with health care organizations in completing spiritual assessments, functioning as the 'cultural broker' and leading cultural and spiritual sensitivity assessments for staff and physicians can be of great value."[41] The Joint Commission has issued new and amended standards that significantly enlarge an institution's responsibilities in this area. The implementation guide features the role of the professional chaplain especially at end of life.[42]

### Participation in the Ethics Process

Since ethical decisions for many patients involve religious beliefs, at least one chaplain should serve on the ethics committee. Given the concepts of multifaith ministry described above, it is not necessary to have all major religious groups represented. The chaplain should develop resources in the local religious community to provide assistance when necessary.

### Quality Improvement

The chaplaincy care department should fully participate in the institutional quality improvement efforts to the same extent as similar departments. The department should have agreed-upon goals for data collection, analysis, and reporting.

## *Final Words*

Health care chaplaincy is emerging from a marginalized role in the process of health care where its task was poorly understood, its practice was apparently random, and it was not considered to be making a contribution to the overall provision of spiritual care into a role defined by standards of practice and increasingly accepted outcomes. The extent to which this change is actualized by chaplains will largely determine the degree to which spiritual care is fully integrated into health care treatment.

### Notes

1. Christina Puchalski et al., "Improving the Quality of Spiritual Care as a Dimension of Palliative Care: The Report of the Consensus Conference," *Journal of Palliative Medicine* 12, no. 10 (2009): 885–904; National Comprehensive Cancer Network, *NCCN Clinical Practice Guidelines in Oncology*, www.nccn.org/professionals/physician_gls/f_guidelines.asp.
2. Daniel Sulmasy, "A Biopsychosocial-Spiritual Model for the Care of Patients at the End of Life," *Gerontologist* 42, no. 3 (2002): 24–33; R. Sean Morrison, "Cost Savings Associated with U.S. Hospital Palliative Care Consultation Programs," *Archives of Internal Medicine* 168, no. 16 (2008): 1783–90.
3. Sulmasy, "Biopsychosocial-Spiritual Model"; Puchalski et al., "Improving the Quality of Spiritual Care"; Centers for Medicare & Medicaid Services, *42 CFR Part 418—*

*Medicare and Medicaid Programs: Hospice Conditions of Participation; Final Rule*, www.cms.hhs.gov/CFCsAndCoPs/05_Hospice.asp.

4. Tracy A. Balboni et al., "Religiousness and Spiritual Support among Advanced Cancer Patients and Associations with End-of-Life Treatment Preferences and Quality of Life," *Journal of Clinical Oncology* 25, no. 5 (2007): 555–60.
5. Sulmasy, "Biopsychosocial-Spiritual Model"; Morrison et al., "Cost Savings."
6. Balboni et al., "Religiousness and Spiritual Support."
7. Ibid.
8. Abigail Sivan, Larry Burton, and George Fitchett, "Hospitalized Psychiatric and Medical Patients and the Clergy," *Journal of Religion and Health* 36, no. 3 (1996): 455–67.
9. Kevin J. Flannelly et al., "A National Survey of Health Care Administrators' Views on the Importance of Various Chaplain Roles," *Journal of Pastoral Care and Counseling* 59, no. 1–2 (2005): 87–96.
10. Balboni et al., "Religiousness and Spiritual Support."
11. Caterina Mako, Kathleen Galek, and Sharon R. Poppito, "Spiritual Pain among Patients with Advanced Cancer in Palliative Care," *Journal of Palliative Medicine* 9, no. 3 (2006): 1106–13.
12. Ibid.
13. Gene G. Ano and Erin B. Vasconcelles, "Religious Coping and Psychological Adjustment to Stress: A Meta-analysis," *Journal of Clinical Psychology* 61, no. 4 (2005): 461–80; Donia Baldacchino and Peter Draper, "Spiritual Coping Strategies: A Review of the Nursing Research Literature," *Journal of Advanced Nursing* 34, no. 6 (2001): 833–41; Kenneth Pargament, *The Psychology of Religion and Coping: Theory, Research, Practice* (New York: Guilford Press, 1997); Crystal Park, Lawrence Cohen, and Lisa Herb, "Intrinsic Religiousness and Religious Coping as Life Stress Moderators for Catholics versus Protestants," *Journal of Personality and Social Psychology* 59, no. 3 (1990): 562–74.
14. George G. Gallup and D. Michael Lindsay, *Surveying the Religious Landscape: Trends in U.S. Beliefs* (Harrisburg, PA: Morehouse Publishing, 1999).
15. George G. Gallup and Jim Castelli, *The People's Religion: American Faith in the 90's* (New York: Macmillan, 1989); Barry A. Kosmin and Egon Mayer, *American Religious Identification Survey* (2001), www.gc.cuny.edu/CUNY_GC/media/CUNY-Graduate-Center/PDF/ARIS/ARIS-PDF-version.pdf?ext=.pdf; Christopher Bader et al., *American Piety in the 21st Century: New Insights to the Depth and Complexity of Religion in the U.S.* (2006), www.isreligion.org/wp-content/uploads/American-Piety-Finall.pdf; Ben Schott, "Who Do You Think We Are?" *New York Times*, February 25, 2007, sec. 4, p. 15.
16. Ano and Vasconcelles, "Religious Coping and Psychological Adjustment to Stress."
17. Leslie Tepper et al., "The Prevalence of Religious Coping among Persons with Persistent Mental Illness," *Psychiatric Services* 52 (2001): 660–65.
18. Harold G. Koenig, David Larson, and Susan Larson, "Religion and Coping with Serious Medical Illness," *Annals of Pharmacotherapy* 35, no. 3 (2001): 352–59.

19. George Fitchett et al., "Religious Struggle: Prevalence, Correlates and Mental Health Risks in Diabetic, Congestive Heart Failure, and Oncology Patients," *International Journal of Psychiatry in Medicine* 34, no. 2 (2004): 179–96; Balboni et al., "Religiousness and Spiritual Support."
20. Harold G. Koenig, "Religious Attitudes and Practices of Hospitalized Medically Ill Older Adults," *International Journal of Geriatric Psychiatry* 13, no. 4 (1998): 213–24; Harold G. Koenig, Julie Nielsen, and Kenneth I. Pargament, "Religious Coping and Health Status in Medically Hospitalized Older Adults," *Journal of Nervous and Mental Disease* 186, no. 9 (1998): 513–21.
21. Anne M. McCaffrey et al., "Prayer for Health Concerns: Results of a National Survey on Prevalence and Patterns of Use," *Archives of Internal Medicine* 164, no. 8 (2004): 858–62.
22. Larry VandeCreek et al., "The Unique Benefits of Religious Support during Cardiac Bypass Surgery," *The Journal of Pastoral Care* 53, no. 1 (1999): 19–29.
23. Kenneth I. Pargament et al., "Spiritual Struggle: A Phenomenon of Interest to Psychology and Religion," in *Judeo-Christian Perspectives on Psychology*, ed. William R. Miller and Harold Delaney (Washington, DC: American Psychological Association, 2005).
24. See Brent Peery, "What's in a Name?" *PlainViews* 6, no. 2 (February 18, 2009), www.plainviews.org.
25. Mark LaRocca-Pitts, "Agape Care: A Pastoral and Spiritual Care Continuum," *PlainViews* 3, no. 2 (February 15, 2006).
26. American Nurses Association and Health Ministries Association, *Faith and Community Nursing: Scope and Standards of Practice* (Silver Spring, MD: American Nurses Association, 2005).
27. Association of Professional Chaplains, *Standards of Practice for Professional Chaplains in Acute Care Settings*, www.professionalchaplains.org/uploadedFiles/pdf/Standards%20of%20Practice%20Draft%20Document%20021109.pdf.
28. George Fitchett and Andrea L. Canada, "The Role of Religion / Spirituality in Coping with Cancer: Evidence, Assessment, and Intervention," in *Psycho-oncology*, 2nd ed., ed. Jimmie C. Holland (New York: Oxford University Press, 2010), 440–46.
29. Association of Professional Chaplains, *Standards of Practice*.
30. Council on Collaboration, *Common Code of Ethics for Chaplains, Pastoral Counselors, Pastoral Educators and Students*, www.spiritualcarecollaborative.org/docs/common-code-ethics.pdf.
31. Joint Commission, *Comprehensive Accreditation Manual for Hospitals (CAMH): The Official Handbook* (Oakbrook Terrace, IL: Joint Commission Resources, 2010).
32. National Comprehensive Cancer Network, *NCCN Clinical Practice Guidelines in Oncology*, www.nccn.org/professionals/physician_gls/f_guidelines.asp.
33. National Quality Forum, *A National Framework and Preferred Practices for Palliative and Hospice Care Quality*, www.qualityforum.org/Publications/2006/12/

A_National_Framework_and_Preferred_Practices_for_Palliative_and_Hospice_Care_Quality.aspx.

34. Puchalski et al., "Improving the Quality of Spiritual Care."
35. George Handzo and Harold Koenig, "Spiritual Care: Whose Job Is It Anyway?" *Southern Medical Journal* 97, no. 12 (2004): 1242–44.
36. Larry VandeCreek and Arthur M. Lucas, *The Discipline for Pastoral Care Giving: Foundations for Outcome Oriented Chaplaincy* (New York: Haworth Press, 2001).
37. Michael L. George, *Lean Six Sigma for Service: How to Use Lean Speed and Six Sigma Quality to Improve Services and Transactions* (New York: McGraw-Hill, 2003).
38. George Fitchett and James L. Risk, "Screening for Spiritual Struggle," *Journal of Pastoral Care and Counseling* 62, no. 1–2 (2009): 1–12.
39. Larry VandeCreek and Arthur M. Lucas, *The Discipline for Pastoral Care Giving: Foundations for Outcome Oriented Chaplaincy* (New York: Haworth Press, 2001).
40. Council on Collaboration, *Common Standards for Professional Chaplaincy* and *Common Code of Ethics for Chaplains, Pastoral Counselors, Pastoral Educators and Students*, www.spiritualcarecollaborative.org/standards.asp.
41. Joint Commission, *Providing Culturally and Linguistically Competent Health Care* (Oakbrook Terrace, IL: Joint Commission Resources, 2006).
42. Joint Commission, *Advancing Effective Communication, Cultural Competence, and Patient- and Family-Centered Care: A Roadmap for Hospitals*, www.jointcommission.org/assets/1/6/ARoadmapforHospitalsfinalversion727.pdf.

## About the Contributor

**Rev. George Handzo, MDiv, BCC, CSSBB,** is the vice president of Chaplaincy Care Leadership and Practice at HealthCare Chaplaincy. Rev. Handzo directs the only consulting service devoted to the strategic assessment, planning, and management of chaplaincy services. HealthCare Chaplaincy employs best practices in strategic planning and clinical practice to maximize the effectiveness of an organization's pastoral care and to align it with the institution's overall objectives. Prior to his current position, Rev. Handzo was the director of Chaplaincy Services at Memorial Sloan-Kettering Cancer Center for more than twenty years and is a past president of the Association of Professional Chaplains. He serves on the Distress Guidelines Panel of the National Comprehensive Cancer Network. Rev. Handzo has authored or coauthored more than fifty chapters and articles on the practice of pastoral care.

# 4

# Assessments

*Chaplain D. W. Donovan, MA, MS, BCC*

Almost all of us have gone through the tedious process of an initial "history and physical" when seeing a physician for the first time. The questions come in a rapid-fire sequence, prompting a series of yes or no answers that sometimes lead to more specific questions, but more often than not seem to be quickly charted and then just as quickly forgotten.

The sad truth is that, even though I should know better after so many years working in health care, half of the time when I'm answering "no," I should be saying, "I don't know." In fact, Doctor, I'm not entirely sure that you didn't just make that word up. Besides, I'm sure I'd remember if I'd ever had pneumonoultramicroscopicsilicovolcanoconiosis.

Of course, most of us are poor historians when it comes to our own well-being. Instead, we trust the medical professional to listen to our story, pulling out the salient facts from amidst our rambling tale, and to fill in the missing pieces based on their extensive education and experience.

What we trust the doctor to do is known to the physician as the assessment process. Physicians are trained to:

- *Listen* to the stories of their patients to identify the relevant history and the current concerns
- *Observe* their patients for signs of other symptoms, which the patient may not mention or may not even be aware of
- *Evaluate* the data they gather to determine the exact nature of the current concerns

- *Determine* what interventions can be used to help the patient return to health and wholeness

In the past few years, several pastoral professionals and researchers have encouraged our profession to adopt a similar methodology for making a spiritual assessment. While some progress has been made, there has also been resistance to thinking in terms of assessments and interventions, perhaps believing that such language takes away from the sacred nature of ministry.

Our own training, particularly in the specialized work of clinical pastoral education (CPE), may have contributed to our slow adaptation of an assessment mentality. Seminary classes and even CPE centers often focus on providing students with the basic tools of pastoral care, which tend to emphasize listening skills over an assessment process. Even those who have benefited from extensive training in CPE often describe their work as:

- Just being there
- Not having an agenda
- Having time to listen
- Being present
- Offering support

While there is no question that the difficult "inner work" of learning to temporarily set aside one's own needs and issues in order to be emotionally available to care for another is critical to training pastoral professionals, a command of those tools alone is no longer sufficient. Virtually every profession today is becoming more focused on measurable outcomes, grounded in an ethical mandate to be good stewards. Professional pastoral care is no different.

Tending to those in crisis has always been an essential part of our overall mission as chaplains. Anecdotally, we know that some pastoral professionals are extremely gifted in this area, while others seem to stumble through the process, unsure of themselves or their role. What guidance might we offer those seeking to become more proficient in this work? Are there best practices from which we can all learn? And finally, are there some basic indicators that would measure our success while simultaneously demonstrating our value?

Borrowing from author Stephen Covey's directive to "begin with the end in mind,"[1] we must first define exactly what we are asking the pastoral professional to do. Several years ago, I worked in partnership with Rev. Dr. Melvin Dowdy, PhD, to develop an organizing principle that would guide the creation of a pastoral care assessment process. To account for a wider range of chaplaincy settings, I have slightly modified our work as follows:

> The role of the clinically trained pastoral professional is to assess the degree to which the client's emotional and spiritual equilibrium has been disturbed by a particular event and to determine what interventions would be appropriate to help the client restore that equilibrium and when such interventions should be employed.[2]

Turning back for a moment to the work of our physician, we know that he or she is guided through the assessment by focusing on the various bodily systems. The pastoral assessment should also be intentional about reviewing certain key areas, although the "systems" we review will be quite different.

In the remainder of this chapter, we will review in some depth a "best practices" process for making a pastoral assessment, including some suggestions as to how your assessment can best be documented for your own benefit or for the benefit of an interdisciplinary team.

I would be remiss if I did not acknowledge that this model draws heavily on the work of many other pastoral professionals and researchers. The work presented here seeks to build upon the best of existing research, while shifting the overall paradigm from an emphasis on faith-based coping mechanisms toward an understanding of how people consciously and subconsciously integrate their values, beliefs, and understanding of the nature of the sacred into the reality of a particular crisis. Those wishing to explore assessments in more detail might begin with the online Reading Room of the Association of Professional Chaplains, found at www.professionalchaplains.org. In particular, the 7 x 7 model for spiritual assessment, developed by George Fitchett[3] and his colleagues, uses a similar approach to my own.

The first of the three elements of the assessment process seeks to identify the relationships and connections that are significant in the life of the person. This includes not only relationships with family and friends, but also with God or a sense of the sacred as understood by the person.

The second of the three elements of the assessment process asks what relationships, values, activities, interests, or beliefs provide a sense of meaning and purpose for the person. It is important to understand that these values and beliefs may be in a state of flux, as the loss of equilibrium demands that previously held concepts be reevaluated in light of the new situation.

The third and final element of the assessment process, while grounded in the work of health care chaplaincy, can easily be translated into crisis work in a range of environments. It asks whether the patient understands his or her current medical condition and is able to apply his or her values and beliefs to that medical condition in a mature fashion.

## *Element 1: Relationships and Connectivity*

Consciously or subconsciously, most of us make an initial assessment of people's key relationships and their sense of connectivity the moment we walk into their space, whether that be their permanent home or a temporary space such as a hospital room. The walls do, in fact, speak to us, giving us hints as to relationships that are most important to this person, and perhaps even giving us clues as to their values and beliefs.

For example, my family and I have just moved across the country, packing up our house of eight years and moving into a rental house until we can find a home of our own. Knowing that we intend to move again shortly, we haven't unpacked the pictures and artwork that made our old house a true home. Nevertheless, even a casual glance around the living room reveals cards sent by our family for the holidays, several framed pictures of our young toddler, far too many toys, and a well-stocked library, displaying books that speak of our professional and personal interests.

What insights might you gain as you enter into our home? You might deduce from the cards that we value those relationships with our family and friends. The prominent pictures of our son, particularly given the lack of any other pictures or artwork, would probably indicate the importance we attach to that relationship. The sheer number of toys, especially in light of an otherwise tidy home, might suggest to you recent visits by doting grandparents. And the heavy oak bookcases, with each book carefully placed and cared for, might provide some insight into both our love of reading and the value we place on the intellectual life. An even closer look would provide insight into our specific interests.

Whether you realize it or not, you've already learned quite a bit about me, and you've only been in my home for thirty seconds. Becoming much more intentional about that process, and building on it through the conversation that follows, is an integral part of the first element of our assessment: relationships and connectivity.

From both a theological perspective and our lived experience, we understand ourselves to be a social people, needing one another to fully experience both the divine among us and what it means to be fully human. Many of our faith traditions suggest that we were created to be in relationship both with the Divine and with one another. When those relationships are flourishing, they provide a sense of security, allowing us to face even the most difficult times with a sense of well-being. On the other hand, when those relationships are fractured, even painful, our overall sense of well-being and security can feel threatened. Thus, an early and accurate assessment of a person's key relationships and his or her sense of connectivity to others, including who or what the person understands to be sacred, is the essential first step in providing care as a pastoral professional.

While it is critically important not to mistake information gathering for an assessment process, there are certain themes you might look to explore or even questions you might ask to help develop your understanding of the key relationships and sense of connectivity. It might be helpful to think of this part of the assessment process in terms of four Ls: what you are *looking* for; what *language* you might use to explore those issues; where that *leads* you; and what you, the patient, the patient's family, and / or the treatment team might *learn* from the pastoral encounter (see Figure 4.1).

There are two important caveats to discuss before we move on to the second element. The first caveat is to acknowledge that you are gathering information and formulating an assessment fairly quickly and often in the midst of some distress. Despite your own training and experience, there is a potential for misunderstanding, and you should allow for that.

I recall working with an Italian family from New York. The patriarch of the family had experienced a severe heart attack while traveling down Interstate 95 from New York to Florida. He was brought emergently to our hospital and admitted to the coronary care unit, where I was working as the staff chaplain. Unfortunately, he was not expected to live long. Throughout the course of the day, family members from up

| ELEMENT 1: RELATIONSHIPS AND CONNECTIVITY | |
|---|---|
| **Looking ...** | To identify the relationships and connections that are significant in the life of the patient |
| **Language** | Tell me about your family and friends.<br>It sounds like he / she is really important in your life.<br>Who are the people that you want close by you in times like these?<br>Do you mind introducing me to your family and friends?<br>You mentioned someone from your church / neighborhood / book club came by?<br>How is (are) your loved one(s) coping? |
| **Leads** | Which relationships support and which relations threaten the person or group's sense of well-being?<br>Are there relationships that cause the person pain or are a source of regret?<br>Is there a person or people who the person feels the need to protect?<br>Is there a person or people who are not emotionally ready to engage in an exploration of the real issues and will try to divert the conversation?<br>Is there a person or people who are threatened by your client's potential for change / growth?<br>Does the person speak naturally about spirituality and those relationships? If so, does it appear to be in an attempt to please you? Does spirituality appear to be an integrated part of his / her relationships, or is he / she reaching out in fear? What appears to be his / her understanding of the nature of the Divine? |
| **Learnings** | What might you share with the patient, the family, or your colleagues (when permissible) to help advance the healing process?<br>For example, it might become clear that when significant issues are discussed, the spouse first tries to divert the conversation using humor, but then grows angry at the person raising the issue. In turn, your most immediate client steps forward to protect his / her spouse, setting up an adversarial relationship with the caregiver.<br>How you address this will vary by your own training and style. However, understanding how those relationships interact is critical to your assessment and, soon thereafter, your ability to help advance the healing process. |

*Figure 4.1*

and down the coast flew in and arrived at the hospital. I moved in and out of the room throughout the day, helping new arrivals adjust to the tragic news and sharing in story after story of this patriarch, whose great-grandfather had brought the entire family from Italy. Typical of my experience with Italian Catholics, they used "God" language with great familiarity, and I learned of the various parishes where families had settled. Near the end of the day, I worked with our cardiologist to facilitate a patient care conference, where the decision was made to withdraw the ventilator and other life-sustaining treatments. At the request of the patient's wife, I gathered the entire family at the bedside for a prayer of commendation. Given their roots, I changed the way that I usually end prayers from "for we ask this, as we ask all things, in Your Holy Name, we do pray ..." to "for we ask this, as we ask all things, in the name of Your Son and our Lord, Jesus the Christ."

An hour or so later, they asked if I might contact a local *rabbi* to help them make arrangements to bring the body back to New York.

Excuse me?

It turns out that great-grandfather had moved into a Jewish neighborhood and been so impressed with the local rabbi that he converted, along with his entire family, to Judaism. Parishes? Oh, that's just how we identify our neighborhoods in that part of New York.

The lesson: even the person or family that you know quite well will surprise you. Don't assume.[4]

This is particularly important given the tremendous diversity of cultures and even faith-based subcultures in our world today. In health care, our major accrediting agency (the Joint Commission) focuses on cultural competence through a revised set of standards. I believe they offer sound advice when they state:

> Do not expect staff to understand everything about every culture; instead encourage staff to engage patients and their families to gather information about individual needs, beliefs, and preferences that may influence care.[5]

The second caveat I would offer as we continue to move through this assessment model might be surprising to some of you. Particularly in the hospital environment, there's a tendency to think that the chaplain deals with spiritual issues, while the cardiologist deals with the heart, the social worker deals with the social situation, and so on.

I would contend that this approach would severely limit the scope and effectiveness of your chaplaincy. Instead, I would advocate for the professional pastoral provider to think in terms of working with the whole person from the spiritual perspective. Mr. Smith is not a Lutheran who happens to be having marital difficulties that can be solved through a purely religious approach. Mr. Smith is having marital difficulties, and as is so often the case, he has reached out to his Lutheran pastor for assistance. Because spirituality is rooted in a set of values and beliefs (a worldview, if you will) that both sustains and is woven through the full range of life experiences, the professional pastoral caregiver is well suited to assist. But it would be a mistake to force the conversation to conform to your own self-expectation that you are "supposed" to focus on purely spiritual issues or use purely spiritual language. Put another way, you are not engaged in an assessment of their spiritual needs; you are assessing how their values, beliefs, and traditions (which we often call spirituality) affect how people and their family / friends will approach a particular situation. As a part of your actual chaplaincy, you may use spiritual tools to assist the patient. But you must remember that if your only tool is a hammer, everything starts to look like a nail.

Now that we have a basic understanding of the first element, relationships and connectivity, let's move our assessment a bit deeper to ask what it is that gives your client a sense of meaning and purpose.

## *Element 2: Meaning and Purpose*

I have spent most of my ministerial life in hospital chaplaincy, and there are many things that we do well. But one area where we struggle, in my opinion, has to do with how we speak to patients or their surrogate decision makers about their religion or faith tradition (if any), spirituality, values, and beliefs.

A significant part of health care is guided by the standards of the Joint Commission. Concerning the spiritual assessment, they recommend the following:

> Spiritual assessment should, at a minimum, determine the patient's denomination and beliefs and what spiritual practices are important to the patient. This information can assist in determining the impact of spirituality, if any, on the care / services being provided.[6]

They go on to suggest several questions that might be asked of the patient or family to help complete the assessment. One example is "What kind of spiritual / religious support does the patient desire?" Another asks, "What are the patient's spiritual goals?"[7]

With due respect to the Joint Commission, this approach suggests exactly the kind of mentality that I warned about in the previous section; namely, reducing spirituality to a series of needs that can be addressed by providing specific services and enacting specific practices, while simultaneously isolating spirituality from a broader understanding of the whole person.

Many years ago, I was both privileged and horrified to visit the remains of the concentration camp in Dachau. As a lifelong Catholic who was just getting started in ministry, I found myself particularly drawn to Block 26, where so many priests had been imprisoned and died. I wasn't naïve enough to think that I would have survived when so many others died. But what I found myself wondering was whether my own *faith* would have survived. Not my faith in God, because I had come to terms with a sense of theodicy, but my faith in people. How could any person treat another person with such disregard for their basic human dignity?

Another few years would pass before I would be introduced to the life and writings of Dr. Viktor Frankl. Many of you know that Dr. Frankl was prisoner #119,104, who rose from the ashes of that horrific experience to become an acknowledged expert in psychology and medicine. What is perhaps his most famous book is titled *Man's Search for Meaning*. Gordon Allport introduces the book by sharing with the readers the startling question that Dr. Frankl would often ask of patients: "Why do you not commit suicide?"[8]

To be sure, Dr. Frankl's question is not gently phrased, and I am *not* recommending it, but it gets to the heart of what a person *lives for*; this is particularly important when your client is a patient facing a terminal disease or another crisis that forces him or her to reexamine his or her own identity or priorities. In the context of the model being presented here, the goal of the second element is to identify what it is that brings meaning and purpose to your client's life.

Imagine for one terrible moment that you were being held in a concentration camp. Or perhaps you might think of Joseph, Jacob's favorite son, "chained and bound, afraid, alone," as the musical describes the scene from Genesis 41.[9] Or perhaps imagine that you are a patient, newly diagnosed with a terminal disease and shocked into silence as you grapple with the idea of an all-too-early death. What would you have to live for?

As we all know, an individual can subscribe to a variety of beliefs, reflecting multiple values that might even, at times, come into conflict with one another. Thus, to help guide my own assessment, I often try to determine what is the "superordinate value" that the person will default to when faced with a conflict among his or her own values. The columnist Dave Barry may have best illustrated how a "superordinate value" functions when he complained, "If a woman has to choose between catching a fly ball and saving an infant's life, she will choose to save the infant's life without even considering if there are men on base."[10]

In other words, when it is crunch time, which value or belief really dominates your thinking and actions?

I once attended a lecture where the instructor told the story of a dedicated physician who worked long hours and was often away from home. For their thirtieth anniversary, his wife had made elaborate plans to celebrate and extracted from him a promise that he would leave the hospital in time to make their 6:00 p.m. reservations. At 5:30 p.m., just as he was changing out of his scrubs and into a tuxedo, he heard the operator announce a "Code Blue," or cardiac arrest, for one of his long-term patients. While there was a resident covering for him, he knew that he was the patient's best chance for survival. Momentarily caught between his personal and professional duties, he glanced through the ceiling toward his patient and muttered to himself, "One of us is in deep trouble."[11]

I've used that story several times over the years, and the conversation that follows is always robust. But what I find interesting is that participants in the discussion quickly adopt one side of the issue or the other and find the opposing perspective not only incomprehensible but also indefensible.

Unfortunately, it is not uncommon for even the closest of family members to have different superordinate values and yet be unaware of how those differences contribute to conflict within their relationship. Consider, for example, a pastoral visit that I made to the home of an older married couple many years ago. They had just learned that his medical condition had worsened significantly and that he would likely die within the next few days. Remarkably, and for better or for worse, he was completely coherent and interactive with others.

During my time with them, many other family members arrived, hoping to provide some measure of comfort and support. So the room where "Dwight" was settled on the couch had become quite crowded, and I found myself circulating through various family members, who themselves were in various stages of grief. But I became aware of a moment of tension between Dwight and his wife, and I drifted back to find out what was happening. Dwight was saying to his wife that he wanted to go through the checkbook with her and that she needed to know where the records were kept and how to keep up with the various financial responsibilities. She kept dismissing him, saying that they would talk about it later or gently reminding him that she knew where the records were. My initial thought was that she didn't want to talk about their financial records in front of their friends and family, but I also thought that she was missing the more important message in his words.

Placing a gentle hand on his wife, I turned to Dwight and asked, very quietly and very gently, "Dwight, are you trying to say that you're worried about your wife being alone?" He immediately began crying and nodded his head. It was obviously a breakthrough for him. What a privilege it was to be a part of such moments, I thought to myself.

And then she responded. And her voice was quiet, barely audible to me and to no one else, but there was steel in it that chilled me to the bone. "Of course that's what he's worried about. Why do you think he called you and every neighbor in a ten-block radius? But God forbid he should be able to talk about his feelings and stop talking about money."

While I had correctly assessed how deeply Dwight cared for his wife, I had not stopped to think how his words were affecting her. At the simplest level, he was a certified public accountant (CPA) and she was a licensed clinical social worker (LCSW). Unbeknownst to me, his tendency to express his love in terms of practicalities, particularly finances, had been a source of tension for many years. He expressed his love in a way that was reflective of his personality, his training, and his work as a CPA. But what she valued more than anything, perhaps as might be true of many LCSWs, was the intimacy of an open and vulnerable conversation. Their superordinate values, those comfort zones where they would fall back to, particularly in times of distress, were in conflict and thus a source of considerable pain.

The issue was not that they did not care for each other; the issue was that those concepts and communication styles that brought meaning and purpose to them were at odds with one another.

Returning to our four Ls framework from element 1, I once again invite you to consider element 2, meaning and purpose, in terms of what you are *looking* for; what *language* you might use to explore those issues; where that *leads* you; and what you, the patient, the patient's family, and / or the surrogate team might *learn* from the pastoral encounter (see Figure 4.2).

Now that we have explored the key relationships and connections in the person's life (element 1) and explored what he or she finds most meaningful or purpose providing (element 2), let us take a brief look at element 3, understanding of the medical condition or current situation and the congruence of response with beliefs and values.

## *Element 3: Degree of Understanding and Congruence of Response*

As you already know, this model was originally developed for hospital chaplains, and I have adapted it to a broader range of pastoral professionals for the purposes of this book. However, I felt that I could most clearly explain element 3 to you by remaining focused on the clinical setting and then inviting you to imagine how you might translate the specialized work of the chaplain to your own area of pastoral expertise.

What truly differentiates chaplains from other pastoral professionals is their understanding of the clinical environment and their ability to integrate seamlessly with the other members of the interdisciplinary team for the benefit of the patient and the patient's family.

When speaking on this topic, I'm fond of sharing a story from my first unit of clinical pastoral education. I had completed a master's degree in theology and was now embarking on the specialized education common to almost all board certified chaplains.

So here I was, brand spanking new, with the whitest (and shortest) jacket on the unit, and I walked into a patient's room to make initial contact and begin my own assessment. With absolutely no affect at all, the patient told me that he had "ESRD." With no clues to help me, I had to ask, "Is that bad?" He didn't know either. Neither one of us understood what the doctor had told him an hour earlier. Leaving the room, I made a

| ELEMENT 2: MEANING AND PURPOSE | |
|---|---|
| **Looking …** | To identify what brings meaning and purpose to the person's life. |
| **Language** | *[Note: The reality is that very few people have considered what it is that brings meaning and purpose to their life. Even if asked directly, their answers are more likely to reflect a desire to please the person asking the question. Therefore, you must listen quite carefully with your "third ear" to search for the meaning behind their words and stories.]*<br>Tell me about yourself. When you're not here, what energizes you?<br>If you could take off a full year to do whatever would be most meaningful for you, what would you do?<br>Tell me about a time when you felt you were at your very best.<br>Your spouse has talked a bit about her faith in X. Where do you find a sense of peace and security? *OR* Where do you find you are most engaged?<br>I'd be happy to pray with you. Help me understand your perspective on this so I can pray with a bit more intentionality.<br>I've heard a little bit about your story / read your chart. But I'm most interested in hearing what has happened from your perspective. |
| **Leads** | Is there a superordinate value that you can identify? If so, does it appear to be in conflict with the superordinate value of other stakeholders?<br>Recognizing the importance of "meaning making" in spirituality, are there ways you can "connect the dots" between those things that the person finds meaningful and the current crisis?<br>Has the person indicated any areas of his / her life where he / she feels a sense of things being unresolved? This can indicate a sense of meaninglessness or unresolved conflict between values.<br>Does the person seem to be "in denial" about a particular aspect of the situation? This can often be an indication that something the person found meaningful or purposeful is being challenged. Similarly, this might also be the case when the person appears compelled to assure you that they feel a certain way. |
| **Learnings** | What might you share with the patient, the family, or your colleagues (when permissible) to help advance the healing process?<br>For example, if the person places a high degree of importance on his / her role as the "head of the household," it might be more difficult for the person to discuss his / her own feelings of loss of control in front of the spouse or other family members. |

*Figure 4.2*

beeline for the internal medicine chief resident, who had befriended me as I found my way onto the unit. As I explained the situation, she smiled and patiently simplified the matter for me: "Renal disease ... bad. End stage ... very bad. End-stage renal disease ... very, very bad."

The point is that I had yet to learn the specialized language that quickly becomes second nature to health care clinicians. I was a missionary who had parachuted into a foreign land to discover that the language was entirely different and the culture was like something from another planet. Until I was able to understand both the language and the unique culture, I would be a student at best and a visiting outsider at worst. I hungered to become a *chaplain*, someone who spoke the language of ministry and medicine with equal fluidity and was an integrated member of the *team*.

It took me a while, but eventually I learned my way around this complex new culture and learned this strange new language. And I learned that a critical element to assess is the degree to which the patient and / or family truly understands the clinical situation. It turns out that most patients also feel like they have parachuted into a strange new land, and they are even less likely to understand what is happening. But for patients to have any chance of being able to cope with their existing situation or make critical decisions in response to a new diagnosis, they first have to understand what it is that the physician and health care team are saying to them.

The next step is to assess whether the patient (or his or her surrogate decision maker) is making decisions in relation to that clinical situation that are congruent with the patient's expressed values and beliefs.

The sample patient care conference I will share with you is quite common in acute care medicine, and yet no less difficult for each family experiencing it for the first time. There are similar examples you can probably think of for hospice, long-term care, behavioral health, and other clinical and nonclinical settings where you might be called up to serve.

Imagine yourself taking part in a patient care conference, either as a chaplain or as another form of pastoral professional. The physician has reviewed the events of the last few days with the family. When "Mrs. Jackson" came into the hospital, we were not sure how bad things were; thus she was placed on a ventilator to protect her airway and help her breathe. However, our tests in the last few days and what the family has shared with us make it clear that we are only prolonging the dying process. The doctor recommends that the family, acting as the patient's surrogate decision maker, discontinue the ventilator and allow the patient to die naturally.

Oftentimes, no matter how much preparation the family has had for this meeting, and no matter how sensitive the physician is, there is stunned silence as the family absorbs this information. And it is quite common at this point for a family member to introduce a faith-based reason why the recommended plan should not proceed. Someone might say, for example, "Well, Doctor, I know you think this is best, but we are believers and put our trust in God and the Lord Jesus Christ. And we know that it is up to God when Mrs. Jackson is called home; our job is to put our faith in God."

This is when every eye in the room will turn toward you. And while I would never address such pain (with perhaps a healthy dose of denial as a reasonable coping mechanism) in such a direct manner, consider the following syllogism:

> God will decide when a person dies.
> Believers put their faith in God.
> Believers allow God to decide when a person dies.

So there is a reasonable question to ask at this point: are you putting your faith in God or in modern-day medicine? The health care team does not have a crystal ball, but they do know that this piece of medical equipment is no longer helping the person. So maybe it is okay to really trust God ... fully and completely ... and to remove the ventilator. Doing so would be congruent with your own values and beliefs and what you have represented to us to be Mrs. Jackson's values and beliefs.

As you can see, it is this final element of the assessment process where the work begins to turn from your own evaluation of the situation toward actual interventions. Again, it is important to remember that assessment is an ongoing process that is interwoven with your pastoral interventions. Fitchett and Canada emphasize this in their definition of the spiritual / religious assessment. Spiritual / religious assessment refers to

> a more extensive [in-depth, ongoing] process of active listening to a patient's story as it unfolds in a relationship with a professional chaplain and summarizing the needs and resources that emerge in that process. The summary includes a spiritual care plan with expected outcomes which should be communicated to the rest of the treatment team.[12]

## *Evidence-Based Ministry: From "Presence" to "Prove It"*

I genuinely hope and pray that the model I have presented here is of value to you and to those you serve. But in these days of tight budgets, it is important to be able to point to some measurable indicators to show that you actually did make a difference. In other words, how do we move the conversation from language of "presence" to "prove it?"

Fortunately, researchers in both pastoral care and related disciplines have begun to consider how quality pastoral care results in measurable outcomes. In the health care setting, much of the attention has been focused on patient-specific outcomes, such as decreased levels of anxiety and depression,[13] an overall reduction of the number of days in the hospital,[14] and an increased sense of "being heard" with a corresponding reduction in lawsuits[15] and a corresponding increase in the patient's likelihood to choose the hospital again when future needs arise.[16] Related research shows benefits to the organization as a whole, with a reduction in staff turnover[17] as the most tangible outcome. If we are engaged in the work of meaning making, it makes sense that our colleagues in ministry would benefit from that as well.

While data clearly exist to support the value of pastoral professionals, I have come to believe that we as pastoral professionals can be our own worst enemies when it comes to advocating for well-trained, well-qualified (and appropriately compensated) chaplains to serve those in our care. Whether driven by an exaggerated sense of humility or something else, we have a tendency to underplay the value of our work. To this end, we must learn to be intentionally *tri*-lingual: "The hospital chaplain understands the workings of the heart (emotions), and the language of the soul (theology) as well as a working knowledge of the body."[18]

Therefore, I have strongly advocated for pastoral professionals to think less about "visiting" or "just dropping by" and to speak (when appropriate, but particularly to resource decision makers) instead of consultations and assessments. Rather than dismiss your presence as "just being there," celebrate that your work is grounded in master's-level training with annual continuing education that feeds both the mind and the spirit.

In addition to the language that you use to verbally define your ministry, some of you may be involved in documenting your work, either as a part of a legal record or for colleagues with whom you collaborate. There may well be a strong temptation to try and summarize this model into a handout or template that can be used by others. *I urge you to avoid this temptation.* I have reviewed literally hundreds of templates for documenting assessments or even screenings, and I have yet to find a model that can deal with the complexities of a true pastoral assessment. Remember that what I have described here is really a process to be followed, not a tool to be utilized. So, in the spirit of the *Dummies* books

## TOP TEN "THOU SHALL NOTS" RELATED TO DOCUMENTATION

**Thou shall not ...**

1. Confuse a pastoral assessment with a list of faith-based interventions. "Baptized baby" is a matter for record keeping; it does little to capture your assessment of why this was done and what difference it made in the life of the parents.
2. Begin by asking about faith tradition or practices.
3. Create checklists of feelings that the person might share with you. It is just not that simple.
4. Reduce highly complex issues to questions that can be answered by Yes / No or True / False. Example: "I expect my Higher Power to help me with healing and health." Instead, you must assess their understanding of how their Higher Power acts in the world and what "help" from such a Higher Power might look like to them.
5. Create checklists of potential outcomes, particularly subjective ones. Doing so says more about our desire to "wrap up" an encounter and does not reflect the complexity of ongoing pastoral care.
6. Use the word "presence" or the phrase "just being there" to describe the intense ministry of pastoral care.
7. Reduce people to their membership in a certain faith tradition.
8. Confuse the tools that you use with an assessment or goals.
9. Put spirituality in a silo separated from the needs of the whole person, nor limit your assessment to purely "religious" variables (e.g., church attendance, frequency of prayer).
10. Use language that promotes a certain faith tradition. For example, use "faith community" rather than "church"; use "pastoral minister" rather than "priest."

*Figure 4.3*

and the Ten Commandments, allow me to finish by listing my top ten "Thou shall nots" related to documentation (see Figure 4.3).

In the next chapter, we'll see to how to use this assessment model to develop a plan for ministering to a particular person and how to document your goals, interventions, and outcomes.

## Notes

1. Stephen R. Covey, *Seven Habits of Highly Effective People* (New York: Simon and Schuster, 1989).
2. Based on D. W. Donovan and Melvin Dowdy, PhD, "The Pastoral Assessment Tool: Developing the Centerpiece of the Pastoral Care Strategic Plan" (unpublished presentation).
3. George Fitchett, "The 7 x 7 Model for Spiritual Assessment: A Brief Introduction and Bibliography," www.rushu.rush.edu/servlet/Satellite?blobcol=urlfile&blobheader=application/pdf&blobkey=id&blobnocache=true&blobtable=document&blobwhere=1144357138306&ssbinary=true. See also George Fitchett, *Assessing Spiritual Needs: A Guide for Caregivers* (Lima, OH: Academic Renewal Press, 2002).
4. Author's note: This story and those that follow are composites of many different encounters from more than twenty years of pastoral work. While remaining true to the events that inspired these stories, key elements have been altered to honor the confidentiality of those involved.
5. Joint Commission, *Advancing Effective Communication, Cultural Competence, and Patient- and Family-Centered Care: A Roadmap for Hospitals*, www.jointcommission.org/assets/1/6/ARoadmapforHospitalsfinalversion727.pdf, p. 42.
6. Joint Commission on Accreditation of Health Care Organizations, *The Source* 3, no. 2 (February 2005).
7. Ibid.
8. V. Frankl, *Man's Search for Meaning* (Cutchogue, NY: Buccaneer Books, 1993), 7.
9. Andrew Lloyd Weber, "Poor, Poor Pharaoh / Song of the King," in *Joseph and the Amazing Technical Dreamcoat*.
10. Dave Barry, www.worldofquotes.com/author/Dave-Barry/1/index.html.
11. Edmund Pellegrino, MD, "Hospitals as Moral Agents" (lecture, Saint Mary's Hospital, Richmond, VA, March 26, 2002).
12. George Fitchett and Andrea L. Canada, "The Role of Religion / Spirituality in Coping with Cancer: Evidence, Assessment, and Intervention," in *Psycho-oncology*, 2nd ed., ed. Jimmie C. Holland (New York: Oxford University Press, 2010), 440–46.
13. Paul Alexander Clark, Maxwell Drain, and Mary Malone, "Addressing Patients' Emotional and Spiritual Needs," *Joint Commission Journal on Quality and Safety* 29, no. 12 (December 2003): 659–70.
14. Ibid.
15. Ibid.

16. T. E. Burroughs et al., "Understanding Patient Willingness to Recommend and Return: A Strategy for Prioritizing Improvement Opportunities," *Joint Commission Journal on Quality Improvement* 25 (June 1999): 251–87.
17. Alexander Tartaglia et al., "Care for the Critical Care Provider, Too?" *American Journal of Critical Care* 12 (2003): 545–47.
18. J. J. Driscoll, "Chaplains and Physicians: Diagnosticians of Care," *Vision*, May 1994.

## About the Contributor

**Chaplain D. W. Donovan, MA, MS, BCC,** currently serves as the mission leader at Providence Holy Cross Medical Center in Mission Hills, California. Board certified since 2001, Donovan has served in hospital chaplaincy since 1997. He served as chief resident of the Pastoral Care Department at the Medical College of Virginia and as the manager of pastoral care at Bon Secours Richmond Health System. Donovan served as committee secretary and general editor in the writing of the *Common Standards for the Certification and Practice of Chaplaincy* and served as the first lead interview team educator with the National Association of Catholic Chaplains (NACC). Highly involved with medical ethics, he is the author of "Defending the Donor's Decision: An Analysis of the Ethical Issues Related to First-Person Declarations of Organ Donation," published in *Health Progress*. He consults on a range of issues related to pastoral care, medical ethics, and liturgy.

# 5

## Creating and Implementing a Spiritual / Pastoral Care Plan

*Rabbi Stephen B. Roberts, MBA, MHL, BCJC; Chaplain D. W. Donovan, MA, MS, BCC; and Rev. George Handzo, MDiv, BCC, CSSBB*

*A spiritual screening tool completed by a nurse indicated that a patient had specific chaplaincy needs. The request for a professional chaplaincy consult was provided to me with no other information other than it was urgent. When I entered the room I noticed how young Sarah was, in her late thirties or early forties. Next to her bed was a picture of herself, a man her age, and a child. Sarah was dying. During our visit she asked me to visit her daughter, Rebecca, who was also currently hospitalized in the same facility. They both had an extremely rare genetic disease, which Sarah only learned about after the birth of Rebecca. Sarah was end stage, and Rebecca was now in the early stages of the disease. Rebecca was only twelve years old, and this was her first hospitalization. It would turn out to be Sarah's last. I met Abraham, the husband / father, at Rebecca's bedside when I went to visit. I also met Terach and Kitura, one set of Rebecca's grandparents, who were at her bedside as well.*

Planning is an important part of our lives. We go to the supermarket with a plan—a shopping list; we drive with a plan—a map; if we are from a liturgical tradition, we worship from a plan—a prayer book. Good planning ensures that we remember the important things and also reach our goals in life.

Yet, chaplains are often resistant to using spiritual / pastoral plans that clearly document assessed spiritual / pastoral issues regarding the patient / resident / family, state goals that we desire to see accomplished based upon the assessed needs, then provide clear interventions and expectations about the interventions, and finally document outcomes based upon the interventions. Even worse, chaplains rarely work to ensure that their plans are fully integrated into the overall plan of care created for the patient / resident. Many chaplains' chart notes are not read because they do not include information useful to the team, including a plan that helps the entire team provide better care to the patient and family.

The focus of this chapter is how to help the reader contribute to the overall plan of care through effective documentation. This chapter is intended to provide specifics on a spiritual / pastoral care plan; discuss how they might differ based upon the institution; explore and provide examples of spiritual symptoms; and discuss in detail the spiritual / pastoral care plan sections that focus on goals and then on interventions that are developed from the goals and that lead directly to expected outcomes related to the goals.

## *Key Assumptions*

The Association of Professional Chaplains' *Standards of Practice for Professional Chaplains in Acute Care Settings* states the first assumption: "The chaplain develops and implements a plan of care to promote patient well-being and continuity of care."[1] We thus assume that all current and future professional chaplains, plus those who educate chaplains, will be interested in developing and implementing expert care plans done on par with the work of other health care departments, such as social work, dietary, physical therapy, medicine, and so on.

The second key assumption is that the spiritual / pastoral plan of care is an integral part of the overall plan of care. Thus, when creating a care plan, the chaplain needs to differentiate between the more general spiritual care sections in which the whole team participates, in particular helping with spiritual screening and history, and the "professional chaplaincy" care sections, which are the specific part of the plan that the professional chaplain does: spiritual assessment, goal setting, and spiritual interventions.

> We support the idea that spiritual care is everyone's job on at least two levels. As caregivers who have our own spiritual dimension, we should be relating to our patients and their loved ones on this level. Furthermore, every professional caregiver, while each has a specialty on the health care team, needs to have an awareness of and a concern for the whole person—physical, emotional, social and spiritual. For example, the chaplain needs to be able to recognize and generally evaluate suicidal ideation, both to be able to pass on this information to those on the team whose job it is to respond to it, and to be able to then properly interpret and treat the depth of the patient's spiritual distress. Spiritual assessment should be a part of a patient's overall assessment by their primary care physician, along with assessment of the physical and psychological domains.[2]

The final key assumption is that there is a difference between spiritual care, which anyone on the team can provide, and "chaplaincy" care, which only a trained clinician in spiritual care can provide (i.e., spiritual assessment, goal setting based upon stated spiritual issues, and then appropriate spiritual interventions). Rev. George Handzo writes in chapter 3:

> The professional board certified chaplain is the spiritual care lead on the health care team. This does not mean that the chaplain is the only one to do spiritual care. It does mean that the chaplain is the spiritual care specialist who oversees the spiritual and religious component of care and is the subject-matter expert for the rest of the team.

With this final assumption is the strong caveat that professional chaplains are responsible for finding ways *and* training the larger team on how to do spiritual screening and provide spiritual care appropriate to their training and skills set. On this second subject our colleague Chaplain Kristopher P. Zygowiec writes the following in *PlainViews*:

> At this time we ask ourselves this question: how can each of us contribute to creating a caring environment for all, regardless of our individual responsibilities? One way is by communicating to our guests that we are comfortable and open to assisting them with the ritual of prayer, if requested. How can we do this in a sensitive way, leaving complete control in the hands of the patient / guest? The words which were shared by a friend: "WOULD a prayer BE HELPFUL?" fulfilled that purpose. We created ID badge tags.... This ID badge tag is available to all members of the St. Helena

> Hospital Region team whether they have direct contact with our clients or not. At the end of every orientation, I often have a few people asking for this tag. As I share the principle of a supportive prayer, I point to the back of the tag where they can read the sample of a short prayer: "Dear God, In times like this we are thankful to place our faith and trust in You. We ask for hope, healing, and peace in Your loving care. Amen." The response has been very positive, and the members of the staff (from Environmental Services to our doctors) who feel comfortable with being asked to pray by our clients are also beginning to wear this tag with their ID badge. In a hospital setting, the chaplain does not have unilateral access to the patients and caregivers. That access is shared by the whole team which is responsible for creating a healing environment, and the number-one spiritual intervention that is requested—a prayer—plays an extraordinary part in it. A similar approach can be implemented in every health care institution (not only faith-based) which takes spirituality seriously.[3]

We know this is a controversial topic, especially in facilities where there is not a standard practice / operating procedure. We had a long discussion about this topic ourselves. While Chaplain Zygowiec's approach represents one option, that option might not be acceptable or advisable in all settings and requires a good bit of oversight and ongoing training by the chaplaincy team. We encourage all departments to have an open discussion with the entire range of stakeholders about this topic. Quality improvement projects are one way to investigate and standardize within your facility. Strategic planning using outcome oriented chaplaincy projects is another approach to this topic.

## *Plans of Care Should Be Specific to Your Type of Institution*

The Psalter found in the Hebrew scriptures includes 150 different psalms. Why? One psalm does not fit every occasion. Nor does one type of care plan fit all institutions. Many health care systems now include acute care (adult and pediatric), behavioral health, hospice, and long-term care within the range of services they offer. Care plans for medicine, social work, nursing, and so on look different within the different lines of service. Our care plans must also accurately reflect the type of chaplaincy we specifically provide, based upon location and service line. There is great commonality, but there are also great differences. In setting up professional, replicable, explainable, and consistent spiritual / pastoral plans of care, each type of line of service needs one specifically crafted for it. There will be overlap between the plans, but there will also be unique features to each plan. Our challenge, as a profession, is to consistently craft these plans so that when our professional colleagues working in other departments move from institution to institution but remain doing the same type of work, they will be able to instantly recognize and feel comfortable with the spiritual / pastoral care plan at the new institution.

## *Only a Detailed Spiritual Assessment Leads to a Plan*

> *I met extensively with Sarah, Rebecca, and Abraham. After a thorough spiritual assessment, it became clear that each member of this family had their unique profound spiritual issues that required professional chaplaincy attention. The assessment also indicated that each person also had more general spiritual needs that could be met by the larger staff.*

There is a major distinction between a spiritual screening and spiritual assessment. A screening is a basic tool that can be done by any member of the professional team. In chapter 3, Rev. Handzo writes:

> The screening should, at minimum, evaluate how important religion and spirituality are to the patient's coping, how well those coping strategies are working at the moment, and whether the patient has any immediate religious or spiritual needs that require chaplaincy care intervention. The success of the referral system depends on the ability and willingness of non-chaplaincy care clinical staff to reliably do spiritual screening.... We recommend a screening system developed by George Fitchett, which has been shown to have a high reliability in identifying spiritual distress.

An assessment, on the other hand, can only be done by a trained professional chaplain. In particular, as stated in chapter 3:

> The assessment should elicit information that will lead to a profile of the patient's spiritual and religious resources and needs, and *a plan of care* with interventions and expected outcomes. (italics added)

## The Plan

First, all plans need to be clear. This is essential so that the information within the plan is understood by members of the team when they refer to it. Remember, our plan will be referenced numerous times when we are not present to answer questions. Second, our plans must be fully and completely incorporated into the larger care plan. This is one way we integrate with the rest of the team—and thus become integral to the overall care plan. Finally, the plan needs to indicate who is responsible for what actions. Without this, no one is responsible for the action. Plans must lead to accountability.

A chaplain who is fully integrated into a larger care team may feel that documenting a plan of care is too time-consuming and even redundant. Such a chaplain would likely have spoken with the relevant physician as well as the nurse caring for the patient. But a health care team taking care of a single patient can easily include twenty or more people, all of whom may benefit in some way from your assessment.

This leads to the second point: documentation must include both your professional assessment of the relevant issues and clear "take-aways" for your colleagues. Consider the following example:

> ***Follow-up with patient and husband:*** *Upon my arrival, both were crying. As we explored their unfolding grief, Abraham noted that he was embarrassed to feel sorry for himself. He spoke of feeling overwhelmed with the prospect of being a single father to Rebecca. He has granted me permission to share this information with the treatment team, whom he feels are often insensitive and make comments that presume the bulk of the work will be done by other women in the family.*
>
> ***Plan:*** *Chaplain will continue to explore this issue with family. Nurse manager will speak to issue with care team members tomorrow, and it will be discussed as a part of rounds the day after.*
>
> ***Recommendations:*** *Although the cultural background of many of our staff is matriarchal, it is important to avoid projecting these assumptions onto this family. Special attention should be given to involving the father in any and all conversations that involve the daughter. This has been discussed in particular with Social Work in terms of helping him plan (emotionally and*

*practically) for the discharge of his daughter in the context of making end-of-life plans with his wife.*

A good plan helps all team members know what is expected of them (they have clarity). Further, it focuses each person who has responsibility for any part of the plan. Focus leads to a productive use of time by all team members, as each person becomes deliberate about what they must do and by when.

## Symptoms and Issues Assessed

*I could have easily written "spiritual distress" for both Sarah and her daughter Rebecca. Yet, that would not have helped me or the staff address their specific spiritual / pastoral issues. Rather, Sarah's assessment in the care plan included: "(1) Sarah is feeling overwhelming guilt related to her impending death, thus depriving her daughter of her time and her guidance, as well as feeling guilty for having passed the genetic illness on to her. This guilt is causing great upset for her and her husband. (2) As the only child of Holocaust survivors, Sarah is also struggling with the deep loss her parents are feeling. This hospitalization has opened old spiritual wounds around loss for the whole family. Sarah feels this spiritual struggle is preventing her from focusing on herself and her daughter. (3) Finally, Sarah is currently unable to comfort her daughter, who is hospitalized for the first time with the same genetic illness. The daughter is being treated in the PICU."*

When a patient / resident is suffering physical pain, it must be documented in the care plan. The person assessing the situation will include the pain's location, amount, onset, and any other issues related to the pain. Only then can the plan continue with treatment. Similarly, it is not enough just to write "spiritual distress" as a spiritual assessment. The documentation must be more extensive. It should be able to include the following:

- What exactly are the spiritual / pastoral issues assessed that need treatment?
- How long have the various issues been going on (did it start as a result of this hospitalization / illness or was it there previously)?

- What is most likely causing each issue?
- How does the issue impact the patient / resident and his or her care?

These bulleted concerns must be clearly included in the care plan. They need to be comprehensible, concise, and understandable by both the chaplains and others who read the chart.

Figure 5.1 lists a sample of spiritual / pastoral symptoms and issues that might come up in an in-depth assessment that should be documented.

While this list is extensive, it is not complete. Different situations will include different issues. For example, someone working in a pediatric intensive care unit might document, "Sibling guilt leading to sibling not wanting to visit" or "Sibling despair as he / she feels helpless and unable to support loved one and what he / she is going through. The patient is thus feeling isolated and in need of support." Someone working in a hospice environment might document, "Spousal spiritual / emotional exhaustion leading to cutting down on visits, leading to patient feeling abandoned" or "Unfinished family issues that patient is spiritually struggling with, causing great spiritual distress." Someone in a long-term care facility might document, "Spiritual loss brought on by loss of independence and private residence. Resident has indicated this loss is leading to feeling sad, gray, without joy, and a distance from God."

Each facility should work from a consistent list developed for their specific type of work. The consistency of assessment will allow other professionals to understand the issues that we assess and address. This also helps them make appropriate referrals to our department when they notice specific issues that we are trained to address.

## Goals

> ***Goals for Sarah:*** *(1) Help Sarah and her husband feel less overwhelmed by spiritual issues of guilt. Help her to directly concentrate on her concerns to help in this goal. (2) Help Sarah to focus more on herself by helping her and her family address the multigenerational spiritually struggles around loss this illness is bringing up. (3) Help Sarah find ways to comfort her daughter, Rebecca, who is currently in the PICU.*

Goals come before interventions. Goals are destinations we seek to reach for the patient / family we are working with. They are based upon

## EXAMPLES OF SPIRITUAL / PASTORAL SYMPTOMS AND ISSUES THAT SHOULD BE DOCUMENTED

- 12-step and spirituality
- Abandonment
  - By family and friends
  - By God
  - By religious community
- Anger
- Courage—spiritual
- Courage to change
- Denial
- Depression—as a spiritual illness
- Faith
- Forgiveness
  - Toward God
  - Toward others
  - Toward self
- God / Higher Power
- Grief / loss
- Guilt
- Hope
- Hopelessness / despair
- How spirituality helps in healing
- Illness as identity / living with chronic illness
- Loneliness
- Love
- Meaning / meaninglessness
  - Of illness
  - Of life
  - Of world
- Peace / peace in adversity
- Prayer / meditation
- Punishment
- Reconciliation
- "Recovery"
- Redemption / renewal
- Relationships
- Repentance
- Rituals and symbols
- Sanctification / sanctity of life
- Serenity
- Sin
- Spiritual emptiness
- Suffering
- Suicide
- Temptation
- Transitions / change
- What is religion?
- What is spirituality?
- Wonder, awe

*Figure 5.1*

the assessed and documented needs, which should come prior in a care plan and which they should reference. The interventions then become the specific tools we use to help all involved reach the destination. Goals need to be specific so they are both "measurable" and leave us "accountable." Goals need to clearly state:

- Spiritual issue being addressed.
- Who should be doing this? (Assumption is the chaplain. When it is not the chaplain, it must be clearly stated who should be working on the issue.)
- Measurable outcome (sometimes stated and sometimes implied).

Sarah's first issue, as documented in the care plan, was not guilt. Rather, it was Sarah's sense of being overwhelmed by the guilt. The specific care plan goal was to help her feel less overwhelmed (not less guilty). It was specific and measurable. In future conversations, staff members, whether from chaplaincy, social work, and / or medicine, can assess and then document whether she states she is feeling the same, less, or more overwhelmed by the "guilt related to her impending death, thus depriving her daughter of her time and her guidance, as well as feeling guilty for having passed the genetic illness on to her."

One way to assess is a closed-ended question such as by a social work colleague who is supportive of our mission: "You mentioned to the chaplain that the guilt you were feeling was overwhelming you. I see in the chart that [*intervention described*]. Has the feeling of being overwhelmed by the guilt lessened, stayed the same, or increased?" The nature of this closed-ended question is a measurement in relationship to a goal. Further, by the specific nature of the goal we are held accountable in a similar way to someone who is treating physical pain.

The second goal is to help Sarah be able to focus on herself. Multigenerational loss is the spiritual issue that needs to be addressed. If we are successful, then we, or any member of the care team, will be able to assess and document that Sarah feels she is better able to focus on herself at this time. Again, by the use of a closed-ended question, one can make this determination. Think of the pain chart test. Using one through nine, the patient / resident indicates how much pain he or she is feeling at that moment. Checking the chart allows the caregiver to know whether the pain is more or less. A specific question that any member of the staff can ask Sarah is: "A couple of days ago you let the team know you were struggling to stay focused on yourself due to the multigenerational loss your family is going through. Are you able to focus more, the same, or less on yourself today?"

We encourage you to think of questions that might determine whether the third goal has been met.

## Goals and Discharge Planning

It is important to emphatically state that chaplains, like the rest of the staff in hospital and rehabilitation facilities, should also tie their goals into discharge planning. Yes, we, as members of a larger health care team, are also involved in discharge planning! The work of helping a patient recover and leave the facility is good chaplaincy on our part. Further, it is good stewardship of limited resources if we help get a patient appropriately discharged without spending unneeded additional days in a health care setting. We know that the longer people stay in a health care facility like a hospital, the more likely they are to develop infections and other secondary health issues.

There are a variety of issues and situations for which professional chaplains are uniquely positioned to help someone leave the facility earlier rather than later. The authors of this chapter have all been actively, repeatedly, and on an ongoing basis involved in setting spiritual / pastoral goals directly related to discharge. The trigger may not come from our assessment, but it may come from another department's assessment. Integrating our care plan into the larger care plan not only allows us to have our notes seen by others, but equally, also allows for us to read other notes and be able to step in and provide needed resources.

Following are a few examples of how chaplains can and should be involved in goals related to discharge:

- A chaplain may discover that a patient is not fully participating in his rehabilitation because he believes that God is punishing him. He may believe that it is thus not proper for him to be free of pain and feeling better and that God will heal him when it is the right time. The chaplain may be able to reframe this belief to include the possibility that God wants and even expects us to participate in our own healing.
- A social work note may indicate that hospital discharge is being delayed because someone needs a ride home and then help into and within her house. If we know the person is active in a house of worship, the chaplain can often help facilitate, with the patient's permission, involving the health ministry / caring committee of the congregation to meet this discharge-specific need.

- A patient care coordinator note may indicate that a patient needs someone to stay with him for a couple of days after discharge but is unwilling to agree to "allow strangers in my home." Often these patients may be comfortable with members of their religious community staying with them. We can thus facilitate this spiritual process of connecting a congregant with his congregation.

Patients hospitalized for behavioral health issues often have their spiritual and religious resources overlooked by other departments when it comes to discharge planning. They are not the experts when it comes to networking and making connections with local houses of worship; we are. Houses of worship and leaders of faith communities are often overlooked as resources to help someone struggling with a behavioral health issue stay well and out of the hospital.[4] In our thinking about discharge planning, we can help document spiritual and religious tools a patient might possess to allow him or her to be discharged. Further, we can then become involved in helping the patient learn to use these resources.

Outcome oriented chaplaincy impels us to work smarter, for the good of the patients and their families, in the specific area of discharge planning. If not us, who? If not now, when?

## Interventions

*Day X: Recommend the following interventions for Sarah: (1) Chaplain explore with Sarah and her husband various spiritual tools from her tradition, such as ethical wills and other similar spiritual tools, that will allow her to guide and accompany her daughter in the years ahead. This might help in lowering her sense of being overwhelmed by guilt. (2) Recommend involvement of Dr. Ben Met of Consult Liaison Psychiatry. His expertise is multigenerational loss. He himself is the child of Holocaust survivors and has extensive experience in this field. His involvement might facilitate patient being able to be less distracted by her family's multigenerational needs around loss. (3) Chaplain will work to arrange a meeting of nurse managers and social workers of both this unit and PICU with patient to strategize on ways to allow her to be further involved in her daughter's care and be able to help provide comfort to her at this time.*

*Day Y [7 days after X]: (1) Over the last week chaplain explored with Sarah and her husband "ethical wills," a spiritual tool found in Judaism (patient's religion). Sarah is starting to make one now. She is also working with her husband to create a series of letters, pictures, and collages to be given to Rebecca, her daughter, at different points in her life that Sarah knows she will not be present for. These include bat mitzvah, sweet sixteen, loss of any grandparent, starting high school, various holy days in the years ahead, finishing high school, starting college, and finishing first semester of college. Sarah stated during our work together that these practical and concrete spiritual tools are helping her feel less overwhelmed by her guilt. (2) Followed up with Sarah after Dr. Ben Met's visit. She indicated that her parents, in particular, found speaking with him helpful and that they planned to continue meeting with him. Sarah articulated a deep sense of relief and felt it easier now (than when we previously spoke) to put the focus back on herself and her needs. (3) As indicated elsewhere in notes (see Social Work and Nursing), Sarah is working closely with staff from both this unit and PICU to find ways to comfort her daughter. She particularly found helpful the picture phone installed in both her room and her daughter's so she can watch, talk, and spend more time with Rebecca. Sarah's face lit up when she recounted how she was able to read to Rebecca from the same book that someone was holding for Rebecca. Her husband indicated that he has not seen Sarah this happy since she was admitted and profusely thanked the staff for the creative ways we have addressed Sarah's sadness.*

Interventions should be based upon goals, either previously stated in a care plan or ones that will be included in the care plan after the visit (i.e., for first visits or in cases in which new issues were assessed during a visit and then treated). Further, interventions should relate and reference specific goals when put in writing.

Equally important, after a first visit, care plans should include proposed interventions based upon the assessment if subsequent visits are planned or needed. Future visits will most likely occur when patients are in intensive care units, have illnesses that bring them repeatedly back to a health care facility (such as cancer), are in a behavioral health facility (where the average length of stay is still longer than a day or two versus a medical facility), are in hospice, or are residents of a long-term care facility (for reasoning on these assumptions see chapter 28). Then in subsequent visits, assuming that a chaplain sees a patient more than once, the care plan should document interventions provided and their outcomes. Our profession is moving toward outcome oriented chaplaincy. Our care plans, to be state of the art and current, need to incorporate this methodology within them.

Chaplains have a wide range of interventions at their disposal. Figure 5.2 lists just a few of the major areas. (See also chapter 27, Figure 27.1 for other interventions.)

A key part of outcome oriented chaplaincy, as it relates to interventions, is documenting our specific and detailed interventions and equally their outcomes—positive, negative, and none. Just as writing "spiritual distress" is no longer state of the art, neither is just documenting "pastoral visit with interventions." Writing "spiritual distress" is the equivalent of a nurse writing "sick" and does little to advance our shared understanding of the issues that need to be addressed. Our care plan intervention notes need to be detailed, clear, and concise. Further, they need to be ones that any member of the team can read and have an understanding of both the goal and the expected outcome of the intervention, whether successful or not.

With Sarah, the patient in this chapter's case, the first assessed spiritual issue was "being overwhelmed by guilt." The stated spiritual / pastoral goal was to "help her feel less overwhelmed." The proposed initial intervention as it related to this issue and goal was exploring spiritual tools directly related to the stated issue—"depriving her daughter of her time and her guidance." The intervention was about working with Sarah to help her gain a sense of control, the opposite of being overwhelmed. A specific outcome was desired and documented.

The follow-up chart note then went into detail about the intervention. It documented the intervention in plain English, so that any member of the team could understand. Understanding of the proposed / actual intervention is essential in a team environment. The chaplain has limited time (i.e., limited resources). The clarity of the note in the care plan allows other team members to become involved in the patient's spiritual care.

To reiterate, the chaplain has the expertise to make a detailed spiritual / pastoral assessment and set up specific goals. We are the subject-matter experts and thus oversee the spiritual care. However, in a team environment, others may help implement the goal—depending on the situation.

## EXAMPLES OF SPIRITUAL / PASTORAL INTERVENTIONS

Exploring and developing spiritual coping resources

Helping patients examine / explore the following from a spiritual perspective:

- Abandonment
- Anger
- Confession
- Courage
- Depression as a spiritual illness
- Emptiness
- Forgiveness
- Guilt
- Hope
- Hopelessness
- How spirituality helps in healing
- Living with chronic illness
- Loneliness
- Meaning
- Meaninglessness
- Meditation
- Negative religious experiences
- Prayer
- Repentance
- Salvation / redemption
- Sin
- Suicide / sanctity of life
- Respect / self-respect
- Ritual(s)

Helping patients examine their image of God and increase their spiritual understanding of that image in relationship to:

- Coping with chronic illness
- Hope
- Their attitudes
- Their behavior
- Their purpose

Helping patients examine their spiritual belief system, including:

- "Beneficial" nature of core religious / spiritual beliefs
- Benefits of individual beliefs
- Congruence of core religious / spiritual beliefs
- Non-"beneficial" nature of core religious / spiritual beliefs
- Reality of beliefs versus symptomalogy of illness
- Role of God / Higher Power in recovery process
- Role of spirituality / spiritual tools in recovery
- Supporting and / or developing religious coping resources

Patients' Pastoral and Spiritual Resources

- Active in religious community
- Active prayer life
- Active religious home life

*Figure 5.2*

With Sarah, the nurses, nurses' aides, doctors, social workers, dietitians, and food service workers could all ask her and her husband about the progress of her projects, thus giving her more of a sense of control and also encouraging her to continue. Equally important is that other team members can sit with the patient and have her talk about the different components of the work she is doing, thus involving the full team in the spiritual / pastoral care plan. Other team members can then also document their involvement and any outcomes they observe that may occur when the chaplain is not present—such as feeling less overwhelmed by her sense of guilt.

Referrals are a key part of the job of a professional chaplain. Knowing when and to whom to refer—both in general and also in a specific facility—should always be part of our ongoing professional development. The care plan in this chapter documented the need for a referral, the goals for a referral, and finally the outcomes from the referral.

We encourage you on your own or as part of a group process to review and discuss / reflect on Sarah's third spiritual issue, the goals related to it, the proposed intervention, and then the documented actual intervention and outcome.

## *Electronic Medical Record and Care Plans*

Electronic medical records (EMRs) are the new state of the art. Soon all charts will be in this format. EMRs offer some clear advantages over paper charting as they relate to documenting assessed issues. At the same time, they bring their own challenges.

Some of the positives of the EMR as they relate to care plans include the following:

- The work of drafting the chaplaincy section of the EMR will help organize the chaplain's work. The chaplaincy section of the EMR should be more than just boxes in which professional chaplains, chaplaincy residents, and clinical pastoral education (CPE) students check off issues they have observed, suggested interventions, and goals they seek. Check boxes may work in many cases (particularly with CPE students and others just learning our field), but the writers of this chapter strongly feel that it also needs to include sections for free-form writing of the details of our care plan for more complete and / or complicated cases. Further, these text boxes help prevent us from moving from "patient-centered care" to "chart-centered care."

- In designing the chaplaincy / spiritual / pastoral care department section of the EMR, those in the department will be obligated to clearly articulate to both those designing and those approving the EMR system the spiritual / pastoral issues they assess, interventions they provide, and goals they seek to accomplish in that particular institution. This clarity then carries over in allowing chaplains to clearly explain and document the work they do, through the EMR, to those they engage with on a daily basis.
- The EMR, if set up properly and with forethought, should help chaplains systematically reflect upon the work we do. Reflection upon the work we do is something we learn as CPE students using verbatims. EMRs can help us keep this skill current and focused.
- Having a chaplaincy section fully integrated into the EMR should help improve communications and interactions between chaplaincy departments and others within the institution.
- Consistency in charting leads to increased accountability as well as increased professional respect and recognition by our coworkers.
- In departments that train in the field of chaplaincy, a well-designed EMR helps those new to the field better understand the role and function they should be seeking to grow into.
- Ultimately, a good EMR departmental section will help each member become more of an effective, outcome oriented professional chaplain.

Some of the "growing edges" of the EMR as they relate to a care plan include the following:

- The challenge of looking at each patient / resident as a unique individual with his or her own distinctive life history rather than just a number that needs to have boxes checked off.

- Time to effectively complete a personalized care plan rather than just using the check boxes to get done quickly.
- Working with management to get the EMR updated as the department changes and its needs and focus of work change.

## *Religious Needs*

Religious needs are not the same as spiritual / pastoral needs. A patient, resident, or family member might have no need for spiritual / pastoral care and yet have high religious needs. The system set up in your institution should be able to separate the two, particularly at the screening stage. A professional chaplain often does not need to provide the religious items, particularly when there is limited staff and high needs. However, the department is always responsible for making sure they are available and provided in a timely fashion. Also, these needs should be documented in the chaplain's chart note so that staff are aware of what the patient's religious practices are. For example, the chart note could say, "Patient prays three times a day around X times" or "Patient eats only kosher food and may therefore be concerned about by-products that could be in medication."

Religious needs include the following:

- Food according to certain religious standards (e.g., halal or kosher)
- Religious items (e.g., sacred scripture, prayer books, rosaries, electric candles for the Sabbath, prayer rugs)
- Access to religious worship (e.g., daily in some traditions; weekly—Friday, Saturday, or Sunday depending on tradition; holy day services)
- Access to sacraments. The most common sacrament needed in the United States at the current time is the Eucharist. It is important to make sure that the chart properly reflects the person's religion, because there is a difference among Protestant, Roman Catholic, and Orthodox traditions as

to who may receive the sacrament from their tradition. Other sacraments often requested are anointing and prayers for healing.

## Notes

1. Standard 2 of Association of Professional Chaplains, *Standards of Practice for Professional Chaplains in Acute Care Settings*, www.professionalchaplains.org/uploadedFiles/pdf/Standards%20of%20Practice%20Draft%20Document%2002 1109.pdf#Project_Update.
2. G. Handzo and H. Koenig, "Spiritual Care: Whose Job Is It Anyway?" *Southern Medical Journal* 97, no. 12 (December 2004): 1242–44.
3. K. Zygowiec, "Asking for a Prayer—Without Asking," *PlainViews* 8, no. 6 (April 20, 2011).
4. Glen Milstein et al., "Implementation of a Program to Improve the Continuity of Mental Health Care through Clergy Outreach and Professional Engagement (C.O.P.E.)," *Professional Psychology: Research and Practice* 39, no. 2 (2008): 218–28.

## Further Reading

Fitchett, George, and James Risk. "Screening for Spiritual Struggle." *Journal of Pastoral Care and Counseling* 62, nos. 1–2 (2009): 1–12.

Puchalski, C., and B. Ferrell. *Making Health Care Whole: Integrating Spirituality into Patient Care.* West Conshohocken, PA: Templeton Press, 2010.

## About the Contributors

**Rabbi Stephen B. Roberts, MBA, MHL, BCJC,** is the editor of this book and coeditor of *Disaster Spiritual Care: Practical Clergy Response to Community, Regional and National Tragedy* (SkyLight Paths Publishing). He is a past president of the National Association of Jewish Chaplains. Most recently he served as the associate executive vice president of the New York Board of Rabbis, directing their chaplaincy program, providing services in more than fifty locations throughout New York, plus serving as the endorser for both New York State's and New York City's Jewish chaplains. Prior to this he served as the director of chaplaincy of the Beth Israel Medical System (New York), overseeing chaplains and CPE programs at three acute care hospitals, one behavioral health hospital, plus various outpatient facilities served by chaplains.

**Chaplain D. W. Donovan, MA, MS, BCC,** currently serves as the mission leader at Providence Holy Cross Medical Center in Mission Hills, California. Board certified since 2001, Donovan has served in hospital chaplaincy since 1997. He served as chief resident of the Pastoral Care Department at the Medical College of Virginia and as the manager of pastoral care at Bon Secours Richmond Health System. Donovan served as committee secretary and general editor in the writing of the *Common Standards for the Certification and Practice of Chaplaincy* and served as the first lead interview team educator with the National Association of Catholic Chaplains (NACC). Highly involved with medical ethics, he is the author of "Defending the Donor's Decision: An Analysis of the Ethical Issues Related to First-Person Declarations of Organ Donation," published in *Health Progress*. He consults on a range of issues related to pastoral care, medical ethics, and liturgy.

**Rev. George Handzo, MDiv, BCC, CSSBB,** is the vice president of Chaplaincy Care Leadership and Practice at HealthCare Chaplaincy. Rev. Handzo directs the only consulting service devoted to the strategic assessment, planning, and management of chaplaincy services. HealthCare Chaplaincy employs best practices in strategic planning and clinical practice to maximize the effectiveness of an organization's pastoral care and to align it with the institution's overall objectives. Prior to his current position, Rev. Handzo was the director of Chaplaincy Services at Memorial Sloan-Kettering Cancer Center for more than twenty years and is a past president of the Association of Professional Chaplains. He serves on the Distress Guidelines Panel of the National Comprehensive Cancer Network. Rev. Handzo has authored or coauthored more than fifty chapters and articles on the practice of pastoral care.

# 6

# Chaplains and Charting

*Rabbi H. Rafael Goldstein, BCJC*

## *Why Chart?*

The patient's medical record is a legal document that maintains a clear and succinct log of all interventions with the patient. As such, every professional member of the health care team is required by the Joint Commission to meticulously document interactions and interventions with the patient. The chaplain is no exception to this rule.[1]

The Association for Clinical Pastoral Education's (ACPE) chaplaincy training curriculum includes writing notes in the patient's medical record as a component of chaplaincy training,[2] and the *Standards of Practice for Professional Chaplains in Acute Care Settings* according to the Association of Professional Chaplains include, "Standard 3, Documentation of Care: The chaplain enters information into the patient's medical record that is relevant to the patient's medical, psychosocial, and spiritual / religious goals of care."[3]

Aside from the legal requirement to make notes in the medical record of patients, charting is a major means of communication between the chaplain and the health care team. A chart note will enable staff to:

1. Know that you have seen the patient.
2. Know the issues with which the patient may be dealing.
3. Provide useful information to the team about the patient about which they may not be aware. For instance, a patient may say to the chaplain that his / her spouse died recently and may not have mentioned this significant life

event to medical staff, who may have been focusing on the patient's physical symptoms.

4. Establish a spiritual care treatment plan.

## *Standard of Practice*

Mount Sinai Medical Center's Pastoral Care Department conducted research on the current standard of practice regarding charting by surveying the top hospitals according to *U.S. News and World Report*.[4] The chaplains at these hospitals were asked the following questions:

1. Does the chaplain have access to the medical record?
2. Does the chaplain make notes in the medical record?
3. Does the chaplain make entries in the electronic medical record?
4. Is there any special credentialing required for chaplains to have access?

Of the "honor roll" (top fourteen) hospitals, 100 percent of the chaplains had access to medical records, made notes in the medical records, and accessed electronic medical records. None required additional credentialing. We then surveyed the *U.S. News and World Report*'s top twenty hospitals in the fields of cancer, geriatrics, and heart. In all three categories, there was only one hospital where chaplains did not make notes in the medical records. However, some hospitals have not fully developed their electronic medical records, and therefore some of the chaplains are not currently making electronic chart notes. All expect they will be included as their electronic medical record system is developed.

This research clearly shows that the top hospitals in the United States, according to *U.S. News and World Report*, include the chaplain in their health care teams and that this is the standard of practice.[5]

## *The Chart Is a Legal Document—Less* Is *More*

While we want the rest of the health care team to know what we have learned, accomplished, plan, think might be useful, and so forth, the chart is a legal document. Discretion is always the better approach. When there is information that should not be kept as a part of a permanent legal record, it may be better to meet with the patient's nurse or other member of the health care team to voice your concerns or questions.

Chaplains should always be aware that their notes might be read by people who do not know them or the patient / resident. They can be part of court cases and legal proceedings. Thus, notes should keep information pertinent, clear, and informative, without violating patient privacy or clergy-congregant relations. Documentation should stay with facts and observations. The language we use should be grounded in our professional field and the work we do as chaplains.

Discretion also applies to when, as a chaplain, we observe something that doesn't seem quite right. The patient / resident complains that he or she has not eaten for four days and has come into the hospital for a headache, or the resident reports that something improper has occurred. While you want to be supportive and bring issues to the appropriate attention, discretion should be the rule, with a note of referral of the general issue to patient services or other appropriate supportive / investigative hospital personnel.

## *What Information / Insights Can Chaplains Provide to the Health Care Team?*

The chaplain is the most qualified person on the health care team to provide "spiritual diagnoses."[6] These include existential concerns, connectedness with God, community, family, anger at God or others, conflicted belief system, despair, loss, grief, shame, isolation, religious concerns, and spiritual struggle.

All patients / residents who enter a health care facility are afraid, either with regard to what will happen to them physically or emotionally or of all of the unknowns that institutionalization entails. Chaplains can identify the sources of the fears and help patients / residents overcome these fears.

Patients / residents will discuss more than fear with chaplains. They will also discuss their hopes and dreams, disappointments in life, and expectations as a result of their hospitalization or entering a long-term care facility or hospice. They will discuss the ways they feel a presence of God in their lives or the lack of that presence, the meaning of religious institutions in their lives or the lack of meaning of these communities. Patients will discuss what they find important and meaningful in their lives and what they know is missing, their growing edges. Significant loss of a loved one, job, or dream will often be something a patient will discuss with a chaplain, as well as issues of guilt, shame, and conflicted feelings; difficult decisions; and considerations of practical implications of their illness. All of these topics could provide helpful insight for the health care team. These issues can affect the course of treatment, and acknowledgment of these struggles can also enhance the patient's perception of being heard by the team, and thus patient satisfaction with the hospitalization experience.[7]

## *Confidentiality and Charting*

The relationship between the chaplain and the patient is a confidential one, as is the relationship with all members of the health care team. The chaplain may learn about significant life events that may impact on the course of the illness and should certainly share this information with the health care team. For example, the patient tells the chaplain that because of this illness and hospitalization, he has been reunited with members of his family from whom he has been estranged.

Another example might be the patient in a long-term care facility who is being treated for gallstones who is eating fried chicken brought by her child when the chaplain comes to visit. It might be significant for the team to know that dietary protocols may need to be explained. This could impact on the course of the illness and is significant for the team to be aware of.

As a professional, the chaplain needs to distinguish between information shared with the chaplain that is medically relevant and that which the patient may not want the rest of the health care team to be aware of. For instance, the patient confesses to the chaplain that he has acted in a manner that he knows is wrong, in a situation that has nothing to do with his current medical issue, and expresses guilt and regret about the incident. While the chaplain might share that the patient is expressing feelings of regret or guilt, the details of the incident should not be shared with the team.

It is a good idea to ask the patient what information to include in a chart note. This discussion can help the patient understand that the chaplain is a member of the health care team, help summarize the accomplishments of the session, reframe and bring closure to the discussion, and provide the health care team with information the patient thinks they should know about his or her spiritual needs and care.

## *Who Reads the Chart Notes?*

The members of the health care team who read chart notes include but are not limited to the following:

- Nurses
- Social workers
- Physical and occupational therapists
- Respiratory therapists
- Doctors
- Other chaplains
- Patient services
- Dietitians
- Legal department
- Just about every professional within a health care setting who has direct patient / resident responsibilities
- Reviewing individuals and organizations for accreditation and many related professionals

## *Humanizing the Chart Notes*

Pastoral / spiritual care is different from many other services the patient / resident receives. While all are concerned for the person's physical and emotional well-being, sometimes there can be a depersonalization in the process of medical care. Pastoral / spiritual care is about making sure the whole human being is supported. One of the ways we can convey that message is to include the patient's first or last name in our notes—to personalize how we experience the person and how we know the person experiences the interaction.

## *Spiritual Care Treatment Plan*

Chart notes should indicate the plan the chaplain has for working with the patient (see chapter 5 for an extensive discussion on this topic). When the chaplain assesses that there is no need for additional spiritual support, the chart note should so indicate. Most treatment plans in chart notes would simply be "continue visiting, with focus on (specific issue)."

When there is significant need for additional support, the treatment plan should also indicate who would be invited to take responsibility for each component. For example, for a patient / resident with multiple complaints about staff and significant spiritual crisis, the treatment plan may include "referral to patient services regarding complaints, referral to social work services for ongoing counseling, referral to community clergy (if appropriate) for prayer and religious support; chaplain will continue visiting to focus on quality-of-life issues."

The treatment plan may include other details of the plan for pastoral care interventions, but for the purposes of the chart note, at minimum, it is most important for the note to indicate that a treatment plan is in place. Details of the plan need not always be specified, particularly if the individual working on the chart is just learning this process. As this is a legal document, remember: "Less *is* more." If specifics of a treatment plan are included, accreditation visits, governmental bodies, and / or legal proceedings may track the plan and its implementation. If the note for the treatment plan is specific, subsequent chart notes should indicate progress based on the earlier treatment plan and indicate when each item has been completed.

## *Forms*

Many chaplains utilize spiritual assessment forms to make chart notes for an initial assessment, for each visit, or for a combination thereof. There is no uniformity in the spiritual assessment tools used by chaplains in health care settings, but in general, spiritual assessment forms should be easy to read and understand and should include the following information:

- Time and place of visit
- Who was in attendance (e.g., family, friends)
- Referral information (both who referred the chaplain to patient / resident, if anyone; and to whom the chaplain made a referral for follow-up services, if anyone)
- If not a permanent part of the chart, the religious affiliation of the patient (if any)
- Religious needs met, such as:
    - Prayer

  - Sacramental services provided (be specific, e.g., Holy Communion; Anointing of the Sick)
  - Religious literature distributed
  - Sabbath candles delivered
  - Patient / resident attended religious services (provide name / time)
- The pastoral / spiritual interventions employed in a visit (e.g., active listening)
- Assessed resident's / patient's spiritual / religious needs / resources (include a space for details about the assessment—more often free-flowing versus canned)
- Spiritual / pastoral issues(s) discussed in the visit, (such as):
  - 12-steps and spirituality
  - Abandonment (e.g., by family, friends, God, religious community)
  - Anger
  - Congruence of core religious / spiritual beliefs
  - Denial
  - End of life
  - Faith
  - Forgiveness (e.g., toward self, God, others)
  - Grief / loss
  - Guilt
  - Hope
  - Hopelessness / despair
  - Illness as identity / living with chronic illness
  - Loneliness
  - Love
  - Meaning / meaningless
  - Peace / peace in adversity
  - Prayer / meditation
  - Punishment
  - Reconciliation

  - Recovery
  - Redemption / renewal
  - Relationship with God / Higher Power / Creator
  - Relationships
  - Repentance
  - Rituals and symbols
  - Sacred scripture / writings
  - Salvation / redemption
  - Serenity
  - Sin
  - Spiritual / religious tools to use in the current situation
  - Spirituality / spiritual emptiness
  - Suffering
  - Temptation
  - Transitions / change
  - Wonder, awe
- Spiritual counseling
- Supporting and / or developing spiritual / religious coping resources
- Discussing personal history
- Follow-up plans
- Place for additional comments

Many chaplains will make more than one visit and complete either the full assessment or write a comment on the progress notes page. The comment should be brief, including the purpose of the visit, date and time, and a very brief description of the encounter: "discussed new diagnosis with patient."

The most minimal form would be a sticker placed in the chart in the progress notes section. It should include the date and time and who visited. It can include a one- to three-word description of the purpose of the visit (e.g., Communion, end-of-life ritual, prayer for the sick).

## *Who Charts?*

It is important to note that as a member of the health care team, the chaplain is required to chart. A distinction is made between members of the health care team and community clergy, who do not have access to medical records and may not make notations in medical records.[8] In order to chart, a chaplain must:

1. be a health care facility employee or contracted by the health care facility, either directly or through an agency, to provide these services
2. have a job description that includes provision of spiritual care, and
3. be clinically trained as a health care professional.

Community clergy are trained to meet the religious needs of a patient, not necessarily their spiritual needs, and community clergy are not employed by the health care facility. Students in clinical pastoral education (CPE), under direct supervision, may chart depending on their particular program and their stage of training.

## *Electronic Medical Records*

When electronic medical records (EMR) are in use, they should include opportunities for chaplains to enter comments and assessments, as would be done in a paper medical record. As the EMR is developed and tailored to the needs and standards of each medical institution, it is essential to involve pastoral care in its development and in establishing forms and procedures for use. As mentioned from the research earlier in this chapter, all of the "honor roll" and top hospitals in the United States (in three categories) provide chaplains with access to read and make notes in paper charts, and the EMR should be consistent with this standard.

## *Final Words*

One component of professional chaplaincy is the accurate reporting of interventions with patients in hospitals. As members of the health care team, it is essential that chaplains access patients' or residents' medical records to be aware of and well informed regarding the treatment plans and services provided and to provide the health care team with spiritual diagnosis and plans for how spiritual care can help. The chart notes should be brief and informative, with a special precaution to provide useful information to the health care team while maintaining appropriate clergy confidentiality.

Chart notes are opportunities for chaplains and the health care team to work together but can never replace the opportunities that actual conversations with the team can achieve. When making notations in the medical record, chaplains provide invaluable insights into the spiritual well-being of patients and their families to the health care team and enable the health care team to be aware of issues, struggles, challenges, accomplishments, and hopes of which they might not be aware. Charting is a way for the rest of the team to see how the spiritual needs and issues of the patient / resident can impact the outcome of their health care experience.

## Notes

1. L. White, *APC News* 6, no. 1 (January / February 2003); Commission on Quality in Pastoral Services, Association of Professional Chaplains, "Chaplains, Assessment, and Documentation: A Template," (2005), www.professionalchaplains.org/uploadedFiles/pdf/assessment-documentation-template.pdf.
2. Association for Clinical Pastoral Education, "Objectives and Outcomes of ACPE Accredited Programs" (2010), Standards 309–19, *Standards & Manuals: 2010 Standards*, www.acpe.edu/NewPDF/2010%20Manuals/2010%20Standards.pdf.
3. Association of Professional Chaplains, *Standards of Practice for Professional Chaplains in Acute Care Settings*, www.professionalchaplains.org/uploadedFiles/pdf/Standards%20of%20Practice%20Draft%20Document%20021109.pdf#Project_Update.
4. This research was conducted in 2010.
5. This research was published in 2011.
6. J. C. Holland, "The NCCN Guideline for Distress Management: A Case for Making Distress the Sixth Vital Sign," *Journal of the National Comprehensive Cancer Network* 5, no. 1 (2007): 3.
7. A. Astrow et al., "Is Failure to Meet Spiritual Needs Associated with Cancer Patients' Perceptions of Quality of Care and Their Satisfaction with Care?" *Journal of Clinical Oncology* 25, no. 36 (2007): 5753; P. A. Clark, M. Drain, and M. Malone, "Addressing Patients' Emotional and Spiritual Needs," *Joint Commission Journal on Quality and Safety* 29, no. 12 (December 2003): 659; Press Ganey, "Press Ganey Knowledge Summary: Patient Satisfaction with Emotional and Spiritual Care," *Press Ganey Preceptor* (2003), http://hmablogs.hma.com/hmachaplains/files/2010/05/Press-Ganey-Patient-Satisfaction.pdf; J. Ehman et al., "Do Patients Want

Physicians to Inquire about Their Spiritual or Religious Beliefs?" *Archives of Internal Medicine* 159 (Aug. 9–23, 1999): 1803.

8. Commission on Quality in Pastoral Services, Association of Professional Chaplains, "HIPAA, Chaplains, and Community Religious Leaders: A Template" (2005), www.professionalchaplains.org/uploadedFiles/pdf/hipaa-definition-of-chaplain-template.pdf.

## About the Contributor

**Rabbi H. Rafael Goldstein, BCJC,** is the director of pastoral care at Mount Sinai Medical Center in New York City. He did his chaplaincy residency at Sharp Memorial Hospital in San Diego, where he served as the Jewish community chaplain for seven years. He is the founder of Dynamics of Hope Consulting (www.dynamicsofhope.com), which provides workshops for health care workers and people living with illness on issues of hope, forgiveness, joy, and life. He is the author of four books, including *Being a Blessing: 54 Ways You Can Help People Living with AIDS* and *The Dynamics of Hope Prayerbook*, for people living with illness, their loved ones, and caregivers, as well as numerous articles, which can be found on the website.

# 7

## Foundational Listening and Responding Skills

*Rev. Robert A. Kidd, MDiv, BCC*

What's so hard about listening? The speaker begins a conversation, then stops talking. The listener takes in what has been said and then makes some sort of response, either verbal or nonverbal. Usually this works well enough, and casual relationships are sustained at a satisfactory level. Spiritually supportive listening, however, is different and takes a great deal of intentionality, skill, and restraint. Allowing a spiritually supportive conversation to unfold naturally does not come easily to many and requires a foundational skill set.

### *What Spiritually Supportive Listening Is and Is Not*

The *sacred work* of spiritually supportive listening is called for when healing, strengthening, or guidance is needed. In these instances, the casual attending of an unskilled listener is not sufficient. Skill, courage, and especially desire to plumb the depths behind the words and emotions being shared are required. Effective listening and responding entail absorbing what the speaker says and then offering it back in order to bring the dialogue to a deeper level. Such transformative listening involves attending to the entirety of the speaker's message, hearing the speaker's words, and discerning the emotions behind them. In such healing interactions, the speaker feels more valued and respected and experiences an emotional completeness unrealized in other forms of discourse. This kind of listening and responding takes practice, patience, and significant respect for the speaker. Such attending is by nature reflective and serves to hold up a mirror for the speaker to hear his or her words in a different, deeper way.

To be effective listeners and responders, chaplains must be willing to relinquish control of conversations. This is often counterintuitive, since most people are acculturated to control or direct conversations through questions or comments. In social conversations, a key objective is to keep the words flowing and to fill in the gaps when a lull occurs. Silences are to be avoided. Social listeners often guide conversations by steering the dialogue toward their personal experiences, or else they try to reroute the conversation to topics they find comfortable. Since the speaker is likely trying the same tactic, much social conversation turns out to be less about listening and more about being heard. Spiritually supportive listening, on the other hand, gives control to the speaker. Patients or family members who seek spiritual support but who instead find themselves in social conversations can often feel unfulfilled, unsatisfied, and even angry.

In fairness, it must be said that spiritually supportive listening is not a therapeutic panacea. The skillful chaplain will not only learn to use this chapter's listening techniques but will also seek other ways to sustain and guide patients into new levels of awareness and self-discovery. Before that happens, however, chaplains first need to learn the foundations of effective listening and responding.

## *Three General Principles for Effective Listening and Responding*

Speaking broadly, three general principles undergird effective listening and responding. These principles supersede mere technique and delineate the overarching philosophy behind such healing interactions. First, *an effective listener encourages the speaker to take all possible conversational initiative.* In spiritually transforming interactions, the listener's remarks are inviting, open ended, and broad. This first principle leads to judicious use of silences, realizing that quiet times create space for the speaker to process what has been said and to move forward thoughtfully. Second, *an effective listener stays attuned to the present.* It is easy for the chaplain's mind to wander, thinking of the next thing to say. It is essential to resist this, focusing instead on what is happening in the moment. An attuned listener notes the speaker's emotional state, ponders the implications of words chosen, observes body language, and is aware of vocal inflections. Third, *effective listeners stay as objective as possible during conversations*. Basically, they stay attuned to their own visceral, inner responses to the speaker. While honoring this personal awareness, they bear in mind that these "gut reactions" reflect their individual experiences and do not necessarily define the truth.

Guided by these three principles, spiritually supportive conversational responses are both skill and art. They entail a number of skills which can be grouped by complexity: basic responses, facilitating responses, and intense interaction responses.

## *Basic Responses*

Basic responses are to chaplains what wrenches and pipe threaders are to plumbers. They are old, well-worn tools, not especially complicated, yet indispensible and consistently effective. Basic responses include literal repetition, reflecting, paraphrasing, and summarizing.

### Literal Repetition

Literal repetition is most useful when the speaker uses a distinctive, striking, or clearly pivotal word or phrase. For example, if a patient says, "When the doctor came into my room and gave me my test results today, I was speechless! I was so afraid of what she'd say." Using literal repetition, the chaplain could say, "You were speechless." If a patient says, "When I saw my new baby for the first time, my heart nearly burst with joy." The chaplain, using literal repetition, could say, "You nearly burst for joy." Literal repetition honors the speaker's choice of words and offers them back as a way of smoothing the way for continued dialogue. Literal repetition also helps the speaker hear what has just been said and so stimulates further reflection on the words chosen.

A caveat about this skill is in order. Used without consideration and without intentionality, literal repetition can sound foolish or even mocking. With this skill in particular, vocal inflection is everything and must be calibrated to match the speaker's in order to convey compassionate listening. Also, this technique can sound ridiculously wooden and parrot-like. It is a clear sign that this skill is being unhelpfully utilized when the patient or family pointedly says, "Why do you keep repeating everything I say?" When this occurs, a wise chaplain will at once switch to another responding style in order to stay in the conversation. Still, used judiciously and with sensitivity—especially when emotions are running high—literal repetition can demonstrate compassionate and careful listening.

## Reflecting

Reflecting is the bedrock, prerequisite skill for effective listening and responding. Reflecting is distinct from other types of listening because it focuses on the emotional content of the patient's words. The importance of diligent reflective listening can hardly be overstated. To those experiencing deep or complex emotions, being in the presence of a caring reflective listener is something like finding water in a desert. Most often the emotional content of daily conversations is discounted, overlooked, or avoided, making reflective listening a great rarity. Consider the case of a furious son who shouts, "I'm angry because that damn nurse won't respond to Mom's call lights!" Commonly, a casual visitor might say, "Now calm down. Being angry won't help." Taking a more rational approach, the son's friend might say, "Well, what do you think is holding your nurse up?" Maybe the acquaintance will attempt to problem solve and say, "Why not phone the nurse's station directly?" The listener might even make some value judgment on the son's emotion by saying, "You're being a pain in the neck. You need to back off." All these responses are amazingly common, and extremely ineffective, serving only to strengthen the listener's efforts to control the conversation.

In the instance above, a reflective listener might say, "Not getting a response from your nurse is really upsetting," or perhaps, "I can tell you are really angry with your mom's nurse right now." In reflective listening, it is less important that the minister responds with the speaker's precise words than that the speaker's emotion is named with reasonable accuracy. Reflective responses are sometimes a bit of a surprise for patients and families, since they are actually accustomed to having their emotional remarks overlooked, minimized, or somehow "managed." A listener who can accurately identify the speaker's emotion communicates that the conveyed emotional content has been honored, received, and deemed important enough for continued attention. Sometimes precise accuracy in naming the expressed emotion is less important than simply attempting to identify the feelings on display. When in doubt, it is often better to understate rather than overstate. Patients and families will frequently fine-tune their responses if the chaplain's response does not satisfactorily match their feelings. To illustrate using the case of the angry son, the chaplain might say, "You seem dissatisfied with your nurse on this shift." Noting that his emotional response has been underemphasized, the son might say, "No, I'm not dissatisfied. I'm furious that my mom is being ignored!" The minister then has even more explicit information about the son's feelings and can use this information for a more accurate, sensitive reply.

## Paraphrasing

Paraphrasing takes small chunks of dialogue and rewords them for the speaker. The goal of this skill is to let patients hear their words from another vantage point and process them further. Paraphrasing helps ease conversations forward without burdening the speaker with requests for additional information, a tactic that slows the conversational flow. Paraphrasing signals that the hearer has understood the speaker and is tracking with the conversation. When paraphrasing, the chaplain may respond with a condensed version of what the patient just said or may augment the speaker's words in order to offer a more nuanced meaning. The point of paraphrasing is to keep the dialogue moving forward smoothly without interrupting it with clarifying questions. For example, a family member may say, "Eddie's condition is worsening by the day. The doctors say that if there's no change after this new medication, there is not really anything much they can do. We'll just have to wait and pray." Using paraphrasing, the chaplain could respond, "Eddie doesn't seem to be responding to his treatments very well. You are standing solely on your faith right now."

In a casual conversation, it would be typical to cut to the chase and respond to the family member's comment with a request for more information: "So what have the doctors done so far with Eddie?" At this juncture, unless the chaplain is also a medical professional, there is little reason to ask such a question aside from simply keeping the conversation going and sustaining the relational contact. Granted, this is not such a bad rationale, and such questions are generally offered as expressions of honest concern. In this instance, however, and others that are emotionally fraught, paraphrasing can be a more inviting response than a direct request for additional information.

### Summarizing

Summarizing is often used as a way to divide a longer discourse into manageable chapters or to terminate a conversation gracefully. Summarization is especially useful in those difficult pastoral conversations that unfold as a seamless sequence of sentences with no break for response. These audio-loop conversations are notable for the way they flow from topic to topic and eventually arrive at the beginning again, retelling things already stated. Summarization can afford the listener with a gentle and sensitive way to stem the tide of such interchanges without leaving the speaker feeling abandoned or cut off. After summarizing what has been said, the chaplain can either channel the conversation in another direction or suggest another chapter like this: "You've told me a lot about your medical history over the years, but I'm wondering how your spiritual life has helped you cope." When necessary, a summarization statement can conclude the conversation with something like, "Now that I know more about you, maybe next time we can pick up where we left off today and talk some more."

## *Facilitating Responses*

Facilitating responses are on the next level of listening and responding complexity. With these, the responder can help the speaker unpack content that may feel significantly uncomfortable, threatening, or overwhelming. Facilitating responses not only help patients / residents communicate with verbal clarity but also help them risk dealing with more difficult emotions. Facilitating responses include open-ended questions, buffering, understatement / euphemism, and tell-me-more / minimal encouragement.

### Open-Ended Questions

Open-ended questions are inquiries that cannot be answered with "yes" or "no." These are process questions that invite the speaker to elaborate on a specific topic. Open-ended questions are best used with intentionality and should be contextualized to fit into the larger conversation. Depending on this context, open-ended questions may include inquiries such as, "How are you coping with the lifestyle changes involved in your heart transplant?" or, "What sorts of things give you the most strength for each day?" Judiciously utilized open-ended questions can provide tremendously rich material for powerful spiritual conversations. Note how much more beneficial an open-ended question can be when compared to a closed-ended question like, "Does prayer give you strength for each day?" When conversations become peppered with open-ended questions, however, potentially spiritually supportive conversations turn into artful interviews that entertain the listener. "How are you today?" is a particular open-ended question to be avoided. Since it is typically posed each time a care team member enters a patient's room, this open-ended question becomes extraordinarily tedious and nearly meaningless. Using some other open-ended question allows patients to start the conversation where they wish and simultaneously indicates the chaplain's openness to more interaction.

## Buffering

Buffering responses help soften the impact of difficult or hard-to-express emotions or topics and clear the way for more vulnerable interchanges. Buffering responses function like a seawall in a coastal town, absorbing and dispersing potentially damaging force. During spiritually supportive conversations, speakers sometimes experience significant discomfort while grappling with deeply felt, carefully guarded topics. Buffering responses help avoid trauma and ensure that the speaker does not feel coerced. Buffering responses include such things as, "You may not want to talk about this now, but ...," or "I don't know how it is with you, but ...," or "Sometimes it's helpful to consider ..." Here is an example of a buffering response in use. Note how this buffering response broaches the potentially upsetting topic but also offers a way around it should the speaker choose to defer this dialogue.

> **Mr. Z:** *The doctors just told me that there's not much they can do about my cancer and suggest an advance directive. Humph ... why talk about that now? I'm a fighter, not a quitter. I'm thinking of signing up as a research subject in a clinical trial.*
>
> **Chaplain:** *Here's another option, Mr. Z.—something you can think about and maybe the two of us can discuss it later. When the doctors say there is not much more to be done medically, sometimes completing an advance directive can be a big help. It can actually help you, your family, and your doctor discuss what kinds of treatments you do and don't want.*

## Understatement / Euphemism

Understatement / euphemism comes into play when people hint at some critically important subject that they seem nonetheless unable to name directly. Often conversations related to death, anger, or sexuality fall into this category. Some examples of understatements or euphemisms follow.

- When discussing a possible death: "My daughter might *pass away*."
- When expressing anger at a relative: "I am really *disappointed* that my grandson didn't come to see me."
- When discussing possible impotence as an outcome of surgery: "I don't know if I'll be able to *function* anymore."

Noting and then using the speaker's own understatements or euphemisms can sometimes clear the way for discussing concerns that might otherwise remain taboo. Skillful listeners will attend carefully to patients' word choices and then assess when and where to employ this responding method. Euphemism should be used advisedly and with sensitivity. Sometimes euphemisms facilitate discussion, keeping the conversation unfolding without being derailed by resistance. With some grieving families, for example, using the words "dead" or "has died" can frequently prompt resistive responses. At the same time, euphemisms sometimes mask content that would be more helpfully named directly. As an illustration of this instance, it may be more helpful to use the word "impotence" openly rather than continue with the speaker's euphemism. Using this word directly and without embarrassment can free the patient for more candid dialogue.

## Tell-Me-More / Minimal Encouragement

Tell-me-more and minimal encouragement responses include a vast array of responses that indicate the listener's desire for more interaction. Tell-me-more responses are easy to use and keep the focus on the speaker. These responses show hospitality and convey interest in what is being said. As a caution, tell-me-more responses tend to foster listener-directed conversation and should be used judiciously. In contrast, minimal encouragement responses allow the speaker to guide the dialogue.

Some examples of tell-me-more responses include:

- "Tell me more about ..."
- "I'd like to hear more about ..."
- "I'd like to focus more on ..."
- "Say more about ..."

Minimal encouragement is the great underappreciated responding skill. These responses include exceedingly brief verbal and nonverbal cues that encourage the speaker to continue. Nonverbal minimal encouragement includes movements like nods and eyebrow raises. Verbal minimal encouragement consists of comments like "Hmm ...," "I see ...," and "Yes, please go on ..." These brief interjections signal that the listener is following the conversational thread and wants additional engagement. Minimal encouragement is underappreciated because it is nearly instinctive in friendly conversations and is mostly noted only by its absence. When a conversation proceeds without minimal encouragement, the interchange will probably seem emotionally distant and chilly, if not frankly hostile.

The downside of minimal encouragement is that it is easy to fake. The alleged listener can be a thousand miles away mentally—totally off topic—and still continue offering minimal encouragement at expected intervals. This of course lacks basic integrity but is done more often than chaplains want to think. The fact that it is easily bluffed, however, does not undermine this skill's usefulness. Minimal encouragement is necessary padding in most conversations and helps ensure an easy, unforced flow of dialogue. It should be used honestly.

## *Intense Interaction Responses*

Intense interaction responses are so named because they are rather like surgical scalpels. They are focused, sharp, and exact. They intentionally steer the speaker in very specific directions to provide needed information. These responses can separate the skilled professional minister from the novice. Because they put conversational control firmly with the listener, this group of techniques should be used with great care and deliberation. They are easily misused by a beginning listener who is uneasy allowing others to guide the conversation. Intense interaction responses include calling attention and hovering.

## Calling Attention

Calling attention responses highlight unconscious or seemingly unnoticed reactions or behaviors. Because they deal with comments, feelings, or behaviors that the patient / resident may not have intended to share, calling attention responses are often best employed after a relational foundation has been established. Even then, these responses may take courage. After all, naming the "hard thing" takes confidence, skill, and discernment. Discernment is especially key in order to know when to press on with calling attention and when to back away and give space. Calling attention responses may include such comments as:

- "I see your tears and wonder what they are saying."
- "I've noticed that you've talked about everyone in your family but your dad."
- "It looks like every time we start talking about leaving rehab and going home your foot starts tapping."

## Hovering

Hovering in a spiritually supportive conversation is a little like piloting a television station helicopter at a breaking news scene. Conversationally, the listener hovers over a topic, not necessarily landing to delve deeply but staying aloft and viewing the topic from several different angles, thus getting a more comprehensive view of the whole. Hovering is beneficial when a topic is painful, seen as risky, or appears potentially overwhelming to the speaker. Hovering is often useful when assisting grieving families, dealing with end-of-life issues, or discussing other emotionally laden life changes. Hovering involves deftly broaching the intended subject for discussion, allowing the speaker to explore it as much as possible, and then gently bringing the conversation back when they stray off topic. The emphasis is on the listener's ability to assess and unobtrusively guide dialogue. For example, when attempting to assist a mourning family with life review, the chaplain using the hovering technique might say something like, "What are some of your most vivid memories of your sister?" The family might begin with a series of mental snapshots of their sister but then, eager for concrete activity, gradually move into a long funeral to-do list. Using hovering, the chaplain might gently say, "You shared some powerful images of your sister.

Are there others that stand out for you?" With hovering, care must be taken to respect the speakers' wishes and boundaries. If they do not wish to be guided back to the desired topic, a respectful listener will back away from the avoided issue for the time being.

## *Verbatim Exercise*

After reviewing these major listening and responding skills, it may be helpful to set them in the context of an actual spiritually supportive conversation to see how they work together. Note how these skills can be used singularly or in combinations. Read the verbatim below with attention to the various listening and responding techniques the chaplain uses. For the various chaplain's responses, please indicate the type of listening response used (see answer key at the end of the chapter). Not all types of response are employed. The following conversation was recorded in The Methodist Hospital by a clinical pastoral education student after visiting Mr. H., a fifty-four-year-old diabetic patient who owns a large farm. Mr. H. is sitting in a wheelchair. He is seriously ill and expects to have his legs operated on shortly. Identifying details in this patient visit have been altered. It is printed with permission from the student.

*C = Chaplain*
*H = Mr. H.*

*C1: Mr. H., I'm Anthony, one of the chaplains here in the hospital. I came by to see you last week. I was checking back to follow up on our last visit.*

*H1: Oh, yes, I remember.*

*C2: I hope things are going well for you today.*

*H2: Well, I'll tell you, they were supposed to operate on me last week. They got me drugged, took me up there, and my heart flew up. They decided they better not try it then. They brought me back down here and I'm supposed to have the operation tomorrow.*

*C3: You say your heart flew up?*

*H3: Yes, my heart rate went all crazy. Scared 'em to death. They thought it might be too risky to go through with it.* [Pause] *I guess I'm ready for the operation. I think I can make it. I'm not ready to die yet. But I think the operation is necessary or I'll lose my legs.*

*C4: You seem pretty calm and peaceful about this.*

**H4:** *Well, yeah. What else am I gonna do? I've got exactly two choices here. Operate or lose my legs and maybe—you know—I might go. Not a real hard choice for a crusty old fellow like me.*

**C5:** *You're not ready to go, but you want something to be done if possible so you won't lose your legs.*

**H5:** *Yeah [*with a nod*]. But if this is the end, well, that's just how it is.*

**C6:** *You have thought about this maybe being the end ... but you can accept that it's just how it is.*

**H6:** *Yeah! Of course, they tell us there's not too much to the operation. They're going to dope me up right here and keep me here until it's time.... They said they're going to put some plastic tubes inside me and that ought to save my legs ... can you believe that? Plastic tubes can help save my legs? Plastic! You see my foot here [*shows me his foot*]? This toe here gets blue when I stand on it. They could amputate here by the ankle, but this way they might save my legs. I'd kinda like to keep them both, you know?*

**C7:** *The operation seems pretty straightforward and you think it's worth it if you can save your legs. And you've got that right ... medical science today is just amazing.*

**H7:** *Yeah, 'course I don't actually* want *to die during the operation or anything. I'd rather die a natural death than die through anesthesia. I do not want to be a vegetable, though. That happened to my daddy. That's really what scares me about this operation—not wakin' up and then just being a vegetable.*

**C8:** *Mr. H., you might not want to talk about this right now, but it's something to think about. Completing an advance directive with your doctor could help your doctor know what you do and don't want if your condition becomes irreversible. Just a thought.*

**H8:** *Yeah, that's right. I actually already did one of those. My daughter hated talking about it, but I thought we needed to.*

*[*Pause*]*

**C9:** *What kinds of things support you spiritually through all this?*

**H9:** *Humph ... Well, hard work takes my mind off my troubles—that and prayer.*

**C10:** *I see. [*Silence*] Well, I'd like to hear what kind of work you do and how prayer helps.*

**H10:** *You know I've got a farm. Farm work never ends. Always a fence to mend, plowing to do, something broken down that needs* *fixing. It's July now, so we got to start picking corn soon. 'Course, I got to gain my strength back first. I figure I'll be ready about the time the crop is ready.*

**C11:** *Mm-hm …*

**H11:** *And prayer, well, I just keep telling the Lord my troubles. He seems to lighten the load somehow. Chaplain, I thank you for coming by to see me today. I want you to pray with me before you go, okay?*

**C12:** *Sure thing, Mr. H. What would you like me to say in my prayer?*

*[*Mr. H. responds and the chaplain prays with him.*]*

**H12:** *Thanks for coming by, Chaplain.*

**C13:** *See you later, Mr. H.*

## *Final Words*

The eleven foundational listening and responding skills in the chapter all support the listener in staying with the speaker, neither lagging behind nor rushing ahead. These skills help chaplains communicate respect and support for those in their care and also provide modalities for gently guiding conversations when necessary. It is helpful to remember that while the skills described in this chapter can help spiritual caregivers through the maze of compassionate conversations, they are as dust and ashes when compared to basic love for others. Strengthened by such love, however, a well-equipped chaplain will not be a mere technician but can become a true healer of souls.

## *Verbatim Answers*

C3: Literal repetition

C4: Reflecting

C5: Paraphrasing and euphemism

C6: Euphemism and literal repetition

C7: Summarizing

C8: Buffering

C9: Open-ended question

C10: Minimal encouragement and tell-me-more

C11: Minimal encouragement

C12: Open-ended question

## Further Reading

Egan, Gerard. *The Skilled Helper.* Monterey, CA: Brooks / Cole Publishing, 1986.

Faber, Hieje, and Ebel Vander Schoot. *The Art of Pastoral Conversation.* Nashville: Abingdon Press, 1965.

Jackson, Cari. *The Gift to Listen, the Courage to Hear.* Minneapolis: Augsburg Fortress, 2003.

McKay, Matthew, Martha Davis, and Patrick Fanning. *Messages: The Communications Skills Book.* Oakland, CA: New Harbinger Publications, 1995.

Rosenberg, Marshall B. *Nonviolent Communication: A Language of Life.* Encinitas, CA: Puddledancer Press, 2003.

## About the Contributor

**Rev. Robert A. Kidd, MDiv, BCC,** is the director of spiritual care and education at The Methodist Hospital in Houston, Texas. He is endorsed by the Alliance of Baptists and is a past president of the Association of Professional Chaplains.

# 8

## Prayer and Ritual

*Chaplain Gerald L. Jones, MA, BCC, ACPE Supervisor*

Health care chaplains have the privilege of sharing deeply meaningful experiences with patients / residents on a daily basis. Prayer and ritual open up opportunities to explore with patients / residents their understanding of the Divine and their relationships with others. Prayer and ritual connect patients / residents and their families to the larger community and to the understanding that they are not alone in the world or in their experiences. Prayer and ritual can also be sacred events that chaplains should feel privileged to enter into with patients / residents. Prayer and ritual also provide an opportunity to reach across the religious divide as chaplains open themselves to the faith journeys of their patients / residents, their families, and also the staff of the institutions they work within.

### *What Is Prayer?*

Prayer is found in most of the world's faith traditions. Those who pray use it to connect with the "other," such as the Divine, community, or nature. In some religious traditions, there is a prescribed time for prayer each day or specific prayers to be said for specific events, such as birth, death, illness, or celebration. In other traditions, prayers are meant to be spontaneous and in the moment. These prayers are tailored to the uniqueness of the individual and her / his present experience. The importance of prayer may vary from individual to individual. For many, prayer is a nominal part of their faith journey, while others rely on it as the most important part of their religious practice.

## *Who Provides Prayer?*

Chaplains are in a unique position when it comes to praying with patients. As the designated "spiritual caregiver" on the health care team, when requests for prayer are received by staff, the chaplain is typically the first person to be called. Community clergy may also be called upon to provide prayer for patients. While a chaplain may be readily available, community clergy bring a tie-in to the patient's home. When community clergy is preferred, chaplains work behind the scenes to facilitate visits from the local clergy and may also offer prayers if the patient / resident so desires.

### Family Prayers

Families may request prayer for their loved ones. These prayers may occur at bedside or separate from the patient. For families who request to pray together with the patient, it is important to get an understanding of the patient's spiritual life. If the patient / resident is religious, a prayer familiar to his / her tradition, such as the Lord's Prayer for a Roman Catholic patient, may be appropriate. If the patient/resident does not have a spiritual life, the prayer may focus more on the family members and less on the patient / resident in order to respect the patient / resident's chosen spiritual path. It is not uncommon for a family member, or even a staff member, to request a prayer even though the patient / resident may not desire prayer. These requests must be handled with sensitivity and understanding for both the family / staff member and the patient / resident. For example, an adult granddaughter requested that a chaplain pray the "salvation prayer" with her comatose grandfather. When the chaplain asked if her grandfather was religious, she informed the chaplain that "he had never really believed in God." The chaplain shared his appreciation for the granddaughter's concern and love for her grandfather, but also noted that to offer such a prayer without the patient's consent would not honor his life's choices. Instead, the chaplain offered to pray with the granddaughter and asked that her love be felt in the heart of her grandfather.

Writing prayers with families for their loved one is also effective. This entails meeting with the family and inviting them to share their thoughts and prayers for their loved one. Then those thoughts are written down, printed, and returned to the family to share with those of their choice. Such prayers are an effective tool in critical care units of hospitals or certain long-term care units where a patient / resident may be non-communicative or in a comatose state. By providing their prayer to staff, friends, and loved ones, the family can feel more confident that their thoughts and prayers will be heard by the patient / resident and that the health care team cares about the physical and spiritual needs of their loved one. An example of a family prayer is as follows:

> Dear God,
> Please bring comfort to Dad.
> Please help him, God, to know that he is loved by his family.
> May your presence be with him, that he be patient.
> Bless him with faith that he may heal.
> Help him to know that healing takes time.
> Let him know that he is not alone in his struggle.
> His family is with him.
> Help him to relax and feel peace when his family is near.
> Thank you, God, for those who helped save his life
> and thank you for the miracles that have been performed for his benefit.
> Thank you for his family, which is present and cares deeply for him.
> Continue to bless him, God.
> Amen.

## Staff Prayers

I have met with many chaplains who have shared mixed feelings about staff praying with patients. Many feel this encroaches on the work of the chaplain, while others share concern that the patient / resident may be the subject of evangelization. I appreciate such concerns and again rely on the patient / resident and the family as the decision makers. If the patient / resident and / or family makes the request of a staff member, and the staff member is comfortable doing so, such prayers provide a valuable service.

If the staff member offers to pray with no indication from the patient / resident that prayer is desired, then the act may be inappropriate and viewed at proselytism. When such an issue arises, it is important to remember that care and compassion are important. In most cases, staff members believe they are helping the patient / resident with their prayers. Education about the role and availability of chaplains and the need to be sensitive to varying spiritual needs can lead to a stronger reliance on chaplaincy in the future (see chapter 5 for other thoughts on this topic).

## *How to Pray*

When asked to pray with a patient, it is important for chaplains to be aware that multiple names for the Divine are used in prayer. Some may prefer to reference God, others may view the Divine as father or mother or both, while others may prefer to address their prayer in a way that removes gender from the equation, such as "Divine Presence." Prayer for many can be very personal and sacred. Chaplains must be sensitive to the reality that prayer can also be seen as invasive or oppressive. For those who have been harmed by a faith tradition, prayer may elicit memories that may cause more harm than good. Therefore, it is imperative to receive the permission of a patient / resident or family member before offering a prayer. Sensitivity to the patient / resident's view of the Divine can enhance the power of a prayer together.

Ending prayer requires additional sensitivity. Christians may be accustomed to ending prayers, "In Jesus's name," but such wording will only aid in distancing the non-Christian patient / resident from the chaplain and may appear to the patient / resident to be an act of proselytism. While ending a prayer in Christ's name may be appropriate for patients / residents who identify themselves as Christian, removing the reference to Christ with non-Christians or those of unknown faith background shows respect for patients' faith journeys and reminds them that the chaplain has no hidden agenda in regard to their faith preference. A simple "amen" would signal the end of the prayer and not be considered offensive by those who request prayer.

### Prayers with Those of Other Faiths

New chaplains often share the common concern of how to pray with those from other faith traditions. While some faith-based health care institutions will cater to one predominant faith tradition, most health care facilities are becoming more and more multifaith. As such, the expectation that a chaplain will pray with persons of any faith is very real. This can lead to soul searching around issues of authenticity if a chaplain is uncomfortable saying prayers from a different faith tradition. In such cases, an honest approach can clarify the situation. A statement such as "Mr. B., while I am not Buddhist, I would be able to read Buddhist prayers with your mother, or would you prefer I contact somebody from her faith tradition?" shares openly that the chaplain is not pretending to be from a different faith, yet it puts the spiritual needs of the patient / resident at the forefront and gives the patient / resident and family the autonomy to make the choice of whether or not to accept the chaplain's offer.

## *When to Pray*

Many chaplains find comfort in their own prayer life, which makes it easy to share that comfort with patients / residents, their families, and others in the health care facility. For chaplains who struggle with the temptation to offer advice and solutions, prayer can become an easy "fix" and be used to bypass in-depth exploration of difficult feelings or experiences. However, the decision to pray is the prerogative of the patient / resident and / or family, not the chaplain or staff member. Most important, prayer is not something that should be imposed, but should be offered in such a way that the patient / resident or family will sense no judgment if they decline.

An example of how to offer prayer in such a way might go as follows: "Mr. Smith, is there anything I can offer before I leave, such as prayer? Or do you feel we have covered enough this visit?" By offering prayer in a way that gives the patient / resident or family an "out," you help them maintain their sense of autonomy while ensuring they recognize you are available to pray if desired.

## *Types of Prayer*

One of the most common ways to pray is vocally and can vary from one person to another. Those from more liturgical, or more ritualistic, traditions may have an expectation that a prayer will be a familiar recitation, such as the Hail Mary, the *Sh'ma*, or Psalm 23. Others may have an expectation that the chaplain will provide a prescribed prayer designated for the particular malady of the patient, such as those found in the Episcopal Book of Common Prayer. For others, the use of a litany, which includes a speaker and a respondent, may be preferred. For those who use such prayer in their own faith journey, the familiar words build a connection to their faith community and provide a strong sense of comfort. Such prayers provide words to experiences that may be too difficult for the patient / resident to vocalize. Liturgical prayers also offer a connection to a patient / resident's or family's faith history and tradition. For chaplains, gaining familiarity with the written prayers of various traditions opens up additional opportunities to care for patients / residents and their religious and spiritual needs.[1]

## Chanted / Liturgical Prayer

Liturgical prayers are often read or chanted with patients. In traditions where prayers or scriptural passages are chanted, the melodic cadence and rhythm can provide a deeper connection to faith and community than can be conveyed through words alone. It is not uncommon for those who have been distanced from their faith tradition to begin chanting a familiar prayer or offering response to a litany as they hear the familiar words and cadences of their youth.

Many chants are repeated in a religiously historical language such as Hindi, Hebrew, Arabic, or Latin and may or may not be spoken or understood by those receiving the prayers. While the language may not be understood, it retains the same importance as the cadence and rhythm. In such cases, a prerecorded prayer may be helpful in patient / resident care. For example, many hospitals have specified chapters of the Qur'an that have been recorded in Arabic in order to facilitate prayer and worship for their Muslim patients.

## Extemporaneous Prayer

Extemporaneous prayers are more conversational in nature and more spontaneous in their wording than liturgical prayers. Typically, such prayers begin with an invocation of the Divine, followed by the thoughts and feelings of the individual offering the prayer. Such prayers may include words of gratitude, requests for blessings and healing, or shared concerns for loved ones. Chaplains may choose to open the prayer up to family members by inviting them to say aloud their own prayers and wishes. The wording and syntax of prayer are also important. Some faiths may use more formal language, such as "thee" and "thou," while others may be more casual in their speech. The amount of reverence demonstrated during prayer can also be difficult to judge. For many, prayers are somber moments where silence of the participants is expected. Others use prayer as an opportunity to be moved by the spirit and may speak up during the prayer with an "amen" or a "praise the Lord." When in doubt, it is best to begin a prayer in a more reverential manner. If the family has a more charismatic approach to prayer, their additions to the prayer will clue you in that it is permissible to change up the energy level.

I have often found that inviting patients / residents to direct their own prayers creates a space for deeper exploration into their experience. For example, while meeting with a woman in her mid-fifties with chronic obstructive pulmonary disease, I explored her frustrations with her health decline, and she asked if I could pray for her. When I asked her what she would like to pray for, she initially stated that she was tired and wanted God to give her strength and understanding. I then asked her to describe "tired." This created a space in which she began to talk about her desire to be finished with treatment and her frustration around her children not wanting to hear her decisions. She believed she needed to hold on for them and did not want to disappoint them or her doctors. As she spoke, I asked permission to write down her statements and then reiterated them in our prayer together. I then asked if she would like a copy of her prayer. She said yes. Her prayer was as follows:

> Dear God,
> I pray for an easy death.
> I hope to be with you
> and not be punished
> for taking the easy way out.
> I pray that my family will be happy
> and accepting of my death.
> I have had a good life.
> I want to be comfortable.
> I don't want to suffer anymore.
> I've been
> pricked,
> plucked,
> sucked,
> and ventilated

and I just can't take it anymore.
Help me to not have fear,
that I can relax and go with it.
Please give me a speedy death.
Amen.

Upon receiving her copy, she shared her prayer with her physician and her family. The results of our discussion led to her filling out an advanced health care directive and going home with hospice. She later shared that seeing her prayer had given her a sense of empowerment to speak up and share her wishes with her loved ones.[2]

### Silent Prayer

Prayer can also be offered silently. The use of silence offers an opportunity for individuals to connect to their deeper sense of spirituality without the distraction that may come from the struggle to find words to pray. Particularly in settings such as the intensive care unit where the patient / resident is often unable to speak due to artificial ventilation or settings such as end-of-life care where the patient / resident is nonresponsive, sitting in silence with a patient / resident can be a very profound and intimate experience. I have often been amazed at the power of silence and the gratitude patients / residents express when they do not feel rushed to speak or receive a response.

## *Ritual*

Ritual and prayer often work together in chaplaincy. Ritual typically involves a familiar action or pattern of actions that works to connect individuals with their larger community. There are many types of rituals, including religious, cultural, familial, and individual rituals. Offering a familiar ritual provides chaplains the ability to help patients / residents create community within their facility, while connecting them to their larger community outside of the hospital. It also can provide a way for patients / residents to feel more grounded as they experience the disorientation of the institutional environment.

### Religious Rituals

Religious communities often designate who may provide ritual, such as an imam, a shaman, a priest, or a rabbi. For religious rituals, it is important to respect the regulations of a patient's faith tradition. For example, only a Roman Catholic priest may provide the Sacrament of the Sick to a patient. While a chaplain can pray and offer words of blessing to the patient, if the chaplain is not an ordained Roman Catholic priest, the rite has not been received. Even when the language may seem familiar, its meaning may differ depending on the faith tradition. For example, when Latter-Day Saints request a "blessing," they do not mean a general prayer, but a specific rite performed by ordained individuals from their faith community.

Some religious rituals, such as baptism, may have additional significance when requested after the death of an infant or fetal demise. While families may request baptism for their deceased child, most faith traditions would note that the sacrament of baptism is a rite for the living. Many hospitals have written policies stating that fetal demise patients are not to receive baptism but the offer of a prayer of blessing instead. Other facilities may have no written policy or procedure regarding fetal deaths. For many chaplains, there is no question that such a request would be honored as a means to comfort the family and assure them that their child had life and family and that God recognizes those facts. For others, baptism of a deceased infant may seem disingenuous and ethically improper. While the internal struggle of whether or not to provide baptism is laudable, such a decision should be made well before a family requests a baptism for their deceased child. A patient's room is not the place for a chaplain to wrestle with her or his own theological dilemmas, as this distracts from the patient's own experiences. A possible solution to a baptism may include a simple prayer of naming and blessing for the child. Regardless of the response, the spiritual and emotional well-being of the family should always be at the forefront.

## Cultural Rituals

Cultural rituals often blend with religious rituals. They are important for patients / residents and families, particularly at the end of life. Such rituals may or may not be available to patients / residents based on local laws. A chaplain is a resource for the family in ensuring that certain rituals are met. Rituals that may include bathing, clothing, and binding a body after death may seem unfamiliar or unusual to staff members. Chaplains can help educate the staff and family about rituals in which cultural needs can be satisfied. For example, in Judaism and Islam, it is preferable that a burial occur within twenty-four hours of death. For many facilities, such accommodations are near impossible due to the legal issues concerning coroner's reports and / or the difficulty that arises in obtaining a death certificate in a timely manner. Even if all rituals cannot be provided, the chaplain's efforts to bridge the cultural gaps will be appreciated. Many cultural and religious rituals can be found in books or on the Internet.[3]

One of the most memorable rituals that chaplains are asked to perform is that of marriage. Many assume that chaplains, as members of the clergy, are also authorized to perform marriage ceremonies. I have experienced occasions where I have been called by a frantic staff member requesting I perform a marriage before a patient / resident expires. While this scenario plays out beautifully in the movies, it is much more difficult to pull off in real life for many reasons. First, the chaplain may or may not be ordained clergy. The religious authority to marry lies with the ordaining body, not with the title "chaplain." Second, the necessary paperwork, such as a marriage license, needs to be prepared and registered prior to the ceremony. Third, local laws and ordinances may dictate where and who can perform marriages, regardless of ordination status. When all three factors fall into place, a bedside ceremony is a memorable experience for family members and staff. When they do not fall into place, chaplains have the opportunity to provide alternatives, such as a "spiritual wedding," which, while not legally binding, allows couples to share a ritual to commemorate their love together. It also offers an opportunity to listen empathetically to the disappointments of those involved.

## Family Rituals

Familial rituals offer an opportunity to better understand a patient / resident and / or family. Such rituals as holiday celebrations, family vacations, and hobbies can connect a family to their loved one and remind them that their time together has forged lifelong connections and memories that will continue after death and loss. Often, in times of grief, creating new rituals can aid the healing process. For example, designating a time to tell stories at family gatherings about those who have passed away or visiting the resting place of a loved one with family may help in the healing process by reminding those left behind of their shared experiences and support.

## Individual Rituals

Individuals also create their own sense of ritual in their daily lives. While the word "routine" is more apt, many of these personal rituals, such as the order in which one starts the day, become disrupted as health declines. Hospitalization / institutionalization removes individuals from their own comfortable spaces and creates new routines. Chaplains have the ability to educate staff about daily rituals and help minimize disruptions for the patient / resident. For example, the chaplain can assist a Muslim patient / resident by offering directionality (toward Mecca) and informing the staff of times, if possible, to avoid disruptions during the patient's prayer schedule. Patients / residents may also find comfort from items used during their daily rituals. The chaplain could suggest that a picture used for daily meditation or a book of scripture used for daily devotions be brought from home to assist in maintaining a daily ritual practice. By recognizing the changes of routine and the feelings that accompany life disruption, patients / residents are better equipped to adapt to their new environment.

Chaplains often work with patients / residents and families to create individual rituals to celebrate, cope, and normalize their experiences. For example, after a birth mother delivered her child, she requested that the chaplain offer a prayer for her baby and for the family that was to adopt the child. After the prayer, the mother asked if the chaplain would be willing to pray with the adoptive parents the next day when they came to receive their new baby. After the chaplain arrived, he recognized that more than a prayer was needed to signify this event. So he invited the birth mother to place the baby in his arms and continue to place her hand on the child; then he invited the adoptive parents to also place their hands on the child. An extemporaneous prayer was offered recognizing the gift of life the birth mother had given, the love and nurturing the adoptive parents would bring, and the love that they all shared for the baby that tied them together. After the prayer, the birth mother took her hand off of the baby and said good-bye. The adoptive parents then took the baby into their arms. Those present appreciated the ritual that had been provided and the tangible feeling of transition from one parent to the other that occurred.

## Use of Objects

Objects are also valuable in creating ritual. By bringing a tangible object to a patient / resident or family encounter, the chaplain has the ability to create a symbol that carries stronger significance than the object itself. For example, many hospitals will place a donated quilt or blanket around a newborn infant. This tangible object later comes to symbolize the moment of birth and often becomes a keepsake for the family and infant later in life. Such rituals using objects may occur spontaneously. For instance, after a young man died in an automobile accident, his mother wanted to say good-bye but did not want to see her son with all his facial injuries. As she struggled with her decision, I remembered that we use "prayer rocks" in our chapel. I excused myself and moments later returned with a small rock. I asked the woman to hold the rock and think of her good-byes for her son. She then kissed it and I took it into his room, placed it in his hand, prayed with him, then touched the rock to his lips. When I brought it back to his mother, I shared what I had done with the rock. She then began to weep while kissing the rock over and over again. As she left, she was holding the rock tightly in her hand, and she felt as if she had been able to say good-bye to her son through this little, tangible object.

## *Final Words*

In my fifteen years of health care chaplaincy experience, I have never found anything as simple and simultaneously complex as prayer and ritual. Prayer and ritual are instant tools that have the ability to connect patients / residents and families to their faith tradition and to the Divine. Yet they have the potential to be easy "fixes" and hidden evangelism. Prayer and ritual have the capacity to enrich a visit or to distance a patient / resident from the chaplain by proving that there was an agenda after all. Added to this mix is the understanding that each patient / resident may interpret prayer and ritual differently. To complicate matters, each chaplain needs to find her or his own comfort level with prayer and ritual in order to use them effectively. It is my hope that this chapter offered some ideas and suggestions in order to make prayer and ritual valuable to both patient / resident and chaplain.

## Notes

1. Websites such as www.beliefnet.com, which focuses on interfaith spirituality, have numerous prayers of multiple faith traditions: www.beliefnet.com/Faiths/Prayer/index.aspx.
2. For more on writing with patients / residents and families, see G. L. Jones, "The Art of Written Prayer," *Chaplaincy Today* 21, no. 2 (Winter 2005): 19–21.
3. See Summa Health for an example of Internet resources on ritual: www.summahealth.org/common/templates/contentindex.asp?ID=3003.

## About the Contributor

**Chaplain Gerald L. Jones, MA, BCC, ACPE Supervisor,** is the director of chaplain services at Sutter Roseville Medical Center, Roseville, California. He is a CPE supervisor with the Association for Clinical Pastoral Education (ACPE) and a board certified chaplain with the Association of Professional Chaplains (APC). He has trained multiple CPE groups throughout northern California on the "Art of the Written Prayer" and has published an article of the same title in *Chaplaincy Today*. He currently serves as the northern California State chair with the APC.

# 9

## Counseling and Interventions

*Rev. Dr. Willard W. C. Ashley, Sr., MDiv, DMin, DH*

### This Is Our Story

> Psychotherapy consists of a gradual unfolding process wherein the therapist attempts to know the patient as fully as possible. A diagnosis limits vision; it diminishes ability to relate to the other as a person. Once we make a diagnosis, we tend to selectively inattend to aspects of the patient that do not fit into that particular diagnosis, and correspondingly overattend to subtle features that appear to confirm an individual diagnosis.[1]

Irvin D. Yalom, MD, professor emeritus of psychiatry at Stanford University, cautions caregivers to avoid diagnosis, except for insurance companies.[2] Clergy and chaplains are called to major in the art of relationships. Our invitation to a person's bedside or moment of crisis is not as a skilled scientist but as a spiritual caregiver. Our call and invitation are to listen, learn, love, and liberate. This is our story.

The purpose of this chapter is to offer a set of tools for clergy as you work with persons who have been admitted to a health care facility or who are in the need of a healing relationship beyond what you are equipped and trained to provide. After reading this chapter you will be able to better understand the difference between pastoral care and psychotherapy. In addition, you will find in this chapter a model for pastoral care that can be used in various health care facilities, congregations, and venues where you are expected to serve as a healing, non-anxious spiritual presence.

There is an Asian proverb that states, "If the only tool that you have is a hammer, every problem will look like a nail." What is in your tool kit?

Chaplains and congregational clergy need an assortment of tools in our tool kit. One size does not fit all. Each situation, each encounter, is unique. The setting / context will impact our response. It is my hope that this chapter adds a few tools to your tool kit and challenges your thinking.

God called me to be a pastor, professor, psychoanalyst, and pastoral care director. Four different congregations over a twenty-eight-year span have looked to me as their pastor. Andover Newton Theological School, Drew Seminary, New York Theological Seminary, Princeton Theological Seminary, Union Seminary, and New Brunswick Theological Seminary have each allowed me to teach their students. Blanton Peale Graduate Institute granted me certificates in psychoanalysis and in marriage and family therapy. Riverside Church, New York City, hired me as a staff psychotherapist for seven years. Barnet Hospital, Paterson, New Jersey, hired me as their director of pastoral care. It was at Barnet Hospital and Hackensack University Hospital, Hackensack, New Jersey, where I supervised six units of clinical pastoral education. Following the tragic events of September 11, 2001, the Council of Churches of the City of New York (CCCNY) hired me to design and implement what has been to date the largest clergy resiliency program in the United States, the Care for the Caregivers Interfaith Program. After that five-year program funded by the September 11th Fund and the American Red Cross, the CCCNY hired me as their director of pastoral care. This is the experience that I bring to this chapter. It is part of my story. How does your story impact what you offer to people?

As a result of this amazing journey, I hear voices. I hear lots of voices. I hear the voices of the choir every Sunday morning. I hear the voices of my students. I hear the voices of victims of domestic violence and the voices of children going to bed hungry. I hear the voices of mothers who lost their sons and daughters to war and to street violence. I hear the voice of God, and Allah, and Jehovah, and other sacred voices. I hear voices. What voices do you hear?

Christina Hoff Sommers and Sally Satel wrote a book together titled, *One Nation Under Therapy: How the Helping Culture Is Eroding Self-Reliance*. Sommers and Satel write:

> On September 14, 2001, three days after the terrorist attacks on the World Trade Center and the Pentagon, a group of psychologists sent an open letter to the American Psychological Association. The nineteen signatories, all established experts in trauma research and

> treatment, were concerned that thousands of people in New York City and elsewhere would receive dubious, even damaging, counseling. "In times like these," the letter said, "it is imperative that we refrain from the urge to intervene in ways that—however well-intentioned—have the potential to make matters worse.... Unfortunately, this has not prevented certain therapists from descending on disaster scenes with well-intentioned but misguided efforts. Psychologists can be of most help by supporting the community structures that people naturally call upon in times of grief and suffering. Let us do whatever we can, while being careful not to get in the way."[3]

How do we support the systems that persons already have in place? How do we "do no harm"? How do we not get in the way? When is it appropriate to encourage a therapeutic relationship? What observations and steps lead to such a conversation? These are the questions that this chapter seeks to answer. This is our story.

We are family. We share the same pedagogical parents. We were birthed together in the same schools, seminaries, seminars, and conferences. We share a common pedagogical memory. We have been supervised and in some cases overly supervised. We have anxiously read aloud our verbatim for our peers and supervisors to celebrate and critique our developmental growth as caregivers. We have run to be with a family in need. We have kept our own doubts and wonderings about suffering and justice in check while we help a father asking, "Why our child?" We have struggles with issues of appropriate boundaries and self-care. We are family.

We speak the same language. We share a similar vocabulary. However, somewhere in our developmental process we hit a wall. It divides some of us from one another. Far too many times we talk around it. And some who do not talk about it at all impose their story instead of actively listening to the patients or parishioners tell their stories.

Like discussions about sexuality in congregations, counseling is the proverbial elephant in the room that we mention in hushed tones. Clergy have allowed other professions to claim expertise as our profession runs from its historic roots. Counseling divides us. It scares us. Granted, if we are not trained, we do more harm than good. However, all it took was one recession for clinicians to concede that when money runs out, people turn to clergy for "free" help. Thus, we as clergy need the proper tools to maintain integrity in our work. There is a point at which a professional counselor is needed. On the other hand, there is a role for us as clergy and chaplains to competently counsel. My personal bias is that worship, celebrations, and congregational gatherings are a form of group therapy. Healing takes place. We help people find meaning in their stories. Crying, shouting, laughing, and applause are permitted. It's therapy!

Invariably, some colleagues are quite correctly thinking I have made some assumptions as to how you practice and what scares you. Some may opt to dismiss this chapter as a projection or, perhaps even worse, some of my narcissistic tendencies. However, I invite you to consider with me, as William James asserted, that there are varieties of religious experience. Within a variety of faith expressions and a multitude of thoughts about the value of counseling, how do we find a proper balance? How can we free persons to find healing in their religious experience and restore hope in their journey?

It is my assertion that to help persons find healing, we must create safe spaces where they can tell the story of their journey under the watchful eye of a caregiver who comes to this sacred moment with creativity, compassion, collaboration, and competence. We walk alongside and at times emotionally lift persons whose story hit a bump or detour or got stuck. We are the guides for those travelers who seem to have lost their way on their journey. We can be of help because we know firsthand what it means to be the wounded storyteller, and our own subjective experience has assisted us in learning how to be a wounded story listener.

Arthur Frank writes in his work *The Wounded Storyteller: Body, Illness, and Ethics*:

> The ill body's articulation in stories is a personal task, but the stories told by the ill are also *social*.... The shape of the telling is molded by all the rhetorical expectations that the storyteller has been internalizing ever since he first heard some relative describe an illness, or she saw her first television commercial for a non-prescription remedy, or he was first instructed to "tell the doctor what hurts" and had to figure out *what* counted as the story that the doctor wanted to hear.[4]

Our task is to free those stories begging to be told. We are to encourage persons to tell their story instead of living up to our comfortable norms and expectations. We are to allow space for both terror and triumph; hell and holiness; divine and demonic; pain and pleasure; satisfaction and shame; ritual and rebellion; morality and meaning; miracles and messiness.

We make ourselves available to hear voices. Our ears are trained to be sensitive to subtle vocal shifts. We not only hear voices, but we also see voices. We visualize victims and victors, along with all the voices that impact a person's story. Society tends to think of clergy more in the role of the storyteller. That is only part of our task as clergy.

We do major in the art of telling a story. However, the stories we tell to listening ears must be infused with a deep appreciation of the human condition and a reflection of the voices and stories we hear from others on their journey. Our story is one who hears voices. The voices we hear tell us stories. Pray with me that all that is holy and sacred will grant us the wisdom and compassion of a wounded story listener. This is our story.

## *Section Two: What Is the Difference Between Pastoral Care and Counseling?*

What is the difference between pastoral care and counseling? The quick answer is that counseling is one aspect of pastoral care. Well, that was easy. Okay, not so fast. What is pastoral care? If you subscribe to the axiom that context makes a difference, allow me to suggest that pastoral care may be defined and practiced differently based on your setting along with the contextual norms and subjective expectations. Reading a multitude of books and articles on pastoral care will lead you to the realization that those clinicians and academicians who spend time thinking about definitions do not agree universally on a meaning of the phrase "pastoral care." As one can imagine, oftentimes the definition affirms a point or perspective the writer is attempting to drive home. Nevertheless, for the purpose of this chapter, we need a definition of "pastoral care." Research suggests that the term "pastoral care" was first used in 1967, as a Christian term to define "helping acts done by representative Christian persons, directed toward the healing, sustaining, guiding and reconciling of troubled persons, whose troubles arise in the context of ultimate meanings and concerns."[5]

Over the years practitioners have expanded the definition to include clergy of all faiths who engage in the work of pastoral care.

This work is a practice that is not limited to one faith expression, and for that matter, is not limited to one methodology.

The following is an inclusive definition of "pastoral care":

> In contemporary American usage, "pastoral care" usually refers, in a broad and inclusive way, to all pastoral work concerned with the support and nurturance of persons and interpersonal relationships, including everyday expressions of care and concern that may occur in the midst of various pastoring activities and relationships.[6]

It is important to note that other faith traditions may use different terminology for this function we call "pastoral care," and so we will find variations of what is an expected and normative practice of care.

Perhaps pastoral care is less about technique and more about our attitude and presence. What would a book like this be without some techniques (which I will offer later in this chapter)? However, the work of the chaplain and clergyperson is about relationships. Techniques provide you with some directions and guides in working with relationships. The most important part of what you will bring to pastoral care is your presence. With that in mind, allow me to add to the definitions of pastoral care that it is a radical relationship. Going even further, pastoral care is showing hospitality in its many forms. Such care is both individualistic and communal. We may work with individuals in the hospital room, senior day care, hospice, prison, or congregational setting. Nevertheless, we are always mindful of returning individuals back into their community with renewed hope, increased wisdom, and spiritual strength. That is pastoral care.

How many of us have sat through those rubber-chicken dinners to honor some caregiver well deserving of recognition, but did it take four hours to say "Thank you"? Usually those who are asked to say a "few" words tell stories of their personal need whereby the caregiver was a healing presence and he or she stayed the course until a new outcome to the problem was possible. We love those persons who seem to break personal boundaries of good self-care and make themselves available to our beck and call. That is not good self-care.

Caregivers need boundaries and excellent self-care habits. Nevertheless, that is usually the model held up as a standard: "He or she was always there for me." Good pastoral care means being available in times of need, but it also means teaching others the valuable lessons of boundaries. My dear professor of marriage and family therapy often told our class, "Even Jell-O needs a container to be enjoyed." Therapists call it the holding environment or frame. Call it structure, boundaries, standards of care, or good common sense, effective pastoral care requires good boundaries. Pastoral care is always about relationships, and those relationships require of us as professionals good boundary setting.

In contrast, what is counseling? Again, you will be hard-pressed to find a universally accepted answer. However, there are some key components of counseling:

> "Pastoral counseling" refers to caring ministries that are more structured and focused on specifically articulated need or concern. Counseling always involves some degree of "contract" in which a request for help is articulated and specific arrangements are agreed upon concerning time and place of meeting; in extended counseling a fee may also be agreed upon, depending on the institutional setting and other considerations.[7]

Clearly there are times when one needs the privacy, focus, and expertise of a trained therapist. This does not rule out or negate the value of the chaplain or clergyperson. A good intervention needs both professions to work together. Clergy and chaplains serve as triage centers. Often your presence, skills, and artful way of building relationships are all that are needed. Those times when a person needs more, we can be the bridge to help persons embrace their need for a professional who can offer more insights into their particular challenges than we are able to provide. Remember, our first goal is always, do no harm. Our only agenda is to be of help.

We can address fears, concerns, and questions about counseling. We can suggest competent counselors for that particular individual and his or her unique needs. Again, counseling is one aspect of the larger ministry of pastoral care.

The comparison can be drawn as follows:

> "Counseling" generally implies extended conversation focused on the needs and concerns of the one seeking help. "Care" in many of its expressions is also conversational, though briefer and less therapeutically complex than counseling, as in supportive or sustaining ministries like visiting the sick. The term is also applied to

> nonconversational ministries in which a significant caring dimension may be present, as in administering communion, conducting a funeral, or pastoral teaching.[8]

We point persons to counseling when cancer has left more questions than answers. We point persons to counseling when the grief process appears in need of a long-term guide to navigate a new reality. We point persons to counseling when their need is beyond our ability and exceeds the amount of time that we can provide to solve the challenges. We point persons to counseling when the illness requires medical intervention and monitoring. We point persons to counseling when our best efforts and expertise have not allowed persons to become unstuck and pull their way out of the quicksand of their daily dilemmas.

What lies ahead is looking at a technique for offering pastoral care that includes a component of counseling. How does the chaplain or clergyperson build trust while assisting persons with difficult decisions and challenging crossroads? How can you be a friend and professional at the same time? What is the difference? Why is it necessary?

How do you make room to be human and tender and show care while being appropriate? What boundaries keep you from burnout yet do not distance you to the point of appearing aloof or insensitive to persons in need?

## *The Compassion Model*

Clergy and chaplains are called by numerous names and ascribed multitudinous images: gardeners, counselors, care specialists, healers, storytellers, story listeners, caregivers, change agents, advocates, wounded healers, and guides, to name a few. The first part of this chapter focused on the definitions of pastoral care and counseling. This section will focus on technique or how you can do it more effectively. My assertion is that effective pastoral care and counseling can be summed up by four actions: listen, learn, love, and liberate.

### Listen

How many times have we heard stories about partners who do not listen to each other? Instead of listening, one partner rehearses his or her next response and simply waits for the other partner's mouth to stop moving in order to jump in with their preplanned response. It is bad communication when partners do this to each other. It is devastating when caregivers demonstrate this type of behavior with the persons who come to us for help. Listening is the most valuable skill that we as caregivers bring to persons in need. Why then is it that far too many caregivers are not good at listening? What can we do to improve our listening skills?

First, listening is a mind-set. Before you walk into the hospital, hospice, rehabilitation, or long-term care room, before the couple arrives in your office, before the board members start to ponder the budget, and before you go into prayer with a family in need, prepare your mind to listen. Perhaps too many of us have had bad models to follow in learning good listening skills. It is hard work. Yes, it is work! (See chapter 7.)

Listening is a mind-set. Active listening, effective listening, compassionate listening, and in-depth listening involve respect and appreciation for the person who is talking. Such listening suggests that what the other person has to say is important and deserves validation. Listening is a decision to engage in another's life story and discern how you can be of help in the shaping of his or her story. Listening does not require us as caregivers to have great answers or be experts in the subject areas. Listening is a commitment to respect you enough to give you my full attention and give you clues and follow-up questions that ensure I received your messages as intended.

Listening is also a social science. Listening requires that we separate facts, feelings, and fiction. Listening requires that in the back of our mind we are asking justice questions:

1. Who is suffering?
2. Why is there suffering? Is it self-induced or systemic?
3. How do families-of-origin issues play into this story? How do my own family-of-origin issues impact my ability to hear this person's story on its own merit?
4. What themes and recurring patterns are in this story?
5. What do I need to help design an effective care plan? What goals, objectives, and outcomes will bring about healing?
6. How do we best collaborate together to bring healing?

We listen with our ears, eyes, head, and heart. We hear words as we also observe body language, facial expressions, tone of voice, rate of speech, affect, degree of difficulty in speaking, Freudian slips, guarded words, inconsistencies, and mannerisms. We play the DVD back to the person speaking: "Let me make sure I heard you properly. Let me repeat what I heard you say. Please let me know whether I accurately captured what you are saying."

We listen because we care. If you are not in this business because you care about people, please get out now. Hurting, hospitalized, hungry, horrified people at the end of their rope or at least standing in need deserve to be heard by someone who cares. We care because we are human and we see the humanity in others. Thus, we listen. Listening builds relationships.

## Learn

Larry King said on his television show, "I learn a lot when I keep my mouth closed." One of the goals of listening is to learn. Consultants are taught to go into a new situation dumb. This does not mean that we check our brains at the front door. What it does mean is that as caregivers, we leave open the very real possibility that we do not know the whole story and what we do know is subjective at best. We will miss something of significance if we do not go into situations with a mind open to learning. To learn as a clergyperson or chaplain is to acknowledge that each case, each situation, is unique, complete with variations, twists, turns, and surprises.

One size does not fit all. Learn what is unique about this person and his or her situation. Both my father and my mother are dead. I have lost other loved ones and friends. In school I studied death and dying along with the various stages of grief. However, the way death impacts another I must learn with each encounter. I only know how death impacts my thinking and actions. As a learner, it is my task to discover how this set of new circumstances impacts the person asking for pastoral care. In learning about someone else, I also learn more about myself. Mom was right: "What did you learn today?" It is a good question to end each visit, each session, each encounter, and each day.

It took me years to realize how my mother prepared me for my life's work as a caregiver, story listener, and adult learner. My mother had a set of stories about growing up in the segregated South as a very tall, fair-skinned, thin woman with natural red hair. She expanded her stories to include her days as a model living in Harlem and later Sugar Hill. It seemed that I had heard the stories over and over and over again. Well, so I thought. What I learned is that Mom really never told the same story the same way. At different times, she included new insights or left out old parts of her story. The lesson became clear: listen and learn.

We create environments and moments where learning can take place.[9] Many writers of sacred literature and the sages show us that the world is our classroom. Some mental health professors teach that everything a person does is informational. Meaning is not attached to actions until we attach the meaning or the person telling the story attaches meaning to his or her own story. Keep your mouth shut in order to learn how this person views her or his situation. What roles does religion play in this person's healing? What measures did the person take to fix the situation? How is it going? How can you be of help? What is the person's expectation of you? Is it realistic and something that you can deliver? What do you need to learn to be of help to this person or be effective in this situation?

We are learning in order to provide better intervention for the person in need. It is not about us. It is about helping someone during a time of need. We are learning about his or her situation in order to make an informed decision: Am I the right person to be of the most help?

## Love

This brief subsection is not about romantic love as we read in novels. This is not about the love we feel for our family and close friends. This is a love that stems from awe at the beauty of the world and being in the world. This is about a special love of persons. Maybe the word "compassion" is more comfortable for you. Love of this sort springs from our connection to the humanity in others. It seems that for us to be effective in our work we are called to love ourselves, love our work, and love the people we serve. If not for love, can we risk our own safety and comfort level to be with another at a time of need? Love pushes us to offer challenges to another's story or at least the subjective retelling of the story. Love sees the good in others and helps hidden strengths be made known. Love is a form of advocacy. We become prophets who in love fight for that which is just and good. Love takes us back to respect and appreciation for someone in need. We love the goodness in other people. We love what creation has made and commit to restore persons to wholeness, health, and happiness. We show love when we ask permission to touch a hand. We show love by being attentive, sincere, and emotionally available. We show love by doing good self-care, which includes vacations, time away, significant romantic relationships, interests outside of ministry, continuing education, and proper compensation for our services. This allows us as caregivers to be fully present with another.

## Liberate

Do not be afraid—this is not a primer on liberation theology. Instead, it is permission to free people of doubts, fears, anxieties, concerns, and conflicts as part of our work as pastoral caregivers. Here we use "liberation" as a religious term to foster justice and fairness. What does this have to do with clergy and chaplains? Sometimes depression can be cured by having a job with a living wage or going to bed without rodents or residing in a home without the threat of violence or not being a target because of sexual orientation. We are challenged to be trustworthy leaders in a world where we are increasingly afraid to trust people with power. Our sense of mission and call is to collaborate with community leaders to bring healing to oppressed communities. If we are to engage in the pastoral care of whole persons, we must liberate persons for whom oppression in its various forms has taken its toll.

## Notes

1. I. D. Yalom, *The Gift of Therapy: An Open Letter to a New Generation of Therapists and Their Patients* (New York: HarperCollins, 2003), 4–5.
2. Ibid., 4.
3. Christina Hoff Sommers and Sally Satel, *One Nation Under Therapy: How the Helping Culture Is Eroding Self-Reliance* (New York: St. Martin's Press, 2005), 177.
4. Arthur W. Frank, *The Wounded Storyteller: Body, Illness, and Ethics* (Chicago: University of Chicago Press, 1995), 3.
5. Emmanuel Y. Lartey, *In Living Color: An Intercultural Approach to Pastoral Care and Counseling*, 2nd ed. (Philadelphia: Jessica Kingsley Publishers, 2003), 21.
6. R. J. Hunter, "Pastoral Care and Counseling (Comparative Terminology)," in *The Concise Dictionary of Pastoral Care and Counseling*, ed. Glenn H. Asquith (Nashville: Abingdon Press, 2010), 22.
7. Ibid., 23.

8. Ibid.
9. Jackson Kytle, *To Want to Learn: Insights and Provocations for Engaged Learning* (New York: Palgrave MacMillan, 2004).

## Further Reading

Lewis, Judith A., Michael Lewis, Judy Daniels, and Michael D'Andrea, eds. *Community Counseling: A Multicultural-Social Justice Perspective.* 4th ed. Belmont, CA: Brooks / Cole, 2011.

Miller, William R., and Kathleen A. Jackson. *Practical Psychology for Pastors.* 2nd ed. Englewood Cliffs, NJ: Prentice Hall, 1995.

Ponterotto, Joseph G., J. Manuel Casas, Lisa Suzuki, and Charlene Alexander. *Handbook of Multicultural Counseling.* 3rd ed. Thousand Oaks, CA: Sage Publications, 2010.

Ramsay, Nancy J., ed. *Pastoral Care and Counseling: Redefining the Paradigms.* Nashville: Abingdon Press, 2004.

## About the Contributor

**Rev. Dr. Willard W. C. Ashley, Sr., MDiv, DMin, DH,** is acting dean and associate professor of practical theology at New Brunswick Theological Seminary. Rev. Dr. Ashley is a psychotherapist and the former assistant dean of students at the Andover Newton Theological School. He is the founder and senior pastor of the Abundant Joy Community Church, Jersey City, New Jersey. Rev. Dr. Ashley was the director of pastoral care at Barnett Hospital, Paterson, New Jersey, and helped start the first unit of clinical pastoral education (CPE) at Hackensack University Hospital, Hackensack, New Jersey. He served as staff psychotherapist at the Riverside Church, New York City; Montclair Counseling Center, Upper Montclair, New Jersey; and the Lutheran Counseling Center, New York City. Rev. Dr. Ashley envisioned and implemented the largest clergy resiliency program in the United States following the attacks on September 11, 2001, the Care for the Caregivers Interfaith Program, a ministry of the Council of Churches of the City of New York. He is the editor of *Learning to Lead: Lessons in Leadership for People of Faith* and coeditor with Rabbi Stephen Roberts of *Disaster Spiritual Care: Practical Clergy Responses to Community, Regional and National Tragedy* (both SkyLight Paths Publishing).

# 10

## *Inspiring Hope*

### Confronting Fear, Guilt, and Shame in Spiritual / Pastoral Care

*Rev. Dr. Glenn A. Robitaille, RPC, MPCP, CPP*

Mark Twain once observed, "If a cat sits on a hot stove, it will never sit on a hot stove again; but it won't sit on a cold stove either." We are not much different than our pets in this regard. We tend to remember events that have shaped our understanding of the world.

Human beings are emotionally complex and shaped by their life experiences. Consider how various people respond to dogs in public places, with some exhibiting warmth and affection toward them and others recoiling to a safe distance. More often than not this behavioral response is based on past experiences with dogs that have shaped people's expectations of them. So, from an objective point of view, neither response really tells us much about dogs. One cannot determine how accurate a perception about a particular dog is without knowing something about that dog, nor can we understand the reaction of one encountering a dog without understanding how that person has experienced dogs in the past.

Understanding emotional responses to religion and spirituality is very similar to understanding people in relation to dogs. People are emotionally shaped and informed by their experiences with religion, faith, and spirituality. We also possess innate emotional qualities that are largely involuntary. According to research, introversion and extroversion profiles can be tracked within the first year of life. While individuals can learn to be more outgoing or less social, introverts will always be most energized by self-directed activities and extroverts by the people with whom they are sharing that activity.

In the world of psychology this dyad between what is learned and what is innate is often called the nature / nurture question.[1] While polarized opinions do exist that would see human responses as largely one or the other, the greater body of evidence would suggest our preferences and responses are the by-product of both nature and nurture, with some tendencies existing in reaction to the experiences we have had and others as part of the package of being who we are.

Beyond that, emotion is important as part of our religious and spiritual experience because how we feel about our beliefs is as significant in developing a healthy spirituality as the beliefs themselves. This concept has been attacked throughout history by everyone from Karl Marx to Sigmund Freud, with religion and spiritual belief being described as the "opiate of the people,"[2] as "neurotic wish,"[3] or other less flattering descriptions. But the simple fact of the matter is people do not experience ideas in a vacuum, whether they are opinions about the weather or a particular spiritual viewpoint. It is not just the religious or spiritual who need to feel secure in their world or who require some confidence in the face of life's many questions and uncertainties. However uncertainty is addressed, the single most important factor affecting human well-being is how we feel about the answers informing our lives. And when it comes to spiritual care, knowing how individuals connect emotionally to their beliefs is critical in providing support.

For many years I went to a hairstylist who held to a very closed and literal belief system. Most of my haircutting experience involved her recounting to me the reasons why her belief was the one and only way to believe and the answer to all of life's questions. Anyone ever trapped by an opportunistic and closed-minded individual will know how annoying such an experience can be. But my desire to understand her overcame my resistance, and over time, I heard about her abusive past and the deep pain she had suffered at the hands of nearly every human being with whom she had risked vulnerability. She openly discussed the pain she felt when her son—a sufferer of a severe and persistent mental illness—took his own life and how close she came to doing so herself. I learned her joy in life was restored by her attachment to this narrow and dismissive religious group. I had the opportunity to disrupt her confidences, like shooting fish in a barrel. Other knowledgeable people of faith she encountered likely tried. But for her, this narrow belief was solid ground in a world that had left her broken and vulnerable. From a spiritual care perspective, how she felt because of those beliefs and how she experienced the world are far more important matters than whether her beliefs make sense. Her closed belief system was likely healthier for her as a coping strategy than the cocaine Sigmund Freud reportedly snorted to deal with his challenges.[4]

Good spiritual care is not about judging the dog. It is taking the time to learn what the dog means to the person and how that special relationship can be strengthened for the promotion of health. It is about hope, peace, and joy and finding meaning amid the unrelenting uncertainties of life. Nor is spiritual care about apologetics or proving the existence of God or any other theological question, but about releasing the healing energy of faith, however it is experienced, and channeling it toward whatever forces are threatening well-being. In healthy individuals, this care is both self-driven and experienced in relationship to others. It is also ongoing, deliberate, and as regular as any other discipline of care, like brushing teeth or taking the stairs. So when it comes to spiritual health, the emotions individuals experience relative to their beliefs are not peripheral or secondary, but central. And understanding the interplay of emotion and faith is fundamental in developing an approach to spiritual care.

For the majority of individuals, the emotions related to faith are positive and affirming. Not many experiencing healthy spirituality seek specialized spiritual care. They practice their faith in whatever way is comfortable for them and find ways to share that experience with others. Because human beings have a natural aversion to painful activities and perspectives, many who are not feeling nurtured by their beliefs will often discard them. The last century has seen an explosion of lapsed believers of all kinds, particularly in the West, and many because they didn't feel any benefit from those beliefs or practices. In the middle of these two extremes are people indulging a spiritual habit—a nominal belief for which they have little energy to cultivate or interest to quit. Others are compelled to plod on in their faith because the cost of not doing so is greater in their minds than the suffering they endure by continuing. For the most part, it is that last group of people, struggling to survive their ambivalence, who present in need of spiritual care. They can be found in synagogues, churches, temples, and mosques, in health care facilities, on the streets, and wherever human beings in need of hope and meaning can be found.

If how a person feels about his or her beliefs determines the degree of well-being experienced in relation to them, then understanding this connection is the first step in spiritual care. Spiritual care from the horizon of the sufferer is that which "sits in the ash pit" with them long enough to learn what is really going on. It does not offer a flight to wellness or stock solutions, but listens to understand the thoughts, feelings, and experiences of the sufferer well enough to be a vessel of hope. A woman suffering a deep depression once used this analogy in describing what she needed from me in times of despair. "I need you to carry my hope for me when I have lost the will to hold it for myself." From that perspective, Job's three friends may not have done much right when they came to comfort Job in his affliction, but sitting and listening was the correct initial approach.[5] Knowing what to listen for and how to recognize complex emotions would have helped them to be better spiritual companions.

Many emotions can potentially underlie a dysfunctional spirituality, but when faith is unhealthy, it is generally marinating in one of three core emotions that capture and inform the full range of negative human emotion: fear, guilt, or shame. These emotions coexist, and the presence of one is often an indicator of the likelihood of the others, but the impact on the spiritual presentation shifts measurably depending on which one is at the fore.

## *When Fear Is Primary*

Silvan Tomkins, creator of affect theory, presented a model for unpacking emotion and motivation.[6] The data he collected has been very useful in every field where understanding human responses is beneficial, whether it be forensics, psychology, or spiritual care. When fear is being experienced, Tomkins identified the affects to be such things as the eyes appearing frozen open, pale skin, feeling cold, perspiration, facial trembling, and the hair standing erect. Most of these affects would be seen most dramatically in a moment when acute fear is being experienced, or terror, but fear can settle and form a baseline in a person's life. The above symptoms are, not surprisingly, also common in anxiety disorders that have fear at the root. For such people, fear is not just an experience of the moment when a real threat is being encountered but an ongoing anticipation, as if the danger is ever present. In such cases, these affects are always simmering under the surface, waiting to be triggered by the slightest thing.

When fear is the primary energy of religious or spiritual experience, the experience possesses the simmering patterns of fear. For the most part, fear manifests as anxiety. Have I done enough to be accepted? Am I good enough to merit inclusion in the company of the faithful? Is God going to strike me down or send me to hell? Will I come back in the next life as a beast of some kind, or will there be another punitive consequence for not having measured up? Often such a pattern emerges following a harrowing experience. It is said that many who heard Jonathan Edward's famous sermon, "Sinners in the Hands of an Angry God" were clutching at the pillars of the sanctuary to avoid being sucked into a fiery pit, so effective was his use of terror in his presentation style.[7]

Fear can also be the consequence of a need for certainty and a lack of compelling information. Agoraphobic individuals have no real knowledge of threat when they choose to remain frozen in a narrow comfort zone; they simply cannot be certain nothing bad will happen if they were to leave it. Spiritual and religious individuals can become fixed in their beliefs and refuse to learn and grow because the safety of where they are in their beliefs is more comforting to them than the possibility of growth that comes with exploration. Others can be trapped in their fear and unable to find their way out.

Ethan was raised in a devout Roman Catholic family. From an early age he aspired to the priesthood, mostly inspired by the colorful vestments and the rituals of worship. The dresser in his bedroom was decorated with the articles of the altar, carefully prepared and placed, so the Mass could be imitated and practiced. By the time Ethan was ten, he could recite the entire Mass from memory along with the Ten Commandments, particular catechism responses, and the required prayers. Things took a turn for the worse for Ethan when, in a moment of anger and frustration, he cursed his older brother and used the name of God in a profane way—a violation of the second commandment. Usually such an occasion would mean a trip to the confessional and the requisite penance; but on this occasion, a Sunday morning stood between him and his next opportunity to confess, and he found himself in the queue waiting for Communion, uncomfortably trapped between his father and his mother. In the end, his fear of his father's questions around why he had not taken Communion overpowered his fear of God, resulting in his accepting the wafer with what he believed to be a mortal sin on his soul. According to his understanding at the age of twelve, receiving Communion when not in a state of grace constituted a sacrilege and required the absolution of a bishop to be forgiven. With any hope of seeing a bishop eclipsed by his age and remote proximity to the diocesan office, Ethan persisted in piling sacrilege upon sacrilege by continuing to receive the sacrament for the next four years. With every passing week, his fear of condemnation grew until he was a neurotic mess. By the time he was sixteen, he was hospitalized for severe gastrointestinal difficulties and was ripe for the picking by any group offering him relief from the terror pervading his life.

According to sociologist Tony Campolo, an inverse relationship exists between power and love; as one increases, the other decreases.[8] Ethan's perspective on God had shifted from being a loving being to whom he wished to dedicate his life, to a malevolent being with the power to condemn him forever. Fear-based faith always connects to power images more profoundly than ones of benevolence or love, whether they focus on a particular deity, karma, or the destructive power of nature itself. Fear removes the possibility of feeling valued or loved; seeing transcendence differently restores hope and moderates the effects of fear.

When people possess a fear-based faith, it is important to connect the belief with what it says about their view of the nature of God. This can often be accomplished by asking, "If what you believe is true, what are you saying God is like?" All theological beliefs connect with a view of the nature of God, and every doctrine we hold makes a statement about how we see God's character. Often people will recognize, in answering this question, a view of God more resembling Adolph Hitler or Saddam Hussein than one of benevolence or understanding.

Using Ethan's story, this connection between beliefs and God's character can be illustrated in the following ways:

- Unless you perform the right ritual, God will not forgive you = God is exacting and cares more about rituals than about human well-being.

- Unless you rightly identify truth, God will condemn you = the bottom line is more important to God than the heartfelt remorse of the person who failed.
- A youthful mistake can cut you off from God forever = God is unkind, unforgiving, petty, and selfish.

In Ethan's circumstance, making these connections enabled him to see the disconnect that existed between his actual view of God and his stated beliefs about God's love. His hope was restored when he was able to see God's character differently and apply the principles of God's love and forgiveness to himself.

The process of providing spiritual care to a person with a fear-based experience begins with attending behavior. It is important that the experience of the individual be affirmed and taken seriously. Often caregivers will rush to contradict material they identify as harmful or destructive, as if the person's problem can be changed with better information. Sometimes fear is the result of bad information, but more often it is how that information has connected with personal background and experience that evokes fear rather than the information itself. To be fearful, a belief must connect with some ambivalence in us. Once individuals understand that connection, it is possible to begin unpacking how particular beliefs are affecting them.

Good spiritual care to those with a fear-based faith experience could reflect the following process:

- Meet them where they are and walk with them. Listen without judgment to their stories.
- Identify the simmering patterns of fear: rejection anxiety, spiritual hypervigilance, inflexibility.
- Engage the fear directly by asking probing questions like "What is your greatest fear spiritually?" or "Does your faith create any fear in you?"
- Ask them to connect what their stated beliefs say about what God is like, using the question, "If what you believe is true, what are you saying God is like?"
- To temper harsh self-criticism, draw material demonstrating benevolence and acceptance of imperfection from their own belief systems.

- Encourage them to continue assessing future beliefs by connecting the content of the belief with what it says about the nature of God / transcendence.

Fear is always most pronounced when it is experienced in isolation. For many people, having a listening and compassionate ear provides a significant measure of relief. It is even more hopeful when a process to address such fears and restore hope is engaged with a knowledgeable spiritual care provider who can uncover the underlying themes informing dysfunctional faith.

## *When Guilt Is Primary*

The theme of regret features prominently in the literature of every culture, in sacred texts, myths, moral fables, parables, and wherever the human condition is discussed. From a purely objective point of view, guilt is the result of entertaining at least two options and selecting incorrectly, resulting in some injury to oneself or to others. Many of these perceived errors can be innocuous and cared for through an admission of guilt and seeking forgiveness. When it is exaggerated and pathological, it could have the behavioral equivalents of "hiding in the bushes"[9] and / or burying the evidence in the ground. Edgar Allan Poe captured the consequence of this strategy in his story "The Tell-Tale Heart."[10] In this account, a woman kills her annoying husband and buries him beneath the floorboards in her home. At first she believes she has hidden the act and beaten the law, but over time she begins to hear his heartbeat penetrating the home like a drum, until she is driven to confess her crime. Guilt often creates background noise that disturbs the sleep and affects digestion.

At other times, guilt has little to do with covering up or hiding the perceived failure and is focused on balancing the scale. The impulse in this guilt response is to make restitution or to make up for the perceived failure in some way. Restitution is good when it has a clear path and a means of providing compensation, but it can become pathological when the offense is believed to be so significant as to be unredeemable. In such cases, it can overwhelm the individual into a state of paralysis and resignation or create a sense of indebtedness so large the individual spends his or her time hammering on a rock pile that never reduces in size.

Hashim was raised in a traditional Muslim family in the suburbs of Toronto. In his earlier years he faithfully participated in the rituals and practices of his faith and was highly regarded by his mentors and peers. While away at university in his early twenties, he began experiencing the symptoms of bipolar disorder, manifesting first in an episode of mania. It was in such an elevated mood that he began experimenting with cannabis and sex and had his first experience with alcohol. With his mind racing and his energy levels soaring, he transitioned from one risky circumstance to another until he found himself behind the wheel of his car, significantly impaired by his elevated mood and alcohol. A short time later, he ran a stop sign at a busy intersection and struck another vehicle, killing the driver instantly. In the months that ensued he was diagnosed as bipolar, deemed not criminally responsible (NCR) by the Canadian courts due to a mental disorder, and transferred for treatment to a forensic psychiatric hospital.

When I met Hashim he had been in the mental health system for years. His illness was stable for the most part, but he bounced in and out of detainment due to an inability to follow the terms of his disposition, generally by leaving his allowed area without reporting. He struggled with bouts of suicidality and was uncomforted by the regular reassurance he was given by his family and caregivers that his behavior was the result of his illness and not his poor character. Hashim felt he had let everyone down, beginning with Allah and ending with himself, resulting in an inability to experience the affection of everyone in between. He believed he did not deserve the reassurances he was given or the forgiveness he was offered. Telling him he was not responsible for the death of the other driver was to provide him with evidence you did not "get it."

Guilt has the aspect of owing a "pound of flesh."[11] Whatever way it is expressed or manifested, it is this dynamic of indebtedness that identifies it as a guilt complex. Pathological guilt is not comforted when the source of the guilt is minimized. Hashim took his offense very seriously; it was disturbing to him that those who interacted with him did not. But he was also paralyzed by his guilt, completely convinced that he could do nothing to balance the scales, leaving him completely bankrupt emotionally and spiritually.

Following an elopement from a minimum-secure forensic psychiatric unit, I met with Hashim to provide a spiritual assessment to his psychiatrist, who believed much of his difficulty was the result of his beliefs. Over the next several days I heard Hashim's story in his own words, delivered without passion or energy. When he was finished, I mirrored to Hashim what I had heard him saying—a man was dead because of him, nothing would bring the man back, and his illness did not change the fact he was responsible for the death of another human being. His eyes brightened when I supported the idea that by whatever means or circumstances, he was the unalterable cause of the man's death and the resulting suffering that had visited the victim's family.

I also pointed out how this event had connected him with the victim in a very deep and intimate way. Because of his guilt, this man was ever present in his awareness. He was in his waking and his sleeping, in his going out and his coming in. A piece of this man had entered his own soul. As a result, two dead men existed, one of them walking and talking and feeling guilty and the other one remaining as the energy determining the quality and content of the existence of the other. Guilt creates an intimate connection to the persons who have been injured. It is not a positive intimacy, but it is deep and strong and has the power to overwhelm the life of the guilty. Sometimes this connection is referred to as moral residue.

This approach served two purposes in my interaction with Hashim: first, it validated Hashim's sense of moral justice and assured him his logic was legitimate; secondly, it supplied a measure of hope that an approach for dealing with his deep pain existed.

When pathological guilt is expressed by deep indebtedness, restitution is the straight path to self-forgiveness. Many faith groups use forms of penance to address this, suggesting everything from pilgrimages and acts of self-abasement to prescribed prayers. In some cases, these approaches do provide a measure of release and are sufficient to restore a sense of peace and well-being. In Hashim's case, no amount of suffering could undo what he had done. My approach to care involved a positive penance intended to allow Hashim to participate in creating a different energy in his life. I explained to Hashim that in causing this death, he had effectively removed the victim's opportunity to make a contribution to the world. As a result, the goodness he would have done while here has been left undone. In some sense, it was this aspect of the man's death that Hashim expressed to be unalterable. I suggested to him that a positive approach to dealing with that deficit would be to do a random act of kindness in this man's name every day. It did not have to be an heroic act—opening a door, talking kindly with someone who was having a bad day, buying someone a coffee could be meaningful enough—but it would have to be intentionally connected to this man in his mind. I also indicated that this is best done with no expectation of compensation or recognition. In addition to this, I suggested he do one random act of kindness per day in his own name to restore his own sense of meaningfully contributing to society at large.

Hashim latched onto this concept with enthusiasm. His depression lifted, and his community involvements increased. Within three months, he was discharged into the community with a measure of well-being unseen in the previous fifteen years, and he rejoined his faith group. Making a contribution in this man's name proved to supply the measure of hope for the future Hashim was lacking.

Providing spiritual care to a person caught in pathological guilt requires an appreciation for the connection that exists between the triggering event and the moral judgment of the person. This moral residue plays like a refrain in the background, affecting the experience of nearly every moment. An approach to spiritual care with those experiencing pathological guilt could reflect the following process:

- Meet them where they are and walk with them. Listen without judgment to their story.
- Identify the prominent patterns of guilt: moral residue, avoidance of spiritual practices, hyperactive conscience, excessive efforts to please, lack of enjoyment of life.
- Engage the guilt directly by asking probing questions like "How has your behavior affected others?" or "How has this circumstance affected you?"
- Validate the experience of the individual by acknowledging the felt indebtedness and the importance of restitution and / or ownership of wrongdoing, where possible.
- Assist individuals in identifying steps that can be taken toward restitution and / or seeking forgiveness.
- Where restitution and / or forgiveness are not possible, suggest a process of positive penance that makes a contribution on behalf of the injured person.

Restitution is critical in restoring hope to someone collapsing under the weight of pathological guilt. When positive penance is a potential spiritual care strategy, the individual in question should decide the degree and depth of the response, the scope—whether it be a lifelong response, a single act, or for a specific time—and the content. Responses addressing moral residue are most effective when they complement the personality and values of the person responding.

## *When Shame Is Primary*

Shame is the visible representation of inferiority.[12] Of all the human emotions possible, shame is the most destructive because it strikes at the core of the identity and deems the self unworthy. No other emotion can so thoroughly dissect a soul, saturate it in despair, and cause it to question the value of its ongoing existence. When healthy shame is experienced, it allows the person to recognize acts that are beneath one's dignity and inspire change; when pathological, it becomes judge and jury to the self. Very often, in such circumstances, shame has nothing at all to do with a shameful act but rather a self-image sculpted in the image of another's abuse.

According to Tomkins, the affect of shame is positioned in the face, with the eyes and head lowered and the gaze averted. Very often it is described as "a loss of face," because the impulse of shame is to block the window to the soul, where it is feared something ugly can be exposed. Shame is not regret about what one has done, although aspects of guilt and fear can also be present; shame is regret about who one is. When fired by religious beliefs offering a dismal assessment of the human condition, shame can be the death of hope and optimism. It is an easy deterioration with religious thought, because shaming doctrines often portray people as onions needing to be peeled back in order to expose the smelly core. Well-meaning educators often work on the assumption that these approaches cultivate humility and create self-awareness in the learner. However, when a person already struggles with shame, regardless of its origin, such techniques merely add the indictment of God to the floundering self-perception of the person overburdened with shame.

Nathan was the kind of man who invited rejection. He experienced so much of it in his life from his family and relatives that he anticipated it in every new relationship he formed. Twice he tried to kill himself with pills and another time by hanging. When he wasn't actively trying to commit suicide, he was passively doing so through chain smoking and junk food. The narrative of his life suggested the theme "I'll give you a good reason to reject me before you reject me for no good reason." It was easier for him to accept the idea he was being rejected for his behavior rather than for not measuring up as a human being. Consequently, he was crude, angry, cynical, and self-sabotaging. If confronted on these behaviors, he was quick and shocking in his responses, often leaving others embarrassed or humiliated. It was easy for others to deem him obnoxious and miss the hopelessness defining him.

Spiritual care of those with pathological shame is predicated on acceptance. This very basic tenet of spiritual care is difficult to practice with shame issues because those who cannot accept themselves often struggle to process the acceptance of others. Nathan knew how to field criticism, but he had no idea what to do with a compliment. When validated, his shoulders, head, and eyes would drop, and he would become silent. Positive statements were generally received as evidence that the affirmer didn't really understand him. Shame projects the underlying script "If you really knew me, you wouldn't like me," rendering any positive reinforcement as impotent.

Acceptance of those with shame scripts requires behavioral affirmation strategies rather than verbal ones. Actions definitely "speak louder than words" for such individuals and are constantly observed, so I approached Nathan with simple tasks and requests. I began by inviting him to take up the Sunday morning offering. He enthusiastically accepted, then did so barefooted with his shirt unbuttoned to the navel. In response, I thanked him for his contribution to the service and ignored his obvious testing. I followed with an invitation to sit on the social committee. He tested the patience of everyone present for the first several years of his participation. Over the next months I invited him for coffee, lunches, and casual chats that had nothing to do with fixing him. Fixing strategies would only have served to reinforce his belief that he was unacceptable as he was. Nathan felt valued by this approach, and his obnoxious behavior diminished. His sense of acceptance within the community of faith increased, and he began to believe in himself. Before long I garnered some trust and was hearing his entire story.

There is no quick fix for shame. The deficit impacts identity and is tenacious, unrelenting, and subject to setbacks. Both the care provider and the sufferer are challenged continually. As such, it is important that realistic goals be embraced. It is more about sustaining hope in the present and keeping the focus on today. While some shame-based individuals do experience remarkable transformations in self-perception, it is more about the journey than the destination—how one is feeling in this moment, on this day and occasion.

Overcoming pathological shame requires the help of a skilled professional. The personality issues underlying the shame profile are too complex for the novice to unpack. Supporting someone working through shame issues requires an accepting heart and the ability to set healthy boundaries.

A supportive approach to spiritual care with those experiencing pathological shame could reflect the following process:

- Meet them where they are and walk with them. Engage in casual conversations.
- Identify the prominent patterns of shame: sagging shoulders, averted eyes, lowered head, self-sabotaging behaviors, addictions.
- Engage individuals indirectly by acts of inclusion and acceptance. Set healthy boundaries respecting your comfort zone.
- Expect testing behavior, setbacks, and potential manipulation.
- Listen without judgment to their story, if shared. Affirm feelings of rejection without offering remedies.
- Look for ways to include them in the group without centering them out.
- See the relationship as a journey rather than a destination. Focus on the good available in the moment.
- If counseling is being considered, indicate that "counseling is a gift one gives oneself" rather than being too enthusiastic about the idea. Use language that is supportive of them rather than focused on deficits needing to be corrected.

Maintaining healthy boundaries is critical. Strategies that are empowering rather than enabling will curtail potential dependency. Without such parameters, well-meaning care providers can do more damage than good, as the erosion of the relationship generally occurring when boundaries are drawn late can reinforce the belief that the person is ultimately unlovable. It is appropriate to help an individual stand up under the load; carrying the person is equally unhealthy for all concerned.

## *Healthy Versus Unhealthy Spirituality*

Effective spiritual care recognizes the central place emotion plays in spirituality. When faith is unhealthy, it is generally the processing of beliefs that is dysfunctional rather than the actual beliefs. Certain viewpoints are more susceptible to creating unhealthy responses, but beliefs have to connect with some emotion in the believer in order to produce an effect. It is the affect of the belief that must be followed in spiritual care.

When faith is healthy, the believer engages the God Presence / transcendence as life-giving, life-affirming, and benevolent. The outcomes of such faith are strengthened resolve to face the uncertainties of life and access to the strengths of one's faith in times of difficulty. When faith is unhealthy, the God Presence / transcendence is cast as severe, exacting, malevolent, and / or indifferent. In such cases, beliefs interfere with the believer's capacity to cope and significantly add to the challenges being faced. Assessing this connection between affect and beliefs is the primary role of spiritual care. Until one follows the emotional trail to this spiritual antecedent, spiritual care is little more than a shot in the dark.

One does not need to be highly trained to offer these assurances. Care providers require the patience to observe what is being said and seen and a willingness to walk alongside. Quick reassurances cannot replace due diligence that is other-centered, without judgment, and supportive. Care providers must also possess the confidence to draw appropriate boundaries. Without such self-care, the energy required to provide spiritual care will be compromised.

People are where they are spiritually because they can be nowhere else. Everyone must occupy the perspectives and attitudes that are reflective of their respective journeys and where they happen to be at a given moment. It is the spiritual care provider's opportunity to share that space and to help identify latent sources of hope.

Generating hope is the primary opportunity of spiritual care. Hope restores life. Sensitive spiritual care providers will center their practice on discovering the glimmerings of light available in each person and help clear the clutter that obstructs its luminescence. Hope is the energy of optimism. Where hope is one is never alone.

## Notes

1. M. McGue et al., "Behavioral Genetics of Cognitive Ability: A Life-Span Perspective," in *Nature, Nurture, and Psychology*, ed. R. Plomin and G. E. McClearn (Washington, DC: American Psychological Association, 1993).
2. K. Marx, *Introduction to a Contribution to the Critique of Hegel's Philosophy of Right: Collected Works*, vol. 3 (New York: 1976), 175, http://marxists.org/archive/marx/works/1843/critique-hpr/intro.htm.
3. A. Freud, *The Ego and the Mechanisms of Defence*, rev. ed. (London: Hogarth Press and Institute of Psycho-Analysis, 1966 [U.S.], 1968 [U.K.]).
4. Sigmund Freud, *The Cocaine Papers*, ed. Robert Byck (New York: Stonehill, 1974), 57–58.
5. Job 2:11–13.
6. Sylvan S. Tomkins, *Affect Imagery Consciousness: The Negative Affects*, vol. 2 (New York: Springer, 1963).
7. D. G. Hart, Michael Lucas Sean, and Stephen J. Nichols, *The Legacy of Jonathan Edwards* (Grand Rapids, MI: Baker Academics, 2003).
8. Tony Campolo, *Which Jesus? Choosing Between Love and Power* (Nashville, TN: Word Publishing Group, 2002).
9. Genesis 3:8: Adam and Eve are portrayed as hiding among the trees of the garden after eating the forbidden fruit.
10. "The Tell-Tale Heart" was first published in the Boston-based magazine *The Pioneer* in January 1843, edited by James Russell Lowell.
11. This metaphor originates in the Shakespearean classic *The Merchant of Venice*, as the security Shylock the moneylender requires of Antonio. When Antonio defaults due to bankruptcy, Shylock demands the pound of flesh for Antonio's act of spitting in his face and defaulting on his loan.
12. Tomkins, *Affect Imagery Consciousness*.

## Further Reading

Bradshaw, John. *Creating Love: The Next Great Stage of Growth*. New York: Bantam Books, 1992.

Fleischman, Paul. *The Healing Spirit: Explorations in Religion and Psychotherapy*. New York: Paragon House, 1990.

Gilbert, Paul. *Compassion: Conceptualisations, Research and Use in Psychotherapy*. London: Routledge, Taylor and Francis Group, 2005.

James, William. *The Varieties of Religious Experience*. New York: Barnes and Nobles Classics, 2004.

Kaufman, Gershen. *The Psychology of Shame*. New York: Springer Publishing Company, 1989.

Tomkins, Silvan. *Affect Imagery Consciousness: The Negative Affects*. Vol. 2. New York: Springer Publishing Company, 1963.

Tournier, Paul. *Guilt and Grace*. New York: Harper & Row, 1962.

## About the Contributor

**Rev. Dr. Glenn A. Robitaille, RPC, MPCP, CPP,** is the director of spiritual and religious care at the Waypoint Centre for Mental Health Care. He is ordained with the Brethren in Christ Church and the founding pastor of Covenant Christian Community Church in Penetanguishene, Ontario, Canada. He has extensive experience in mental health chaplaincy and has been instrumental in establishing spirituality as a clinical variable in mental health care. He is a member of the Canadian College of Professional Counsellors and Psychotherapists (CCPCP), a registered professional counselor and master practitioner of counseling psychology with the Canadian Professional Counsellors Association (CPCA), and a certified pastoral counselor with the International Association of Christian Counseling Professionals (IACCP). Rev. Dr. Robitaille is a contributing author in *A Peace Reader* and *Leaving Fundamentalism: Personal Stories* and has published thirty articles in various magazines and journals in the field of theology and counseling.

# 11

## *Life Review*

*Rev. Nancy Osborne, MDiv, ACPE Supervisor*

*If there's anything worth calling theology, it is listening to people's stories, listening to them and cherishing them.*[1]

MARY PELLAUER

What better definition of spiritual care could there be than Pellauer's words above, "listening to people's stories, listening to them and cherishing them"? And yet there are many ways to listen to people's stories and to cherish them. In this chapter, I will discuss three of those many ways of listening and cherishing, all with links to spiritual care: life review, reminiscence, and a way I think is most closely kin to spiritual care, as we chaplain-types might practice it; it is a way I will call "life synthesis," an emotional and cognitive process of knitting together in love our own life stories and / or the stories of those for whom we care.

We are, if nothing else, creatures in time and who move through time. The Roman god Janus, the god for whom January is named, is described as having a two-sided head with two faces—where one face looks forward and the other looks backward.[2] At the intersection of the two faces is a sacred territory, a liminal space. Life review, reminiscence, and the work of life synthesis all occur, if they occur at all, in that liminal space, and it is onto that holy ground that one steps, whether self, psychiatrist, chaplain, or other spiritual caregiver for reflection. And it is surely into this world that life review takes us. Life review is a process where time converges, where one stands in the present time and looks forward to a reality marked by death and at the same time looks backward on a life full of joys and sorrows, successes and failures, well-integrated and unresolved events. Reminiscence and "life synthesis" also take place in liminal spaces, though with different temporal foci and dynamics. Surely the God who holds all of time is the God of this work.

When I was asked to write this chapter on life review, however, I hesitated. What came immediately to mind was the process I had been introduced to a long time ago, the counseling process described as "life review" and the long list of questions often associated with doing life review with oneself or with another.[3] I had been introduced to this process and to these lists as a young college student interested in aging and in working with persons in their later years. And while I have worked with aging and elders, I have not regularly used such a list in my spiritual care. To me, the list seemed not only overwhelming and unwieldy, but also oddly detached and impersonal, despite the personal significance of many of the questions. I just as surely knew, however, that I had been about the work of life review, of some sort, though perhaps without being in that formal category, with many, many people in my spiritual care practice: with the elderly, absolutely, but also with prisoners and homeless persons, with patients and families, with volunteers and staff members, in birth centers and emergency departments, at bedside services and funeral homes, and in just about every imaginable place, with persons experiencing just about every situation. In addition to introducing life review and reminiscence, it is that life review "of some sort" that I will seek to define and explore here.

## *Chapter Preview*

In this chapter, I will briefly describe the work of life review as it has been presented and defined by Robert N. Butler, the psychiatrist with whose name and work it is almost synonymous. I will also briefly set it in the context of a more broadly defined and more ancient life review. With help from Kathleen Woodward's work, I will then define the difference between life review and reminiscence and will propose that most spiritual care lies somewhere between the two, with common and distinct elements. I will call this middle process, this work of heart and soul, "life synthesis." I will draw both on the work of Mary Bateson in her book *Composing a Life* and on Arthur Frank's work *The Wounded Storyteller* to assist us in this journey.

In the second section, the process of life synthesis in some of the particular settings mentioned above briefly will be explored, followed in the third section by further spiritual / theological reflection on the process of life synthesis, the process of working to stitch together the parts of our lives and the parts of the lives of others for whom we care.

## *Traditional "Life Review": Robert Butler*

Presenting his understanding and research on life review in the journal *Psychiatry* in 1963, Robert Butler writes, "I conceive of the life review as a naturally occurring, universal mental process characterized by the progressive return to consciousness of past experiences, and, particularly, the resurgence of unresolved conflicts."[4] He goes on to say that "presumably this process is prompted by the realization of approaching dissolution and death, and by the inability to maintain one's sense of personal invulnerability."[5] He writes that this life review process can contribute both to "certain late-life disorders (particularly depression)" but may, on the other hand, have "impressive," "positive," and "constructive" effects. It may lead to severe depression, panic, intense guilt, obsessional rumination, increased rigidity, or even suicide,[6] or it may be related to the development of such characteristics as "candor, serenity, and wisdom among certain of the aged."[7] It is through the life review process, says Butler, that the past, including unresolved conflicts, is "surveyed and reintegrated."[8]

Butler challenged other psychiatrists who had tended to see this self-reflective process as simply a result of some dysfunction or decline in the elderly rather than as a natural developmental process. He insisted that the positive, affirmative changes reported by the aged themselves as a result of their life review also be noted. Butler recognized that this life review process might occur as well in younger persons or in any persons if they, too, are expecting death. His awareness was that while all people reflect on the past, for most, the principal concern is the present.[9] I would also add, from personal as well as spiritual care experience, that the death of others close to you (perhaps especially in age or life situation) also can stimulate this reflection upon life, its meaning and limits, its continuities and discontinuities.

Of the life-enhancing dimensions of life review, Butler writes, "As the past marches in review, it is surveyed, observed, and reflected upon by the ego. Reconsideration of previous experiences and their meanings occurs, often with concomitant revised or expanded understanding. Such reorganization of past experience may provide a more valid picture, giving a new and significant meaning to one's life; it may also prepare one for death, mitigating one's fears."[10] And sometimes, he says, this work "proceeds silently without obvious manifestations."[11]

## *Differences between "Life Review" and Reminiscence Therapy: Butler and Woodward*

Butler defines reminiscence as "the act or process of recalling the past"[12] and writes that "life review is not synonymous with, but includes, reminiscence."[13] Kathleen Woodward, professor of English and director of the Simpson Center for the Humanities at the University of Washington for nearly two decades, presented "Telling Stories: Aging, Reminiscence, and the Life Review" at a panel discussion at the University of Wisconsin, Milwaukee, in March 1997 under the sponsorship of the Doreen B. Townsend Center for the Humanities at the University of California, Berkeley. The text of this panel discussion shows that Woodward defines life review and reminiscence as more distinct from one another than does Butler, though in a related way to his distinction.

Woodward emphasizes that life review functions to evaluate life as a whole and is a "psychological process, under pressure of the coming ending, to see life as a whole, a coherent narrative." She identifies what she calls "totalization" in life review, a comprehensive process and one that emphasizes what's known, judged, evaluated. It is an analytical, cognitive process, inclusive of emotional responses, according to Woodward, but "primarily for the purpose of understanding."[14] Life review is, then, analogous to autobiography, she says, a summing up of an entire life and primarily analytical in nature. Analysis is the primary mode of life review.

Reminiscence, on the other hand, Woodward says, is a fragmentary and partial process concerned with a certain moment or moments. And while there might be, but not necessarily is there, a social dimension to life review (for example, it can occur in solitude), she sees reminiscence as more fundamentally a social interaction. It is a non-totalizing, social, less analytical and cognitive process than life review. Reminiscence is, she goes on to write, less concerned with finding the truth than with creating a certain "atmosphere of companionableness," with creating a mood that is "generative or restorative" and marked by "hope for trust and security."[15] Reminiscence, then, is analogous not to autobiography, she writes, but to certain moments in an autobiography. The mood or quality of the experience of remembering is the primary mark of reminiscence.

## *An Introduction to Life Synthesis*

Spiritual care occurs with persons experiencing all kinds of situations, events, and feelings. It includes analysis (as in life review) and emotional experience (as in reminiscence), and it seeks healing and wholeness to the greatest degree possible. It happens at times Walter Brueggeman, Hebrew Bible scholar and writer, calls the original orientation[16] or original organization—that is, in the everydayness of life. It also occurs in periods of disorientation or disorganization—in time of crisis and chaos.[17] Life review, in Butler's sense of the term, does not occur in the midst of times of situational crisis, but would certainly include reflection back over the causes, turning points, results of choices, and changes in life brought on by these times. Life review is more of a reflection with some distance from the events for the purpose of integration. Reminiscence is a memory experience with primary emphasis on the moment itself. Life synthesis is not equivalent to Brueggeman's new orientation[18] itself, but attempts to live into and to express the dynamic or energy (the call of God?) within every situation, life, relationship, or community, the energy that calls us toward and is about creating wholeness and *shalom*, even in the most disrupted and torn of the realities of life.

As I understand it, then, spiritual care in the form of spiritual counseling might be more likely to use the longer, more complete and cognitive, life review work. Spiritual care in its more traditional and multicontextual forms, such as chaplaincy or spiritual care in the context of a local worshiping community, is, like reminiscence, shorter term (though sometimes only relatively so), is a less formal and structured process, is a more emotional and relational work, and also hopes to be generative and restorative. Unlike reminiscence, however, spiritual care, as I am defining the term here, or life synthesis work, is attuned to much more than moments, does concern itself with the truth, and has both analytical and emotional dimensions. Another distinction is that life synthesis work, as I am defining it, occurs even with those unable to tell a story, to remember a conflict, or to participate in the integration when it is occurring. That is, this kind of spiritual care, life synthesis work, may occur not only by the subject of the reflection but also by others in relationship to that person.

Figure 11.1 provides a comparative visual.

In their journal article "Life Review in Pastoral Counseling: Background and Efficacy for Use with the Terminally Ill," Robert LeFavi and Marcia Wessels describe the formal process of life review as originating in Europe in the twelfth century, when a person facing death created what was basically a moral balance sheet in his or her last will and testament. In pre-industrial United States, life review was used to pass on instructions to the next generation, they write, but with the shift from rural to urban life, generations were separated, the knowledge and skills of elders became less valued, and the formal process of life review fell into disuse. Butler, they believe, revived interest in this process with his 1963 work and originated the term "life review."[19]

In her book, *Composing a Life*, writer and cultural anthropologist Mary Catherine Bateson describes the constructions of the sense of self

| COMPARING PROCESSES | | | | |
|---|---|---|---|---|
| **Process** | **Scope** | **Primary Means of Processing** | **Extent of Exploration** | **Degree of Relationship** |
| 1. Life review | Entire life | Thinking / analytical | Complete | Solitary or social |
| 2. Reminiscence | Momentary | Feeling / experience | Partial | Social |
| 3. Life synthesis | Momentary, situational & overarch-ing | Thinking & feeling, experiential & reflective | Partial & / or complete | Solitary, social & spiritual |

*Figure 11.1*

for each of her five protagonists as being acts of improvisation—acts more like the weaving together of a patchwork quilt than the sculpting of a single work from a massive tree trunk. Just as Woodward's understanding of reminiscence is less systemic and structured, Bateson describes the work of "composing a life" for many people to be more "interrupted and discontinuous" than "purposeful and monolithic."[20]

Spiritual care or counseling through life review is more like the monolithic autobiographical work. Life synthesis work occurs more often in the midst of the interrupted and conflicted workings of life. Life synthesis is the attempt to recognize both the beauty and the bravery, and perhaps even to participate in the stitching together of a life (however interrupted and conflicted). The recognition within life synthesis includes the work of acceptance and reconciliation. Reminiscences are the building blocks for both life review and life synthesis.

In *Composing a Life*, Bateson writes, "This is a book about life as an improvisational art, about the ways we combine familiar and unfamiliar components in response to new situations, following an underlying grammar and an evolving aesthetic."[21] She describes her own life as a "desperate improvisation in which I was constantly trying to make something coherent from conflicting elements to fit rapidly changing settings.... A good meal, like a poem or a life, has a certain balance and diversity, a certain coherence and fit."[22] She adds that oftentimes "the biography of exceptional people is built around the image of a quest, a journey through a timeless landscape toward an end that is specific, even though not fully known."[23] For many people, she insists, however, their story is not like that but instead, because of the constantly changing landscapes of work, home, love, and technology, they are like refugees, displaced by the discontinuities of custom and economics, and "a new, more fluid way is needed to imagine the future."[24] I think a "new, more fluid way" is also often needed to interpret the present and the past. She compares the difference between understanding achievement in life as a purposeful and monolithic endeavor, "like the sculpting of a massive tree trunk" into a single work of art, and a life "crafted from odds and ends, like a patchwork quilt."[25]

Life review is perhaps more like the quest for a single work of art from the massive tree trunk of life's events. The bulk of spiritual care, I believe, is more the improvisational work of patchwork quilting with the patchwork folks we call God's people, all people. My theory papers for ACPE supervisory certification were titled "Knit Together in Love." It is love—ours, others, God's—that allows the stitching together of the pieces of a life, perhaps not into a great single masterpiece but certainly into a patchwork quilt of value. It is that love that holds together and uses all the scraps; that serves as the backing for the quilt.

## *A New Delineation in Spiritual Care: Life Synthesis*

So, perhaps a new delineation in spiritual care, somewhere between the analytical and systematic work of Butler's "life review" and the momentary feeling experience of "reminiscence" as Woodward describes it, is the patchwork composing of life work, sometimes elicited by the awareness of the approaching death of oneself but sometimes brought on by the death of someone close or simply by the meaning-making work of relational spiritual care. "Spiritual care, life synthesis, re-membering, being knit together in love" are all ways I am seeking to name what I see as this "both / and" reality. In each of the three—life review, reminiscence, and life synthesis—disowned parts or experiences of our story, of our self, of our past, present, or future may find acceptance and are reconnected in love and understanding to the whole. Life synthesis is the experience of being about healing, of being reunited to parts of our story, of "re-membering," we might say, ourselves and attending to that process with others, of mending spirits. It is the experience of seeing and hearing, of being seen and heard, where we experience the coming together of broken and scattered pieces, individually or in community. Spiritual care through life synthesis is a meaning-making meeting of souls where the desire for a whole fabric of life, stitched together in love, can be experienced and explored, emotionally, cognitively, and spiritually.

## *Life Review in Specific Contexts: Hearing the Stories*

Arthur W. Frank, physician and author of *The Wounded Storyteller*, writes that we are above all else storytellers, and his writing seems especially helpful to this discussion. He writes that we are people in time and of story, with past, present, and future parts of our stories.

The story we would naturally tell about our lives, our future, would not include the crisis that is at hand. It would move instead from the experiences past, through the present, and into the future as we had planned or anticipated it to be. With a crisis, in the wake of the unchosen events, we become people of a "narrative wreck."[26] We struggle to live the story we have been handed, the one that includes this occurrence. Only enormous energy begins to move us from the chaos narrative to the quest narrative, not the monolithic quest of which Bateson writes, but the quest to create a story that can hold this loss or disorienting event within a larger, more complicated story. Spiritual care, "life synthesis" work, occurs as we live into this story with hope, a transformed hope, but nonetheless very real hope.

Spiritual care is most profoundly significant at these times, in the midst of these times, where the story cannot yet fully be told, cannot yet be held by the one whose story it is most fully. Spiritual care is often about the standing in the chaos with another in faith that God's story has room and will work to redeem even this wreckage. Yet it is not always an analytical, cognitive process in which the person him- or herself comes to some resolution or even to some reconciliation. What of the person who has Alzheimer's and who can by no means do the cognitive work of life review or hardly even, if at all, the work of reminiscence? What of the person in a persistent vegetative state or a coma or so seriously psychotic as to be in a completely other realm? What of the person who has committed suicide and so is no longer present for the review? Life review is not, in these moments, an option at all, and yet spiritual care, life synthesis, life review "of some sort" is a profoundly important spiritual work.

## Birth Center

In a birth center, for example, life synthesis occurs in many ways—certainly as the celebration of new life and all the hope in the birth of a child is experienced, but also at the time of tearing pain at the death of a child. As a man and woman stand at the edge of parenthood, they often look back and review their life together and even the individual lives that brought them to this moment. They project their story into the future of raising this child, already pointing toward that future in all the numerous preparations of space, external and internal, that have preceded this day. The families from which they came, their parents and siblings, their intentions regarding becoming parents, and their hopes for this child and for themselves are all a part of the life review "of some sort" of this moment and place. When a death happens so close to this expected joy, life's fabric is torn, and holding and mending are profoundly important.

## Emergency Department

Life synthesis occurs in an emergency department, where the day began like any other for the couple there. The anticipated future for them included taking their basketball-crazy son to his girlfriend's house to go to the sports center, but it never included his breaking his neck in five places in the ball pit. It never included sitting in the waiting room as he was rushed to surgery to try to find out why he could not move his legs or how serious the damage was. It never included the possibility of their son being paralyzed or of not having their son at all, of his dying. Janus-like, they look back, and at the same time try not to look forward, into a future that for years now has always included this young man, their son, in every frame but that may now be so different. Could a future exist that is so discontinuous from the one they had envisioned? The care and support of a spiritual caregiver, the work of life synthesis comes, sits down with them, as their story demands attention. In the hearing and in the holding of the inexpressible pain of this moment, this period, "life synthesis" is occurring.

## Aging

And certainly as we age, life synthesis occurs. There is sometimes a deeper tenderness toward life and toward the living of it that comes with age. "I thought somehow that I would always be young. Yet now, I look in the mirror and I am no longer young or even 'not old.' I am the older neighbor; I am the grandparent; I am the one for whom others give up their seat or lift the bag, or speak louder." When we hear or think about the reality of our life and of our aging, life synthesis work is occurring.

## End of Life

And as I live on past more and more of my friends' deaths, my own life dances before me. Someday it will be over. It is so hard to imagine and yet so inevitable, so obviously so as siblings and friends and acquaintances cross through the veil. Looking back, remembering, regretting, and rejoicing, wondering why and wondering when and wondering how—the "whys" and "whens" and "hows" of the past and of the future are here with us in the present days. Life synthesis work is occurring.

### Bereavement

And life synthesis occurs as we experience bereavement, as we grieve the death of others. As we ritualize their leaving this world, we look back at life with them, and at least briefly, we look forward, toward a future without them. We reflect on their life, on what stitched it together and where it was frayed; on our relationship, on where it was strong and where it was tattered. And perhaps in this work, we live into the future in ways that ever more tightly stitch us together with the ones we love and in the ways we hope to live.

### Community

And in a community setting, life synthesis can occur as well. I once worked as a chaplain in a small community when a patient no one knew, a circus worker, was dropped off as the train continued south to Florida. The community tried to get to know him as much as was possible when he was so ill. The community reviewed its life and his and all the connections the persons there had, and this man became a member of the community. He needed a place to be cared for until he died, and the local hospital staff rallied around him. He needed a place to be buried, and the local church donated a spot. He needed a family to mourn him, and his new family mourned, looking back at how he might have become so disconnected from persons in his past and looking forward to a time when he would be fully at peace. Life synthesis, beyond even his single individual life, was occurring.

## *What We Learn about God in This Process*

And what is it that we learn about God as we do this life review, life synthesis, reminiscence work? We experience the holiness of life, torn and tattered, sewn together by listening and love. We can never return the cloth to its original form, but we experience the power of the One who can hold everything and the gift of being one of the number in the communion of saints, encircling all that we can only pick up with tenderness but cannot stitch together yet—to hold and see or hear, to smell or taste, to feel in the mysterious moments of life. We experience a God who can stitch forgiveness and eternity into every quilt, can find a balance and sometimes a fierce beauty in the fullness of it all. As spiritual care companions, perhaps we hold a weary hand as the stitching happens, perhaps we help sift through the scraps for a matching or contrasting or fitting pattern to balance the life of the one with whom we commune. And hopefully we experience the warmth of shared life, heightened by the pause or brief stop in this portion of the journey even as the larger journey continues.

## Notes

1. Mary Pellauer in Kathleen Norris, *Dakota: A Spiritual Geography* (Boston: Houghton Mifflin, 2001), 69.
2. Robert N. Butler, "The Life Review: An Interpretation of Reminiscence in the Aged," *Psychiatry* 26 (1963): 67.
3. Gloria J. Swanson, *Down Memory Lane* (Rosemount, MN: Prince of Peace Lutheran Church, 1991, 2008), 1–14.
4. Butler, "The Life Review," 66.
5. Ibid.
6. Ibid., 68–69.
7. Ibid., 65.
8. Ibid., 66.
9. Ibid., 73.
10. Ibid., 68.
11. Ibid., 67.
12. Ibid., 66.
13. Ibid., 67.
14. Kathleen Woodward, "Telling Stories: Aging, Reminiscence, and the Life Review," *Doreen B. Townsend Center Occasional Papers*, no. 9 (1997): 2.
15. Ibid., 3.
16. Walter Brueggeman, in Logan C. Jones, "The Psalms of Lament and the Transformation of Sorrow," *Journal of Pastoral Care and Counseling* 61, nos. 1–2 (2007): 51.
17. Ibid.
18. Ibid., 53.
19. Robert G. LeFavi and Marcia H. Wessels, "Life Review in Pastoral Counseling: Background and Efficacy for Use with the Terminally Ill," *Journal of Pastoral Care and Counseling* 57, no. 3 (2003): 282.
20. Mary Catherine Bateson, *Composing a Life* (New York: Plume, 1990), 4.
21. Ibid., 3.
22. Ibid., 3–4.
23. Ibid., 5–6.

24. Ibid., 8–9.
25. Ibid., 4.
26. Arthur W. Frank, *The Wounded Storyteller: Body, Illness, and Ethics* (Chicago: University of Chicago Press, 1995), 53–55.

## Further Reading

Butler, Robert N. *Why Survive? Being Old in America*. New York: Harper & Row, 1975.

Kenyon, Gary, Phillip Clark, and Brian de Vries, eds. *Narrative Gerontology: Theory, Research, and Practice*. New York: Springer Publishing Company, 2001.

Kimble, Melvin A., Susan H. McFadden, James W. Ellor, and James J. Seeber, eds. *Aging, Spirituality, and Religion*. Minneapolis: Augsburg Fortress Press, 1995.

## About the Contributor

**Rev. Nancy Osborne, MDiv, ACPE Supervisor,** is the director of chaplaincy and clinical pastoral education at the Good Samaritan Society, University Specialty Center in Minneapolis, Minnesota. From 1995 to 2005 she served as the manager of pastoral care at Rex Healthcare in Raleigh, North Carolina. Rev. Osborne is a member of and is certified as a clinical pastoral education supervisor by the Association for Clinical Pastoral Education (ACPE). She is an ordained Alliance of Baptists clergyperson.

# 12

## *End-of-Life Chaplaincy Care*

*Rev. Brian Hughes, MDiv, BCC*

End of life (EOL) can only be accurately declared in hindsight. Much chaplaincy care is provided during this period in a person's life, and the chaplain's work includes the patient, family, and staff. Although ideally each person's own religious faith leader would be present throughout his or her illness and dying, this tends to be the exception. Consequently, the chaplain's role, whether long term, hospice, or acute care, is more important now than ever in addressing the spiritual, emotional, ethical, communication, and even logistical issues that arise as a person faces life's end.

Not long ago, a person might appear relatively healthy and then get ill, suffer shortly, and die. EOL might be a week from the time anyone knew anything was wrong to the time when the person died. Now, with modern medicine and the health care complex accompanying it, this can often be extended indefinitely. A person can now live with a formerly fatal disease or illness for months, years, even decades, and events that used to be fatal are now potentially survivable. It is helpful to visualize these changes to EOL trajectories (see Figure 12.1).

Each of these descriptive trajectories brings unique challenges for providing quality chaplaincy care, as each is a different experience for the patient / resident, the family, and the health care facility staff. Sudden death may result from a traumatic incident such as a motor vehicle accident or an undiagnosed heart condition. This allows little possible interaction with the patient, though providing chaplaincy care for the family is essential, as the death is likely quite unexpected.

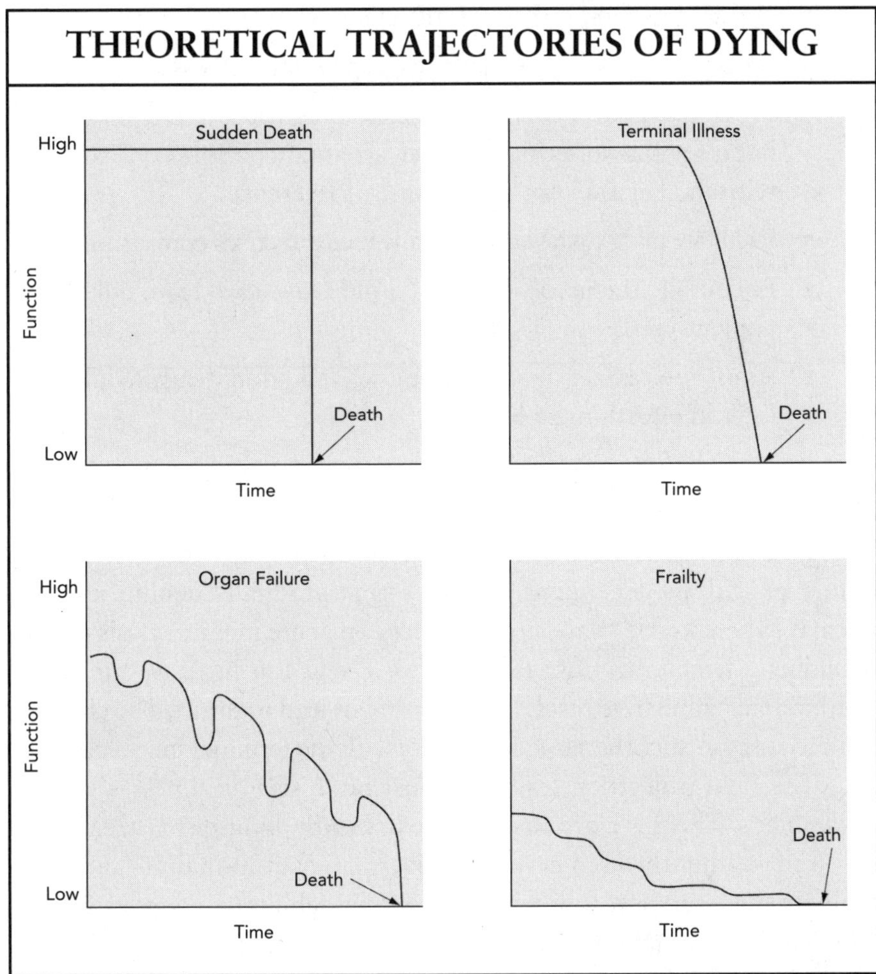


From J. R. Lunney, J. Lynn, and C. Hogan, "Profiles of Older Medicare Decedents," *Journal of the American Geriatrics Society* 50 (2002): 1108–12.

*Figure 12.1*

In the terminal illness trajectory, the time from the original diagnosis to death has been extended significantly due to medical intervention. A person with this trajectory is seen as healthy until a given diagnosis, a terminal cancer, for example. There was "normal" life, then the diagnosis, then treatment, and ultimately death. This can take days, months, or even years. Among the ways a chaplain can help this patient / resident is to:

- Guide this person through the stages of grief.
- Assist the patient / resident with spiritual distress.
- Provide reassurance of God's active presence and redemptive hope for the suffering or other spiritual comfort consistent with the person's spiritual frame of reference.
- Facilitate a life review and / or advance directives conversation.
- Encourage the involvement of a palliative care team when appropriate.
- Assist the person in articulating what a good death would look like for him or her.

The organ failure trajectory is increasingly common and shares many of the chaplaincy care issues with the extended terminal illness patients. This type of patient has a chronic condition—perhaps congestive heart failure or dialysis-dependent diabetes—that gradually debilitates from normal, where every "flare-up" produces an acute medical crisis—often including a hospitalization, followed by a new, less healthy, "normal." The gradual cumulative result of this cycle can lead to death. The chaplain can provide much of the same support as with the terminal illness patients.

The final trajectory, frailty, is most often seen in illnesses such as Alzheimer's. There is a gradual decline in health, long-term care is often involved—either through home caregivers or institutionally—and eventually the person dies, following a lingering debilitative condition. The chaplain has a potential long-term role with patients on this trajectory, with many of the same goals as the previous two entries.

With the vast majority of the last three death trajectories, the basic issue can be that *it is extremely difficult to know where the line is between prolonging life and prolonging the dying process*. Medicine has near-miraculous procedures, equipment, and medications that can work well in patients experiencing an acute medical crisis, but those same interventions can also extend the physiological experience of dying. The difficulty is in knowing when it is helping healing and when it is prolonging dying. In the moment, the best physicians can only speculate and make informed guesses. Chaplains must find ways of being present in this gray zone somewhere between living a normal life and dying an extended death, not only with the patient / resident and the family but also with the staff attending them.

## *A Good Death*

A good death is "one that is free from avoidable suffering for patients, families and caregivers in general accordance with the patients' and families' wishes; and reasonably consistent with clinical, cultural, and ethical standards."[1] It also "comes with reasonable warning, occurs in the company of loved ones, and provides the opportunity for people to reconcile with families and friends and achieve the kind of meaning, peace, or transcendence that is relevant and significant for them and those close to them."[2] In one study, only 62 percent of cancer patients' families stated that their loved ones died a good death.[3] The chaplain's role is integral for patients, families, and staff in navigating complex circumstances surrounding many deaths. Chaplaincy care with dying patients should be focused on making meaning and finding peace and transcendence. Chaplains should facilitate open and honest, respectful communication in this emotionally charged situation.

For patients and families, this is a once-in-a-lifetime state of affairs with intense emotional and spiritual energy due to the crisis. They are asked to navigate extremely complex medical situations with minimal to no medical knowledge or background. But for staff, the dying patient may be a common occurrence. The staff will also be more detached because the patient is not a close family member or friend. This can then lead to conflict. For example, a physician may think a family is not responding in the way she has seen that "worked well" and seek to steer this family toward that more familiar or comfortable trajectory. A chaplain can be an arbitrator or a translator, helping both "sides" understand the position, goals, and needs of the other.

## *Sudden Deaths*

The abrupt nature of unexpected deaths creates different issues than expected deaths. Inevitably, unresolved issues, things unsaid or undone, and last actions or words weigh heavy with surviving family. A chaplain can encourage family, even after the patient's death, to express pain, fears, regrets, love, anger, or remorse directly to the patient.

### Traumas

Traumas are among the common scenarios for sudden deaths. Chaplains are often directly involved as a part of the trauma team and may contact family of the trauma patient. Trauma deaths can be difficult because they are abrupt for the family, and they may first hear about the trauma from a phone call from the hospital—a call where little information can be given. There is often a considerable wait from the time they arrive until they can speak directly with a doctor who can give them a reliable medical update on their loved one, and it is often the chaplain who is the liaison between the family waiting for updates and the medical team.

## Codes

Codes are also a common scenario for an unexpected death. A code occurs when either breathing or the heart stops, creating a crisis where a specific medical team responds, often with chest compressions (CPR) and the possibility of the patient being put on a mechanical ventilator. Chaplains are often a part of the code team and respond to the spiritual and emotional needs of the family. This may include contacting the patient's family—though it is advantageous to partner with a nurse or medical person for the medical update.

Unlike codes on medical TV shows, if a person who is already in the hospital codes, he or she is unlikely to do well. In one study, only 17 percent of hospitalized patients who coded survived long enough to be discharged from the hospital.[4] A chaplain can assign patients who have coded a high priority for visitation and seek to develop a pastoral relationship with the family, which may prove helpful as events unfold following the code.

## Fetal Demises

A fetal demise may not always be sudden, but it is often unexpected. It occurs with younger families who may not have much experience with grief or suffering and may have already painted a nursery or had baby showers in expectation of the joy of a newborn baby. The loss of an unborn child can be wrought with complex grief, as few share much about their experience with others, and consequently the parents know little about what to expect logistically and emotionally and have few avenues of support.

The parents often want common religious rites provided to newborns of their faith tradition, such as baptism—even if the baby has already died. This is worth exploring in training and in preparation, so that a chaplain will know how he or she intends to respond to various religious requests. An important chaplaincy question is "What am I communicating to this grieving family about God if I do *X* (e.g., baptize or anoint a dead baby, religiously name the child, have a formal religious funeral), and what am I communicating if I do not?" For example, while it may not be "good theology" to baptize a dead baby, it can be good pastoral care.

As with most crises, a chaplain can connect the grieving parents with support outside of the hospital—family, friends, and faith community. There is a program called Resolve Through Sharing that I have found to be extremely helpful.[5] Other spiritual care interventions include naming ceremonies, assisting the parents in choosing whether to hold the baby and spend time with him or her, baptism / blessing / anointing, prayers, and formal religious funerals. It is important for chaplains to understand that they will likely see or even touch a premature, sometimes deformed, fetus at many stages of development. This can create issues for the chaplain, and the chaplain should be prepared for the intensity of the experience.

Finally, as has been emphasized throughout this book, it is extremely important that chaplains, prior to a fetal demise, get to know the social workers and similar staff that they will be professionally teaming with in these situations.

## Expected Deaths

Many expected deaths follow a chronic gradual decline in health. This can be the case with diseases such as Alzheimer's, cancer, diabetes, congestive heart failure, and many others. For persons with chronic conditions, a longer-term relationship with a chaplain can develop and be incredibly helpful.

Research[6] has shown that family concerns regarding care at EOL for those with chronic conditions include the following:

- Inadequate help for patient's emotional stress
- Not enough emotional support for family
- Not enough contact with physicians
- Poor communication with the physicians
- Patient not always treated with respect
- Inadequate family information about what to expect when the patient was dying

The vast majority of these issues can be addressed through chaplaincy care.

One of the difficulties in an EOL situation for a person with a chronic condition is that he or she likely survived numerous "scares" and previous hospitalizations, and the EOL hospitalization can look indistinguishable from previous ones. The difficult question becomes: how is the patient, family, and staff to know that "this is the time"?

## *Advance Directives*

The more frequently a person is admitted to the hospital, the higher the potential need for a structured conversation around advance directives, which the chaplain can help facilitate.

Advance directives are treatment preferences and the designation of a surrogate decision maker in the event that a person should become unable to make medical decisions on his or her own behalf. Advance directives generally fall into three categories: living will, health care proxy, and durable power of attorney. They also include "Do not resuscitate" (DNR) medical orders.

- **Living will:** A document that specifies which medical treatments are desired. It can be specific or general. A common statement in a living will might be as follows: "If I suffer an incurable, irreversible illness, disease, or condition and my attending physician determines that my condition is terminal, I direct that life-sustaining measures that would serve only to prolong my dying be withheld or discontinued." More specific living wills may include information regarding an individual's desire for services such as pain relief, antibiotics, hydration, artificial nutrition, and ventilators or CPR.
- **Health care proxy:** A legal document in which individuals designate someone to make health care decisions on their behalf if they are rendered incapable of making their wishes known. The health care proxy has the same rights to request or refuse treatment that the individual would have if capable of communicating decisions, but only acts in that position when the patient is incapacitated. This should not be confused with a durable power of attorney.

- **Durable power of attorney:** A legal document allowing a person to sign checks, make bank transactions, and so on.[7]
- **DNR—do not resuscitate order:** A physician order given a patient, often in response to a plan of care conversation with the patient and / or family, that would preclude a code from being called when the patient's breathing or heart stops.

A chaplain is often involved in the advance directives discussions with patients / residents and families, depending on a health care facility's protocols and procedures. The chaplain can serve as a bridge between the non-medically informed family in the midst of an emotional crisis and the "we-see-this-all-the-time" technology-dependent medical staff by being involved in the conversation with patients and families regarding advance directives. A chaplain must be careful to "stay in one's own lane" and not to over function, as some of the medical specifics of the discussion are beyond the scope of the chaplain's training and expertise. However, a chaplain can spend the requisite time with a patient / resident or family in order to determine what their wishes may be if things do not go as hoped.[8]

## *Patient / Family–Physician Plan of Care Conferences*

Chaplains are often involved in patient / family–physician plan of care conferences, where diagnosis, prognosis, treatment options, and potential decisions are discussed. It is only when the patient and family are aware of the specific prognosis that they can accurately and most realistically articulate their EOL care preferences.

Unfortunately, many medical personnel speak with one another and the patient / family in terms of diagnoses, not prognosis. For example, when a physician tells the nurse that the patient has metastatic pancreatic cancer, both understand the implicit grim prognosis. However, for patients and families, this mutually understood medical background is not present. One of the difficulties often seen in many plan of care conferences is when a physician explains a diagnosis well and skims over or even omits the prognosis, which ultimately for the patient and family is the "so what" of the diagnosis. I have found coaching the families to ask about prognosis directly or asking about it myself in the midst of a plan of care conference to be helpful in clarifying the implications of a specific diagnosis.

Research demonstrates that communication skills could be improved and that there is a need for communication training among physicians and nurses.[9] Prognoses are seldom disclosed unless the patient or family asks the physician directly, and this potentially impedes EOL planning. A physician seeking to communicate a poor prognosis who lacks competence or confidence (many are nervous about such conversations) may appear callous or overly blunt, deliver a monologue rather than a dialogue, or even avoid the conversation altogether.

Professionally trained chaplains often have considerably more training in communication than most medical staff. Professional chaplaincy training also often makes board certified chaplains (BCCs) more attuned to the emotional / spiritual distress and its impact on the patient's / family's ability to navigate the complex medical issues. Thus, I would encourage a chaplain to speak up, keeping in mind that it is important to "stay in one's own lane" and not to over function. The more a chaplain can "pre-game" the plan of care conference with the medical team involved, and the better the chaplain knows the team and has established rapport, the more effective the chaplain can be in these conferences.

## *Pediatrics*

Research demonstrates that the fifty thousand children who die in America each year do not consistently receive compassionate physical, emotional, and spiritual care.[10] A dying child can challenge the spiritual fortitude of the most experienced chaplain. The unfairness of a child nearing the end of life is tragic, and chaplains should be especially attuned to compassion fatigue for themselves and the medical staff working alongside of them. A child life specialist—whose training and position can bring a depth of knowledge and experience in developmental, psychological, and child-centric issues—is a strong ally. A chaplain should also be familiar with local resources, support groups, and other social, emotional, and spiritual support that grieving parents can access both during and following hospitalization. (Chapter 20 focuses solely on pediatric issues. You are encouraged to become familiar with this chapter.)

## *Death in the ICU*

In the United States, approximately 20 percent of all deaths occur in the intensive care unit (ICU), the majority following withdrawal of life-prolonging treatments.[11] This runs contrary to most people's preference of the "good death" of dying with family present, not in pain, and not connected to a lot of machines.

Chaplains' work, primarily with families in the ICU, is one of the most time intensive and emotionally involving circumstances in an acute care setting. The chaplain's role is much more effective if the chaplain has been involved before the decision has been made to withdraw treatment, having been able to establish a relationship with the patient and family. Chaplains in the ICU often provide some religious ritual, prayer, scripture, and ongoing empathic presence for families. As discussed previously, chaplains can also be integral in helping initiate, facilitate, and participate in patient / family–physician plan of care conferences.

## *Quality of Life Decisions*

Quality of life is an important concept in EOL care and ethics. Quality of life is a patient's ability to enjoy life and experience well-being. For many, spirituality is integral to quality of life. As the end of life approaches, different treatments or interventions may extend a person's life chronologically, but lower the quality of life. In the discussions regarding these treatments, it is important to allow the patient to define what would be an "acceptable outcome" of a treatment or an intervention and where that line is between acceptable and unacceptable.

Ethically, a chaplain's role is to encourage patients or families to articulate their wishes and to help the team honor those without creating competing ethical issues of doing harm. Regardless of how the chaplain feels about their decision, the chaplain should explicitly express non-abandonment of the patient and family. My own experience in numerous ethical consults is that there is often a miscommunication and / or lack of trust at the core of the dispute, and a chaplain's role can be integral in helping facilitate better communication without an agenda.

There does come a point in some EOL cases where "futility" is reached. This can be defined as "an intervention that is unlikely to be of any benefit to a patient, and will not achieve the patient's intended goals."[12] This echoes the fine line between prolonging a person's life and living and prolonging their death and dying. The difficulty is in knowing when this line is reached.

As emphasized earlier, professional chaplains receive extensive training to understand our emotions in relationship to those with whom we work. Most physicians do not receive this sort of training. As a result, when some physicians near this line when medical action changes from prolonging life to prolonging the dying process, they do not explicitly communicate it to the patient and family and internally build up an emotional dissonance with the medical care they provide. The longer this goes on, the more likely the physician will, from the patient's and family's perspective, abruptly switch from going along with the provision of aggressive care to strongly advocating that it is past time to discontinue such efforts. The physician's experience of it was a slow boil crescendoing into a position of moral distress, and then the aggressive care became too much. But from the patient's or family's perspective, it appears that the physician agreed with them, even shared their optimism regarding treatment, and then abruptly did a one-eighty and shifted from being an ally to being an adversary. The chaplain would do well to be in communication with both the physician and the patient and family. When it becomes apparent that the patient or family has expectations that differ greatly from the physician's, the chaplain is in a position to encourage more explicit communication.

## *Organ Donation*

The family of each person near death is most often required by law to be asked about organ donation. This "ask" is usually coordinated and executed by a geographic region's organ procurement organization (OPO). A chaplain can be helpful in clarifying for a family the different religious traditions' perspectives on organ donation, as many are unaware of their own tradition's views on organ donation.[13] If at all possible, I personally feel the chaplain for a patient or family should not be the person approaching that family regarding organ donation, as this can confuse the chaplain's role as spiritual caregiver. Each hospital has its own policies and procedures, and it would be worthwhile for chaplains to be familiar with these in their own facility.

## *Palliative Care and Hospice*

Palliative care is defined as follows:

> Palliative care is an approach that improves the quality of life of patients and their families facing the problem associated with life-threatening illness, through the prevention and relief of suffering by means of early identification and impeccable assessment and treatment of pain and other problems, physical, psychosocial and spiritual. Palliative care:
>
> - provides relief from pain and other distressing symptoms;
> - affirms life and regards dying as a normal process;
> - intends neither to hasten nor postpone death;
> - integrates the psychological and spiritual aspects of patient care;
> - offers a support system to help patients live as actively as possible until death;
> - offers a support system to help the family cope during the patient's illness and in their own bereavement;
> - uses a team approach to address the needs of patients and their families, including bereavement counseling, if indicated;
> - will enhance quality of life, and may also positively influence the course of illness;
> - is applicable early in the course of illness, in conjunction with other therapies that are intended to prolong life, such as chemotherapy or radiation therapy, and includes those investigations needed to better understand and manage distressing clinical complications.[14]

Hospice is defined as follows:

> Hospice focuses on caring, not curing and, in most cases, care is provided in the patient's home. Hospice care also is provided in free-standing hospice centers, hospitals, and nursing homes and other long-term care facilities. Hospice services are available to patients of any age, religion, race, or illness. Hospice care is covered under Medicare, Medicaid, most private insurance plans, HMOs, and other managed care organizations.[15]

Hospice is also focused on the patient's family, providing grief and bereavement services for up to a year or more following a patient's eventual death.

Chaplains are often integrally involved in both hospice and palliative care teams. Palliative care can be used in conjunction and simultaneously with curative care for a person with a chronic and debilitating disease. It is like two ropes hanging from the ceiling—one is curative, aggressive care; the other is hospice, which forgoes curative care in favor of a focus on maximizing a patient's quality of life. Palliative care can be seen as having one hand on each rope. Palliative care is also a good transition ultimately from curative to hospice care. Palliative care, in an inpatient setting especially, is often finally utilized far too late in the patient's journey and would benefit everyone by moving farther upstream in a patient's course of illness. Recent studies also show that, counterintuitively, some patients who received palliative care earlier in the course of their journey actually outlive their counterparts who seek more aggressive curative treatments.[16]

## *Bereavement and Grief*

Grief is the normal response to a loss. In defining the five stages of grief in 1969, Elisabeth Kübler-Ross had as her focus dying cancer patients. The stages that many are familiar with—denial, anger, bargaining, depression, and acceptance—are intended to describe the experiences of those facing their own impending death but have since been expanded to include loss such as bereavement. This is a descriptive rather than prescriptive model. These are stages through which people can cycle back and forth. Just because a person has been angry and moved on to bargaining does not mean he or she will not be angry again at some point in the future, and successful healing does not require one to experience all or even any of these stages.

Bereavement is the experience of losing a loved one to death. For many family members of patients near or at EOL, anticipatory grief allows family members to gradually come to terms with the reality of pending loss and potentially seek some closure in the relationship with their loved one. Normal or common grief is experienced as the gradual acceptance of the loss, and being able to maintain typical daily living (though acute struggles with extreme emotion may still occur), and is time limited—beginning at the time of loss and lasting usually for roughly one year. "Complicated grief" occurs when a person does not exhibit the characteristics of common grief. This is described in more depth in chapter 25.

One of the best things a chaplain can do in the acute experience of grief and bereavement is to help normalize it, affirming that feeling this way is okay and will not be permanent. It helps the person experiencing these new and overwhelming emotions to name or articulate the feelings, and a chaplain can listen to any religious meaning making or spiritualizing of the experience. For some, God will provide a resource of comfort or solidarity in suffering. For others, the suffering may be interpreted as punishment for past sins, as rejection or judgment by God, or as a spiritual / supernatural struggle with evil, the devil, or darkness. It is important in these circumstances to not challenge someone's theological assumptions, which can risk distancing the chaplain from a position of positive influence. However, a chaplain can listen for so-called "negative" theological interpretations and seek to accompany the person in the midst of the suffering and offer alternative interpretations that are consistent with the person's religious or spiritual perspective, but that might also reframe it more positively.

## Notes

1. M. J. Field and C. K. Cassel, eds., *Approaching Death: Improving Care at the End of Life: A Consensus Report of the Committee on Care at the End of Life, Institute of Medicine* (Washington, DC: National Academies Press, 1997), 24.
2. Ibid., 24.
3. Commonwealth Fund, *Family Perceptions of Quality of Care at End of Life: A Performance Snapshot*, www.commonwealthfund.org/Content/Performance-Snapshots/Experiences-with-Care/Family-Perceptions-of-Quality-of-Care-at-End-of-Life.aspx.
4. M. A. Peberdy et al., "Cardiopulmonary Resuscitation of Adults in the Hospital: A Report of 14,720 Cardiac Arrests from the National Registry of Cardiopulmonary Resuscitation," *Resuscitation* 58 (2003): 297–308.
5. More can be found at www.bereavementservices.org.
6. Commonwealth Fund, *Family Perceptions of Quality of Care at End of Life.*
7. www.medterms.com/script/main/art.asp?articlekey=2158.
8. A great resource for the discussion is called Five Wishes, www.agingwithdignity.org/five-wishes.php.
9. K. I. Pollak et al., "Oncologist Communication about Emotion During Visits with Patients with Advanced Cancer," *Journal of Clinical Oncology* 25, no. 36 (2007): 5748–52.
10. *When Children Die: Improving Palliative and End-of-Life Care for Children and Their Families: A Consensus Report of the Committee on Palliative and End-of-Life Care for Children and Their Families, Institute of Medicine* (Washington, DC: National Academies Press, 2003).

11. D. C. Angus et al., "Use of Intensive Care at the End-of-Life in the United States: An Epidemiologic Study," *Critical Care Medicine* 32 (2004): 638–43; R. J. Curtis et al., "Use of the Medical Futility Rationale in Do-Not-Attempt Resuscitation Orders," *Journal of the American Medical Association* 273 (1995): 124–128; T. J. Prendergast and J. M. Luce, "Increasing Incidence of Withholding and Withdrawal of Life-Support from the Critically Ill," *American Journal of Respiratory and Critical Care Medicine* 155 (1997): 15–20.
12. L. J. Schneiderman, N. S. Jecker, and A. R. Jonsen, "Medical Futility: Its Meaning and Ethical Implications," *Annals of Internal Medicine* 112 (1990): 949–54.
13. The vast majority of religious traditions actively encourage organ donation. For a representative list, see www.organdonor.gov/aboutRelViews.asp.
14. "WHO Definition of Palliative Care," World Health Organization, accessed October 5, 2011, www.who.int/cancer/palliative/definition/en.
15. www.nhpco.org/i4a/pages/index.cfm?pageid=4648&openpage=4648.
16. J. S. Temel et al., "Early Palliative Care for Patients with Metastatic Non–Small-Cell Lung Cancer," *New England Journal of Medicine* 363, no. 8 (2010): 733–42.

## Further Reading

Chen, Pauline W. *Final Exam: A Surgeon's Reflections on Mortality*. New York: Vintage, 2008.

Committee on Care at the End of Life, Institute of Medicine. *Approaching Death: Improving Care at the End of Life*. Washington, DC: National Academies Press, 1997.

Didion, Joan. *The Year of Magical Thinking*. New York: Vintage, 2007.

Karnes, Barbara. *Gone from My Sight: The Dying Experience*. Vancouver, WA: Barbara Karnes Books, 2008.

Kübler-Ross, Elisabeth. *On Death & Dying*. New York: Scribner, 1997.

Lester, Andrew D. *Pastoral Care with Children in Crisis*. Louisville, KY: Westminster John Knox Press, 1985.

Matlins, Stuart M., ed. *The Perfect Stranger's Guide to Funerals and Grieving Practices: A Guide to Etiquette in Other People's Religious Ceremonies*. Woodstock, VT: SkyLight Paths Publishing, 2000.

Nuland, Sherwin B. *How We Die: Reflections on Life's Final Chapter*. New York: Vintage, 1995.

## Resources

Center to Advance Palliative Care: www.getpalliativecare.org

End of Life and Palliative Care Resource Center Fast Facts and Concepts: www.eperc.mcw.edu/EPERC/FastFactsandConcepts

National Cancer Institute website on grief, bereavement, and mourning: www.cancer.gov/cancertopics/pdq/supportivecare/bereavement/healthprofessional/allpages

National Hospice & Palliative Care Organization: www.nhpco.org

Pediatric Chaplains' Network: www.pediatricchaplains.org

## About the Contributor

**Rev. Brian Hughes, MDiv, BCC,** is a chaplain certified through the Association of Professional Chaplains, where he serves as Education Committee chair. He attended Princeton Theological Seminary and completed nine units of clinical pastoral education in New York City; Temple, Texas; and Phoenix, Arizona. He has served as a hospital staff chaplain in Phoenix, Arizona; Irving, Texas; and Philadelphia, Pennsylvania. He recently authored *Handbook of Evidence-Based Best Practice for Spiritual Care Provision for those with Post-Traumatic Stress Disorder (PTSD) and Traumatic Brain Injury (TBI)* for the U.S. Navy Bureau of Medicine and Surgery (BUMED).

# 13

## *Ethics and the Care of the Sick*

### An Overview for Professional Chaplains and Other Spiritual / Pastoral Care Providers

*Dr. Nancy Berlinger, PhD, MDiv*

### *Why Chaplains Must Be Present to Ethical Dilemmas*

What is the difference between a dilemma and a problem? The short answer: problems can be solved, dilemmas cannot. What is an ethical dilemma, then? Another short answer: an ethical dilemma involves a set of moral choices in which no option is clearly right or clearly wrong. So, if ethical dilemmas arising in the care of the sick cannot be solved, and if they present themselves in such murky (and time-consuming) ways, can professional chaplains and other spiritual care providers just leave these dilemmas where they find them and go about doing whatever good they can?

No, they cannot. Complacency about ethical dilemmas in health care is hazardous to professionals and patients alike. Ethical dilemmas present choices about ways to respond to suffering. They may present themselves with urgency: something must be done, *now*, to prevent greater suffering or other avoidable burdens. For chaplains, complacency with respect to ethical dilemmas undermines their professional ethos of striving to be "present" in the face of suffering and with those who suffer. Being present to suffering involves being alive to moral complexity in health care and being prepared to address ethical dilemmas as they arise, whether at the bedside or as organizational challenges.

This chapter offers an overview of ethical issues arising in the care of the sick, with particular attention to the hospital setting and with some attention to other health care settings. It is written for professional chaplains, mindful of the special ethical responsibilities that chaplains bear as members of patient care teams and, often, as members of clinical ethics consultation teams, ethics committees, or institutional review boards (IRBs). It should also be helpful to other spiritual care providers and to local clergy who are involved in the care of the sick and need to be aware of the ethical dimensions of this work.

Cases can be useful ways to explore ethical dilemmas. At the outset of this discussion, it can be helpful to bring an ethical dilemma to mind by reflecting on one's own professional experience and recalling a situation marked by uncertainty and distress: someone was suffering, and someone else did not know what to do in response to suffering. Uncertainty and distress are characteristic of ethical dilemmas in the care of the sick. Any chaplain can recall situations like these, which can be haunting experiences for health care professionals and for other caregivers.

## *Three Ways of Thinking about Ethics*

The word "ethics" can be used in various ways, whether in everyday speech or in different specialized contexts. Three ways (among others) in which "ethics" can be invoked in the health care setting are as the search for the good, as rules to live by, and as the critical analysis of morality.

### Ethics as the Search for the Good

The questions of the ancient Greek philosophers—How ought we to live? What way of life best supports human flourishing? How can we avoid harm in the pursuit of the good? What are our reasons for pursuing one way of life over another?—are questions that are still alive today. They can assist our efforts to resolve ethical dilemmas, to teach and model ethical behavior, and to craft ethically sound policy that can support good practice. Being alive to these living questions keeps our thinking fresh and reminds us that these questions are likely to matter to patients, too. Taking patients seriously as persons means being attentive to the values that have shaped their lives and aiming to support their values and preferences concerning medical treatment, while recognizing that wishes are not the same as choices. What a patient wants—or what a patient's surrogate thinks a patient would have wanted—may not be attainable through the actual choices available to this patient. However, sometimes an opportunity to support the patient's values and preferences has been overlooked. A chaplain who is skilled at listening is not an empty vessel or solely a witness to suffering. Rather, a chaplain should recognize that he or she has the potential to be a channel between a person's vision of the good, as expressed, in part, through values and preferences relevant to what is going on in this person's life right now, and the health care professionals and systems that can help support this vision under present circumstances. Human flourishing can continue even amid suffering, even when a person is near death.

## Ethics as Rules to Live By

Being alive to ethics as the continuing search for the good also helps avoid reducing ethics to the application of rules and to rules compliance. However, various types of "rules"—including policies, processes, laws, regulations, forms, and so on—are important in ethics. When they represent consensus, rules can guide good practice and avoid hasty, ad hoc measures. Thus, ethics in health care settings typically includes various forms of consensus guidance concerning issues such as patients' rights and how to honor them; the protection of patients enrolled in research trials; how to discuss and document patients' wishes and preferences concerning medical treatment; or how to conduct a clinical ethics consultation or resolve a conflict. When such rules are (or seem) arbitrary, unfair, or unduly burdensome to one group, they are unlikely to be viewed as trustworthy guides to good practice; while the reason for a rule may have been a good one, that reason is no longer apparent.

Health care systems are complex systems in that they are always changing. The doing of ethics in a complex system requires ongoing attention to the usefulness of guidance intended to support ethical practice: Is this policy outdated, or does it still do its job of helping clinicians honor patients' rights and understand ethically challenging situations? How will clinical practice change in response to a new law or public policy development? Do we need to develop a new policy to respond to a frequently occurring dilemma, or would better clinician education be a more effective response?

Making it a rule to maintain a vibrant forum to address ethics issues in an institution is its own challenge. In 1992, the Joint Commission mandated that hospitals have some means of addressing ethical issues in patient care. (The federally regulated IRB system for institutions that conduct research involving human subjects dates from the early 1980s.)

Nearly all American hospitals satisfy this accreditation requirement through an ethics committee that includes a consultation service. However, in too many institutions, the ethics committee lacks training and clear authority, consults on or reviews only a handful of cases each year, and meets too infrequently to sustain a practice of substantive and productive discussion. Chaplains, who frequently serve on ethics committees and may be assigned the difficult task of chairing an unproductive committee, should seek to contribute to this aspect of ethics by improving their own knowledge of the good-seeking goals of ethics as a clinical service, finding opportunities to participate in peer education networks of clinicians involved in ethics consultation, and sharing research and consensus concerning good practice with colleagues in their own institutions. These tasks should not be left to chaplains alone, but on occasion it will be up to the chaplain to promote change.

As a health care profession, chaplaincy has produced its own set of ethics rules. *The Common Code of Ethics for Chaplains, Pastoral Counselors, Pastoral Educators and Students* was adopted in 2004 by the six organizations in the United States and Canada with authority to certify professionals and training programs. This code of ethics sets out principles that should inform relationships in professional practice, including relationships with clients, between supervisors and students, with faith communities, with other professionals and in the community, with colleagues in providing spiritual care, in advertising, and in research.

Members of any profession should be familiar with their profession's standards of conduct as articulated in a code of ethics, with the understanding that mere compliance with standards is insufficient as a guide to ethical practice. For supervisors and other mentors responsible for guiding the professional development of chaplains, the *Common Code* offers one way to encourage the practice of ethical reflection, including critical reflection on this code itself. For example, the *Common Code*'s reliance on the word "client" seems problematic. Clinicians in acute care settings usually do not view patients as "clients." Nor do clinicians who work in nursing homes, home care, or hospice. If this standard is intended to suggest a chaplain and a client in a one-to-one therapeutic relationship, it may be useful with respect to professional conduct but inadequate with respect to situations in which a chaplain in an institution is simultaneously providing care to a patient, to members of that patient's family, and to colleagues on a team and is also functioning and being supervised as a member of that team.

As this example demonstrates, the limited scope of a professional code means that citing a code is not sufficient as ethics guidance. Because codes of conduct for community clergy may not address the health care context and the special duties of health care professionals and organizations to patients, chaplaincy organizations and health care institutions that involve community clergy should aim to offer some ethics education for community clergy involved in patient care.

Dilemmas can arise in ways not anticipated by a code of ethics. Some indispensable features of ethically sound practice are difficult to codify or do not apply to one profession in isolation. In health care, clarifying the medical facts relevant to a situation at hand is an example of indispensable information for any participant in a clinical ethics consultation, case discussion, or policy review. Dilemmas involve competing interests, and in health care, the best interests of patients often compete with powerful organizational and professional interests. Interpersonal conflict and the distress arising from experiencing or witnessing suffering can complicate efforts to resolve ethical dilemmas in health care. For these reasons, ethics education for chaplains cannot be limited to the context of chaplaincy. Indeed, it is possible that there is no such thing as "chaplaincy ethics," or "nursing ethics," or other professional ethics in isolation from other professions and disciplines and from the particular context of a unit, an institution, or a patient population. Chaplains must know their own rules, and they must also have some idea of the rules that others live by and what their colleagues may think of those rules.

## Ethics as the Critical Analysis of Morality

Looking critically at rules brings us to another way of looking at ethics, as the difference between "is" and "ought." Looking uncritically at morality—for example, the moral norms of a department, a hospital, or a nation—means settling for "That's the way things are around here, they'll never change," and abandoning all hope (and all responsibility) for social change. Looking critically at morality means asking, "Why are things like this, and what would need to change to make things better?" A philosophical commitment to social justice means looking critically at different levels of society, including systems of care for the sick, and asking whether these social systems are placing the best interests of the sick first. Those who benefit from these systems as employees or consultants have a special responsibility to think critically about them; health care is never just a business, a means to a paycheck, or a way to live out one's own vocation or values. It is difficult, even impossible, for patients to improve health care while they are seriously ill. They may see the flaws in the system, they may suffer as the result of these flaws, but they usually cannot correct these flaws on the spot and they lack the authority to repair broken systems even if they wish they could do so.

Chaplains who view themselves as having a moral obligation to be truth tellers or justice seekers should ask, as part of their own critical reflection, *how* they are challenging systems that they observe to be harmful or unfair. For example, chaplains who work in nursing homes or in intensive care units are likely to observe long-standing practices of transferring frail elderly nursing home residents to the hospital when they are near the end of life. They may wonder why this practice exists and whose interests it serves. Is this really what this debilitated patient wants? Has anyone tried to find out what this patient wants or what the patient's surrogate thinks an incapacitated patient would have wanted? What are the economic factors that may drive "revolving-door" practices? Is there a different way to care for these patients? Would some of these patients prefer to be cared for in a different way? And what can the chaplain, in the nursing home or the intensive care unit (ICU), do from his or her position in a health care system to encourage colleagues, including leadership, to look critically at this situation and the ethical questions it raises?

This is not easy to do—the chaplain may not have much authority within the system. However, the chaplain has more power than the patient he or she is observing, and the chaplain has an obligation not only to be present to suffering but also to question conditions that appear to promote or add to suffering.

Doing ethics in complex and inherently imperfect health care systems usually requires working at all three of these levels: searching for the good, making good rules and questioning problematic ones, and thinking critically about the morality of health care systems and acting to improve them. Time is a limited resource in health care. The opportunity to act to prevent or relieve a patient's suffering may not permit professionals to ascertain, definitively, what a good life consists of. The resolution of an ethical dilemma usually cannot wait for the drafting of policies and processes or for optimal social conditions. The resolution of an ethical dilemma in real time often involves the identification of the "least worst" option among available options, the one that does the least harm. Chaplains and their colleagues should not lose sight of opportunities to do better than the least worst, even if this cannot be done at the bedside but must be accomplished through consistent attention to education, to policy development—and even to the art of conducting a productive ethics consultation or ethics committee meeting—so as to spend available time well.

## *Doing Ethics in the Context of Science and Contemporary Society*

Over the past fifty years, the consideration of ethical dilemmas raised by new and emerging medical treatments and technologies and by research into how health-related benefits and burdens are allocated within and across societies has become known as bioethics or biomedical ethics. While bioethics centers are often located in medical schools or academic medical centers, bioethics was initially conceived of neither as its own academic discipline nor as a profession, but as a mode of interdisciplinary inquiry. Questions that did not belong solely to the practice of medicine, to the sciences, to law, to philosophy, or to theology became the subject of deliberation and debate: What is the nature of suffering? What are the goals of medicine? What values and policy should guide the fair allocation of tragically scarce resources such as transplantable organs? How can death be determined if technology can sustain a body's vital functions? What does it mean to be a person? Is there a right to health care? Is there a right to health? What does it mean to make an informed choice about medical treatment or participation in research? Are we our genes? Are we our brains? The list of questions at the intersection of ethics, science, and society is endless. Some of these questions reflect ancient concerns—questions of medical ethics arose well before the advent of contemporary technological medicine—

while others take shape as a technology is introduced or is used in more than one way.

The working vocabulary of bioethics has long been informed by Western philosophy. Ethics education for chaplains and other clinicians should include some basic definitions of influential moral theories, with the reminder that bioethics, as a form of applied ethics, rarely functions along hard philosophical lines. It is useful to know what a "utilitarian" argument is and how it differs from a "deontological" argument. (Respectively, these refer to an argument in favor of an option whose consequences include the most good for the greatest number, and an argument that gives priority to moral obligations, such as truth telling.) It is usually less useful to try to make an ethical dilemma fit the requirements of a particular theory. Resolving the case at hand tends to involve looking at it from different perspectives, including different moral theories and the interests of different actual and imagined stakeholders.

Another important reminder concerning the doing of ethics in health care concerns the limits of what is sometimes termed the "principlist" approach. This term refers to the work of Thomas Beauchamp and James Childress, whose *Principles of Biomedical Ethics*, first published in 1971, has become immensely influential in the teaching of bioethics. Beauchamp and Childress proposed and have continued to refine an approach to bioethics that is grounded in four ethical principles. The principle of autonomy or self-determination refers to respect for patients as persons capable of "self-rule" and to practices that support the ability of patients to make informed choices. The principle of nonmaleficence refers to the duty to avoid harm to patients, while the principle of beneficence refers to the duty to do good and to act in patients' best interests. The principle of justice refers to considerations ranging from nondiscrimination in the treatment of patients, to the equitable allocation of resources and the use of fair processes, to respect for law.

Principles are tools. We do not simply "have" principles; we use them to help us sort out what to value and how to act. Using them to help us think through the ethics of a situation requires us also to think about how this approach shapes our perspective. In clinical settings, Beauchamp and Childress's principle-based approach can be a starting place for discussion, with the understanding that there can be more than one reasonable way to look at an ethical dilemma and that reducing this approach to a formula (or to four bullet points on a slide) is unlikely to be sufficient as a guide to using these tools or to being alive to moral complexity in the care of the sick.

Even when only one patient is involved, getting a grasp on the ethical issues at stake in a particular case can be difficult. A patient with a psychiatric condition affecting thought may have the capacity to make some decisions under some conditions. Can this patient make an informed choice concerning medical treatment for a life-threatening condition if this patient is incapable of making an informed choice concerning psychiatric treatment? Or is this patient's underlying psychiatric diagnosis impairing the patient's capacity to make the medical decision? If so, is it in the patient's best interests to receive medical treatment over objection? And how would this work, as a practical matter? Or, consider a case in which a patient wishes to receive a medical treatment that is likely to create economic or other burdens for family caregivers: to what extent do their interests matter? Certain dilemmas, such as how to care for patients under conditions of extreme resource scarcity and rapidly changing conditions, as would occur during a public health emergency, are likely to require special tools for ethical deliberation under abnormal rather than normal clinical conditions.

Chaplains should also keep in mind that there are dimensions of their own practice that can aid in interdisciplinary moral reasoning concerning the ethics of a clinical or an organizational situation. For example, chaplains and other clergy tend to value hospitality—the reception of guests and of strangers—as part of good spiritual care and a practice that is historically associated with the care of the sick: "hospitality," "hospital," and "hospice" share Latin roots. Hospitality can be expressed in ways that are not ethically problematic, such as by offering family caregivers a place to rest or to have private discussions. It can also be a useful way of looking at an ethical challenge within an organization. What does a hospital owe the "stranger" at its gate, whether this stranger is a person who lacks health insurance, an undocumented community resident, a newly arrived group whose interests are competing with those of a long-established group, or a previously uninvolved family member who is now seeking to become involved in a patient's care? And how can a chaplain, as a participant in clinical ethics consultation or in organizational policy development, work from hospitality as moral practice to develop a reasonable argument for a moral theory of hospitality that acknowledges the gray areas of dilemmas and constraints?

## *Toward Ethically Competent Spiritual Care: Integrating Ethics into Chaplaincy Education and Practice*

Ethics education should be part of professional formation and clinician education. Professionals responsible for the care of the sick should be prepared for the moral, psychological, and social issues they will encounter in this work and should be equipped to address ethical dilemmas and interpersonal conflicts as they arise amid the organizational complexity of a particular health care setting: the emergency department, the ICU, the neonatal ICU, the psychiatric unit, the room on the medical floor where a "difficult conversation" is about to take place.

Clinical pastoral education (CPE) supervisors, in their capacity as clinician educators, should take responsibility for integrating bioethics into the CPE curriculum, as the ethical dilemmas chaplains will confront will rarely be limited to the practice of chaplaincy in isolation from other professions. To this end, CPE supervisors should have a vision for bioethics education in the context of CPE residency programs and the needs of residents. What are the fundamentals that any CPE resident should learn and incorporate into practice, even if this resident does not plan to become a professional chaplain? What skills and areas of knowledge must a resident master in preparation for a career in chaplaincy? What opportunities for cross-training in ethics exist or can be created within an institution, at the residency level and also for staff chaplains? (For example, are residents and staff encouraged to attend ethics grand rounds offered by medical departments and by interdisciplinary services?) How valued is bioethics education at an institution, and how can CPE supervisors participate in strengthening this area of the institution? How are CPE supervisors improving their own knowledge and skills concerning bioethics education for clinicians and concerning bioethics as a clinical service in which they and their residents are likely to participate?

Chaplaincy directors—and, indeed, all professional chaplains and other spiritual care providers—should recognize continuing education in bioethics as integral to clinical excellence. Whether or not they also function as CPE supervisors, chaplaincy directors should seek out opportunities to learn from other professions and to share knowledge and skills with other professions, with the common goal of supporting ethically sound practice.

## *Getting Better at Doing Good: What Chaplains Should Master*

Chaplains, other spiritual care providers, and those responsible for their education have a special obligation to master the areas of clinical and organizational ethics in which the involvement of a chaplain is foreseeable or desired by patients and loved ones or in which a chaplain's skills may be helpful in promoting a patient's best interests. With respect to the care of seriously ill patients, and often chronically ill patients, these areas include the following:

### Palliative Care

Palliative care is part of good care. It is ethically mandatory with all treatment plans for seriously ill patients, including but not limited to plans to forgo medical treatment.

Palliative care includes continuous pain and symptom management and continuous access to other palliative care services, including mental health services, social services, and chaplaincy services.

### Collaborative Decision Making

The involvement of professionals with expertise in communications can support the practice of collaborative decision making involving parents, physicians, and pediatric patients, aimed at identifying a child's best interests. Collaborative decision making may also be appropriate for some adult patients who lack decision making capacity but are capable of expressing preferences and who wish to participate in decision making with physicians and surrogates. Social workers, chaplains, mental health specialists, and nurses can assist the collaborative process as discussion facilitators, as continuity between discussions, and by offering support to participants.

### Advance Care Planning

Asking patients about their values and preferences and documenting and using patient preferences are integral to good care. A professional responsible for the care of a seriously ill patient should know how to initiate advance care planning and to use documents resulting from this process. Nurses, chaplains, and social workers may share responsibility with physicians for advance care planning.

## Decisions about Food and Feeding When a Patient Is Near the End of Life

Including a chaplain or another member of the health care team with strong communications skills may be helpful in clarifying the nutritional needs of the dying person in the context of good end-of-life care, with appropriate reference to social values concerning food, feeding, and caregiving. The chaplain, in particular, should be well informed about religious teachings concerning feeding near the end of life, as these teachings may be unfamiliar to or misunderstood by other participants in the discussion.

## Discussing "Hope" in the Context of Treatment Decision Making

The language of hope can be prominent (and confusing) in decision making near the end of life. Because this language may be associated with religious beliefs and practices, the involvement of a chaplain may be helpful in facilitating communication during treatment decision making.

## Objections to a Determination of Death

Acknowledging objections to the declaration of death, including objections to the neurological criteria for making a determination of death, does not alter the physiological state of the deceased patient. However, some religious groups acknowledge only cardiopulmonary death. Sometimes a family will express a nonspecific religious or moral objection to the determination of brain death or will use religious language ("we're praying for a miracle") that may indicate a belief that the patient is still alive or reflect an inability to acknowledge that death has already occurred. The involvement of a chaplain with experience caring for bereaved families and who is familiar with how grief and other emotions may be expressed in religious terms may be helpful in such situations.

## Religious Objections to Treatment Decisions

Involving a chaplain as soon as any religious objection to a treatment decision is expressed is more productive than paging the chaplain to intervene in a standoff. If a religious objection is an effort to halt a decision-making process, the chaplain may be able to elicit the underlying source of distress or serve as a nonconfrontational presence.

If the objection reflects a religious struggle or an unmet religious need, the chaplain can collaborate with others to provide appropriate care to loved ones while protecting the patient's best interests and supporting the decision maker. A chaplain may also be able to collaborate with outside clergy trusted by a patient or loved ones but who is unfamiliar with clinical settings.

### Policy Supporting Good Practice

Because chaplains are responsible for meeting any specific religious and related cultural needs of a patient or family, including rituals associated with the care of the sick or the dying, institutional policies and processes should ensure that chaplaincy, mental health services, and social services are routinely alerted to cases identified by medical and nursing staff as situations in which end-of-life decisions are being made.

## *Final Words*

Good chaplaincy does not exist in a bubble. It is connected to other professions, to teams, to units, and to organizations, as well as to patients and their loved ones. The maturation of chaplaincy as a health care profession will include the expectation that chaplains are well informed about the ethical dimensions of the care of the sick and are prepared to participate in ethics consultation, ethics education, and the analysis and development of ethically sound policy.

### Further Reading

These readings and web-based collections of resources reflect the interdisciplinary nature of bioethics. While professionals in all disciplines, including medicine, should read beyond their own disciplines, much of the professional literature in bioethics is written by physician-ethicists or concerns research conducted by physicians, so chaplains should expect to read medical journal articles. All of the books, articles, and websites listed here include extensive bibliographies for those interested in pursuing specific topics.

#### BOOKS

Beauchamp, Thomas L., and James F. Childress. *Principles of Biomedical Ethics*. 6th ed. New York and Oxford: Oxford University Press, 2008.

Dubler, Nancy N., and Carol B. Liebman. *Bioethics Mediation: A Guide to Shaping Shared Solutions*. New York: United Hospital Fund of New York, 2004.

Ford, Paul J., and Denise M. Dudzinski. *Complex Ethics Consultations: Cases That Haunt Us*. Cambridge: Cambridge University Press, 2008.

Lo, Bernard. *Resolving Ethical Dilemmas: A Guide for Clinicians*. Philadelphia: Wolters Kluwer Health / Lippincott Williams & Wilkins, 2009.

Post, Linda Farber, Jeffrey Blustein, and Nancy N. Dubler. *Handbook for Health Care Ethics Committees*. Baltimore: Johns Hopkins University Press, 2007.

Ravitsky, Vardit, Autumn Fiester, and Arthur L. Caplan. *The Penn Center Guide to Bioethics*. New York: Springer, 2009.

Steinbock, Bonnie, ed. *The Oxford Handbook of Bioethics*. Oxford: Oxford University Press, 2007.

## JOURNAL ARTICLES

Block, Susan D. "Psychological Considerations, Growth, and Transcendence at the End of Life: The Art of the Possible." *Journal of the American Medical Association* 285, no. 22 (2001): 2898–2905.

Curtis, J. Randall, and Robert A. Burt. "Why Are Critical Care Clinicians So Powerfully Distressed by Family Demands for Futile Care?" *Journal of Critical Care* 18, no. 1 (2003): 22–24.

Curtis, J. Randall, et al. "The Family Conference as a Focus to Improve Communication about End-of-Life Care in the Intensive Care Unit: Opportunities for Improvement." *Critical Care Medicine* 29, no. 2 Suppl (2001): 26–33.

Fox, Ellen, Sarah Myers, and Robert A. Pearlman. "Ethics Consultation in United States Hospitals: A National Survey." *American Journal of Bioethics* 7, no. 2 (2007): 13–25.

Lynn, Joanne, and Nathan E. Goldstein. "Advance Care Planning for Fatal Chronic Illness: Avoiding Commonplace Errors and Unwarranted Suffering." *Annals of Internal Medicine* 138, no. 10 (2003): 812–18.

Meier, Diane E., Anthony L. Back, and R. Sean Morrison. "The Inner Life of Physicians and Care of the Seriously Ill." *Journal of the American Medical Association* 286, no. 23 (2001): 3007–14.

Meisel, Alan, Lois Snyder, and Timothy Quill. "Seven Legal Barriers to End-of-Life Care: Myths, Realities, and Grains of Truth." *Journal of the American Medical Association* 284, no. 19 (2000): 2495–2501.

Quill, Timothy E., Robert M. Arnold, and Frederic Platt. "I Wish Things Were Different: Expressing Wishes in Response to Loss, Futility, and Unrealistic Hopes." *Annals of Internal Medicine* 135, no. 7 (2001): 551–55.

Solomon, Mildred Z., et al. "New and Lingering Controversies in Pediatric End-of-Life Care." *Pediatrics* 116, no. 4 (2005): 872–83.

Steinhauser, Karen E. "Factors Considered Important at the End of Life by Patients, Family, Physicians, and Other Care Providers." *Journal of the American Medical Association* 284, no. 19 (2000): 2476–82.

Sulmasy, Daniel P. "Spiritual Issues in the Care of Dying Patients: '... It's Okay between Me and God.'" *Journal of the American Medical Association* 296, no. 18 (2006): 1385–92.

Wendler, David, and Annette Rid. "Systematic Review: The Effect on Surrogates of Making Treatment Decisions for Others." *Annals of Internal Medicine* 154, no. 5 (2011): 336–46.

White, Douglas B., J. Randall Curtis, Bernard Lo, and John M. Luce. "Decisions to Limit Life-Sustaining Treatment for Critically Ill Patients Who Lack Both Decision-Making Capacity and Surrogate Decision-Makers." *Critical Care Medicine* 34, no. 8 (2006): 2053–59.

## Resources

Center to Advance Palliative Care (research and education in palliative care): www.capc.org

The Hastings Center: www.thehastingscenter.org

Kennedy Institute for Ethics (bioethics library): http://bioethics.georgetown.edu

Public Responsibility in Medicine and Research (research ethics): www.primr.org

PubMed, U.S. National Library of Medicine, National Institutes of Health: www.ncbi.nlm.nih.gov/pubmed

Spiritual Care Collaborative, Council on Collaboration, *Common Code of Ethics for Chaplains, Pastoral Counselors, Pastoral Educators, and Students* (2004), www.spiritualcarecollaborative.org/docs/common-code-ethics.pdf

## About the Contributor

**Dr. Nancy Berlinger, PhD, MDiv,** is a research scholar at the Hastings Center, an independent, nonprofit bioethics research institute located in Garrison, New York. Her research and teaching focuses on health care ethics, related topics in public health ethics and in human rights, and ethics education for health care professionals, including chaplains. Dr. Berlinger is the project director for the forthcoming revision of the Hastings Center guidelines on end-of-life care and has a special interest in ethical issues related to cancer as a chronic illness. She teaches health care ethics to graduate students at the Yale School of Nursing. She serves on the Bioethics Committee at Montefiore Medical Center, Bronx, New York, and on the Board of Directors of the Westchester End-of-Life Coalition. Dr. Berlinger is the author of *After Harm: Medical Error and the Ethics of Forgiveness* and coauthor of "Ethical Dilemmas and Spiritual Care Near the End of Life," in *Living with Grief: Spirituality and End-of-Life Care.*

# 14

## *Spirituality Groups*

*Rev. Lynne M. Mikulak, MDiv, MSW, BCC, ACPE Supervisor*

This chapter is divided into three sections. The first section provides a general overview of the purpose and function of spirituality groups, including a group protocol. The second section introduces two group models developed by this chapter's author that are used by chaplains and clinical pastoral education (CPE) students at NewYork-Presbyterian Hospital, Payne Whitney Westchester Psychiatry Division. These two models, in addition to spirituality group guidelines, can be used in general or specialized health care settings, as well as any community worship setting by clergy, with a particular emphasis on multifaith and multicultural diversity. The third section includes a resource list highlighting contexts for spirituality groups as found in literature review.

## *The Purpose and Function of Spirituality Groups*

### The Purpose of Spirituality Groups

The one-on-one pastoral visit is the primary focus of a chaplain's training, certification, and continuing professional development. The chaplain at the bedside offering reflective listening, spiritual care, and prayer is the iconic image held by chaplains, patients, families, and hospital staff as the ideal for what a chaplain can and should provide to those who are ill or suffering. However, both the influences of the Joint Commission and other regulatory bodies and the expectations of hospital administration and clinicians regarding the treatment of the whole patient are continuously shifting and expanding.[1] Chief among this trend is an expectation for chaplains to facilitate inpatient and / or outpatient spirituality groups to address cultural, spiritual, and religious needs.[2]

Seminary training generally provides cursory resources and skill building in group and systems theory and facilitation of spirituality groups.[3] In CPE programs, didactics on the "how-to" of spirituality groups are scarce if it is a critical care setting where spirituality groups are rarely or never held on patient units; likewise, there is little clinical literature available written by chaplains about spirituality groups.[4] If a request or a mandate for a spirituality group on a patient unit is made, this gap in the training creates uncertainties for the chaplain about how to proceed with resources, developing a format, and clinical facilitation. As health care organizations continue to integrate best practices for patient safety and provision of care standards, considerations become increasingly important for pastoral care and clinical treatment teams about multicultural and multifaith dialogue, meeting the health care facility's and the unit's clinical standards and protocols for groups, ensuring that the chaplain's approach is in line with treatment outcomes for any given patient, and ensuring that the clinical team possesses an understanding of the chaplain's role.[5]

Changing definitions of terms need to be qualified. Standards are being revised by the Joint Commission requiring cultural competence among health care staff and for meeting cultural needs in tandem with emotional, spiritual, and religious needs of patients / residents and families.[6] Pastoral care organizations such as the Association for Clinical Pastoral Education and the Association of Professional Chaplains continue to update and shift their standards in the same direction.[7] Spiritual and religious needs are no longer an isolated focus in standards of care as they had been in the past. Wilson-Stronks' and Galvez's Joint Commission publication recommends the following definitions for guiding best practices and provision of care:

- **Culture:** Integrated patterns of human behavior that include the language, thoughts, communications, actions, customs, beliefs, values, and institutions of racial, ethnic, religious, or social groups.
- **Cultural competence:** A set of congruent behaviors, attitudes, and policies that come together in a system or agency or among professionals that enables effective interactions in a cross-cultural framework.[8]

Chaplains are poised through their own training and professional standards to be able to incorporate cultural competence into the facilitation of spirituality groups.

An important place for the chaplain to start is by asking a signal question: "What is the purpose of this group?" From the question of purpose, the chaplain can review and draw upon the variety of clinical, cultural, and theological resources widely available through pastoral care networking, professional organization resources, and hospital library and online resources to plan the direction and focus of the group. While intensive one-on-one pastoral care to a patient / resident can be spiritually and emotionally healing for that person and vocationally rewarding for the chaplain, that same patient / resident invited to a spirituality group facilitated by the chaplain may experience broader dimensions of insight about self-care, compassion for others, and awareness about illness and the human experience through the sharing of narratives.[9] Likewise, the chaplain's skills and level of understanding about patients' / residents' sufferings are enhanced through group process.

Religious expression has a communal root. Although health care chaplains' theological formation and endorsement process must be based in a chosen religious denomination, they center their pastoral care and work, as addressed in *Standards of Practice* and as expected by health care institutions, in multifaith and multicultural perspectives. A spirituality group in a health care setting automatically provides for a collective wisdom from a broadly diverse population. In the communal gathering of a multifaith, multicultural spirituality group, group members share experiences and stories, invoking multiple dimensions of the Holy and creating a sacred space for healing and transformation.[10] This space provides a foundation for building and creating mutual respect and a common language (see also chapter 32). Group members' consciousness and awareness are expanded through exposure to new cultural and spiritual perspectives. Building the foundation for mutual respect and common language is critical for a positive outcome in the context of a multicultural, multifaith spirituality group.[11]

Later in the chapter, I provide two group models that can aid in the chaplain and the patients / residents building the foundation together. In my tradition as an ordained United Church of Christ minister, I understand that "where two or three are gathered" (Gospel of

Matthew 18:20) the group and I are collectively building and experiencing with the potential for each individual to reach out beyond one's own concerns and worries. My observation as a group leader is that spirituality groups provide the possibility of opening group members up to compassion and empathy for each other, which helps diminish individual feelings of isolation and aloneness.

## The Function of Spirituality Groups

When formulating a design for a spirituality group in inpatient or outpatient health care settings, criteria for spiritual assessment can be inclusive in the function of the group and can provide for creative freedom for the group format. In the Joint Commission document "Spiritual Assessment," areas that a chaplain and / or a clinical team can address—but are not required to—in spiritual assessment for patients and families also provide useful elements for exploration in spirituality groups:

- Who or what provides the participant with strength and hope?
- Does the participant use prayer in his or her life?
- How does the participant express his or her spirituality?
- How would the participant describe his or her philosophy of life?
- What type of spiritual / religious support does the participant desire?
- What is the name of the participant's clergy, minister, chaplain, pastor, rabbi?
- What does suffering mean to the participant?
- What does dying mean to the participant?
- What are the participant's spiritual goals?
- Is there a role of church / synagogue in the participant's life?
- How does faith help the participant cope with illness?
- How does the participant keep going day after day?
- What helps the participant get through this health care experience?
- How has illness affected the participant and his / her family?[12]

In addition to providing ideas and function to the design of a spirituality group, established provisions and guidelines (whether from accrediting bodies or from within an institution's own vision, values, or mission statements) assist the chaplain in creating spirituality group formats that are congruent with the institution and multidisciplinary practices. Pastoral care departments tend to silo themselves from other clinical departments because of the generally smaller size of pastoral care departments and barriers to direct knowledge and interface with clinical treatment, depending on the setting. Spirituality groups run by chaplains serve to integrate the chaplain into the patient unit and care team. There is also a broader function when spirituality groups are open to inpatients, outpatients, families, and the community. Groups create an important bridge between the health care facility and the community.[13]

The design and function of a spirituality group requires dialogue with the clinical care team and administration. Necessary considerations in these dialogues could include but are not limited to the following:

- Choosing a space that would promote a respectful and reflective experience for the group
- Respecting time limits related to unit schedules for meetings, rounds, and so on
- Having proximity to the nurse's station and whether the group space should be secluded or closer to other clinical team members in the event of a need for medical assistance
- Including a co-leader or guest facilitators from other members of the multidisciplinary team
- Making sure the group design meets standards and hospital protocols

Tending to these logistics ahead of time will provide for fewer interruptions of the functioning of the spirituality group once it gets under way.

At the Westchester Division of NewYork-Presbyterian Hospital, spirituality groups are included in a document used for education and training that lists all group protocols on patient units (see Figure 14.1).[14] This spirituality group protocol was approved by operational and nursing administration of the hospital. It includes a variety of possibilities to engage in for spirituality groups facilitated by CPE students, chaplains (including this chapter's author), and other members of the multidisciplinary care teams collaborating with the pastoral care department. Spirituality groups are offered weekly on all adult, children, and adolescent inpatient units.

## *Introducing Group Models*

### Spirituality Group Guidelines

Opening each spirituality group with stated guidelines provides clarity and boundaries for the patients / residents attending the group. Furthermore, it provides a grounding of pastoral authority for the chaplain facilitating the group. With the concerns of illness and treatment on participants' minds, the guidelines help members focus on their treatment goals and a group task. Group members might have some anxiety about whether such an assembly would go against their religious practices or beliefs, and the guidelines would clarify those concerns. Chaplains at our facility, depending on their personal preference and the group setting, will read the guidelines out loud, paraphrase them, pass the guidelines around for the group to read different paragraphs, or ask for a volunteer to read. Particularly in psychiatry on units with cognitive-behavioral treatment models, having patients volunteer or take turns reading the guidelines promotes a sense of personal ownership and group cohesiveness.

#### *Example*: Pastoral Care Department Spirituality Group Guidelines

- The purpose of this group is to discuss topics or participate in exercises related to spiritual and cultural needs that will aid in your discovery and awareness about your own beliefs and resources. This group is usually facilitated by a chaplain or occasionally another member of the care team. We will begin with an explanation of the exercise and how the group time will be shared.
- If at any time you are uncomfortable with this group, you may opt to leave quietly. If you feel an issue or topic is too difficult for you and you would like to meet with the chaplain one-on-one, you may make that request with a unit staff member or by calling the chaplain directly at ext. ___.

## SPIRITUALITY GROUP PROTOCOL SAMPLE

**Name of group:** Spirituality Group (depending on the patient unit, the group has a specific name, such as "Meditation Group," "Sacred Texts," "Beliefs and Values").

**Purpose:** To help patients share their spiritual beliefs, values, cultural traditions and contexts, ritual needs, creative processes, and sacred texts with other patients; to help patients identify what their emotional, spiritual, religious, and cultural needs are and to speak from their own experiences; to give a forum for patients to express their spirituality while learning about and being respectful of other people's faith experiences.

**Objectives:** At the end of this group, the patient will:

- Understand and identify the difference between negative spiritual coping (i.e.,"God has abandoned me") and positive spiritual coping (i.e.,"God is present for me")
- Identify her / his personal stories through the text, topic, or exercise
- Understand his / her behaviors and attitudes related to his / her religious upbringing, spiritual beliefs, and practices
- Have a better sense of other people's religious and spiritual practices
- Be introduced to a new text, topic, or exercise that adds to positive coping

**Place of group meeting:** On each patient unit in the group / meeting room.

**Time, length, and frequency of group meetings:** 30 min.–1 hour, once a week.

**Group leader(s):** (List of chaplains and CPE students. This protocol is revised annually.)

**Supervisor:** Chaplain Adama Eve, Pastoral Care Coordinator (contact information listed, including phone extension, pager number, e-mail).

**Selection criteria for patients:** Patients cannot be mandated to attend this group due to patients' rights regarding freedom of religion; however, the Westchester Division mandates that the group be provided. Participation is considered an elective based on patients' emotional, spiritual, religious, and cultural needs. A list of patients is made prior to the start of the group by the Psychosocial Rehabilitation Therapist or charge nurse based on spiritual assessment and patients' medical and mental health status.

**Usual number of patients in the group:** Varies from 5–20.

**Materials:** Materials can include poems, psalms, spiritual or cultural-based writings; sacred texts of a variety of religious traditions; educational information regarding religious observances; paper for drawing, painting, journaling, or writing; mandala or labyrinth drawing exercises; 12′ x 12′ portable canvas labyrinth for walking meditation brought onto the unit; escort provided for the outdoor courtyard 40′ x 40′ brick labyrinth.

**How is group attendance documented?:** Charted on computer, and individual unit paperwork if required.

*Figure 14.1*

- Because of the nature of this hospital and the diversity of its population, this group cannot be the focus for any particular religious affiliation or viewpoint. Hopefully, you will be able to share from your own unique perspective about your experiences, struggles, and strengths while also being respectful of other people's beliefs, practices, traditions, and experiences.
- Please keep in mind that this is not a group to debate religious differences or to discuss current events that have a religious significance. This is a group to share your experience and matters of a spiritual, religious, or cultural nature that may be pertinent to your treatment and well-being.
- Please regard general guidelines for all groups on this unit: (1) do not interrupt or have private conversations while another person is talking; (2) remain engaged in the activity of the group and with the direction of the facilitator; (3) maintain confidentiality. Thank you.

## The Sacred Texts Spirituality Group

The sacred texts group format below developed at the Westchester Division by this chapter's author was designed with two specific foci: addressing patients' emotional, spiritual, religious, and cultural needs; and creating a spirituality group format that aligns with the clinical treatment goals for improving cognitive functioning for patients with mental illness, learning and literacy needs, and social functioning. This group was first created for the Second Chance unit, an adult social-skills unit for chronically mentally ill patients.

### *Example*: The Sacred Texts Spirituality Group

- Begin the group with Spirituality Group Guidelines.
- Present one, two, or three brief sacred text readings, depending on the length of each and similarities in themes. These consist of psalms, lessons, stories, sayings, parables from any religious tradition, including the Hebrew Bible, Christian Bible, Qur'an, Buddhist canon, Hindu texts, Native America stories, and other ancient sources. You can

also use extra-canonical or extra-biblical resources such as anthologies and collections of stories, prayers, and parables from a variety of traditions and cultural contexts.

- Vary the presentation and length of the readings based on the group's needs, illness status, and group size. If it is a smaller group (fewer than ten), ask for one or two volunteer readers. If it is a large group, have the entire group read the texts, with each person reading a paragraph or phrase. This helps promote the team's treatment goals for cognitive improvement, coping, personal growth, and empowerment. Say: "If it is your turn to read and you are not comfortable for any reason, please say 'pass.'" If it is a large group with chronic illness, medication issues, and learning disabilities, the facilitator can read the readings, as a pastoral therapeutic act and a non-anxious presence.
- If one text is presented, begin the discussion with the following questions: "How do you relate to this story? How does this text relate to your own personal experience?"
- If two or more texts are presented, ask the second question above also, but replace the first question with this: "How are these readings similar or different? What themes do you hear?"[15]

## The Multifaith Devotional Encounter

This format was designed to meet a specific spiritual problem on our patient units. An administrative decision was made to replace larger group worship held in the auditorium with small services on each unit. This decision resulted from the fact that many patients could not attend the larger worship for one of two reasons: if a patient was on a watch status and could not leave the unit, or if there was a weekend shortage of staff escorts (there is a one staff to three patients escort ratio at Westchester). Since our only large worship service was Roman Catholic (approximately 50 percent of our patient census is Roman Catholic), we recruited more Eucharistic ministers and now have weekly Catholic Communion services on all of the units.

The goal in creating the Multifaith Devotional Encounter (MFDE) is to provide an interfaith worship opportunity on the patient units that is also congruent with the spirituality group format.[16] The MFDE serves to enhance and support the function of the spirituality group, not replace it. A psalm used for discussion in a sacred texts spirituality group can also be used that week for the MFDE to provide continuity and cognitive cohesion for the patients. The MFDE has some elements of a spirituality group and some elements of worship. This format was granted administrative approval, with a consensus that only psalms would be used as the sacred text. This format was created to give chaplains general guidelines with an understanding that they have creative freedom within the design of the format (see Figure 14.2).

## *Spirituality Group Contexts*

A literature review of spirituality groups—formats and research studies—in health care settings reveals that a diverse range of clinicians engage in the facilitation of spirituality groups, including medical doctors, psychiatrists, psychologists, social workers, nurses, and rehabilitation therapists. As Kehoe, Popovsky, McCorkle, and others note, there is little literature written by chaplains about spirituality groups facilitated by chaplains, and what is written generally comes from chaplains working in the field of psychiatry.[17]

While facilitating spirituality groups on acute care units and general medical floors presents many challenges to patient safety and care, it can and has been done with thorough planning. As literature by chaplains grows for presenting models and methods for spirituality groups in any setting, barriers to group care can be analyzed and addressed. The formats presented in this chapter will hopefully add to a growing lexicon of resources to assist chaplains and clergy to facilitate spirituality groups in a variety of medical settings, long-term care institutions, community centers, and places of worship.

Figure 14.3 lists a sampling of topics or settings of spirituality-focused groups run by clinicians other than chaplains or clergy, as found in the literature review.[18]

In closing with this list, it is my hope that possibilities will spark initiation and dialogue between chaplains and their administrators and create stronger collaboration with health care providers for designing and implementing spirituality groups as a pastoral care best practice.

## THE MULTIFAITH DEVOTIONAL ENCOUNTER SAMPLE

**Opening**

Hello, I'm Chaplain ____________. Welcome. This is a multifaith devotional encounter, offered once a week at ___o'clock, open to anyone of any spiritual or religious tradition. We will read a psalm and reflect together about its meaning in each of our lives. (*You can state here whether you will include music and other activities.*)

**Prayer**

Let us begin in prayer. Oh Holy One, be with us today as we gather, hear our prayers and concerns of the community of people on this unit, nurture us with your words as we seek your comfort, presence, and healing. Guide our thoughts and intentions as we spend this time together. Amen.

**Psalm**

And now a reading from Psalm _________________. *Read out loud. Choose a full psalm, a verse, or a couple of verses. Carefully choose verses that reflect messages for healing, Divine Presence, and community strength.*

**Meditation**

I would like to offer you a reflection about our reading for today.... *You may do whatever feels comfortable for you here. Offer some reflective words or a brief sermon on the psalm passage you just read; you may cite authors who have commented on this text. You can also invite silent meditation and / or play music before, after, or during this time.*

**Community Reflection**

At this time, I invite anyone to reflect on the reading and meditation as it relates to your life experience and journey. You may also offer prayers for yourself or others.

**Closing Blessing**

*Using the language of the psalm you used*: Oh Gracious God, or Holy One *(or whatever name for the Divine that feels comfortable and is not exclusively related to one religion)*, you have heard the prayers of this community. We ask that you bless each person, all patients and staff, walk with them, make your presence known to them through your kind ways. Nurture them and give them hope and peace, and be with their loved ones. And may each of you be a blessing to each other as you continue in your journeys toward healing. Amen.

**General Suggestions**

You may adjust your wording in whatever way is comfortable within your own pastoral style, keeping in mind that this is a multifaith and multicultural context. Music should be used with some caution, avoiding specifically oriented religious music. Suggestions for music include meditation music, classical music, instrumental music, or a song form of the psalm that was read. The length of an MFDE could range from 15–45 minutes, depending on the size and needs of the group.

*Figure 14.2*

## TOPICS AND SETTINGS OF SPIRITUALITY-FOCUSED GROUPS

Anxiety
Aromatherapy
Cardiology
Chronic pain
Community centers
Correctional facility spiritual issues
Domestic violence
Dream analysis
Eating disorders
Educational institutions
Elder care & geriatrics
Empowerment
End of life
Family systems
Forgiveness
Genograms
Grief / loss / bereavement
HIV / AIDS
Hope
Hospice
Inner city / urban life
Jewish Orthodox & ultra-Orthodox community issues
Meditation & mindfulness-based practices
Mental health & psychiatry
Military service
Mind-body
Oncology
Pediatrics / children & adolescents
Rehabilitation facilities
Religious conflicts
Sacredness & sacred space
Self-esteem & self-awareness
Sensory stimulation
Sexual abuse
Sexuality & sexual orientation
Stress
Substance Abuse
Trauma / crisis / disaster

*Figure 14.3*

## Notes

1. Joint Commission, *Advancing Effective Communication, Cultural Competence, and Patient- and Family-Centered Care: A Roadmap for Hospitals* (Oakbrook Terrace, IL: Joint Commission, 2010), chaps. 2–3.
2. Joint Commission, *Standards Supporting the Provision of Culturally and Linguistically Appropriate Services* (2009). The inclusion of spirituality groups can address the following standards: p. 13, Standard PC.1.10, Element of Performance (EP) 8: After screening, clients are matched with the care, treatment, and services in the organization most appropriate to their needs; p. 15, Standard PC.4.50: Clients are encouraged to participate in developing their plan for care, treatment, and services, and their involvement is documented; EP 1: The organization has a process for involving clients in their care, treatment, and service decisions; p. 16, Standard PC.6.10: The client receives education and training specific to the client's needs as

appropriate to the care, treatment, and services provided; EP 2: The assessment of learning needs addresses cultural and religious beliefs, emotional barriers, desire and motivation to learn, physical and cognitive limitations, and barriers to communication as appropriate; p. 20, Standard RI.2.10, EP 2: Each client has a right to have his or her cultural, psychosocial, spiritual and personal values, beliefs, and preferences respected.

3. D. B. Clark, "Working with Groups, Families and Couples, Clergy as Systems Analysts," in *Guide to Pastoral Counseling and Care* (Madison, CT: Psychosocial Press, 2000), 243–73. On p. 243, Clark makes the distinction that seminaries train clergy to speak in front of groups, yet clergy are not adequately taught about group process and theory, and group facilitation techniques.
4. M. Popovsky, "A Spiritual Issues Discussion Group for Psychiatric Inpatients," *Journal of Pastoral Care and Counseling* 61, nos. 1–2 (Spring–Summer 2007): 119–128.
5. Amy Wilson-Stronks and Erica Galvez, *Hospitals, Language and Culture: A Snapshot of the Nation, Exploring Cultural and Linguistic Services in the Nation's Hospitals—A Report of Findings* (Joint Commission, 2007), p. 52, Domain Four: Patient Safety and Provision of Care, recommendation and observation (R&O) 4-3: Hospitals should take advantage of the internal and external resources available to educate them on cultural beliefs they may encounter; R&O 4-5: Patient safety and quality improvement leaders need to have dialogues with language services coordinators, diversity officers, and pastoral care workers about issues relating to cultural and language that can impact patient safety.
6. Joint Commission, *Roadmap for Hospitals*. This document will help prepare hospitals for the revised 2010 Joint Commission standards. Joint Commission surveyors began evaluating compliance of the revised standards January 1, 2011, p. 57.
7. Association for Clinical Pastoral Education, "Objectives and Outcomes of ACPE Accredited Programs," *Standards & Manuals: 2010 Standards*, www.acpe.edu/NewPDF/2010%20Manuals/2010%20Standards.pdf. A sampling of standards: For supervisory education, standard 308.9.5 states requirement for multicultural theory; CPE Level I outcome standards include: 311.1 articulate the central themes of their religious heritage and the theological understanding that informs their ministry, and 311.2 identify and discuss major life events, relationships, and cultural contexts that influence personal identity as expressed in pastoral functioning; CPE Level II outcome standards include: 312.1 articulate an understanding of the pastoral role that is congruent with their personal and cultural values, basic assumptions, and personhood, and 312.2 provide pastoral ministry to diverse people, taking into consideration multiple elements of cultural and ethnic differences, social conditions, systems, and justice issues without imposing their own perspectives.

   Association of Professional Chaplains, *Standards of Practice for Professional Chaplains in Acute Care Settings*, www.professionalchaplains.org/uploadedFiles/pdf/Standards%20of%20Practice%20Draft%20Document%20021109.pdf#Project_Update. A sampling of standards: Standard 1, Assessment: The chaplain gathers and evaluates relevant data pertinent to the patient's situation and / or bio-psycho-social-spiritual / religious health; Standard 7, Respect for Diversity: The chaplain models and collaborates with the organization and its interdisciplinary team in respecting and providing culturally competent patient-centered care.

8. Wilson-Stronks and Galvez, *Hospitals, Language and Culture*, 15.
9. R. A. Kidd, V. Maripolsky, and P. Smith, "The Use of Sacred Story in a Psychiatry Spirituality Group," *Journal of Pastoral Care* 55, no. 4 (Winter 2001): 353–64.
10. B. H. McCorkle et al., "'Sacred Moments': Social Anxiety in a Larger Perspective," *Mental Health, Religion & Culture* 8, no. 3 (September 2005): 227–38. The authors, in referring to the work and research of Pargament and Mahoney, state that people perceive sacredness through a variety of forms, and "therefore, any person, place, object, event or relationship might be considered sacred, and no particular religion or theology is implied in the perception of sacredness" (p. 228).
11. N. Kehoe, "Spirituality Groups in Serious Mental Illness," *Southern Medical Journal* 100, no. 6 (June 2007): 647–48. Kehoe, a nun and psychologist, has written extensively on spirituality-focused groups she has led for those who suffer with mental illness. She has designed fundamental guidelines for such groups, which include the following:
    - Each group member must be able to listen respectfully to another's beliefs and be able to tolerate religious differences.
    - No member can impose his / her beliefs on another or judge another.
    - The group is a discussion group, not a prayer or study group.
12. Adapted from Joint Commission, "Spiritual Assessment," in *Provision of Care, Treatment, and Services*, www.jointcommission.org. In standard PC.3.100, the Joint Commission requires assessment of a patient's spiritual orientation and religion.
13. C. O'Rourke, "Listening for the Sacred: Addressing Spiritual Issues in the Group Treatment of Adults with Mental Illness," *Smith College Studies in Social Work* 67, no. 2 (March 1997): 185.
14. While the Joint Commission has revised standards in the past decade regarding protocols for behavioral health, such a document with group protocols is not required. It is a Westchester Division best practice. Development of the protocol for spirituality groups was initiated by this author's predecessor, Rev. Amy Manierre, who coauthored the following article about a spirituality group she ran at the Westchester Division: G. Goodman and A. Manierre, "Representations of God Uncovered in a Spirituality Group of Borderline Inpatients," *International Journal of Group Psychotherapy* 58, no. 1 (2008): 1–15; material originally presented at the American Psychoanalytic Association conference in Seattle, WA, on June 11, 2005.
15. These questions are designed to be integrative with the treatment team's approach for clinical treatment. The Westchester Division uses both cognitive behavioral therapy in groups and dialectical behavior therapy in groups, and these questions and the format of this spirituality group have been deemed congruent by unit staff with those approaches. As written about in this author's theory papers for

supervisory certification in the Association for Clinical Pastoral Education, from a theoretical standpoint, this is a constructivist approach for meaning making and healing through storytelling and narrative. If a person shares a personal story in response to the readings, the chaplain affirms the story and then asks the group who else would like to share and also asks for responses to the story or experience just shared, encouraging a response that maintains the integrity of the previous sharer. In this format, the stories build upon each other, interweaving the texts with the shared experiences of the group as a whole, for a shared learning encounter.

A description of this group, which included an interview with this author, was published in S. W. Cook, L. S. Dixon, and M. A. Fukuyama, "Integrating Sacred Writings in Therapy," in *Spiritually Oriented Interventions for Counseling and Psychotherapy*, ed. J. D. Aten, M. R. McMinn, and E. L. Worthington (Washington, DC: American Psychological Association, 2011).

16. The name for the MFDE evolved from a discussion with CPE students about the design and format. I credit Rabbi Hillel D. Gold with creating this name.
17. Kehoe, "Spirituality Groups in Serious Mental Illness"; Popovsky, "A Spiritual Issues Discussion Group for Psychiatric Inpatients"; McCorkle et al., "'Sacred Moments': Social Anxiety in a Larger Perspective."
18. At least fifty references came up in a literature review for spirituality-focused groups run by clinicians other than clergy and chaplains. Therefore, the above list is not meant to be comprehensive. For the purposes of this chapter, this topics list is useful for initiating ideas. The majority of the topics listed above were generated from numerous clinical articles by multiple authors in clinical roles other than chaplain.

## Further Reading

Anderson, R. G., and M. A. Fukuyama, eds. *Ministry in the Spiritual and Cultural Diversity of Health Care: Increasing Competency in Chaplains*. New York: Haworth Pastoral Press, 2004.

Artress, L. *The Sacred Path Companion: A Guide to Walking the Labyrinth to Heal and Transform*. New York: Riverhead Books, 2006.

Brussat, F., and M. A. Brussat. *Spiritual Literacy: Reading the Sacred into Everyday Life*. New York: Scribner, 1996.

Hirshfield, J. *Women in Praise of the Sacred: 43 Centuries of Spiritual Poetry by Women*. New York: HarperCollins, 1994.

Hopkins, E., Z. Woods, R. Kelley, K. Bentley, and J. Murphy. *Working with Groups on Spiritual Themes*. Duluth, MN: Sacred Heart Medical Center, 1995.

O'Donohue, J. *To Bless the Space Between Us: A Book of Blessings*. New York: Doubleday, 2008.

Roberts, E., and E. Amidon. *Earth Prayers from Around the World: 365 Prayers, Poems, and Invocations for Honoring the Earth*. San Francisco: HarperCollins, 1991.

## About the Contributor

**Rev. Lynne M. Mikulak, MDiv, MSW, BCC, ACPE Supervisor,** is coordinator of pastoral care and education at the Payne Whitney Westchester Psychiatry Division of NewYork-Presbyterian Hospital. She is a certified supervisor with the Association of Clinical Pastoral Education and an ordained minister in the United Church of Christ. She has run spirituality groups for the past fifteen years in a variety of parish, community, and clinical settings, with a focus on spiritual, theological, and cultural awareness and development.

# 15

## *Spiritual Care of Staff*

*Rev. Robin C. Brown-Haithco, MDiv, ACPE Supervisor*

Prior to my current position as director of staff support with the Emory Center for Pastoral Services, I served as director of chaplaincy and CPE at a level-1 trauma center. Looking back on it, my experience working in a trauma setting prepared me for the work I find myself doing today. Let me explain. I've always understood that creation brought order out of chaos. Working in trauma helped me develop more fully my theology of chaos, that is, I learned to create order in disorder, not necessarily eliminating the disorder, but more an ordering of the disorder. Sometimes the work I find myself doing as a staff support chaplain is helping staff create order (find their center) in the midst of their chaotic personal and vocational lives.

Health care is constantly in flux. Change is the order of the day. Learning how to live within this context that is constantly changing requires a particular sense of one's self. It requires an ability to center one's self and invite calm, and sometimes this can only be done in the context of a space that invites the presence of the sacred. As director of staff support, I help staff create a space of calm by inviting them to take a "pause," by inviting them to step inside that centering space within their own spiritual self to reflect on their vocational purpose and calling. Sometimes in a hectic context we can lose sight of that which is most important and lose our sense of balance in the process. Staff support is a way to offer staff a space to regain their sense of balance and meaning and purpose.

When I arrived at Emory in June 2006, I was both excited about this new venture and anxious. I came with ten years of experience working in a level-1 trauma center. My knowledge of staff support theory was limited. I did staff support at my old job, but it was "off the cuff" using the knowledge I had of chaplaincy and spiritual care of patients and families. In many ways it was the same, yet different. So my first task when I arrived at Emory was to research the literature. I found only one article; it provided me with a frame with which to begin the work before me.

What I have learned in my role as director of staff support is that staff support chaplaincy has been in many ways an assumed role of the chaplain, with no formal training in methodology or theory of staff support. As a result, spiritual care of staff has become an informal or secondary role of the chaplain. This chapter will invite us to see staff support as a primary role of the chaplain.

## *Staff Support—What It Is and What It Looks Like*

So, what is staff support, and what does it look like? For the purposes of this chapter, when I speak of staff support, it will refer to support of staff within health care contexts.

I have been in my current position as director of staff support for four and a half years. In many ways, I am still developing my role. I am still working to define what it is that I do. I am still finding ways to live out my role in ways that are distinct from as well as similar to the role of the chaplain whose primary role is to provide spiritual support for patients and families. The staff support chaplain focuses primarily on the needs of staff who work within the health care context who are responsible for the care of patients and families who come to us for healing. This includes staff across disciplines—nursing, physicians, support staff, and administrators.

I often introduce myself to staff as the "chaplain for staff." This has come to mean I am solely theirs. I am the person who is there to help them find a way to live in the critical situations to which they are called on a daily basis. It means being a consistent and supportive presence, a constant companion who is willing to walk alongside staff during critical times in their vocational space as well in their personal lives. As the chaplain for staff, I have become the one nurses turn to for support when a patient with whom they have worked for months and sometimes years finally dies. I am the one to whom nursing managers and directors turn when their staff is overwhelmed with the stress created by high acuity and staffing shortages. I am the one to whom hospital administrators turn when they want to take the "pulse" of the organization. What are staff feeling and thinking about working in this place? What are their primary issues, and how do we need to address their concerns? I am the one staff turn to when they receive the news of the death of a colleague as a result of a sudden, tragic accident or a protracted illness. I am the one staff turn to when they receive news of the death of a loved one. I am the one staff turn to with sensitive issues of cultural diversity such as injustice, unfairness, and managerial practices that are unfair and unsupportive. I am also the one staff turn to when there is a major accomplishment or celebration in their life.

Staff support is about creating a hospitable space. It is about creating a safe and vibrant work environment where staff can live out their vocations with a sense of affirmation and support and appropriate challenge. Staff support is about being a supportive presence for all who work within the organization, including administration. Staff support is about calling *all* who work within the organization to their highest purpose and meaning, to their spiritual vocation, to the divine intent for which the organization was originally formed or created.[1] In the health care context, we are called to "service," serving those who have come to us for health and healing, and serving each other in a way that allows that service to others to be done with integrity, honesty, and respect.

## *Staff Needs*

So what are the needs of staff? When I arrived at Emory, I was charged with providing spiritual and emotional support for all staff within the institution. What has become my reality is that the bulk of my time and energy has been consumed by the needs of nursing staff. This does not, however, mean that staff from all disciplines are not in need of staff support. It simply means that often nursing staff most consistently express their needs. For the purposes of this chapter, I will focus primary attention on nursing staff.

In a 1981 article, the most frequent causes of stress among nursing staff in hospice, surgery, oncology, cardiovascular surgery, and medicine were "work load, death and dying, and inadequate preparation to meet the emotional needs of patients and their families."[2] In a 2004 article, stressors specific to oncology nurses included the following:

> The nature of cancer as a disease, complex treatments, caring for high acuity patients, dealing with death, communication issues, intense involvement with patients and families, interdisciplinary conflicts, ethical issues, terminal or palliative care issues, surrogate decision-making, workload, isolation outside the workplace, role overload, role conflict, lack of control, role strain, and work environment issues.[3]

Several weeks before I began writing this chapter, I sent out an e-mail survey to my colleagues in the Association for Clinical Pastoral Education (ACPE) inviting them to respond to seven questions related to staff support (see Figure 15.1).

The last question addresses the primary needs of staff within their institutions. Their answers are found in Figure 15.2.

It is clear that the issues found to create the most stress among nurses in 1981 and 2004 are similar to those currently being experienced by staff today. I believe the following issues have increased the stress I see among staff today:

1. **Our country's current economic crisis:** More and more staff are arriving at work each day with added stress related to meeting financial and family responsibilities; these stressors compound the stress inherent within the workplace.
2. **The high acuity of patients:** Patients are arriving at the hospital sicker, many with end-stage diseases, and staff are therefore seeing more and more difficult death and dying situations.
3. **The current nursing shortage:** The shortage has increased the workload of staff. Staff are finding it more and more difficult to take breaks and to tend to their own self-care needs.
4. **Cultural diversity:** Many of our health care contexts are becoming more diverse. Staff do not know how to engage the diversity, which results in conflict and tension among staff as well as dysfunctional team functioning and ineffective and inefficient care of patients.

| E-MAIL SURVEY |
|---|
| 1. Do you have a designated staff support program in your institution? |
| 2. If so, is it located within your pastoral care department? |
| 3. What are the components of your staff support program? |
| 4. What kinds of programs / services do you offer to support staff? |
| 5. How does your CPE curriculum address staff support needs? |
| 6. Do you have chaplains whose primary role is staff support? |
| 7. What would you say are the primary needs of staff in your institution? |

*Figure 15.1*

| PRIMARY NEEDS OF STAFF | |
|---|---|
| Overworked | Diversity issues |
| Grief and loss | Underappreciated |
| Patient and family abuse | Stress management |
| Trauma | Workplace violence |
| Critical incident debriefing | Moral distress |
| Vicarious grief | High acuity of patients |
| Intrapersonal conflict | Interpersonal conflict |
| Nurse-to-patient ratio | Bereavement support |
| Loss of satisfaction in job | Staffing shortages |
| Lack of support from coworkers | Difficult patient and family situations |
| Communication issues between patients / families and staff | Communication issues between staff |
| Lack of trust in management / administration | Complexity / intensity of work |
| | Loss of meaning and investment in work |
| | Lack of team building |

*Figure 15.2*

5. **Moral distress:** This occurs when staff find themselves going against their own ethics, morals, and integrity when providing care for patients who want aggressive treatment that is not medically indicated or futile.
6. **Compassion fatigue:** This is the experience of burnout; that which once gave them a sense of fulfillment now drains them and exhausts them.

7. **Organizational change:** Health care is in a constant state of flux. Staff often get caught in the changes and feel pulled in many different directions, with no clear understanding of their role or the system's expectations of them. This lack of role clarity creates ambiguity and confusion and often leads to increased probability of mistakes, as well as interpersonal tensions and conflict.
8. **Lack of appreciation and affirmation:** One respondent to the survey wrote that staff want to be related to "as persons and not just cogs in the corporate wheel."[4]
9. **Leadership:** Health care organizations tend to function using a hierarchical model. This style of leadership does not lend itself to mutual relationships. Staff often feel disempowered and that their opinions don't count.

This list is by no means exhaustive; it does indicate that providing for the spiritual and emotional needs of staff is needed and important.

## *Staff Support—Current Practice*

I received twenty-two responses from colleagues in ACPE to my e-mail survey. Figure 15.3 highlights responses to questions 1, 2, and 6. The data indicate that most institutions have employee assistance programs (EAP) designed to address counseling and financial needs of staff. Many of those EAP programs work closely with the pastoral care departments within their institutions. What I had hoped to find, but did not, was more staff support programs within pastoral care departments, with designated chaplains assigned primarily to do staff support. It seems that staff support continues to be a part of the chaplain's role.

| RESPONSES TO SURVEY QUESTIONS | | | | |
|---|---|---|---|---|
| Question | Yes | No | Shared | Type |
| #1 | 18 | 3 | | EAP |
| #2 | 1 | | 4 | |
| #6 | 1 | 20 | | |

*Figure 15.3*

The literature review was sparse, but I did find several articles that might be beneficial for chaplains who are working with staff within health care contexts (see further reading). One of those articles provides a model for staff support in an outpatient setting that could be easily transferable to other contexts. In that article, the authors describe four programs:

> 1. *Finding Soul at Work*: designed to help staff find meaning in their work; 2. *Existential Expedition*: designed to provide spiritual and emotional support for staff; 3. *After Book*: designed to help staff bring closure with patients; and 4. *Labyrinth Program*: designed to nurture the spirituality of staff.[5]

In an article referenced earlier, a one-day retreat called the "Circle of Care Retreat" is described. "This retreat program is intended to acknowledge the human side of caring for patients ... by nurturing the *spirit* of the interdisciplinary ... care team members."[6]

Finally, I would like to conclude with the program of staff support in my health care system. Even though this program has a twenty-eight-year history, it is still evolving. My office is on the main thoroughfare, adjacent to the hospital's chapel. The very first thing I did when I arrived was open the door. Staff saw this open door as an invitation to enter. I created a welcoming space with a sacred corner—a place for staff to come in and find peace and get away from the chaos and disorder of the hospital.

In the four years that I have served as the director of staff support, I have implemented some new programs as well as maintained traditional programs from our history.

## Traditional Programs

- **Annual holiday "Cookie Run"** (formerly known as the "Bagel Run"): This event is an opportunity to celebrate and honor our night and weekend staff who often feel the most neglected within our system.
- **Blessing of the hands:** Every year during nursing and health care workers' weeks, we do a blessing of the hands of all staff.
- **Services of remembrance:** These services invite staff to remember and honor patients, coworkers, and family members who have died. Services are offered in the chapel and in clinical areas.

- **Special services in the chapel:** Services are offered during holy days and Martin Luther King Jr. Day. Memorial services are also offered throughout the year for deceased staff.
- **Critical incident debriefings:** We provide debriefings for staff following critical incidents.
- **Staff support and grief groups:** These groups are requested and offered by chaplaincy staff as needs arise.
- **Individual support for staff:** Spiritual and emotional support is offered to staff as needed. Staff are referred to our EAP program when appropriate.
- **Conflict mediation:** Managers and directors often consult with me when their staff is in conflict. I serve as a mediator and help staff reconcile their differences.

## New Programs Implemented Since 2006

- **Spiritual care grand rounds:** These were implemented in December 2009. Topics include working with complicated patient and family situations; moral distress; patient- and family-centered care.
- **Educational in-services:** These focus on clinical areas of team building, conflict management, cultural diversity, communication, compassion fatigue, moral distress, self-care, grief, and loss.
- **Collaborative training:** We provide educational in-services with our EAP program.
- **Centering and meditation service:** This is midweek for staff.
- **Evening and weekend staff support chaplains:** The chaplain for our main campus was hired in January 2007; the chaplain for our midtown campus was hired in September 2010.
- **Ethics grand rounds:** The executive director of our Pastoral Services Program is the chair of ethics for our health care system. These grand rounds have been in place at our Geriatric Center since 1991. We implemented them for our other hospitals in 2009.

- **Creative arts program:** This program will be implemented in 2011. The aim is to offer opportunities for patients, family, and staff to find renewal through a variety of artistic modalities, including but not limited to music, visual art, literature, and movement.
- **Consultant to nursing leadership and hospital administration:** I meet with the chief nursing officer and chief operating officer quarterly to address staff issues and concerns.

## *Future Vision*

Our center has had a designated chaplaincy staff support program for the past twenty-eight years. An article written by Fred L. Smoot and Donald E. Wells in 1985 discusses how the program got started.[7] The literature review revealed two other designated staff support programs within pastoral care departments, one in Canada[8] (implemented in 1996) and one in Indiana[9] (implemented in 1980). It is clear, however, from the literature, collegial input, and personal experience that spiritual care of staff is important. It is my belief that staff support should be done by chaplains hired specifically for staff support. I further believe that staff support training should be included in every CPE curriculum. I invite directors of pastoral care and CPE training programs to advocate for staff support programs within their institutions and for funding for a designated chaplaincy position(s). The staff support program will be a visible reminder to health care administrators of the importance of caring for the soul and heart of staff who care for patients and families within their health care institutions. A lot of research is being done on creating healthy work environments. It is my belief that caring for staff is primary to creating this healthy work space.

### Notes

1. Walter Wink, *The Powers That Be: Theology for a New Millennium* (New York: Doubleday, 1998), 4–6.
2. Pamela Gray-Toft and James G. Anderson, "Stress among Hospital Nursing Staff: Its Causes and Effects," *Social Science and Medicine* 15A (1981): 640–41.
3. Jacqueline Medland, Josie Howard-Ruben, and Elizabeth Whitaker, "Fostering Psychosocial Wellness in Oncology Nurses: Addressing Burnout and Social Support in the Workplace," *Oncology Nursing Forum* 31, no. 1 (2004): 4.

4. Dick Haines, e-mail message, November 10, 2010.
5. Stephen D. King, Debra Jarvis, and Marilyn Cornwell, "Programmatic Staff Care in an Outpatient Setting," *Journal of Pastoral Care and Counseling* 59, no. 3 (2005): 263–73.
6. Medland et al., "Fostering Psychosocial Wellness," 50–53.
7. Fred L. Smoot and Donald E. Wells, "Staff Support Services: Room by the Side of the Road," *Journal of Religion and Health* 24, no. 2 (1985): 167–73.
8. Deborah R. Damore, John A. O'Connor, and Debby Hammons, "Eternal Workplace Change: Chaplains' Response," *Work* 23 (2004): 19–22.
9. Pamela Gray-Toft and James G. Anderson, "A Hospital Staff Support Program: Design and Evaluation," *International Journal of Nursing Studies* 20, no. 3 (1983): 137–47.

## Further Reading

Burke, Sylvia, and Ann R. Matsumoto. "Pastoral Care for Perinatal and Neonatal Health Care Providers." *Journal of Obstetric, Gynecologic and Neonatal Nursing* 28 (1999): 137–41.

Haines, Richard B., and Bobbye T. Cohen. "When the Caregiver Needs Care: A Review of an Interdisciplinary Team Response to Stressful Events in a Tertiary Care Setting." *Journal of Pastoral Care* 54, no. 2 (2000): 167–72.

Pullman, Darryl, and Bill James-Abra. "Care for the Caregiver: Effective Pastoral Support for Nursing Home Staff." *Journal of Pastoral Care* 55, no. 1 (2001): 35–45.

## About the Contributor

**Rev. Robin C. Brown-Haithco, MDiv, ACPE Supervisor,** is the director of staff support at the Emory University Hospital in Atlanta, Georgia. This program is located in the Pastoral Care Department. Prior to assuming the position at Emory, Rev. Brown-Haithco was the director of chaplaincy and CPE at the Grady Health System. Her publications include "Standing on Holy Ground: The Vocation of Pastoral Supervision," in *Journal of Supervision and Training in Ministry*, and "Decisions at the End of Life: A CPE Supervisor's Personal Reflection," in *Journal of Pastoral Care and Counseling*. She also presented a paper titled "Effective Pastoral Care in HIV / AIDS Contexts" at the McAfee School of Theology in 2007 and at the New Baptist Covenant Celebration in 2008. Rev. Brown-Haithco is ordained in the American Baptist Churches, USA.

# 16

## Gender Issues in Pastoral Care

*Bishop Dr. Teresa E. Snorton, MDiv, DMin, BCC, ACPE Supervisor*

Academics, the clinical setting, and most of society have come to recognize gender as a distinct factor in determining an individual's perception and experience. Thus, the idea that gender has an impact on how pastoral care is given or received should not be surprising.

It is tempting here to elaborate on the origins of gender differences, particularly from the spiritual texts, such as the Bible. As enticing as that may be, the purpose of this chapter is not a theological discussion, but a practical discussion of the gender issues in pastoral care that bear attending, in order to provide effective, relevant pastoral / spiritual care.

Maxine Glaz, noted pastoral theologian and author, reminds us about the inherent bias toward males found in traditional pastoral theology, which is dependent on both classical psychological and developmental theories. From Glaz's perspective, paying attention to the broader, more inclusive notion of gender that includes both male and female perspectives is crucial. "Because pastoral theology has given credence to psychological theology and because a male psychological bias exists, we must also critique the male norms within pastoral thought and practice. We can learn from new interpretations of women's psychological experience just as we do from current discussion of gender issues in the fields of biblical studies, church history, and theology."[1] Therefore, the consideration of gender issues in pastoral care is a corrective to traditional praxis that may have included male bias, but more importantly, such consideration is toward a more inclusive understanding of the dynamics of pastoral care relationships, which include male and female caregivers, as well as male and female care receivers.

There is little evidence to suggest that gender determines such things as intelligence or emotional and psychological characteristics. Nevertheless, there are ways in which the spiritual care provider must pay attention to the real ways in which persons are different. Our attention is not just on biology, but also on cultural definitions that have been imposed because of one's gender. We must pay due attention to the ways in which those definitions impact people's perception of their experience, and hence their needs for spiritual care.

## *Definitions*

A number of traditional definitions will be helpful in this discussion, particularly definitions of gender identity and gender roles. "Sex" refers to the biological distinctions between male and female, characterized by the genitalia, sex chromosomes, and hormones. "Gender," on the other hand, refers to the personality traits ascribed to persons based on their sex. Gender identity can actually be subdivided into two different constructs: gender identity as determined by biology, and gender identity as determined by personal choice. In actuality, while one's sex is determined by biology, gender is an overlay of a cultural definition of what those biological differences mean and how they manifest themselves within the culture. So, the first way in which we can understand gender is as a culturally defined construct based on one's biological sex. Male and female are the typical ways in which this construct of gender is subdivided and are often referred to as one's gender identity.

However, it is important for the spiritual caregiver to recognize that individuals often modify their gender identity. Subcultures may also make alterations to traditional definitions of gender. Transsexuals, for example, are persons who have chosen to identify themselves with the gender opposite from the one that their sex would suggest. In addition, the majority cultural group or the individual herself may identify a person as a "tomboy," as a way of suggesting that a person (a female in this case) has embraced an identity that is opposite from her sexual identity. If the premise of spiritual care is to "meet people where they are," then the responsible care provider cannot afford to ignore the gender identity that is embraced by the person, not just the one that is culturally imposed.

A definition of gender roles, as determined by culture, is also critical to formulating effective spiritual care. Hand in hand with culturally defined gender identity is the notion that the culture then defines the roles for each gender. Gender role socialization is imparted by the society through parenting, peer relationships, education, religion, and the media. Such socialization may be overt (e.g., cheerleading and gymnastics summer camps for girls, and baseball and basketball summer camps for boys), though much of it is covert and even unconscious. Yet, through repetitive messaging, individuals embrace (or reject) the assigned gender roles and live out their experiences through those assigned roles.

It is important for the spiritual caregiver to give appropriate note to the way in which gender identity and gender roles play a part in the unfolding story that is revealed through the pastoral care encounter. Persons often have feelings of guilt and shame when they have not lived up to the gender role expectations or when they have rejected them. Religious and doctrinal beliefs may add to their sense of guilt and shame. Individuals may attempt to live into the gender roles assigned to them, stifling emotions that are appropriate to the current experience, but perceived by the larger culture and the individual to be inappropriate for one's gender (e.g., a male who just received bad news being reluctant to cry).

As cultures change, so do gender descriptions. The effective spiritual care provider must also recognize that such change often means that individuals struggle with how to behave and how to express themselves, out of a desire to be socially / culturally appropriate, but unsure what is appropriate in the current circumstances. The spiritual care provider or chaplain is often privileged to accompany persons in their initial experience with crisis, illness, and death. And in such uncharted territory, the individual may add to the task by attempting to define what is the gender-appropriate response to the situation. A skilled pastoral provider's intervention can facilitate the individual in a process of transcending the social / cultural expectations of gender in general, to the discovery of the individual's inner and outer emotional, physical, and spiritual needs.

## The Spiritual Care Encounter

The spiritual care encounter is a typical communication loop that involves messages between the care provider and the care receiver. Figure 16.1 suggests the way in which this takes place.

Both caregiver and care receiver have internal and external gender perceptions of themselves as well as of one another. The care receiver may or may not be aware of these perceptions. To provide appropriate professional spiritual care, the caregiver must be aware of these perceptions—both his or her own and those of the care receiver.

### Care Receiver to Caregiver Issues

In addition to being aware of the gender identity and gender role issues that may be operative in the care receiver's life, there are some particular dynamics that the spiritual caregiver must be able to recognize and assess in the pastoral care encounter. The first is transference reactions. In the *Dictionary of Pastoral Care and Counseling*, John Patton writes that transference

> is the human tendency to relate to persons in the present as if they were persons from the past. Psychologically, in the minds of others, a pastor is not only an individual human being but also a representative of other significant authority figures—parents, teachers, and so forth. This means that parishioners and counselees often relate to him or her on the basis of their experiences with other authority figures who were important to them. A parishioner may be "in love" with her or his pastor or feel rejected by her or him because of prior rejecting experiences.[2]

Transference reactions can lead to a variety of behaviors toward the caregiver—erotic (as in Patton's description), dependent, or hostile. These three manifestations of transference, according to Sigmund Freud, who coined the term, relate to the parent-child relationship and any unresolved conflicts within that relationship.[3] In applying Freud's ideas to theology, Loomis suggests that transference is related to a person's relationship and unresolved conflicts with God.[4] Thus, the spiritual caregiver and the pastoral relationship become the arena in which these conflicts are acted out, since the caregiver becomes God's representative in the pastoral care encounter.

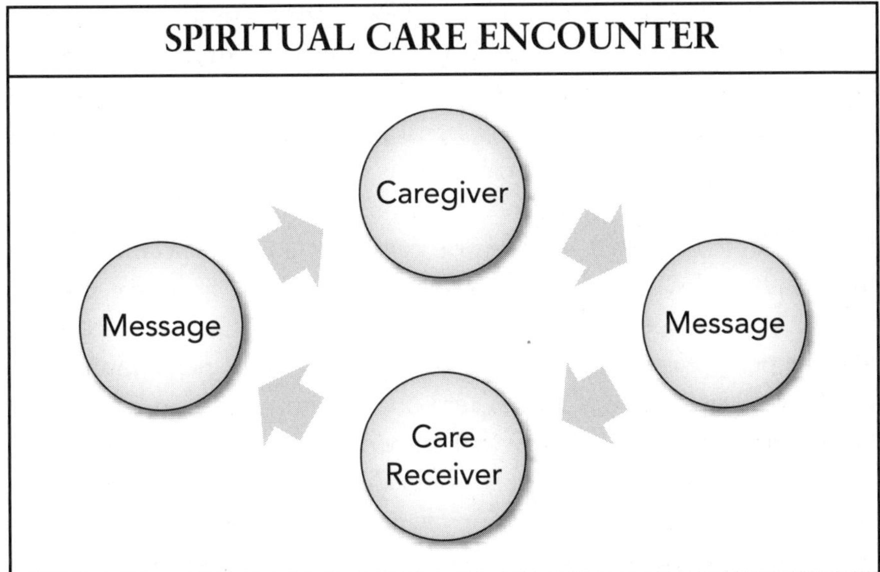


*Figure 16.1*

Harry Stack Sullivan preferred the term "parataxic distortions" as a broader way of talking about transference as it occurs in all relationships, not just in a psychotherapeutic relationship.[5] Sullivan's expanded way of viewing transference is helpful to the pastoral caregiver in recognizing that a number of kinds of relationships in the care receiver's past may be influencing how the current pastoral relationship is being perceived. For example, transference may relate to relationships with persons perceived by the individual to be persons of authority (teacher, police, judge) or relationships with persons to whom one feels inferior (an abusive spouse, a demanding boss).

The task of the spiritual care provider is to be *aware* of transference reactions and *intentional* in formulating a response to them. Patton advises: "Although pastors who have become skilled in psychotherapy have been supervised in using this 'transference' from the past in their work, the relatively untrained pastor deals with this phenomenon by concentrating upon the practical dimensions of the problems presented rather than the relationship with the counselee."[6] The professional spiritual caregiver should be somewhere in between the skilled psychotherapist and the untrained pastor, able to recognize the transference dynamic and determine its impact on caregiving. Intentionality means that the caregiver will be aware of but may choose to ignore the transference dynamics, may choose to address them verbally, or may choose to address them behaviorally. The key is that the caregiver incorporates the transference dynamics into a spiritual care response and care plan that will meet the real and current needs of the care receiver.

In addition to transference reactions, there are core and cultural beliefs that may impact the pastoral care relationship, specifically, sexual beliefs and sexism. The caregiver must note and listen for ways in which the care receiver's sexual beliefs may impact the crisis experience and the perception of the need for care, as well as the perception of the caregiver. The receiver's beliefs may make him or her uncomfortable talking about parts of his or her experience. The receiver may feel embarrassed or ashamed to talk about details of his or her life experience that are sexual in nature or intimate. He or she may have conscious or unconscious "rules" about such personal self-disclosure. The gender of the caregiver may complicate the care receiver's ability to be transparent and open. The caregiver must be sensitive to these dynamics and monitor them, so they do not become an impediment to the pastoral care relationship. Referrals are mandated when the impediment is too great to dispel.

The care receiver's experience with sexism could also have an impact on the pastoral care relationship. Women, who have been taught by the larger culture that they are inferior and that their concerns are secondary, may have difficulty expressing their needs. In describing the experience of women who have experienced systematic sexism at the social and personal level, Mary Field Belenky writes of these silenced women:

> The actions of these women are in the form of unquestioned submission to the immediate commands of authorities, not to the directives of their own inner voices.... Feeling cut off from all internal and external sources of intelligence, the women fail to develop their minds and see themselves as remarkably powerless and dependent on others for survival. Since they cannot trust their ability to understand and to remember what was said, they rely on the continual presence of authorities to guide their actions.[7]

Caregivers must be able to assess whether dynamics of sexism are operative and hindering the mutuality that is essential in the pastoral relationship.

Women who have experienced sexism may need permission to explore and reflect, two processes that are often assumed as the norm by professional caregivers who have been saturated in an environment that affirms the development of an inner authority.

## Caregiver to Care Receiver Issues

When care receivers express their transference issues, there is the danger of a countertransference reaction from the caregiver. Broadly, countertransference is understood as the unconscious reactions of the caregiver toward the care receiver, the opposite direction of transference. Some theorists suggest that countertransference is related to the caregiver's unresolved issues, while others suggest that it is purely related to the caregiver's responses to the transference reactions of the care receiver. Third, countertransference is sometimes understood as any emotional response that the caregiver has toward the care receiver.[8] Regardless of which of these dynamics may be operative, it should be clear that the caregiver must be proactive in monitoring and diligent in addressing all countertransference issues.

When it comes to issues of gender, the caregiver must examine his or her beliefs about gender, including the social, cultural, and religious values to which one has been exposed as well as embraced. This kind of careful scrutiny of one's core and cultural beliefs is vital in minimizing the possibility that one's own unresolved issues related to gender (or sexuality or sexism) would interfere with the pastoral relationship. In addition, the ability to recognize transference reactions is vital in crafting an appropriate response to the transference, rather than blindly responding to the distortions of the care receiver. Finally, the effective caregiver will utilize consultation as a venue for addressing countertransference and other emotional responses to the care receiver and his or her experience. This kind of personal accountability is a prerequisite to the institutional, ecclesiastical, professional, legal, and ethical accountability that is incumbent upon the spiritual care provider who provides care "in the context of complicated issues and potentially compromising situations."[9]

Another caregiver issue that bears attending is "caring style." According to David Augsburger, every culture has a preferred metaphor for what it means to help, to be helped, and to change. In his book *Pastoral Counseling across Cultures*, Augsburger examines the following list of cultural metaphors:[10]

- **Hide-and-seek:** Inducing the patient to look for the secret of his or her distress with the help of the caregiver
- **Choice and change:** Helping the patient discover choices, embrace the idea of change, and make corrections
- **Sanctioned retreat:** Encouraging a respite from life tasks, social accountability, communal expectations, and personal responsibility to allow for reorganization of one's life process and a reintegration of values
- **Teacher and student:** Elements of learning, unlearning, and relearning are employed to help patient with values, worldviews, belief systems, life goals, and a sense of meaning
- **Scientific technique and skill:** Using therapeutic techniques in concert with the relational qualities of caring
- **Therapeutic communication:** Using a shared frame of reference along with presence, self-disclosure, opening up to the other, sharing in suffering, reconciliation, and mutuality
- **Healing relationship:** Using warmth, empathy, genuineness, and unconditional positive regard
- **Human transformation:** Facilitating deep change
- **The healing community:** Using a positive network of persons (e.g., family system, support groups) to enable health, growth, or human transformation
- **Host and guest:** Understanding the relationship with the counselee as host (who owns the life story and human experience) and the counselor as guest, both respecting the principle of hospitality
- **The wounded healer:** Using one's woundedness (vulnerability) *and* healing powers to help another

Augsburger urges the caregiver to be aware of the preferred metaphor of the care receiver. In addition, an awareness of one's own preferred style is assumed and necessary. The ability to employ multiple styles, dependent on the cultural view and needs of the care receiver, is an essential pastoral skill. This kind of development of the "intercultural pastoral counselor" results in a caregiver who is "aware of values—their nature, universality, uniqueness, variety, and power in directing life—and sensitive to the core values of culture, group and person" and "aware of the inequities of gender roles, sensitive to the exploitation and abuse of women, and committed to work for justice and the liberation of all who suffer oppression."[11] If the caregiver's preferred caring style is incongruent with the care receiver's preferred metaphor, confusion and frustration are the likely result, rather than care and compassion.

## *Cultural Impact on Gender Definitions*

The cultural impact on gender definitions, from the perspective of both the caregiver and the care receiver, must be understood as an evolving, rather than a static, process. Cultures have a tendency to accept some level of inconsistency within its own gender definitions. Age, socioeconomic status, or religion may allow for variations in gender definitions. The male-female definitions for school-age children may vary from those for adults or senior citizens. Persons of means (e.g., economic, education) may be permitted to function as males and females differently from persons of lesser means in the same culture. For example, the gender definitions for men and women in African American life in the pre-civil rights years varied significantly from those for men and women of the majority culture of the same era. Cultures that are or are becoming multicultural may (or may not) affirm gender differences based on religious beliefs. For example, American culture to a great extent accepts the differences assigned to women who are Christian versus those who are Muslim, in terms of dress, family, and social life.

The competent spiritual care provider will always be aware of the emerging cultural patterns of the current geographical location of one's pastoral care. In addition, any particular locale may have multiple cultural value systems operative within the culture—some generational, some ethnically or similarly defined. The spiritual care provider's initial orientation to the community in which he or she is working should include a thorough survey of these kinds of definitions and dynamics, including those that are historic, those that are present, and those that are emerging.

## *Common Dynamics in the Health Care Setting*

In the health care setting, the caregiver's first task is to understand the depth of authority that he or she inherently represents for the patient / resident and patient's / resident's family (both biological and as defined by the person you are working with). Some of this assigned authority may also be embraced by the health care staff. While the caregiver may perceive him- or herself as having modest or moderate authority compared to that of physicians and other members of the medical team, for patients / residents and families, the spiritual caregiver's symbolic authority as a representative of God (or the transcendent) unquestionably puts the burden on the caregiver to simultaneously be open to all gender definitions and expressions and be present as "neutral" in terms of expectations for the person and the family. This is a fine line to walk, as the caregiver also is an embodied self who will be perceived as male or female, as well as bound by his or her own maleness or femaleness or sexuality. Maintaining the authentic self, open to the authentic selves of others, who may or may not experience gender congruence within their own cultures, is the foundation for all spiritual caregiving.

Another dynamic that requires attention is the operative patterns of relating among the staff and other caregivers. Given the historic male-female dichotomies assigned to the doctor-nurse dyad, issues of authority, respect, and communication among the medical caregivers not only impact their relationships to each other but also have the potential to impact how patients' / residents' experiences are being interpreted, how medical decisions are being made, and how care is being offered. As a part of the medical team who stands outside of the medical team, the spiritual care provider's input and guidance can assist the staff in maintaining an environment of care that is embracing of (rather than judging or suppressing of) all individual and cultural gender expressions. For example, during the early years of the emergence of AIDS-related deaths, spiritual caregivers who were willing to suspend and challenge judgments being made by the larger community about homosexual persons were instrumental in helping medical personnel, as well as families, maintain openness to the physical and emotional needs of those patients. Over the years, mothers of sick children, previously regarded as a problem or complication for the care team to manage, have been more positively enlisted as a part of the child's care team, as the care team has evolved in being more diverse and more embracing of the different modalities of holistic care. The spiritual care provider, as a part of the interdisciplinary (holistic) team, reinforces the notion that physical care is not the only task in the health care setting. Nurture and community / family care join physical and spiritual care to provide an approach to the whole of the person's life. The spiritual caregiver is often the bridge between the two, encouraging the "high-tech" medical team members to join hands with the "high-touch" family and community in caring for the patient.

A final dynamic to note in the health care setting relates to the evolving and emerging changes to gender definitions within the larger culture. For years, male and female have been sufficient gender distinctions within most cultures. However, as homosexuality has been less hidden, the vocabulary of gender has expanded to include gay, queer, lesbian, and so on. In addition, transgendered persons, transsexual persons, or others who express their engendered selves in non-traditional ways have become more open with those self-definitions. The institutional setting, on the other hand, still primarily utilizes the male-female dichotomy as its primary gender definition. Fortunately, a number of issues that emerge from this gap in a multiply defined patient population and a dichotomously defined institution are being addressed by changes in health care. For example, where shared rooms used to be the norm, private rooms are quickly becoming the norm in newer health care facilities. Where shared rooms still exist, the institution must be prepared to respect the gender identity of the patient / resident. Spiritual care providers in behavioral health and correctional facilities, where shared accommodations and bath facilities remain the norm, may find themselves educating the institutional staff about these differences and helping the staff make appropriate adjustments for, increase their sensitivity to, and amend their judgments about patients or clients who want to be identified with a gender other than that suggested by their genitalia. Because of religious beliefs, these kinds of situations are often highly charged and filled with tension. Yet, the spiritual caregiver can be highly instrumental in conveying the need and modeling care for all persons with professional integrity, regardless of our own faith community's beliefs on this subject.

## *Strategies for Addressing Gender Dynamics*

As the spiritual caregiver prepares for effective, relevant caregiving, there are a few strategies that can assist in maintaining an inclusive, welcoming posture. Without much elaboration on each, see these as steps that can be a part of the preparation for the professional chaplaincy process (i.e., clinical pastoral education), a part of preparation for chaplaincy in a specific setting, as well as a part of preparation for the individual pastoral encounter:

1. **Be aware of your own gender issues.** *Example*: I was not aware of how my own pain about divorce was operative in my spiritual care until the day I said to a patient who was sharing the pain in her marriage, "Men are just like that."
2. **Be open to differences in gender definitions, identity, and expressions.** Read, learn, be informed. Understanding is not the same as acceptance. The care provider can still have his or her personal beliefs but must discover an inclusive framework and model for care.
3. **Assess potential problem areas in advance.** *Example*: I once worked in a psychiatric facility for adolescents. We were unprepared for our first transsexual patient, a biological male who did not want to shower with the other male patients.
4. **Be prepared for assumed problem areas not to emerge and for others not anticipated to emerge.** No matter how much preparation we make, it is difficult to anticipate every possibility. For example, there are cultures in the United States where unofficial polygamy is accepted, in addition to those we traditionally are aware of.
5. **Know the cultural specificity about gender of the primary ethnic, racial, and religious groups served by the institution.** A tool, called the culture-gram, can assist in gathering this kind of information. Local planning agencies and universities also have extensive demographic information about the local population. A number of texts—written for psychology, sociology, and religion—elaborate on the

cultural traditions and norms of many cultures, including gender roles and expectations.

6. **Ask questions for clarity and in a way that does not convey bias.** Rather than assume that an elderly woman would be "Mrs. Jones," ask, "What name do you prefer I use when I talk to you?"

7. **Expand your comfort zone, while maintaining cultural humility.** The effective spiritual caregiver will invest time and energy in exposing him- or herself to a variety of cultures, observing the gender dynamics and definitions of each, and cultivating the ability to respond to multiple expressions of gender. Finally, a posture of cultural humility means that the spiritual caregiver always sees him- or herself as learner. Mistakes will be made in addressing all the possible variations around gender in spiritual care. New information and awareness will be needed. Old assumptions will become dated. However, humility will enable us to learn, to extend apology, or to ask for help as we seek to meet the needs of the persons in our care.

## Notes

1. Maxine Glaz, "A New Pastoral Understanding of Women," in *Women in Travail and Transition*, ed. Maxine Glaz and Jeanne Stevenson-Moessner (Minneapolis: Fortress Press, 1991), 12.
2. John Patton, "Sexual Issues in Pastoral Care," in *Dictionary of Pastoral Care and Counseling*, ed. Rodney Hunter (Nashville: Abingdon Press, 1992), 1148.
3. Sigmund Freud, "Fragment of an Analysis of a Case in Hysteria," in *Complete Psychological Works* (London: Hogarth, 1953), 77–122.
4. E. A. Loomis, Jr., *The Self in Pilgrimage* (New York: Harper and Bros., 1960).
5. Harry S. Sullivan, *The Interpersonal Theology of Psychiatry* (New York: W.W. Norton, 1953).
6. Patton, "Sexual Issues in Pastoral Care," 1148.
7. Mary F. Belenky et al., *Women's Ways of Knowing: The Development of Self, Voice and Mind* (New York: Basic Books, 1986), 28.
8. Richard S. Schwartz, "A Psychiatrist's View of Transference and Countertransference in the Pastoral Relationship," *Journal of Pastoral Care* 43, no. 1 (Spring 1989): 42–43.
9. Naomi Paget and Janet R. McCormack, *The Work of the Chaplain* (Valley Forge, PA: Judson Press, 2006), 96–100.

10. David Augsburger, *Pastoral Counseling across Cultures* (Philadelphia: Westminster Press, 1986), 346–73.
11. Ibid., 372–73.

## About the Contributor

**Bishop Dr. Teresa E. Snorton, MDiv, DMin, BCC, ACPE Supervisor,** is the former executive director of the Association for Clinical Pastoral Education. She is a certified clinical pastoral educator (CPE supervisor) and a board certified chaplain in the Association of Professional Chaplains. She is an ordained minister in the Christian Methodist Episcopal Church and the presiding bishop of the denomination's Fifth Episcopal District. She is the first female to be elected by the CME Church to serve as bishop. Bishop Dr. Snorton has more than thirty years of experience in pastoral ministry, chaplaincy, and clinical pastoral education. She is coeditor, with Dr. Jeanne Stevenson-Moessner, of the book *Women Out of Order: Risking Change, Creating Care in a Multicultural World.*

# 17

# *Working with Community Religious Resources*

*Rev. Marcia Marino, DMin, BCC*

Health care facilities and chaplains regularly collaborate to offer resources to their local community. They do this in a variety of ways. This chapter is divided into two sections. The first provides specific ways in which you and your health care facility can work collaboratively with your local community. The second looks at resources offered by the religious communities for chaplains to use in their work.

## *Program Ideas for Collaborations between Health Care Institutions and the Local Community*

Health care facilities and chaplains have worked together offering a range of innovative workshops to educate local clergy. What follows is a sampling. The goal is to get you to think about what your facility can provide in your local community. To be effective and helpful, all projects and programs need to be tailored to individual locations and populations.

- HIPAA (Health Insurance Portability and Accountability Act of 1996) training is available for congregational clergy who need further information about appropriate ways of accessing information about hospitalized congregation members. This type of proactive outreach helps later when priests, imams, rabbis, ministers, and so on seek to find out specific information regarding their members when they are hospitalized, in a long-term care facility or are with a hospice program.

- With advancing technology changes in health care and the more visible presence of bioethics committees, hospitals have offered a variety of workshops on bioethics. Local clergy have the opportunity to reflect on some of the complex health care issues that come up before bioethics committees, including those around end of life.
- Hospitals have offered intensive workshops (sometimes known as a "cancer residency") where clergy have had in-depth conversations with cancer survivors, actually spent time on non-active radiation therapy machines in order to reflect on how that might feel for patients receiving radiation therapy, held tumors in their hands, and talked with immunologists in the hospital gene lab where the staff were growing cells to battle cancer cells. These types of workshops have had a profound impact on the pastoral care skills of clergy who attended them.
- Hospices, long-term care facilities, and hospitals have all offered workshops on death and dying to leaders of faith communities in order for them not only to become more comfortable with the concepts around death and dying, but also to have the chance to interact with dying patients / residents themselves. This writer witnessed clergy interviewing dying patients who were not their congregants. They had the opportunity to ask them pertinent questions, such as "What did your priest / minister / rabbi / imam do for you that was particularly helpful or not helpful?" "What do you wish that you might have received in care from your priest / minister / rabbi / imam?" "What do you celebrate about your spiritual life?" "What do you most regret?" Once again, these conversations had an enormous impact on the pastoral care of those clergy taking part in them. They were also quite moving for the dying patients who shared their spiritual story in a meaningful manner.
- Some hospitals offer clinical pastoral education (CPE) to interested clergy, religious, and laypersons. The largest and

oldest established certifying organization for CPE centers and supervisors is the Association of Clinical Pastoral Education (ACPE). Their accredited sites can be accessed at www.acpe.edu. Clinical pastoral education is "experienced-based theological education which promote(s) the integration of personal history, faith tradition, and the behavioral sciences in the practice of spiritual care."[1]

- Hospitals host multifaith activities during times of crisis. Many offered a multifaith response on September 11, 2001, that drew hospital staff, patients, and visitors to auditoriums and hospital chapels around the country. Chaplains of many faiths were able to provide comfort and inspiration by offering readings, prayers, inspiration, and a symbol of spiritual unity as they worked together to offer these services. Multifaith services happened again when the Indonesian tsunami struck in December 2004. People appreciate gathering in common need during times of crisis and stress.
- Health care facilities have trained advance care planning teams that include their chaplains. These teams provide both forms and training for filling out the forms. The teams travel into the local community to offer workshops and to hand out forms. After seeing a video regarding end-of-life decisions and perhaps listening to a panel discussion, the participants can then walk through the forms themselves and gain a deeper understanding of the potential decisions to be discussed with their family members and their health care agent. Workshops have targeted elders, large groups of people gathered in congregations, and groups in public library settings to help people give serious consideration to their end-of-life decisions.
- Chaplains also offer their expertise by taking part in community-wide crisis teams and disaster teams. They participate alongside other community volunteers at the scenes of major disasters (such as September 11) and other local disasters (such as a plane crash). They also provide follow-up for those who are grieving a loss after major events in a local community (e.g., the death of a high school driver, the

crash of a military reserve aircraft, a stillborn death, or the suicide of a college student).

## *Resources Offered by Religious Communities*

This chapter will now look at the resources offered by the various religious communities to chaplains, chaplain students, and clergy. In particular the focus is on religious and spiritual groups not usually studied in traditional seminary programs that have a focus on Judeo-Christian religions. With the continued influx of immigrants from around the world, it is helpful for chaplains to have at least a basic familiarity with the customs of a lesser known faith tradition in the United States and Canada in order to be familiar with proper religious etiquette when offering spiritual care to a member of that tradition.

Helpful websites include the following:

- Buddhism: www.buddhanet.net
- Ethical Culture Society: www.answers.com/topic/ethical-culture-society-for
- Hinduism: http://hinduism.about.com/od/basics/p/hinduismbasics/htm
- Islam: www.islam101.net
- Taoism: www.patheos.com/Library/Taoism/Beliefs.html
- Unitarian Universalism: www.uua.org

Chaplains learn about the diverse religious and cultural practices surrounding death and dying as they complete their training in clinical pastoral education and meet clergy of various world faiths. They might learn, for example, that many Jewish families do not use embalming, so funeral services will take place soon after a death. Also, cremation is not approved by many in the Jewish community.[2]

In the Theravadan Buddhist tradition, it is believed that cremation sets the soul free. The body is placed with the head pointing toward the west with an oil lamp beside it. Often a photograph is placed beside it. At some Buddhist funerals, the grieving loved ones will eat pumpkin and salt-fish. It is believed that pumpkin is good for the grieving heart and that the salt-fish replaces the body's natural salts, lost from crying.[3]

In the Hindu tradition, most rites are performed by the family. The head of the dying person is placed facing east, and she or he is encouraged to concentrate on his or her mantra. (Others may say it for her or him.) At the time of death, holy ashes or Vedic paste are applied to the forehead, and Vedic verses are chanted. The head of the person who has died is placed facing south, and the body is placed on a cot or laid on the ground, symbolizing a return to Mother Earth. Embalming and organ donation are forbidden. Religious pictures are turned to the wall.[4]

Taoists do not believe that death is the end of life. They see death as the transformation of life into the life of the soul. Thus, Taoists perform rituals for the soul. They help guide the soul to its new home. They believe that the soul of the person who has died is always watching over them. The sons of the person who has died symbolically wash the body of the person. They are washing away his or her past. The water that is used is seen as the waters that come from heaven. The body is then covered with seven layers of "longevity" clothing. This is supposed to help the body remain in as good a condition as possible for as long as possible.[5]

It is important for chaplains to be sensitive to specific communities in their area, so that they might offer effective spiritual care to them. Several communities will be discussed in this chapter as examples. You are encouraged to learn about the various faith and cultural communities that your facility serves so that you can provide better professional care.

## *Example*: Hmong Community

The Hmong community's culture, like the culture of every community that a chaplain encounters, requires attention and respect. Anne Fadiman addressed it in *The Spirit Catches You and You Fall Down: A Hmong Child, Her American Doctors, and the Collision of Two Cultures*:

> Failing to work within the traditional Hmong hierarchy, in which males ranked higher than females and old people higher than young ones, not only insulted the entire family but also yielded confused results, since the crucial questions had not been directed toward those who had the power to make the decisions. Doctors could also appear disrespectful if they tried to maintain friendly eye contact (which was considered invasive), touched the head of an adult without permission (grossly insulting), or beckoned with a crooked finger (appropriate only for animals).[6]

## *Example*: GLBT Community

The culture of the gay / lesbian / bisexual / transgendered (GLBT) community is diverse. I encourage you to read chapter 22, which is devoted to this community. Many members of the GLBT community have been deeply wounded by early childhood experiences where they felt judged or excluded by their religious communities. Thus, sometimes chaplains meet challenges in building relationships of trust with GLBT patients, especially when inpatients are hospitalized for short stays. It is important that chaplains maintain a welcoming stance and let GLBT patients know that they are available to them for spiritual support.

GLBT partners have serious concerns about recognition within a medical setting. It is important that they be recognized, respected, and taken seriously. Some GLBT patients may not be in contact with their families of origin. Others may have developed deep attachments to a "family of choice" over the years.[7]

Several denominations have developed websites that are supportive to members of the GLBT community. These websites can be located as follows and the list continues to grow:

- United Church of Christ: www.ucccoalition.org
- Presbyterian: www.mlp.org
- United Methodist Church: www.umaffirm.org
- Reform Judaism: http://rac.org/advocacy/issues/issuegl
- Unitarian Universalist Association: www.uua.org/welcomingcongregation

GLBT community centers have grown into hubs of recreational, political, and cultural GLBT activity in larger cities. These centers assist young people who are coming out, elders who are isolated, those who are struggling with addictions, members of the community who have been diagnosed with AIDS, people who want to network with other GLBT community members, those who are interested in organizing a pride parade, book groups, and affinity groups of all kinds. GLBT community centers can most easily be found via the Internet, a phone call to a local GLBT bookstore, or ads in the local GLBT newspaper.

## *Resources Offered by Pastoral Counselors*

Chaplains and chaplain students also benefit from the resources provided by pastoral counselors. These resources are helpful in two ways:

1. Chaplains are able to make referrals to pastoral counselors when they feel that patients are in need of in-depth counseling for depression or other serious issues.
2. Chaplains themselves might need occasional follow-up with pastoral counselors when dealing with multiple losses or protracted grief situations.

More information about pastoral counseling is available at http://aapc.org. See also chapter 9.

## Notes

1. Mission Statement of the Association of Clinical Pastoral Education, www.acpe.edu.
2. Guide to Jewish Funeral Practice, www.uscj.org/Guide_to_Jewish_Fune6211.html.
3. Buddhism Practices: Buddhist Funeral Rites, www.maithri.com/articles_new/Buddhism_Practices_Buddhist_funeral_rites.htm.
4. Rites of Transition: Hindu Death Rituals, www.beliefnet.com/Faiths/Hinduism/2001/02/Rites-Of-Transition-Hindu-Death-Rituals.aspx.
5. Religion's Perspective, http://library.thinkquest.org/11518/customs/taoism/death.htm.
6. Anne Fadiman, *The Spirit Catches You and You Fall Down: A Hmong Child, Her American Doctors, and the Collision of Two Cultures* (New York: Farrar, Straus, and Giroux, 1997), 65.
7. Wendy Peters, "Providing Spiritual Care to Gay and Lesbian Couples," *PlainViews*, http://plainviews.healthcarechaplaincy.org/archive/AR/c/v7n8/pp.php.

## About the Contributor

**Rev. Marcia Marino, DMin, BCC,** currently serves as the transition minister of the First Unitarian Church of Saint Louis, Missouri. She previously served as the regional director of pastoral care for Aurora Health Care in Milwaukee, Wisconsin. She is a board certified chaplain with the Association of Professional Chaplains. She is the Finance Committee chair and the interim treasurer for the Association of Professional Chaplains. She holds dual standing with the Unitarian Universalist Association and the United Church of Christ. She wrote "Living with a Big Heart," in *The Spirit: An Ecumenical Spirituality Newsletter*.

# 18

## *Transdisciplinary Relationships*

*Chaplain Linda F. Piotrowski, MTS, BCC*

Most health care clinicians are trained to work in a medical setting within health care systems that attempt to meet patients' needs mostly through medical interventions. As medical care evolves, health care professionals are gradually moving toward providing care that is biopsychosocial-spiritual in an attempt to meet whole-person needs. Rather than as a problem to be solved or a series of systems that are malfunctioning, the patient / resident is seen primarily as a person in a series of relationships.

From a philosophical point of view, Canadian Jesuit priest Bernard Lonergan (1958) has argued that when one knows (literally) any "thing," what one is really grasping is a complex set of relationships, whether that thing is a quark, a virus, a galaxy, or a patient.[1] Thus, sickness, rightly understood, is a disruption of right relationships.[2] It is not, as medical professor Dr. Daniel Sulmasy states, "looking at a bad body inside an otherwise healthy body."[3]

One of the cornerstones of philosophical anthropology is that human beings are intrinsically spiritual. This is based on the notion of the human person as a being in relationships.

Thus, one can say that illness disturbs relationships both inside and outside the body of the human person (Figure 18.1). Inside the body, the disturbances are twofold: (1) the relationships between and among the various body parts and biochemical processes, and (2) the relationship between the mind and the body. Outside the body, these disturbances

| INTRAPERSONAL AND EXTRAPERSONAL RELATIONSHIPS |
|---|
| **I. Intrapersonal:**<br>A. Physical relationships of body parts, organs, and physiological and biochemical processes<br>B. Mind-body relations—multiple relationships between and among symptoms, moods, cognitive understandings, meanings, and the person's physical state |
| **II. Extrapersonal:**<br>A. Relationship with the physical environment, including interpersonal—family, friends, communities, political order<br>B. Relationship with the transcendent |

Adapted from D. Sulmasy, "A Biophysical-Spiritual Model for the Care of Patients at the End of Life," special issue, *Gerontologist* 42, no. 3 (2002): 26.

*Figure 18.1*

are also twofold: (1) the relationship between the individual patient and his or her environment, including the ecological, physical, familial, social, and political nexus of relationships surrounding the patient; and (2) the relationship between the patient and the transcendent.[4]

## *Transdisciplinary Health Equals Collaboration*

Transdisciplinary health care involves reaching into the spaces between the disciplines to create positive health outcomes through collaboration. This model of care effectively integrates clinicians such as physicians, nurses, social workers, physical therapists, complementary and alternative medicine practitioners, physician assistants, community health workers, and other health care providers to create a team that provides comprehensive preventive primary care.[5]

Transdisciplinary care is a process by which health care professionals put aside their professional territoriality to listen and plan for the best possible care of a patient. In truly interdisciplinary care, others outside of the core care planning group (when possible, including the patient) are incorporated into the plan of care. Transdisciplinarity represents the highest progression in the process of patient care. Figure 18.2 illustrates a care continuum model.

As health care becomes increasingly specialized, care itself is in danger of becoming more and more fractured. Multiple specialties increase the possibility of communication failures. Patients and families become extraneous to the process of health care rather than the reason for health care. Time pressures and multiple responsibilities make it increasingly more difficult for health care providers to gather as a team to plan for patient care. However, the patient care plan remains the blueprint and the heart of a patient's road to health as well as a means of communication with community health providers.

The professional board certified chaplain plays a key role in patient / resident care. Both the key elements of spiritual care as well as the main responsibilities chaplains embrace put the chaplain in an excellent position to initiate, advocate, educate, and facilitate care planning meetings and / or patient rounds.

| CARE CONTINUUM | |
|---|---|
| *Unidisciplinary:* | Feeling confident and competent in one's own discipline |
| *Intradisciplinary:* | Believing that you and fellow professionals in your own discipline can make an important contribution to care |
| *Multidisciplinary:* | Recognizing that other disciplines also have important contributions to make |
| *Interdisciplinary:* | Being willing and able to work with others in the joint evaluation, planning, and care of the patient |
| *Transdisciplinary:* | Making the commitment to teach and practice with other disciplines across traditional disciplinary boundaries for the benefit of the patient's immediate needs |

Adapted from *UCPA Staff Development Handbook: A Resource for the Transdisciplinary Process* (New York: Bureau of Education for the Handicapped, United Cerebral Palsy Association, 1976).

*Figure 18.2*

A professional chaplain, as a fully integrated member of a health care team, is in an excellent position to advocate for excellence in healing. One way professional chaplains do this is by advocating for the establishment of care teams and regular interdisciplinary rounds. Membership on a care team varies depending on the services required to address the identified expectations and needs. An interdisciplinary team typically includes one or more physicians, nurses, social workers / psychologists, chaplains, pharmacists, personal support workers, and volunteers. Other disciplines may be part of the team if resources permit.

By actively participating on a team in the care planning process, a chaplain fulfills his or her role as educator and coordinator. Implicit in the role of coordinator is that of communication. Utilizing his or her assessment skills, the chaplain contributes insights valuable to other team members.

Transdisciplinary team care requires that each member summon the courage to address patient needs and speak from the expertise of one's own discipline while at the same time respecting the knowledge and insights provided by others from various disciplines. Patient care rounds as well as inter- and transdisciplinary team meetings are sacred times in which the inherent value and respect needed for each person—staff, team member, patient, and caregiver—are held as sacred. Disciplinary lines blur and at the best of times disappear as the group engages in uncovering what will best serve patient needs.

The interdisciplinary process is more than just several health professionals gathered around a table to discuss a patient. Rather, each sits down and, in essence, brackets his or her professional-discipline identity, places it to the side, and assumes the new identity of "team member." Integrated, smooth, coordinated, and congruent care, with the patient's immediate needs at the center of the effort, makes transdisciplinary care. Individuals come together without territorial professional boundary needs to guide their role and responsibilities. This is what makes it the highest form of care.[6]

Spiritual and / or religious beliefs can have a powerful impact in the clinical setting. This can include but is not limited to the following:

- Understanding of illness
- Making health care decisions (e.g., feeding tubes, advance directives, use of pain medicines, level of alertness)

- Choosing a support person or decision maker (might be clergy or spiritual care professional)
- Choosing treatments (e.g., medication use, prayer)
- Choosing treatment plans (e.g., chaplain referral, meditation, yoga, complementary therapies)
- Helping patients cope and deal with illness
- Developing resiliency of spirit
- Connecting to God / other as well as others in personal relationships
- Finding meaning, hope, love
- Finding social support
- Becoming comfortable with mystery, the unknown
- Reframing death to alleviate death anxiety
- Experiencing a sense of control over what seems out of control[7]

The chaplain member of a team brings awareness of all of these characteristics to the table but possesses the ability to listen at many levels to the various patient needs, contributing from his or her field of expertise related to spirituality and religion and considering the contributions of other team members.

## *Four Major Functions of a Chaplain*

Professional board certified chaplains have four major functions within a health care setting: (1) assessor, (2) advocate, (3) educator, and (4) coordinator. Each function is described with a focus on its role within a care team.

As **assessor**, spiritual care professionals (board certified chaplains):

- Focus on spirituality in context of clinical care
    - Serve the patient and care team by assessing all aspects of a patient's condition with a primary focus on spiritual assessment (board certified chaplains are trained to complete spiritual assessments)

- Identify resources, assess supports, pray, and celebrate rituals according to the patient's / caregiver's needs and desires
- Assist in training other members of the health care team to complete a spiritual care screen in order to:
    - Recognize spiritual themes, issues, resources of strength, and conflicts
    - Provide an environment where patients can share these concerns if the patients so desire (noncoercive)
    - Make timely referrals to other board certified chaplains

As **advocate**, spiritual care professionals (board certified chaplains):

- Focus on spirituality in the context of clinical care
- Take risks and stand up for the nontraditional path
- Navigate the work culture
- Use language and definitions that are broad
- Develop practical tools
- Support the mobilization of both religious and nonreligious spiritual resources in response to the stresses of illnesses, hospitalization, and treatment
- Support and counsel regarding goals of care and, when appropriate, end-of-life decisions

As **educator**, spiritual care professionals (board certified chaplains):

- Work with staff and in-services within the institution
- Model for and educate staff regarding spiritual care issues as they relate to palliative care
- Outside the institution:
    - Develop and deliver presentations
    - Present workshops
    - Serve on committees
    - Publish writings
    - Educate religious congregations

As **coordinator**, spiritual care professionals (board certified chaplains):

- Document and communicate their assessment, care plan, interventions, and ongoing work with patients through attendance at team meetings and through appropriate charting and other means of electronic and in-person communication
- Communicate with teams and other professionals within the medical setting
- Initiate, build, and sustain professional helping relationships
- Work with community resources
- Serve as a liaison with community-based religious leaders and communities to provide specific counsel and services consistent with the patient's religious traditions and beliefs (if requested by the patient or caregiver)

Transdisciplinary care advocates call for broadening our notion of primary care to include a multiplayer team working together to alleviate the burdens borne by patients with multiple comorbidities and extenuating social circumstances.[8]

Transdisciplinary care is the highest form of patient care planning. The board certified chaplain, by virtue of training and call, brings many of the necessary qualities to the group care planning process. In these days of heightened fiscal concerns and the demand for increased professionalism as well as productivity, the board certified chaplain is in a unique position to model the humility and maturity required to function in an interdisciplinary and transdisciplinary manner.

By advocating for patients' spiritual needs, assisting patients in making connections with faith communities, educating transdisciplinary team members, and alerting religious leaders and congregations to the critical role they can play in supporting patients and families in times of serious illness, death, and dying, the chaplain on the transdisciplinary team ensures that the patient and family receive the best care possible.

The chaplain on a transdisciplinary team fills many roles. The chaplain's primary responsibility to the patient is to complete a spiritual assessment, ensuring that the spiritual and religious needs of the patient and family are appropriately and professionally addressed.

Assessing a patient's spiritual needs is the way in which the chaplain can then fulfill other roles as advocate, educator, and coordinator.

Spiritual assessment completed, the chaplain becomes the patient's spiritual advocate, claiming a place at the health care table. Along with other team members, the chaplain assists in the development of a comprehensive care plan that acknowledges and incorporates the patient's spiritual needs (see chapter 5 for details on the care plan).

Education related to spirituality and religion and their role in patient care is an ongoing responsibility. It takes place through formal educational presentations throughout the institution and informally through interactions at the patient bedside and in transdisciplinary team meetings. Creating an awareness of the spiritual, training other team members to screen for patients' spiritual needs, and educating other team members regarding the necessity of referrals to the chaplain are all critical components of the ongoing education provided by the chaplain team member.

Transdisciplinary care is the highest form of patient care. Progressing through the levels of caregiving required to reach truly transdisciplinary care is a lifelong process. At times, teams move back and forth through the various levels. Truly transdisciplinary care is elusive. Each team member must remain open to learning from other team members, keeping the patient's needs and interest foremost, maintaining a sincere appreciation for one's team members, and respecting the patient's knowledge of his or her needs and resources. All of these actions contribute to the creation of transdisciplinary care processes and patient care plans that help the patient's consistent movement forward toward health and wholeness.

## Notes

1. B. J. F. Lonergan, *Insight: A Study of Human Understanding* (San Francisco: Harper and Row, 1958), 245–67.
2. D. Sulmasy, "A Biopsychosocial-Spiritual Model for the Care of Patients at the End of Life," special issue, *Gerontologist* 42, no. 3 (2002): 26.
3. Ibid., 25.
4. Ibid., 26.
5. C. Davis, "Philosophical Foundations of Interdisciplinarity in Caring for the Elderly, or the Willingness to Change Your Mind," *Physiotherapy Practice* 4 (1988): 24–25.
6. Ibid.

7. C. Puchalski, "Spirituality and the Care of Patients at the End-of-Life: An Essential Component of Care," *Omega: Journal of Death and Dying* 56, no. 1 (2007): 33–46.
8. B. Ruddy and K. Rhee, "Transdisciplinary Teams in Primary Care for the Underserved: A Literature Review," *Journal of Health Care for the Poor and Underserved* 16, no. 2 (May 2005): 248–56.

## Further Reading

*UCPA 1976 Staff Development Handbook: A Resource for the Transdisciplinary Process.* New York: Bureau of Education for the Handicapped, United Cerebral Palsy Association, 1976.

## About the Contributor

**Chaplain Linda F. Piotrowski, MTS, BCC,** is the pastoral care coordinator and chaplain for the Palliative Care Service at Dartmouth-Hitchcock Medical Center and the Norris Cotton Cancer Center in Lebanon, New Hampshire. Previously, she was the founding chaplain of the Pastoral Care Service at Central Vermont Medical Center in Berlin, Vermont, and regional director of spiritual care for the Covenant Healthcare System in Milwaukee, Wisconsin. Chaplain Piotrowski is coauthor of "Teamwork in Palliative Care: Social Work Role with Spiritual Care Professionals," in *Oxford Textbook of Palliative Social Work*. She is also published in *Living with Grief: Spirituality and End-of-Life Care*, the companion book for Hospice Foundation of America's (HFA) 2011 Living with Grief program.

# PART III

## *Spiritual / Pastoral Care with Special Populations*

# 19

## *Spiritual / Pastoral Care in Worlds Beyond*

### Ministry to International and Immigrant Patients

*Rev. Yoke Lye Kwong, BCC, ACPE Supervisor*

### *Losing the Baby*[1]

A two-year-old girl of Southeast Asian origin was brought into the pediatric intensive care unit after nearly drowning in the swimming pool that served the apartment complex where the family lived. Upon arriving at the hospital, the child was intubated and kept on the ventilator. Soon it was determined that the child showed little to no brain activity. The signs of life were dim and the beautiful Hmong child was declared brain dead. Imagine the depth of grief of the family, and imagine the utter helplessness and smallness the medical team felt.

To make things worse, in the midst of this profound loss were huge language and cultural barriers. The medical team was not equipped to address the real cultural needs of the Hmong, and the family was up against the formidable bureaucracy of an institutionalized medical culture. A clash of worldviews and cultures was about to happen.

As a medical community of spiritual caregivers along with nurses, physicians, and social workers, how do we mitigate cultural divides and language barriers effectively for immigrants who every day walk our cold linoleum hospital hallways and face white-lab-coat medical professionals entrenched in a medical culture so foreign to immigrants? Are we as "medical professionals" equipped to meet a world of many colors within our health care facilities? As immigration of peoples and cultures continue to grow exponentially in twenty-first-century America, can the spiritual caregiver or chaplain be an effective broker of cultures in the delivery of medical care?

## *The Future Is Now: Demographic Majority-Minority "Flip"*

In his book *Trails of Hope and Terror*, Miguel A. De La Torre writes:

> Why would people in their right mind pack up their family and their meager belongings to cross hazardous borders in order to enter a country with different customs, traditions, and languages?... As difficult as it may be for most of us to imagine leaving behind the country that witnessed our birth and the family that defined us for a new life in a strange land, more than two hundred million migrants (almost half women) throughout the world made this decision in 2008.... The modern movement of people across international borders, as a consequence and component of globalization, may very well become a defining characteristic of the new millennium.[2]

This is the reality. In the next ten to thirty years, the population in the United States will be unprecedented in its changing demographics. Immigrants from international countries will reach 54 percent, and single-race whites will drop in population from 66 to 46 percent. One in three persons will be Latino, and Asians will double to 9.2 percent. Immigrants will make up one in nine U.S. residents, one in seven U.S. workers, one in five low-wage workers, and one in two new workers. Seventy-five percent of the children in immigrant families will be U.S. citizens.[3]

The acute demand for cultural awareness in clinical settings is challenged by the fact that the number of minority physicians and medical students has not been increasing proportionately.[4] Medical schools are making attempts to respond by implementing cultural immersion programs and cultural competency curricula that include either a clinical rotation in a foreign country or local exposure with native communities. In 2002, 38 percent of U.S. medical students participated in international electives, compared with 6 percent in 1982.[5] Cultural competence curricula are typically case-based, small-group contexts on cultural issues and health beliefs of various ethnic groups, complementary and alternative medicine, language barriers, racism, classism, sexual orientation, age, sexism, and other factors. Research that documents the outcomes of cultural competency training is scarce. Hence, it is not clear whether medical students' abilities to be culturally relevant and sensitive to diverse patients have increased after they have gone through such programs.

"How shall we sing the Lord's song in a strange land?"

*¿Cómo cantaremos cántico de Jehová En tierra de extraños?*
(Spanish)

*Bagaimanakah kita menyanyikan nyayian Tuan di negeri asing?*
(Malay)

我们怎能在外邦唱耶和华的歌呢？
(Chinese)

Immigrants themselves already face enormous economic, social, language, cultural, and identity challenges simply by being in a country and culture that is not their own. These factors alone make accessing health care in the United States very difficult. For their prominent non-American accent, the color of their skin, and an overall unpolished non-American look, immigrants are perceived as uneducated, inferior, and poor. Thus, these real factors and perceptions bring about a great disparity in health care access between immigrants and the typical American. In fact, there is compelling evidence that race and ethnicity correlate with persistent health disparities. Many immigrants are not enrolled in health care programs due to the lack of an effective support system to help them navigate the health care bureaucracy. Many do not know how to apply, receive, and maintain health benefits from Medicaid due to these barriers.

The Joint Commission developed proposed accreditation requirements for hospitals to implement effective communication, cultural competency, and person / patient-centered care. Systematic strategic planning and execution of organizational cultural assessments and interventions with measurable outcomes are needed so that health care may be effectively delivered in a culturally relevant manner to diverse immigrant populations.

With the quickly changing demographics of America, the role of the spiritual caregiver / chaplain in health care must take on new ethical dimensions: (1) as an advocate for immigrants in accessing health care, and (2) as a cultural broker between the health care system and the patient / resident and family whose culture is different from ours.

The spiritual caregiver must become the embodiment of cultural humility. It is in that posture that cultural appreciation is nurtured, cultural knowledge grown, and the cultural broker raised. The cultural broker should understand differences in the hierarchy of needs between Western and Eastern cultures, especially immigrants of the latter, as shown below.

**Western Hierarchy of Needs—Abraham Maslow[6]**

- **Physiological needs:** hunger, sex, thirst, sleep, relaxation
- **Safety needs:** security, trustworthiness, reliability, consistency
- **Social mobility:** the need to climb the socioeconomic ladder
- **Social acceptance:** the need to be accepted in a bigger group
- **Esteem needs:** achievement, competence, independence, freedom
- **Self-actualization:** reaching one's full potential

**The Southeast Asian Hierarchy of Needs[7]**

- ***Pagkabayani*:** the need to be esteemed and revered
- **Social needs:** the need to be accepted in a bigger group
- **Social mobility:** the need to climb the socioeconomic ladder
- **Reciprocity:** the need to be reciprocated
- **Physiological needs:** hunger, sex, thirst, sleep, relaxation
- **Familism:** the need to belong

Spiritual caregivers or chaplains ministering to immigrant patients / residents and their families should refer to Figure 19.1 for simple yet important tips to follow when making the initial contact, establishing rapport, and developing a trusting and helpful relationship in the process.

## *Saving the Family*

It was as if the entire Hmong community had come—the immediate family, the extended family, relatives, and friends. Their faces downcast, their eyes a hollow stare with a feeling of uneasiness in the hospital setting they

| WORKING WITH IMMIGRANT PATIENTS / RESIDENTS | |
|---|---|
| **NEEDS / ISSUES / BARRIERS** | **INTERVENTIONS** |
| **Language:** The rights of limited English proficient (LEP) patients | • Use qualified interpreters. A language line may be used to ensure the patient-chaplain communication takes place.<br>• Do not use minor children, family members, or friends to provide medical interpretation / translation.<br>• Reminder: not all interpreters share the same belief system of the patient / family she / he serves.<br>• Reminder: all persons speak with an accent. |
| **Culture** | • Practice "cultural humility."<br>• Use a "cultural broker" to negotiate with the patient and health system toward a compassionate, holistic, and effective outcome. |
| **Name** | • Respect the patient's personhood by making an effort to pronounce her / his name in her / his language.<br>• Practice cultural humility by saying, "I need your help to say your name correctly." |
| **Meaning of illness** | • Remain curious and open about the patient's worldview and culture to learn about how they relate their illness with their spiritual heritage.<br>• A sudden death may be experienced as an attack by an evil spirit that takes a community to resist it by invoking a collective ritual. |
| **Support system** | • Identify and explore ways to bridge issues of disparity both internally and externally. Accommodation may be necessary so the patient / family can practice their rituals with their community. |

*Figure 19.1*

were not used to. Within the circle of the gathered community, the presence of one another communicated a quiet support for the family. The nurses and doctors were readying their best efforts to break the news on the hopeless situation and to explain "brain death." The Organ Procurement and Transplantation Network personnel were waiting.

The meeting unfolded with the ten-year-old brother of the patient interpreting until the arrival of the professional interpreter. The meeting ensued, the professional interpreter arriving and taking over the task of explaining "brain death" in Hmong on behalf of the medical team. The spiritual leader of the Hmong community had been requested and was on the way. The medical team and the interpreter, for fear of giving any false hope, conveyed the futility of shamanic interventions to revive the child. Tensions were high; grief was all around. Obvious distrust emerged from the Hmong toward the professional interpreter, who knew the language but missed the cultural nuances of community and honor and respect for traditional ways.

The on-call chaplain who responded to this crisis felt a great deal of helplessness due to the language barrier. His inadequacy bred a sense of powerlessness to advocate for the family spiritual leader to heal the child. It was at this juncture that the chaplain called me for support. I could not speak the language but was familiar with the Eastern worldview and culture of community and honor and so could act as a "cultural broker," to bridge between the medical team, their interpreter, and the grief-stricken Hmong and to negotiate a culturally supportive outcome for the family.

The presence of the spiritual leader validated the Hmong identity, tradition, and community. As "simplistic" and "senseless" the Hmong rituals were to hard, cold, scientific data, the ritual in the collective experience of the Hmong offered the family and community an anchor to tradition and gave meaning to their tragic loss. The presence of the community elder and the work of the spiritual leader did not revive the child, but immense healing was invoked upon the family and throughout the community.

The presence of the community elder was as vital to the family's and community's spiritual healing as, in the same situation, a Roman Catholic priest doing an anointing or a rabbi leading those gathered in the *Sh'ma* prior to death would be. As professional chaplains, our duty is to make sure that appropriate, culturally sensitive spiritual care takes place for all.

## *The Blessing*

I do not remember his name. He was a white physician who took care of a Chinese patient in room 8. The doctor paged me to make a visit with the patient because he knew I was Chinese. I learned that the patient was found on the road after being hit by a car. The physician said he needed my help to interview the patient. He stood on the right side of the patient's bed while I stood on the left. I reached out to hold the patient's hand and the physician did the same. The doctor began to speak with the patient in fluent Chinese Mandarin. However, the patient's face was turned toward me, looking into my eyes for connection. As the patient responded to the doctor's questions, the patient's eyes stayed on me. I came away realizing that a profound connection was happening for the patient on two levels: the doctor speaking with the patient in her own language, and my sense that she saw her face in mine. Upon reflection, I wrote this prayer:

Compassionate God,
Our God who understands the unspoken
Who knows the unexplainable
And touches those who are in despair
May I recognize the face of God in my patient's face
Just as she recognizes her face in my face.

Now may God's face shine upon you, and be gracious to you
May God lift up God's countenance upon you
and give you peace.
Amen.

*This chapter is dedicated to the loving memory of my beloved mother, Chung Sook. Her journey as an immigrant from China to Malaysia gives me courage and faith to overcome the unspeakable obstacles as an immigrant in the United States.*

## Notes

1. The story has been adapted to protect the true identities of the institution, patient, and family.
2. Miguel A. De La Torre, *Trails of Hope and Terror* (New York: Orbis Books, 2009), ix.
3. Quay Kester, "Medical Competency," (paper presented at an Evoke Communications workshop, 2010).
4. Genao I. Bussey-Jones et al., "Building the Case for Cultural Competence," *American Journal of Medical Science* 326 (2003): 136–40.
5. I. S. Mutchnick, C. A. Moyer, and D. T. Stem, "Expanding the Boundaries of Medical Education: Evidence for Cross-Cultural Exchanges," *Academy Medicine* 78 (2003): S1–S5.
6. A. H. Maslow, "A Theory of Human Motivation," *Psychological Review* 50, no. 4 (1943): 370–96.
7. Dennis Wayman, "A Model for Pastoral Care to Filipinos" (unpublished manuscript, 1998).

## Further Reading

Andrulis, Dennis P., et al. *Patient Protection and Affordable Care Act of 2010: Advancing Health Equity for Racially and Ethnically Diverse Populations.* Washington, DC: Joint Center for Political and Economic Studies, 2010. www.jointcenter.org/sites/default/files/upload/research/files/Patient%20Protection%20and%20Affordable%20Care%20Act.pdf.

## Resource

CDC Office of Minority Health and Health Disparity: www.cdc.gov/omhd/About/about.htm

## About the Contributor

**Rev. Yoke Lye Kwong, BCC, ACPE Supervisor,** is the director of spiritual services, Howard Regional Health System, Kokomo, Indiana. She is an Association for Clinical Pastoral Education (ACPE) supervisor and an Association of Professional Chaplains (APC) certified chaplain. She is the author of "Silent Cry: In Search of Harmony on Gold Mountain—The Yin-Yang Way of Pastoral Care," in *Women Out of Order—Risking Change and Creating Care in a Multicultural World,* and "The Integrity of Tao," in *Journal of American Association of Pastoral Counselors.*

# 20

## Pediatric Chaplaincy

*Rev. Dr. Dane R. Sommer, MDiv, DMin, BCC*

There is more to pediatric chaplaincy than playful encounters. For me, every day I spend in the hospital is an encounter with God. When I look at any child, I am reminded of what it means to be human. Who but a child can show us so much about what it means to be human?

Providing pastoral care for children who are critically injured or seriously ill or who are dying or have died is often a great existential and theological struggle. There are, indeed, many methods of providing pastoral care with children that engage them in playfulness and expression of their faith. This article, however, will focus on some of the elemental issues that are faced by chaplains in moments when families must face the unthinkable—unexpected pediatric illness up to and including the possibility of the death of their child. This article also reflects the reality that much of the pastoral care that occurs in a children's hospital is directed to parents, grandparents, and staff. There are four primary topics that will be addressed: children and suffering, theodicy, faith, and the suffering of chaplains.

### Children and Suffering

Anyone who works with extremely ill children is forced to observe and participate in human suffering. One cannot be close—in the room—when death is near to a child and not feel all the elements of suffering. It is different with adults. There are times, for adults, when death is welcomed, when it is a friend that takes us to a better place where all the pain of life goes away. Indeed, our efforts to build effective palliative care programs and our shift from aggressive end-of-life treatments to "allow natural death" declarations result from our desire to acknowledge that life has limits.

But it is not so with children. No one can stand idly by and just watch as a child suffers. Everyone is drawn into the pain and sorrow of the moment. Everyone is affected, touched, influenced by the sadness and sorrow that occur when a child is in pain or is afraid of what is happening. The primal mechanism of a child crying is designed to set everyone in motion to bring comfort and reassurance. We know, though, that sometimes just as it is almost impossible to stop a child's tears, it is also impossible to bring an end to a child's suffering.

That is because suffering has overwhelming power. We suffer when we are acted upon by a force or an entity over which we have no control. When we have control over something—whether it is pain, or treatment options, or the timing of treatments, or even whether or not we are treated—suffering is lessened. But when pain or nausea or exhaustion cannot be controlled, suffering raises its ugly head. Many years ago I sat with a seventeen-year-old girl who relapsed with leukemia for the fourth time. She talked openly about the prospect of dying without shedding a tear. She abruptly collapsed into the deepest spasms of sorrow when she came to the realization that her hair would once again fall out, the only thing that she felt she could not control if she pursued one last round of chemotherapy (which she inevitably did). Again, we suffer when we are acted upon by a force or an entity over which we have no control.

Sometimes children suffer because of the physical limitations that are part of their mortality. An infant is born three months early, before his or her lungs have had time to mature fully. The medical team uses the latest technological wizardry. Sometimes the lungs have enough time to grow, but sometimes they do not. An infant is born with a genetic or congenital anomaly, a toddler is diagnosed with Wilm's tumor, a teenager is diagnosed with an astrocytoma, or a young adult has a sickle cell crisis. We often know why these things happen but still do not know what to do to make them go away. Suffering occurs when there are no effective treatments. Suffering occurs when nothing can be done to help.

And sometimes the suffering that we witness is caused by one human acting on another. We protect children because of their innocence and physical weakness. Tragically, these are the reasons that children are often harmed by others. Horrendous injuries occur because adults ignore their responsibilities: seat belts ignored, cigarette lighters left out, handguns unlocked. We say that these injuries are the result of "accidents," but they are really not accidents at all; they are careless breaches of responsibility that cause suffering. Children are also harmed by non-accidental trauma. They are beaten, choked, thrown, burned, even drowned because a parent or caregiver has an egregious lapse of control. Children are harmed or even killed while being sexually abused by adults. In some of these situations, adults want to blame the children or say that children have control over what happened. Unfortunately, children have no control, and they suffer.

Whether the suffering is caused by the uncontrolled forces that affect our physical limitations or by the actions of one human harming another, there is a great need for pastoral care that recognizes how children suffer. Our presence—our complete presence—with an understanding of what has happened may be the only clear and truthful voice in the midst of many thoughts and opinions of why something has occurred. The pastoral voice can be the one voice that helps families move beyond quick clichés to an honest understanding of how fragile life can be. Our pastoral voice can be the source of compassion and justice when families want quick answers.

## *Suffering and Clinical Interventions*

There are two important interventions that can be offered in the context of pastoral care. Both are somewhat counterintuitive to what most people would think the role of the chaplain should be. First, we can express valid concern for the suffering of a child by not being quick to take away a perpetrator's sense of guilt. Guilt is the natural human awareness of wrongdoing. One stereotype of chaplaincy that needs adjustment is the perception that we are quick to comfort and forgive those who have done something wrong. In the context of a children's hospital, it may seem almost natural to help parents and grandparents not feel so bad when an accident has occurred. It may seem natural to say, "Everything will be okay," to a grandmother who didn't bother to make sure that a toddler was secured in a car seat as she sits in an emergency room after a motor vehicle accident. Or it may seem compassionate to say, "It's not your fault," to a father who left a handgun unsecured as he sits in a pediatric intensive care unit following a life-threatening gunshot wound. Every quick and easy answer actually impedes the personal journey through which individuals must go after their actions have caused harm to another, especially when the person who is harmed is a child. By withholding our absolution, we encourage others to look more closely at what has happened and how they may be responsible for the suffering of another.

Second, we can add our voice to the other clinical voices who give children and their families as many choices as possible. If we understand suffering as being acted upon by forces or entities over which we have no control, then all clinicians—and especially chaplains—must offer as much control to children as possible. Everyone must do everything that can be done to eliminate suffering, but the chaplain has a unique role of listening to the narratives of children. Sometimes the chaplain is the first clinician to learn that a patient is in pain or afraid. Sometimes we learn that a child's questions have not been answered. Sometimes we learn that there is a discrepancy between what a patient wants and what his or her parents want. Sometimes the chaplain is the first to suggest options: what to eat, how to play, what medications to take, and most important, what to believe. Our role can be instrumental in helping children and families figure out what they believe about the cause of their suffering and how God is present in their lives.

## *Theodicy*

Whenever there is an interface of children and suffering, there must be a discussion of theodicy. When I made the transition from working in a large adult facility to working in a children's hospital I was immediately struck by the frequency with which I found myself discussing with others the nature of God, such as:

- Where is God in the midst of all the suffering that occurs in a children's hospital?
- Why does suffering exist if God is present in our lives?
- Why does God seemingly allow suffering to occur in the lives of some children and miraculously lifts the burden from others?
- Why is God testing me with this enormous burden?

- What have I done to be punished like this?
- Why does God seem so distant?
- Why doesn't God do something about this?

Our culture, by and large, is one that reflexively causes us to raise these questions when we face suffering. We are a culture that is steeped in traditional theism, believing that God is all-loving, all-knowing, and all-powerful. We have a formulaic response to suffering. The formula gets expressed in a number of ways but usually manifests itself in sadness, guilt, and anger. We believe, for example, that since God is all-loving, all-knowing, and all-powerful, God could remove our suffering and chase death away if God wanted. Since God has not done this, we must not be expressing our beliefs strongly enough, or we must have done something wrong, or we must not be religious enough. Or maybe we just lack God's infinite wisdom. The focus of this interpretation is upon us, our humanity, our mortality, our imperfection that summarily becomes the cause of God's lack of intervention. Or, conversely, in a small number of cases, we believe that since we are good and righteous, God must be not-loving, not-knowing, or not-powerful. The focus of this interpretation is upon God, God's inattentiveness, God's capriciousness, God's vindictiveness. The great challenge is that *our culture has taught us to respond to our suffering with these formulaic responses; our culture has taught us these images of God.*

Sometimes this challenge means the chaplain becomes a real-life representative of God. We are there, in the room, when God is not. We try to extend ourselves to those who believe that they are unworthy of anyone's care, including God's. We try to be present for those who have given up on God. We try to be present in situations that are emotionally draining. It is often best to listen and affirm others who are struggling with the enormous burden that is caused by feeling guilt or estrangement because of God's immanence or transcendence. It is often best to allow others to confess that they feel abandoned or tricked by an inconsistent, unloving God. And yet, if we listen carefully to what parents are saying, and if we carefully define for *ourselves* how God is present in the midst of suffering and death, there is so much that we can say and do. Presence alone makes a difference. This is embodied by our not joining the rush of others to leave or find fault or cast blame. Simply expressing respect, openness, acceptance, and tenderness by our presence reminds others that they have not been completely abandoned. This open and affirming presence may help others feel—somehow—that "another" is present in the midst of their crisis. It is especially important for children and their parents.

The mistake that many clergy make is that they believe that presence alone is enough. A colleague once told me that it is best not to say anything when nothing can be said. This admonition addresses the reality that many clergy speak to others out of their anxiety because they, themselves, are uncomfortable with the experience through which they are going. Families experiencing the suffering of a child need someone who can speak directly to them. We are a verbal culture. Presence alone is often interpreted by others to be an affirmation of what they have said. Through prayers, rituals, explanations, and leadership, clergy have an opportunity to say, with appropriate emotion and repetition, that God *is* present in the midst of our most difficult moments. We can share that all human life is fragile and that death is never far from anything that is alive. We can share that God's power offers us the ability to continue to pray for a miracle and ask for God's help. Our presence and our words can help others rethink the manner in which they justify God's presence or lack of presence in their lives and in the suffering of their child. Chaplains, more than any member of the clinical team, can help families "rebalance" their understanding of how God is present in the midst of suffering.

## *Children and Faith*

Much has been written about spiritual and religious development of children and adolescents. Just as children grow physically in somewhat predictable ways, they also grow spiritually from one phase of thinking to another. It is helpful for chaplains to understand how children grow in their thought and faith. Rather than thinking of these changes as literal or figurative, it might be more helpful to think in terms of "helpful-God" versus "unhelpful-God." Sometimes a superhero God is exactly what a toddler or an adolescent really needs. And sometimes a lonely child just needs a God—a voice, a spirit, a promise—who will somehow bring comfort in the middle of a long night. The task of pastoral care is not to correct the logic or catechetical implications of a child's description of God, but rather it is to strengthen and encourage what a child believes.

It is helpful to understand that children often believe that they are the center of the universe. They believe in the power of their own magical thinking. Children often think that their thoughts and actions cause bad things to happen. Their sense of guilt can be much more pervasive than an adult's, thinking that God has caused their suffering because of something they did or did not do. If they become sick, they may think that their illness was punishment because they were bad. If a sibling gets sick, they may believe that it was because they had a random retaliatory thought, such as "I wish you would just go away and die!"

At times it is hard for children to express what they believe because they rely on the direction and instruction of parents and others. *It is imperative that pastoral care include open opportunities for them to talk freely about who God is to them.* Maybe this begins with a question like "Why do you think kids get sick?" or "How do you suppose all of this started?" Maybe it begins with a story: the forces of light and darkness, the struggle of good over bad, the story of creation, the story of restoration, the story of rebellion ... all of these stories are part of every faith group. And as the story is told and retold, we can ask, gently, sometimes repeatedly, what a child really believes about the world and what he or she really believes about God. Most of the time children will start talking about God as a powerful force who controls everything that occurs. But as they talk, their notion that God controls everything and causes everything may fade in importance to their understanding that God is a source of love, healing, and courage. It may be that our quiet intervention keeps us circling on an internal question as we talk with children and their parents: "Do they believe what they really believe?" Religious traditions and instruction are vitally important, but in the face of great personal struggles and in the face of suffering, everyone needs to get honest about who God is.

## *Our Own Suffering*

Pastoral care with children and their families causes us, the caregivers, to suffer. We are drawn into the suffering of children because of the unfairness and unacceptability of it. We are affected because there are times when we want to change the outcome of a situation but find *ourselves* powerless. There is little that we can do to compartmentalize or objectify the sadness and fear that are expressed by parents and others.

Their sadness and fear become our sadness and fear. And just as there are times when they get angry, we get angry also. Pastoral care with children requires disciplined self-scrutiny so that we can understand exactly how we are affected by all the suffering to which we are exposed. For many of us, it means developing the skill to separate what is happening to the children we see in the hospital from our own children. It may mean developing our own therapeutic relationship with a counselor or spiritual director so we have a place to go with our emotions and thoughts.

For most pediatric chaplains, this great challenge means developing a theological infrastructure that allows for children to be born and live in a world where suffering occurs. The need to reiterate, tweak, and reaffirm one's theology or belief over and over because of the challenges of theodicy can be physically and emotionally exhausting. Eventually it becomes almost impossible to be present when another child is coding or another child has died. The zeal and enthusiasm with which we started our first jobs just disappear. To be successful, we must be able to understand that God is present with *us* in our journey. Not unlike Jacob at the Jabbok, there are times when God wrestles with *us*, and then sends angels to show *us* the way. There are times when we are hungry and God gives *us* a small portion to help *us* get by. There are times when God sends strangers to *us* to bring *us* healing and hospitality … or a small cup of water. And sometimes, we just have to believe that God will be present with *us*—and with every child—no matter what we face.

## About the Contributor

**Rev. Dr. Dane R. Sommer, MDiv, DMin, BCC,** has been the director of Chaplaincy Services at Children's Mercy Hospitals and Clinics since 1987, where he is also the assistant director of Bioethics Policy and Practice. He is the founder of the Pediatric Chaplains Network. He is also adjunct professor of bioethics at the Kansas City University of Medicine and Bioethics. Rev. Dr. Sommer is the author of several articles related to children and illness, including "Exploring the Spirituality of Children in the Midst of Illness and Suffering," in *The Advocate*, and "A Premature Infant with Necrotizing Enterocolitis Whose Parents are Jehovah's Witness," in *Pediatrics*.

# 21

## *Behavioral Health*

*Rev. Michele J. Guest Lowery, MDiv, BCC*

It's ironic that behavioral health is considered a chaplaincy specialty, given our origins. Not only did Anton Boisen, pioneer founder of clinical pastoral education (CPE), start the first unit of CPE at Worchester State Hospital, a psychiatric facility, but he himself lived with schizophrenia. Many of the early CPE training centers were at state psychiatric hospitals.

Today, few psychiatric hospital-based CPE centers remain; behavioral health training for chaplains is largely limited to the occasional general hospital psychiatric unit rotation. Understandably, chaplains may feel ill prepared to serve those with mental disorders.

This chapter is divided into two sections. The first provides a brief introduction to behavioral health, including need-to-know basics for chaplains in this setting. The second section focuses on spiritual issues in behavioral health, including resources for effective ministry.

## *Basic Orientation to Behavioral Health Chaplaincy*

### What Is Behavioral Health?

"Behavioral health" refers to the field of mental health care. It comprises mental disorders (including substance-related disorders) and process addictions.[1] It represents a movement from focusing on illness symptoms to behaviors that can promote stabilization and wellness. This functional focus helps people find ways to live effectively in the midst of oftentimes profound illness, which blends well with a chaplain's role to help people find meaning and hope in and throughout all of life's circumstances. *(Note: Because of the literature abundance on addictions and spiritual care, the focus of this chapter will be mental illness.)*

## Understanding Mental Illness[2]

"Mental illness" is a collective term for a group of disorders that affect how a person thinks, feels, and / or behaves. Serious mental disorders compromise all aspects of a person's daily functioning—work, relationships, self-care. While what exactly causes someone to develop a mental illness is not fully understood, the following factors are to be considered:

- **Heredity:** There appears to be a genetic predisposition to mental disorders.
- **Biochemistry:** Brain chemistry imbalances are linked to mental disorders, which is why mental illness is considered a brain disease. These imbalances cause the brain's neurotransmitters—chemicals that allow brain cell communication—to malfunction.
- **Environmental factors:** Childhood trauma / neglect, relationship dysfunction / loss, substance abuse, and other significant stressors may trigger the onset of mental illness in vulnerable persons or exacerbate its symptoms.

## The Diagnostic and Statistical Manual of Mental Disorders (DSM)[3]

The *DSM* is a useful resource for learning about the various mental disorders. Published by the American Psychiatric Association, it provides diagnostic criteria, statistics, prognosis, and optimal treatment approaches for all mental disorders. It uses a multiaxial or multidimensional approach.

Axes I and II identify the specific mental disorders:

- Axis I covers clinical disorders (major mental illnesses), categorized according to patterns or clusters of symptoms. Examples include mood, psychotic, eating, and anxiety disorders. (See Figure 21.1 for a synopsis of major symptoms of and tips on working with people diagnosed with these clinical disorders.)

- Axis II covers personality disorders and mental retardation. Personality disorders are rigid, ingrained, self-defeating patterns of thought, feeling, and behavior that damage one's matrix of relationships. Examples include borderline, schizoid, dependent, and antisocial personality disorders.

The remaining axes identify contributing factors: Axis III, physical conditions; Axis IV, psychosocial stressors; Axis V, level of functioning.

## Stigma and Mental Illness[4]

Despite progress in the understanding and treatment of mental illness, misconceptions persist, fueled by media portrayals of people with mental disorders as violent, lazy, and / or unable to live productive lives. Many still attribute mental illness to moral weakness or personal failure. Some faith communities directly teach or subtly suggest that mental illness is rooted in wrong belief, inadequate faith, or demonic possession. Because of such misconceptions, mental illness carries a stigma, resulting in discrimination and marginalization, and discouraging people from getting treatment. Chaplains are not immune to these misunderstandings. We must address our own biases in order to help patients heal from whatever misconceptions they have internalized as negative core beliefs.

## The Importance of Language

The language we use about mental illness either contributes to its stigma or promotes understanding. Always observe the following language guidelines:

- Never label people with mental illness as "crazy," "loony," "split personalities," "frequent fliers," and other inappropriate descriptors. Such labeling perpetuates negative stereotypes.
- Avoid labeling people by their diagnosis. Instead of referring to someone with a specific mental illness as "a schizophrenic" or "a bipolar," identify her or him as "a person with schizophrenia" or "an individual with bipolar illness."

Remember, people with mental disorders often overidentify with their illness and thus struggle to see themselves in a fuller context. This can contribute to a diminished—and damaged—sense of self. By using respectful, "people first" language, we subtly remind them that they are more than their illness, thus creating a sacred space for remembered wholeness and thus healing.

## Group Focus in Behavioral Health

In general hospitals, chaplaincy largely takes place bedside, while in behavioral health settings patients are expected to participate in therapeutic groups and other milieu activities throughout the day. Spiritual care delivery is thus group-focused, with facilitation of spirituality (and other) groups a core chaplain function. Opportunities for individual work come from connections made in these groups and treatment team referrals.

## Boundaries Revisited

Boundaries take on especial importance in behavioral health given the impact of mental disorders on a person's perceptions, thought processes, and emotion regulation skills. Not only must appropriate physical, emotional, and spiritual boundaries be meticulously maintained, but also at times rigid boundaries are necessary to protect the sensibilities of vulnerable patients and / or keep people safe.

An example of this is therapeutic touch. While often encouraged in other health care settings because of its healing potential, touch can be provocative in behavioral health. People with autism spectrum disorders, for example, are hypersensitive to touch. For those with a history of physical or sexual abuse, touch can trigger painful memories. Sensory abnormalities and cognitive distortions complicate even incidental physical contact, which is why touch of any kind is discouraged in behavioral health, and in many settings, disallowed.

This can be challenging for chaplains accustomed to working in other settings, where care is often communicated through the holding of hands during prayer and other forms of healing touch. It is also challenging because many patients desire and expect such forms of touch from the chaplain.

In behavioral health, expect that any and every "button" you have will be pushed—and welcome this as both gift and task! Honing your observation and intuitive skills, practicing mindfulness, and being a committed student of self will help you navigate the sometimes maze of boundary challenges.

### Treatment Team Role

Given psychiatry and religion's uneasy history, chaplains sometimes feel the need to present themselves more like therapists than spiritual care specialists when interacting with treatment teams in order to gain respect. This is a mistake, as the value we bring lies precisely in our distinctiveness as clinically trained religious professionals.

Treatment teams are charged with both gathering the information needed for accurate diagnosis and developing treatment plans that maximize patients' recovery potential. While clinicians are experts in most aspects of behavioral health, they may have inadequate cultural and religious training and thus may pathologize some non-mainstream religious expressions, practices, or experiences.

For example, "religiosity" is often identified as an illness symptom, but clinicians may not always differentiate between certain devoted religious beliefs / practices and illness-mediated excesses / distortions. Professional chaplains can play a significant role on treatment teams by identifying normative cultural and religious values, beliefs, and practices and showing their adaptive value as recovery resources.[5]

## *Providing Effective Spiritual Care*

This section addresses spiritual needs, special issues, and spiritual care interventions.

### Spiritual Struggles in Behavioral Health[6]

Spiritual struggle is best understood in the context of holism, which affirms that humans are multidimensional and that the different dimensions of life (physical, emotional, mental, spiritual) are transactional, that is, they influence each other. When healthy, the spiritual dimension of life grounds us in hope and helps us find meaning and purpose in life. Conversely, spiritual struggles can contribute to or exacerbate vulnerabilities in all areas of life, including the experience of illness. Common spiritual struggles in behavioral health include the following:

- **Spiritual struggle of disconnection:** A pervasive spiritual struggle in mental illness, disconnection can manifest as a fragmented sense of self, a deep sense of aloneness, and a damaged relationship with God, often expressed as feelings of abandonment by or anger at God. It's reinforced by stigma and results in isolative behaviors, which are relapse triggers for most mental disorders.

- **Spiritual struggle of guilt:** Guilt—what we feel after doing something that violates our values—is normally helpful, motivating us to choose behaviors that honor what's important to us. However, guilt is complicated for people with mental disorders for the following reasons:
  - An exaggerated sense of guilt can be an illness symptom. People with depression, for example, often feel extreme guilt for insignificant things or may feel guilty most of the time for no reason. They also feel a disproportionate amount of guilt for personal mistakes and transgressions.
  - Impaired judgment is a symptom of many mental illnesses. During the manic phase of bipolar illness, for example, people may engage in risky, impulsive behaviors that cause a world of harm in their lives and the lives of those they love most. The resulting guilt can be overwhelming. A compounding factor is that they may not remember what they did and thus have difficulty coming to terms with the behavior(s) and resolving the guilt.
  - In both cases, people may feel their illness as a punishment from God.
- **Spiritual struggle of shame:** Given the stigma of mental illness, it's easy to see why shame—a deep sense of self as basically "bad," "a failure," or otherwise flawed—is such a potent struggle among people with mental disorders. Rooted in invalidating relationships / environments, internalized shame creates a distortion of self, resulting in damaged self-esteem and negative core beliefs.

  Shame is powerfully reinforced when judgment and condemnation are taught in religious context. Thus people with mental disorders who are also active in judgment-focused faith communities often feel unworthy of God's love and can become hyper-focused on concerns about the eternal state of their souls.

- **Spiritual struggle of diminished sense of meaning:** Chronic mental illness can negatively impact all areas of life, resulting in a plethora of losses: relationships, employment, housing, functional capacities, independence. This can precipitate a crisis of identify and faith, marked by questions like "Why is this happening to me?" "Where is God in this illness?" "What is my purpose in life now?" This struggle to find meaning in life can lead to despair, a suicide risk factor.

## *Facilitating Spirituality Groups*[7]

Spirituality groups offer a unique forum for addressing spiritual struggles, enhancing chaplain interventions with the collective wisdom that can emerge through group process. A well-facilitated group is a haven of healing, providing moments of connection, glimpses of the profound truth that we are not alone. By creating safe spaces for shared stories and connecting these to the Divine, chaplains help patients remember who they are and what matters most.

### General Considerations for Inpatient Spirituality Groups

Patients are vulnerable and may be reactive, intrusive, or impulsive. It's thus important for groups to be well structured, with clear behavioral guidelines, established group format, and wise containment of sharing. This helps participants feel safe and stay grounded.

Patients are struggling with both illness symptoms and medication side effects, making it difficult to concentrate. Keep group content simple, with clear discussion questions and easy activities. This helps participants both focus and contribute, which increases a sense of connection and self-esteem.

Group facilitation in behavioral health is both a skill set and an art. Like the proverbial herding of cats, effective facilitators must become adept at keen observation, graceful redirection, skillful de-escalation, and firm but gentle boundary setting / keeping.[8]

### A Model for Inpatient Groups

At the facilities where this writer has worked, spirituality groups are considered part of treatment, exploring the spiritual dimension of life and how it can be utilized to assist one's recovery. This dimension includes core beliefs, values, and the need / capacity for connection (to self, others, and God), which provides a helpful framework for spirituality group content. The following are presented as possible guidelines:

- Begin with a brief overview of the spiritual dimension of life and the chaplain's role as facilitator. This clarifies the nature / purpose of the group.
- Review the general group guidelines, which should minimally include the following: listen respectfully to different viewpoints, experiences, and beliefs; do not interrupt or engage in private conversations when someone is speaking; maintain confidentiality—"What is said in group stays in group." This helps participants feel safe.
- Initiate group introductions, with a brief icebreaker activity ("Tell us your name and favorite color, animal, etc."). This helps participants connect.
- Lead a mindfulness exercise (e.g., observe your breathing, describe an object, tense / relax different muscles). This helps participants ground. Relate the exercise to the recovery strategy of staying in the moment: we can deal with difficult situations moment-by-moment, but become overwhelmed when we add to the moment regrets of the past / fears about the future.
- Introduce the topic and how it relates to spirituality and illustrate with appropriate materials (e.g., quotations, multicultural parables, inspirational stories, poems, music lyrics), inviting participant response. Specific discussion questions and topic-related activities can help participants stay focused on the group theme instead of voices or other internal stimuli, as well as relate the theme to their lives.
- End the group by inviting patients to identify one thing they learned in this group, and then close with a blessing or prayer.
- Helpful group topics include the following: forgiveness; self-acceptance; gratitude practice; hope versus wishful thinking; healing images of the Divine; self-love; spiritual

practices to cope with distress; self-care when grieving; recovery-centered values; finding a faith that "fits."

### Outpatient Groups

Outpatient groups provide opportunities for more complex content and increased sharing, as clients are more stabilized. Since outpatient programs generally focus on relapse prevention and strategies for promoting wellness, spirituality groups can help by addressing spiritual struggles that may trigger or contribute to relapse and by accessing community-based spiritual resources.

Outpatient groups may be larger than inpatient groups and have a psycho-educational format and focus, requiring more substantive material preparation and the creative blend of interactive lecture-style presentation and smaller group breakouts for discussion.

Examples of outpatient spirituality groups developed by this writer include the following:

- Are we there yet? Learning to live in the here and now
- Workouts for spiritual fitness
- Everyday uplifts: seeing the sacred in all of life
- From shame-based to grace-filled living
- Good grief: finding ways to heal from loss
- I gave up guilt for Lent: reclaiming values in recovery
- Forgiveness as a way of life
- There's no place like home: connecting with a spiritual community

## *Practical Tips for Working with Different Patient Populations*

Figures 21.1 through 21.4 highlight four primary clinical disorders, with both special concerns and suggested approaches to effective ministry.

While by no means comprehensive, I hope this brief introduction to behavioral health chaplaincy has piqued your interest, inviting further exploration of this challenging yet richly rewarding field. The resource section that follows offers suggestions for further study.

| PRACTICAL TIPS FOR WORKING WITH DIFFERENT PATIENT POPULATIONS | |
|---|---|
| **EATING DISORDERS** | |
| **Major Symptoms** | People with eating disorders (ED) have extreme attitudes about food and weight, resulting in self-destructive, potentially life-threatening behaviors to maintain their distorted body image.<br>People with anorexia nervosa:<br>• See selves as fat despite extreme thinness<br>• Self-starve, resulting in malnutrition<br>• Develop eating rituals (cut food into tiny pieces / rearrange on plate to give impression of eating; will only eat "safe" foods)<br>People with bulimia nervosa eat large amounts of food in short periods of time, and then secretly purge (laxatives, self-induced vomiting, excessive exercise). |
| **Special Issues for Spiritual Care** | People with ED are often perfectionists who never measure up to their unrealistic expectations. Those who are religious often focus on scriptures that seemingly reinforce their sense of not measuring up and thus justify self-punishing behaviors.<br>Low self-esteem, shame, and difficulty seeing self as worthy of love are frequent struggles among people with ED. They tend to focus on care of others while neglecting self-care and may confuse self-care with selfishness.<br>Rigid, "either-or" thinking and emotional avoidance are common traits of people with ED. |
| **Intervention Strategies** | People with ED have significant anxiety. Follow strategies in anxiety disorders section as appropriate.<br>Focus on grace vs. works as basis of relationship with God, self. Redirect to scriptures supporting positive change within context of loving self-acceptance.<br>Help people identify strengths / abilities, use affirmations to counter fusion with negative self-beliefs and reduce experience of shame.<br>Promote self-care, self-responsibility as healthy spiritual practices; assist with self-forgiveness.<br>Assist movement from "either-or" to "both-and" thinking, using spiritual paradox theme. |

*Figure 21.1*

| PRACTICAL TIPS FOR WORKING WITH DIFFERENT PATIENT POPULATIONS | |
|---|---|
| **ANXIETY DISORDERS** | |
| **Major Symptoms** | Anxiety is a normal reaction to stress, rooted in the fight, flight, or freeze response to fearful situations. Anxiety disorders, though, interfere with the ability to live a normal life. There are many types of anxiety disorders—symptoms may include:<br>• Exaggerated worry<br>• Excessive fear reactions<br>• Physical symptoms like heart pounding, nausea, trembling, shortness of breath, chest pains<br>• Recurrent, unwanted thoughts and repetitive behaviors (obsessive-compulsive disorder—OCD)<br>• Flashbacks (reliving trauma), nightmares (post-traumatic stress disorder—PTSD)<br>• Behaviors that are avoidance-based, which reinforces fears |
| **Special Issues for Spiritual Care** | People with anxiety disorders have difficulty with uncertainty and may seek you out for reassurance about religious concerns. However, like scratching a bad itch, reassurance paradoxically increases anxiety and interferes with treatment.<br>Scrupulosity is a form of OCD where the obsessive thoughts and repetitive behaviors are religiously themed. One may worry continuously about sinning, going to hell, etc., and try to ease these fears by excessive religious practice. While these are illness symptoms, not religious issues per se, rigid religious belief systems exacerbate the fears. |
| **Intervention Strategies** | Reinforce normalcy of religious uncertainty, exploring sacred stories of faith as journey vs. faith as belief certitude.<br>Use mindfulness practice to help people focus on the present moment vs. fear-based worries about the future, both fostering distress tolerance and promoting acceptance vs. avoidance as a faith-filled life stance.<br>Assist in creating value-based action steps to increase experience of purposeful living.<br>Assist in identifying any cognitive distortions of religious beliefs.<br>When appropriate, offer reframing of rigid beliefs to lesson grip of fear and promote balance. |

*Figure 21.2*

## PRACTICAL TIPS FOR WORKING WITH DIFFERENT PATIENT POPULATIONS

| MOOD DISORDERS | |
|---|---|
| **Major Symptoms** | Difficulty regulating mood and affect: inappropriate, inflated, or limited range of feelings.<br>Major depression is a common mood disorder typified by persistent sadness, hopelessness, loss of interest in activities once enjoyed, sleep / appetite troubles, and thoughts of death or suicide. It's also called unipolar depression to distinguish it from bipolar disorder.<br>Bipolar disorder is marked by extreme swings in mood, thought, energy, and behavior, ranging from depression to mania. Symptoms include racing thoughts, irritability, excessive energy / decreased need for sleep, impaired judgment, grandiosity, pressured speech. |
| **Special Issues for Spiritual Care** | Depression is a major risk factor for suicide. When a person with depression asks if people who kill themselves go to hell, he / she may be seriously considering suicide and the fear of hell may be his / her only remaining deterrent. Resist the urge to comfort / assure; instead, reinforce the concern. Notify doctor / charge nurse and document patient inquiry.<br>Working with someone in the manic phase of bipolar illness is like dancing: you must anticipate the movement of your partner. Astute observation and flexibility will help you respond effectively to roller-coaster emotions and impulsive behaviors.<br>Remember, depressive symptoms can resemble spiritual struggle. |
| **Intervention Strategies** | Explore hope stories and experiences.<br>Clarify true guilt vs. illness symptoms.<br>Explore doubt as part of authentic faith and support "holy struggle."<br>Assist safe expression of feelings.<br>Encourage movement from God who "fixes" life to God who companions through life.<br>When working with someone experiencing mania, stay calm, observe closely, model proxemics, redirect intrusive behavior. Listen for / validate experiences of distress. When patient is more stable, explore spiritual themes.<br>Self-reproach for illness-influenced behaviors is both common and a recovery barrier; assist with self-forgiveness. |

*Figure 21.3*

| PRACTICAL TIPS FOR WORKING WITH DIFFERENT PATIENT POPULATIONS | |
|---|---|
| **PSYCHOTIC DISORDERS** | |
| **Major Symptoms** | Delusions (false beliefs), often religiously themed. Examples: beliefs that others are controlling your thoughts or scheming to harm you, and / or that you have special powers.<br><br>Hallucinations (false sensory perceptions): auditory hallucinations are the most common.<br><br>Disordered thoughts and behaviors (fragmented thinking, trouble sorting out what's relevant / nonrelevant to a situation, erratic behavior).<br><br>Schizophrenia is the most common psychotic disorder. |
| **Special Issues for Spiritual Care** | Don't assume certain spiritual experiences are always illness symptoms. People with psychosis can have authentic encounters with God, and people without psychosis can have non-normative religious experiences—common throughout religious history / in some cultures.<br><br>Don't confront delusions; this is futile / may cause agitation.<br><br>Use care with religious language / when discussing scripture: people with active psychosis are often literalistic. |
| **Intervention Strategies** | Listen for lucid moments, when what matters most shines through. Reflective listening can help patients sustain reality focus.<br><br>Religiously themed delusions / psychotic experiences can contain kernels of truth: explore to find spiritual needs and sources of hope.<br><br>Strengthen positive religious coping by helping patients access and use appropriate resources.<br><br>Model / teach social behaviors to increase the ability to connect. |

*Figure 21.4*

## Notes

1. Addictions to mood-altering behaviors.
2. Two helpful, user-friendly resources for information about mental illness are the National Institute of Mental Health's website (www.nimh.nih.gov) and the Surgeon General's report on mental health, accessible online (www.surgeongeneral.gov/library/mentalhealth/home.html).
3. *DSM-IV TR* is the edition referenced, with the next update (*DSM-V*) released in 2013.
4. P. Corrigan, ed., *On the Stigma of Mental Illness: Practical Strategies for Research and Social Change* (Washington, DC: American Psychological Association, 2005). A compilation of the Chicago Consortium for Stigma Research, this is a good resource for examining the impact of stigma on the experience of mental illness.
5. See chapter 31, on cultural competencies. Also, for a different clinical approach that integrates psychospiritual worldviews and East-West spiritual practices, see S. G. Mijares and G. S. Khalsa, eds., *The Psychospiritual Clinician's Handbook: Alternative Methods for Understanding and Treating Mental Disorders* (Binghamton, NY: Haworth Reference Press, 2005).
6. This section is drawn from the author's almost twenty years of experience in behavioral health, including lectures on the spiritual dimension of life and various surveys / patient self-assessment tools developed to identify areas of spiritual struggle. To explore research in this area, some authors to consider are Harold Koenig, Kenneth Pargament, George Fitchett, and Kevin Flannelly.
7. See chapter 14 of this book, written by Rev. Mikulak (another behavioral health chaplain), for a full orientation.
8. I. D. Yalom and M. Leszcz, *Theory and Practice of Group Psychotherapy*, 5th ed. (New York: Basic Books, 2005). This definitive work contains everything you need to know about therapeutic and support group facilitation.

## Further Reading

Address, R. F., ed. *Caring for the Soul—R'fuat HaNefesh: A Mental Health Resource and Study Guide*. New York: Union of Hebrew Congregations Press, 2003.

American Psychiatric Association. *Diagnostic and Statistical Manual of Mental Disorders (DSM-IV-TR)*. 4th ed. Washington, DC: American Psychiatric Association, 2000.

Boehnlein, J. K., ed. *Psychiatry and Religion: The Convergence of Mind and Spirit*. Washington, DC: American Psychiatric Press, 2000.

Fitchett, G., L. A. Burton, and A. B. Silvan. "The Religious Needs and Resources of Psychiatric Inpatients." *Journal of Nervous and Mental Diseases* 185, no. 5 (1997): 320–26.

Fitchett, G., and J. L. Risk. "Screening for Spiritual Struggle." *Journal of Pastoral Care and Counseling* 63, nos. 1–2 (2009): 1–12.

Kehoe, N. *Wrestling with Our Inner Angels: Faith, Mental Illness and the Journey to Wholeness*. San Francisco, CA: Jossey-Bass, 2009.

Koenig, H. *Faith and Mental Health: Religious Resources for Healing*. West Conshohocken, PA: Templeton Foundation Press, 2005.

Kurtz, E., and K. Ketcham. *The Spirituality of Imperfection: Storytelling and the Journey to Wholeness*. New York: Bantam Books, 1992.

Lelwica, M. M. *The Religion of Thinness: Satisfying the Spiritual Hungers behind Women's Obsession with Food and Weight*. Carlsbad, CA: Gurze Books, 2009.

McConnell, K. M., K. I. Pargament, C. G. Ellison, and K. J. Flannelly. "Examining the Links between Spiritual Struggles and Symptoms of Psychopathology in a National Sample." *Journal of Clinical Psychology* 62, no. 12 (2006): 1469–84.

Osborn, I. *Tormenting Thoughts and Secret Rituals: The Hidden Epidemic of Obsessive-Compulsive Disorder*. New York: Dell Publishing, 1999.

Pearmain, E. D. *Doorways to the Soul: 52 Wisdom Tales from Around the World*. Cleveland, OH: Pilgrim Press, 1998.

Weiss Roberts, L., and A. R. Dyer. *Ethics in Mental Health Care*. Arlington, VA: American Psychiatric Publishing, 2004.

## Resources

Muslim Mental Health Ministries: www.mentalhealthministries.net

National Alliance on Mental Illness (NAMI): www.nami.org

Pathways to Promise (interfaith resource center for ministry to people with mental disorders): www.pathways2promise.org

## About the Contributor

**Rev. Michele J. Guest Lowery, MDiv, BCC,** is coordinator of the Center for Spiritual Care at Alexian Brothers Behavioral Health Hospital, Hoffman Estates, Illinois. She is an ordained minister in the United Church of Christ and a board certified chaplain with the Association of Professional Chaplains, with almost twenty years of experience in behavioral health chaplaincy. Other publications by Rev. Lowery include "Just Another Manic Monday" (2008), "God in the Odd" (2008, 33–34), and "Practicing the Presence of Pavement" (2008).

# 22

## Gay, Lesbian, Bisexual, and Transgendered (GLBT) People

*Rev. Nancy K. Anderson, ACPE Supervisor, and Rev. Jo Clare Wilson, ACPE Supervisor*

### *The Experience and the Problem (The Action)*

In 1990 I received a phone call from a hospital chaplain and a pastoral counselor in South Carolina. He knew of me because of the work I had done with the Association of Pastoral Clinical Education (ACPE) in establishing a gay, lesbian, bisexual, and transgendered (GLBT) network for education and support within the organization. One of the functions we served was to be available for consultation to supervisors and chaplains around issues regarding GLBT persons.

This chaplain asked if I would be willing to speak with one of his counselees who had been struggling with issues of coming out as a gay man. This young man was the son of a Southern Baptist minister, and his struggle was highlighted by questions of integrating his faith and his orientation. He felt that a conversation with a clergyperson who was also gay would be quite helpful and thus the referral for a conversation.

A few hours later my phone rang; the young man identified himself and we spent a few minutes establishing connection and structure for the conversation. About fifteen minutes into the conversation the young man hesitated and said he really had a question that seemed to be at the root of his struggle. After pausing he asked: *"Do you believe God really loves you as a gay person?"* I admit to being a bit taken aback at first; I had expected a few possible scenarios having to do with parental disapproval, work-related issues of coming out, and certainly struggle with faith. I don't think, however, I was prepared for such a poignant question. Its power was in the simplicity *and* the power it held for this young man. His sincere and earnest concern was born out of years of hearing the strong language of sin and evil associated with his very being. In the depths of his soul, he believed he was fundamentally not okay.

This experience has stayed with me for years as I have encountered many persons of faith who have wrestled with a variety of issues related to self-esteem and their sexual orientation. And I always remember this young man's question. He even worried aloud that his question would appear somehow trite or simplistic. He commented that intellectually the answer seemed obvious, but the roots of his emotions were intertwined with his spirituality, and the sense of his nature being *unacceptable to God* ran deep.

For GLBT persons who struggle with issues of faith, coming to terms with their sexual orientation *and* their relationship with God requires a struggle that can be transformative. In *Coming Out Within*, the authors suggest that the process of working to integrate identity with faith is often the potential for transformation, and as a consequence, there may be a higher form of spiritual evolvement for GLBT persons precisely because there is such a struggle to reconcile and work toward their spiritual wholeness.[1] So the question of acceptance and knowledge that a person is acceptable to God is at the very heart of how GLBT people of faith understand themselves.

Out of this dilemma comes questions. Who do GLBT persons of faith turn to as religious authorities when they are struggling? How do they know that the person they choose will be safe for them to bring this struggle for help? How do they determine the religious authority's openness and ability to help them with this struggle? And then, what about all the other issues that surround GLBT persons as they navigate through life? For all of the milestones that occur in everyone's family, such as birth, death, transitions, illness, crisis, marriage, and so on, do they assume that their religious leader is going to be helpful? Will that person understand the issues that often accompany a person who lives as someone "outside the gates"?

## *A Theological Foundation (The Reflection)*

Consider the gates of Jerusalem. There are people who live inside the walls, who can travel back and forth whenever they so choose. And there are those who live outside the walls who can never go inside the walls. There are those who have lived inside the walls, but because of decisions to live authentically, they find themselves living outside of the gates, never to be able to live inside again. Where we live in relation to those walls not only defines and shapes our beliefs and values but also participates in creating the culture in which we live.

What does it mean to live inside the gates? Those are the ones who live culturally entitled and who live by the circumscribed norms of our society. We still live in a culture where the norm is defined as white, often male, heterosexual, married, and with a respectable job. Anything that deviates from this is considered optional, thus the norm requires and bears the burden of finding the similarities so that trust, conversation, and acceptance can occur.

Often, we hear from those who are within the gates that they "understand" what it is like to be on the outside. There are some who are even willing to celebrate those on the outside of the gate. Sometimes this is defined as tolerance and appreciation of diversity. But what would it look like to change the norm? How would it be that instead of tolerating and accepting diversity that diversity becomes the norm? After all, our values become what define us.

We say this because there can be a tendency among those who are able to go in and out of the gates to equate knowledge of the other as understanding the world of the other. An individual consciousness among our liberal friends does not qualify gay, lesbian, bisexual, and transgendered people to enter or live within the gates of Jerusalem. That is an important distinction to bear in mind.

To attend and even perform heterosexual weddings when there is no recognition of same-sex couples who have a committed love relationship is disconfirming. To have to hold back physical expressions of affection in public creates a sense of invisibility. Regardless of how liberal and accepting you are as a heterosexual person, your pastoral / spiritual caregiving to a GLBT person will always be done out of the paradigm of privilege.

There are places where we hold privilege and it is never easy to think of extending ourselves to actually imagine the world of the other. Sacrifice and action are part of change. Language helps build trust, as does the willingness to move out of your own comfort zone.

## *The Hope in Spiritual Care (The Implications for Spiritual Care)*

As two clinical pastoral educators, we start with the familiar model of teaching: the action and then the reflection. We hope to have this touchstone as a beginning point of considering the pastoral and spiritual care of GLBT people. For us, it captures the legacy of the struggles inherent in this task, even as we live in a world that has begun to see a different environment than the world of 1990. In the past several years we have seen much advancement for GLBT persons and their families. But, to tackle the issues involved in providing pastoral care, it is always important to know the depth and breadth of the problem. After all, when we are practicing the art of pastoral and spiritual care, we carry the depth and breadth of our traditions, of our beliefs, and of our knowledge. The question becomes framed in attempting to know *what we can do in our practice* to communicate our skills and our capacity to be a safe place for this struggle.

### Language and Communication

Those of us in the religious world would agree that words and how they are used are essential in communicating our values and beliefs. How we are able to convey something of who we are can impact significantly on someone's opinion of whether we might be safe. David Switzer, in *Pastoral Care of Gays, Lesbians, and Their Families*, noted his experience of a gay man in his congregation who felt free to come and speak with him as a result of hearing his sermons and determining he would be able to trust him.[2] Because of the *content* of his words, he was perceived as safe.

The GLBT community will listen to the language of someone to determine the safety of and the opinions about perceptions of sexual orientation. When persons who are religious leaders make a spiritual or pastoral visit, attention must be given to the issue of language. The words we choose in introductions, in questions asked, and in general conversation will be listened to carefully and used to determine whether a person is open and knowledgeable about issues of sexual orientation. The seemingly simple action of introduction and asking questions is important. Naturally this is important in all conversations that are involved in offering spiritual care, but there are certain language terms that hold meaning for the GLBT population.

As noted above, a person felt comfortable because of the pastoral leader's sermons. He had heard the words that conveyed to him that this person was open and safe. Religious leaders in congregations need to be aware of the words used when talking about relationships, when noting families (are you speaking as though all families are heterosexual?), and when inviting participants to events. A simple way of making sure you are inclusive is by *not* assuming that everyone is heterosexual. This means that you refer to loved ones as spouses, partners, and so on. It is important to know that persons who are in a heterosexual marriage might be struggling with their sexual identity; they may have married in an attempt to be "normal."

When a spiritual care provider enters the room of a patient or long-term-care resident and begins to discern information for assessment, are questions asked with an eye toward inclusivity and openness? Is there an assumption that persons are heterosexual (until proved different?), and if so, are all questions or inquiries about family or relationships phrased in terms that correspond to heterosexual roles—for example, noting a woman in a man's room and asking, "Are you his wife?" Or do you ask the general and inclusive question of "Are you family or friend?" in order that they might know you are aware and acknowledging of all options. Instead of asking "Are you married?" which limits options, you ask, "Who is your family?" or "Who is of primary support to you?" You do not just assume heterosexual privilege. You must develop the skill to ask questions with an eye toward inclusivity, not limitations. This is in order to send the message that you are not assuming and that you are allowing for a variety of answers.

## Our Ability to Sit with Comfort

What does your body language convey when you are in conversation with people? Are you making eye contact? Are you aware of shuffling your feet or speaking in a hurried fashion because you are in a hurry to depart or you are anxious about what you might hear?

It is helpful to remember that most GLBT persons *expect* religious persons to see them as less than, as sinners, as persons who are in need of *correction*. One of the most distasteful responses to make to a GLBT person in an attempt to somehow convey that he or she is acceptable in your eyes as a religious person is the phrase "Hate the sin, love the sinner." All that says to a GLBT patient / resident is "You are doing something wrong, and once you correct your maladaptive behavior, your life will be approved in the eyes of God and the religious community." Many GLBT are familiar with the large range of religious organizations that are in the business of providing conversion therapy. The awareness of these realities makes it incumbent upon spiritual care providers to articulate not only through language the words that are welcoming but also through gestures that express their comfort in the discussion.

In order to do this, we suggest that spiritual care providers need to take the time to explore and understand their own views, attitudes, and beliefs about GLBT persons. The language and the comfort a spiritual care provider is able to convey are determined by the truth of your convictions and the willingness to imagine the world of the other.

You might be a spiritual care provider with a faith tradition or belief that does not approve of a GLBT person. If that is the case, we recommend that integrity requires you to be honest about your own position and allow the person to seek spiritual counsel somewhere else. If, on the other hand, you are a spiritual care provider who wants to be open and supportive but you are not informed about potential issues as well as some idea of what it means to be GLBT, then you need to seek knowledge and experience.

## Knowledge

Some years ago when persons in the religious world began looking at the reality of domestic violence and sexual assault within their congregations, they were told at conferences and workshops to make sure their office shelves contained books that reflected they had knowledge about the issues. It was also recommended that the books be read, not just displayed. There is a difference between knowing what you *think you know* about GLBT people and actually being familiar with the issues and the experiences.

To gain knowledge about the issues requires more than reading; you need to spend some time in dialogue with GLBT persons. Ask questions about the spiritual issues facing them or the struggles they have had within their religious and spiritual communities. If you are one of those persons who might say you are not aware of knowing any GLBT persons, please understand the reality that there are GLBT persons in your life; more than likely they haven't told you.

An experience worth understanding is the following simple situation. Just recently, we were traveling between Connecticut and California. One of our connecting flights landed, and we were departing into the connecting airport to spend an hour waiting for the next leg of our trip. As we walked through the aircraft ramp into the waiting area, the TV was on, and the first words greeting us loudly was that of a popular TV evangelist stating that "the homosexual lifestyle is just not acceptable for Christians who believe the Bible." In this interview he was stating the familiar litany of words we have heard throughout our life about how wrong, how sinful, how the homosexual person is going against God and needs to know that God "loves the sinner, but not the sin." For whatever reason, the TV was turned up extra loud, and there were about twenty-five people gathered around listening with rapt attention. Can you imagine what it might be like for you to be walking in a public place while a loud voice is reminding you that who you are *in your essence* is bad? Despite having been out for more than twenty-five years, I felt it was still hurtful and it made me feel self-conscious even if no one was necessarily looking. If you can sit with that reality for a moment and imagine what it would be like for you to hear over a loudspeaker that who and what you are is wrong, then perhaps you can begin to understand the debilitating effects that still occur in our world of progress.

## *The Actions of Pastoral and Spiritual Care (What to Do)*

### Advocate

To be able to live out the above directions of language, comfort, and knowledge is to recognize the specific ways GLBT persons might need pastoral and spiritual care. Imagine being in an acute care, rehabilitation, long-term care, or hospice setting and worrying whether the institution and / or the staff will recognize *who is family for you*. How might your care be impacted, and who will be your advocate?

## Acknowledgement and Recognition

Think of what it might be like for a GLBT person to face going into long-term care surrounded by people who will be a new community in which perhaps another "coming out" will be necessary. At the onset of dementia, who will remind you and keep the memories close at hand if you have no friends around or family who are accepting? Are there skilled nursing facilities and or assisted-living arrangements where a GLBT person will be accepted and feel safe? What about someone who is transgendered? Who helps those caring for this person understand and treat with sensitivity the particular issues? Are the proper pronouns used? Do people stare and behave in ways that are isolating?

## Inclusion

Are the people you consider family able to be present and around you? Is your partner of many years considered in the making of decisions about end of life? What if your entire life you have lived closeted and now face dying without being able to have your beloved with you in the way you are familiar with and live at home? Will your partner be included in the planning of your funeral? Will he or she be forgotten? Who will make sure she or he is given spiritual care and able to grieve openly?

How will you, as the pastoral and spiritual care provider, be a voice for those who might otherwise not have a voice? If your pastoral and spiritual care is characterized by thoughtful and inclusive language, the ability to convey comfort with the "other," and as much knowledge coupled with experience that you can bring, then perhaps together we will begin to remove the bricks in the wall, even if one by one.

## Notes

1. Craig O'Neill and Kathleen Ritter, *Coming Out Within: Stages of Spiritual Awakening for Lesbians and Gay Men* (San Francisco: HarperSanFrancisco, 1992).
2. David K. Switzer, *Pastoral Care of Gays, Lesbians, and Their Families* (Minneapolis: Fortress Press, 1999).

## Further Reading

Carl, D. *Counseling Same Sex Couples.* New York: W.W. Norton and Company, 1990.

Marshall, J. L. *Counseling Lesbian Partners.* Louisville: Westminster John Knox Press, 1997.

O'Neill, Craig, and Kathleen Ritter. *Coming Out Within: Stages of Spiritual Awakening for Lesbians and Gay Men.* San Francisco: HarperSanFrancisco, 1992.

Switzer, David K. *Pastoral Care of Gays, Lesbians, and Their Families.* Minneapolis: Fortress Press, 1999.

Tigert, L. M. *Coming Out While Staying In.* Cleaveland: United Church Press, 1996.

## About the Contributors

**Rev. Nancy K. Anderson, ACPE Supervisor,** is director of spiritual care at Bridgeport Hospital in Bridgeport, Connecticut, and is regional codirector of the Eastern Region of ACPE. She is an ordained United Methodist clergy.

**Rev. Jo Clare Wilson, ACPE Supervisor,** is director of pastoral care and education at Griffin Hospital in Derby, Connecticut, and is regional codirector of the Eastern Region of ACPE. She is a past president of ACPE and a Disciples of Christ minister.

# 23

## *Spiritual / Pastoral Care with People with Disabilities and Their Families*

*Rev. Bill Gaventa, MDiv*

Pastoral care with people with intellectual, developmental, sensory, and / or physical disabilities, their families, and other caregivers has too often been seen as "special ministries to special people," usually in segregated settings. Far more people with disabilities live in community settings. They are born in acute care and community hospitals and come as patients throughout their lives, sometimes because of their disability but more often because of normal health issues. In cases of severe behavioral or psychiatric problems, they may end up in behavioral health settings with "dual diagnosis" or a mistaken diagnosis. Toward life's end, nursing homes, long-term care facilities, or hospice may be involved. Add the growing numbers of people with acquired disabilities from accident, traumatic brain injury, war, and trauma who often go from acute care to rehab to long-term care, sometimes with stops in behavioral health care and later into hospice. Then add disabilities emerging as part of aging that mirror intellectual and physical disabilities. The numbers are huge.

### *Disability and Pastoral Care*

Far too many stories from people with disabilities and their families are not about the trauma of hospitalization for an illness but about the assumptions and attitudes that more "typical" caregivers have about their disability or "the disabled" as a whole. Who are the people with disabilities?

Most would now say, along with their caregivers, "See me as a person first!" Person-first language, which, beyond a person's name, means using language like "John Smith, the patient *with* cerebral palsy in room 214." That rule has exceptions, such as "the deaf" who consider themselves a culture, not a disability. Some adults with autism claim their identity as "autistic" rather than "neurotypical," hence another form of diversity. When in doubt, ask how they prefer to be addressed and / or have their disability discussed.

The World Health Organization's three-level definition of "disability"[1] is helpful:

1. An impairment of some biological, physical, or psychological origin (e.g., an extra chromosome [Down syndrome]; lack of oxygen at birth [cerebral palsy]; accidents; or environmental, genetic, or unknown causes).
2. That impairment then causes some level of "dis-ability," an activity limitation or inability to function in some usual way, which can vary in different contexts.
3. A participation restriction, affecting involvement in life situations.

However, what we think about the impairment and functional limitation—our assumptions, values, and attitudes—is often the biggest "handicap."

Pastoral care with people with physical disabilities, blindness, or hearing impairments involves the same strategies as with anyone else, perhaps with supports such as the use of sign language interpreters, sensitive use of touch and voice to let someone who is blind know who and where you are and when you leave, and sensitive placement of eye levels for conversations with someone with physical disabilities.[2] My primary experience is with people with intellectual and developmental disabilities (including autism)[3] and acquired disabilities like traumatic brain injury.[4] Here, assumptions often get made about communication, reason, and the capacity to understand.

This chapter will look at four roles of the pastoral caregiver organized in a gradual exploration of life stages:

1. Presence, being there, at crucial and critical periods and over the long haul

2. Guide, as people struggle with questions of God's will and purpose, healing, vulnerability and limitation, hope, and in this arena, barriers of attitude, architecture, and lack of supports
3. Shepherding, the biblical name for advocacy and protection
4. Community building, empowering a wider body to care and support[5]

A theme of this chapter is that those dimensions of pastoral care apply not just to people with disabilities but to everyone.

## *Acute Care*

### At Birth

Pastoral care may start at the beginning when a child is born or diagnosed with unexpected impairments or health conditions, or perhaps, even earlier, as expectant parents seek specialized services because of unexpected prenatal testing results. Those can be times of shock and fear, as they struggle to change expectations, questioning themselves and everyone else, trying to find out: "What's wrong?" "Why us?" "Why our child?" "What do we do now?" It is often a grieving process, where shock, guilt, anger, and lamentation need to be heard as chaplains support the families who wonder, "Where is God in all of this?"

But the role goes deeper. A chaplain's very attitude and presence can convey that this baby is still a child, someone greater than the health issue or disability, someone who needs the typical love that any baby needs, along with the special services or procedures being called for. A resource for chaplains can be other parents with older children with the same kinds of issues and / or disabilities.[6]

Be there, listen, pray, help them ask questions of the care team, and support a family's network to provide the kinds of supports that only a mobilized congregation or network of friends can do. Be very careful with euphemisms that may miss a family's feelings (e.g., "Your baby is a 'special child' born to 'special parents'"). They may arrive at an answer or sense of purpose that may or may not be your own. That may be a long time coming. The key is presence on the journey.

## Avoid Spiritual Abuse but Embrace Its Pain

In that life journey, parents, family members, and people with disabilities often have had to deal with the absence of pastoral care but also with forms of abusive care, leading to disenfranchisement from clergy and congregational care. It happens in two ways:

1. When an individual or family, already struggling with "Why did this happen?" gets asked, explicitly or implicitly, "What did you do that God sent you this child?" Chaplains can help families as they struggle with the "why" of suffering and can help them or others see that this is the same question for almost any unexpected disease or accident.
2. When the assertion is made that "if your faith were strong enough, you could be healed." I know of no single case of a person with Down syndrome, cerebral palsy, other forms of intellectual or developmental disability, blindness or deafness from birth, and so on, who has been cured from that impairment by prayer, faith, or "faith healing." Those who make that assertion are acting out of their own helplessness and / or inability to be with others in their spiritual, psychological, and physical journeys. Harold Wilke (a United Church of Christ clergyman without arms and a leading pioneer in inclusive ministries with people with disabilities) used to tell a story about a man with an obvious disability who was approached on a street by someone who asserted, "My brother, if your faith were strong enough, you could be healed." (Almost any person who uses a wheelchair or has a physical disability can tell you a similar story.) Whereupon, this man simply said back, "My brother, if your faith were strong enough, you could cure me." Thus, if at first people with disabilities and / or their families are very leery or suspicious of you as a chaplain, it may take pastoral sensitivity and time for them to trust that you are a religious authority who is not wielding that kind of weapon.

## From Childhood into Adulthood

Children with disabilities may have repeated hospitalizations because of the disability or simply because of an unrelated health issue. Hopefully, their pastor and congregation are providing the nexus of care,[7] but your role may be to guide the child, family, and other caregivers through the valleys of complicated procedures and often incomprehensible language.

Be with kids as you would any others in your hospital. If there are communication barriers, find out from parents, therapists, and / or teachers, both secular and religious, what works—touch, smiles, pictures, simple signing, rituals, augmentative communication aids, and so on. What do they love? How do they express their fears and questions? In current "person-centered planning" strategies[8] for children and adults with disabilities, the question is not just "What is important for this child or adult?" but also "What is important to them?"

Both siblings and parents may need other forms of attention. Parents may be so understandably focused on their child with special needs that other siblings feel left out. Chaplains can pay sensitive attention to siblings when they visit, helping them understand what their brother or sister is going through, and hearing their questions or feelings. In exhausting stretches of acute or chronic care, one support for parents is respite care—biblically, a Sabbath—helping families find ways for a break and their own self-care: "We'll make sure they are entertained or looked after today; you all go do something for yourself or with your other kids."

## Adults

Hospitalization evokes a wide range of feelings for adults with disabilities, just as it does for everyone. Communication issues may necessitate interpreters, clear English, pictures,[9] or other communication aides. Using simple, clear language does not have to be childish. Just because people do not respond does not mean they do not understand or feel both verbal and nonverbal communication.

When uncertain, turn to the people who know them best for guidance. They may be aging parents, siblings, and / or staff from support agencies. Direct care staff are increasingly immigrants, who may also feel at a loss in hospital settings. You then face diversity of culture as well as of disability. Those staff can help you get to know someone and may deeply appreciate a chaplain asking about their own stories and caregiving roles.

Pastoral initiative in getting to know an adult with an intellectual or developmental disability can speak volumes to direct care staff, families, and / or other hospital staff, as it would with any marginalized population. Lack of frequent visitors does not mean there are not people who have poured sweat, heart, and tears into their caregiving. If an adult comes from his or her own home or a residential service, who are his or her housemates or friends in day services and programs? Chaplains can help them understand what is happening and ways to support their friend.

Finally, be open to stories of disconnection from a faith community or, conversely, how much it means to the patient / resident. Has the adult ever participated in faith communities of his or her choice and tradition, and / or been through rites of transition, such as baptism, confirmation, bar / bat mitzvah, and so on?[10] Your advocacy can help that happen, making it an incredibly powerful form of reconciliation and comfort for individuals and families who have been turned away.

## Behavioral and Psychiatric Care

Children and adults with developmental, intellectual, physical, or sensory disabilities can also have psychological problems, behavioral problems, and / or addictions. Adults with physical and sensory disabilities can be provided pastoral care in a behavioral health program just like anyone else. However, both children and adults with some forms of intellectual and / or developmental disability may end up in psychiatric settings because of behavior misinterpreted as a psychiatric issue when it may be related more specifically to their disability (e.g., some on the autism spectrum or others with limited verbal skills). There are too many stories of people with disabilities being overly restricted by restraints or medication because professionals did not understand their behavior.

The message, as chaplains in these settings know, is that all behavior is a form of communication. "Challenging behavior" gets frequently attributed to a person's disability or a mental illness when it may be a response to loss, trauma, abuse, pain, grief, or other issues that someone has not been able to communicate other than by "acting out" behavior. Professionals are learning that key treatment strategies may not first be medication or behavior modification, but determining what that person is trying to communicate and / or get from that behavior, and then developing detailed, guided, alternative ways to help them meet those needs. Chaplains can help other staff remember that patience, space, and time are needed with an individual who may test any authority figure before trust develops. Pastoral attitude and presence, listening with eyes and ears for the meaning of pain or issues that are being expressed in behavior, and supporting families and other caregivers in what can be incredibly hard roles are all key areas for chaplains.

## *Long-Term Care*

Pastoral care skills such as touch, presence, prayer, worship, ritual, and music are all powerful ways of communicating comfort and care with people with intellectual and developmental disabilities, just as they are with people with Alzheimer's and other aging conditions. Pastoral presence that helps everyone remember the person beyond or behind the label is crucial. The spiritual tasks of aging for a person with a disability may take unique forms but are essentially the same as with anyone: maintaining connections, life review, giving and receiving blessings, reconciling relationships, and maintaining dignity in the face of aging and faith in the face of loss.[11]

One population in long-term facilities needs a different form of pastoral care. Far too often, people sixty and younger end up in nursing homes or long-term care facilities because of complicated issues in physical care. Isolation and depression can then follow because they don't feel themselves to be old and have vastly different generational interests. Those issues need attention and addressing, perhaps even by helping search for more appropriate placements.

## *End of Life and Hospice*

People with disabilities are living longer even though a developmental or acquired disability may also contribute to an earlier than expected death. They are also aging and dying in community settings instead of behind institutional walls. Again, the starting point for pastoral care is that their needs, and those of families, caregivers, and friends, are just like and just as important as anyone else's.

There are some unique challenges, opportunities, and resources that can be part of this vital ministry:

- Be cautious with assumptions that people with intellectual or developmental disabilities are not feeling grief or struggling for understanding with what is happening. Words, pictures, analogies, concrete images, stories, memory objects, music, and behavior may all be ways of communicating.[12] Direct and concrete communication is much better than allusion. Participation in rites and rituals of leave-taking and mourning is both verbal and nonverbal communication and care. New resources on end-of-life planning and advance directives help honor individual needs and preferences for people with developmental disabilities, resources that can be used for and by anyone who needs simple, clear communication.[13]
- For families and others who have poured years of care and commitment into the growth and development of a person with a disability, death can sometimes seem like a double injustice: "Why death on top of the disability?" For others, it is relief, although hard to voice. If you get to know parents well, you may hear an often unspoken hope that their son or daughter dies just before they do, a feeling coming out of their despair about who will care for their "child" after they are gone.[14]
- Aging and death can be an anathema in service systems geared toward growth and development of potential. Teachers and / or direct care staff are often young and / or from a wide variety of cultures, thus with either little experience with death or a huge diversity of cultural experiences. Many deaths in the past, and sometimes present, have been caused by abuse or neglect, leading to a first reaction by systems: "Who's fault?" All involved need pastoral care.
- People with disabilities can be well known in their communities for their unique gifts and life story and may have huge numbers of people impacted by their death.

- People with intellectual and developmental disabilities have often been shielded from illness, grief, or death because of mistaken assumptions about what they can handle or understand. That's true when a parent or another relative dies and also true when an individual with a developmental disability dies and the questions are from their friends from school, day programs, or residential settings. Lack of intellectual understanding may make participation in rites, rituals, and other communal, behavioral traditions of mourning even more important. A chaplain can help inclusive participation by providing and / or organizing supports to a person with a disability so his or her direct family does not have to worry about issues of behavior. In my experience, however, many people with developmental disabilities are often more open and able than others regarding their questions, feelings, and understandings of death.
- When inclusive participation in communal rituals of grief is not possible, a redeeming pastoral role can be leading a memorial service that allows housemates, friends, and staff to mourn, remember, and celebrate someone's life. If a chaplain does not know the person well, then learn from the staff, family, and friends and also figure out ways for them to participate in the service. A memorial service that allows for expressions of grief while celebrating someone's gifts, story, and relationships can literally reframe the way a person's life has been seen by families and communities. I have heard chaplains, clergy, and funeral directors say that those are some of the most memorable funerals they have ever done. Conversely, the stories about funerals led by someone who knows little more than a name and disability and / or nothing about planning and leading participatory services illustrate a final act of disconnection.

## *Final Words*

The challenge is adapting the pastoral roles of presence, guide, shepherd / advocate, and community builder / bridger through all of these health care settings and life stages. New strategies in communication can lead to new skills in verbal and nonverbal communication, lessons that may serve you well with many other people. Chaplains will also walk and work in situations where profound questions are raised about what it means to be human (both created in the image of God and with a disability), the meaning and purpose of all created life, and what it means to be in community.[15] The all-too-frequent marginalization of people with disabilities in civic society and faith communities may lead to unique opportunities for re-membering people to faith communities and traditions, reconciling past experiences of spiritual wounding and pain, and redeeming / celebrating lives too frequently devalued.

Those ethical and social justice dimensions underlie core issues that run throughout the experience of people with disabilities in many health care settings. Their oral and written histories from a not-too-distant past include the eugenics movement, automatic institutionalization, medical experimentation without consent, and ways that people with severe or multiple disabilities, in particular, are too often assumed to have little or no "quality of life." Those assumptions are easier to make about someone other than your friend, family member, or self. People with disabilities are often the ones around whom critical ethical issues in health care are framed and debated (e.g., Baby Doe, Terri Schiavo, the Ashley case, Peter Singer, and Sandra Jensen). Then they are serving as the "canary birds" in the dangerous ethical mines full of issues that ultimately come back to be about all of us. Pastoral and theological presence in those arenas is crucial. Key skills in the face of those issues are reversing the question, that is, asking what we would do with anyone else and including the perspectives of friends and people with disabilities.

In those ethical minefields, and through the lives and voices of people with disabilities and their families and caregivers in far more "normal" situations, chaplains also have the opportunity to learn from, if not be awed by, the resiliency, determination, and, indeed, faith embodied in their lives. That faith, depending on the disability, is sometimes defined as "childlike," yet we applaud and celebrate the faith of children. Or that faith may be hidden behind the assumptions of who "we" think "they" are. Indeed, they are us.

## Notes

1. World Health Organization Definition of Disability, www.who.int/topics/disabilities/en/ and http://en.wikipedia.org/wiki/Disability#cite_note-0.
2. *The Ten Commandments for Communicating with People with Disabilities*, www.disabilitytraining.com. Excellent twenty-five-minute video for pastoral care and other hospital staff.
3. W. Gaventa, A. Walsh, and M. B. Walsh, eds., *Autism and Faith: A Journey into Community* (New Brunswick, NJ: Boggs Center, 2008), http://rwjms.umdnj.edu/boggscenter/products/Product_FaithBased.html.
4. W. Gaventa and W. Berk, eds., *Brain Injury: When the Call Comes; A Congregational Resource* (New Brunswick, NJ: Boggs Center, Brain Injury Association of New Jersey, and New Brunswick Theological Seminary, 2001), http://rwjms.umdnj.edu/boggscenter/products/Product_FaithBased.html.
5. W. Gaventa, "Pastoral Counseling with People with Disabilities," in *Clinical Handbook of Pastoral Counseling*, vol. 3, ed. Richard D. Parsons, Robert J. Wicks, and Donald Capps (Mahwah, NJ: Paulist Press, 2003).
6. Most states have parent-to-parent networks, or search online for disability-specific organizations.
7. Erik Carter, *Including People with Disabilities in Faith Communities: A Guide for Providers, Families, and Congregations* (Baltimore: Paul Brookes Publishing, 2007).
8. www.inclusion.com, www.elpnet.net. Also talk to parents, teachers, or agency staff about the patient's individualized education program (IEP) or plan.
9. See titles in the Books Beyond Words Series, www.rcpsych.ac.uk/publications/booksbeyondwords.aspx.
10. See, e.g., the film *Praying with Lior*, www.prayingwithlior.com.
11. William Gaventa, "Spirituality Issues and Strategies: Crisis and Opportunity," in *End-of-Life Care for Children and Adults with Intellectual and Developmental Disabilities*, ed. Sandra L. Friedman and David T. Helm (Washington, DC: American Association of Intellectual and Developmental Disabilities, 2010).
12. M. Markell, *Helping People with Developmental Disabilities Mourn: Practical Rituals for Caregivers* (Ft. Collins, CO: Companion Press, 2005), www.centerforloss.com; see also http://rwjms.umdnj.edu/boggscenter/projects/end_of_life.html.
13. L. A. Kingsbury, *People Planning Ahead: Communicating Healthcare and End-of-Life Wishes* (Washington, DC: American Association of Intellectual and Developmental Disabilities, 2009).
14. See *Supportive Care in the Congregation* and other resources, www.adnetonline.org.
15. Audiotapes, Institute on Theology and Disability, http://rwjms.umdnj.edu/boggscenter/projects/faith_based.html.

## About the Contributor

**Rev. Bill Gaventa, MDiv,** serves as director of Community and Congregational Supports at the Elizabeth M. Boggs Center on Developmental Disabilities and as associate professor at Robert Wood Johnson Medical School, University of Medicine and Dentistry of New Jersey (UMDNJ), New Brunswick, New Jersey. In his role at the Boggs Center, Rev. Gaventa works on community supports, training for community services staff, spiritual supports, training of seminarians and clergy, aging and end-of-life / grief issues, and cultural competence. He has edited four books, written a number of book chapters and articles, and served as the editor of the *Journal of Religion, Disability and Health* for fourteen years.

# 24

## *Chronic Illness*

*Rabbi Zahara Davidowitz-Farkas, MHL, BCJC, CPSP*
*Diplomate Supervisor*

The prevalence of chronic illness in the United States continues to grow at a disturbing rate. Some basic statistics:

- In 2005, almost one out of every two adult Americans had at least one chronic illness.[1]
- That number is projected to increase by more than 1 percent per year by 2030, resulting in a chronically ill population of 171 million people.[2]
- Ninety-six percent of those with chronic illness live with a condition that is invisible to others.[3]
- Sixty percent of those with a chronic illness are between the ages of eighteen and sixty-four.[4]
- Seven out of ten deaths each year are from chronic illness.[5]
- Fifty percent of all deaths each year are from heart disease, cancer, or stroke.[6]
- The average health care costs for someone who has a chronic illness is five times greater than for someone without a chronic condition.[7]
- Chronic diseases account for three of every four dollars spent on health care.[8]

- Expenditures in the United States on health care surpassed $2.3 trillion in 2008, more than eight times the $253 billion spent in 1980.[9]

## *As Chaplains, We Know It Is NOT about the Numbers*

Although we get certain kinds of information from the statistics above, they teach us nothing about the human experience of living with a chronic illness. They do not tell us about the cost in human dreams and endeavors, in human pain, suffering, and isolation. They also do not tell us about the courage and determination of those ill and about the love and patience of their caregivers.

Chronic illness includes arthritis, hypertension, multiple sclerosis, cancer, lupus, diabetes, chronic pain, AIDS, mental illness, and mental impairment, to name just a few. It may be described as a condition that lasts more than six months, that requires long-term therapy, and where a return to a state of normalcy is the exception rather than the norm.

Chronic illnesses differ in their rate of progression—some may result in complete or partial disability or even lead to death. Illnesses such as coronary artery disease and cancer begin with an acute phase and then become chronic conditions. Others, such as chronic obstructive pulmonary disease, are known for stabilization and destabilization. Arthritis and multiple sclerosis may go into periodic remissions and exacerbations.[10] Regardless, chronic illnesses are all permanent and nonreversible. They cause an individual to significantly alter day-to-day activities because of factors such as decreased endurance, mobility, or cognitive functioning. One's usual lifestyle becomes permanently disrupted.[11]

However, the one thing that all of these ailments have in common is the element of uncertainty, and it is this uncertainty that defines the life of an individual living with chronic illness. Symptom onset, duration, intensity, location, and the consequent degree of incapacity are unpredictable by nature.[12] There is no obvious light at the end of the tunnel.

In contrast, the trajectory of an acute illness is quite different. Acute illnesses are characterized by symptoms of rapid onset and progression and of short duration. Immediate and urgent care is frequently called for. An episode of acute disease results in recovery to a state comparable to the patient's condition of health and activity before the disease. It is significant that while an acute illness is treated primarily by experts, chronic illness requires extensive management by the patient.[13]

## *Chronic Versus Acute—What It Means for Us as Chaplains*

In his book *The Nature of Suffering and the Goals of Medicine*, Eric Cassell posits that "suffering occurs when an impending destruction of the person is perceived; it continues until the threat of disintegration has passed or until the integrity of the person can be restored in some other manner.... Suffering can be defined as the state of severe distress associated with events that threaten the intactness of person."[14]

It is this "intactness of person" that chronic illness overwhelms and frequently destroys. It leaves no part of a person's life untouched. It affects the sufferer's physical, psychological, social, existential, and spiritual well-being by impacting social functioning, relationships, economic stability, role identity, faith, daily routines, lifestyle, plans, and dreams for the future.

In a chronic illness, losses are cumulative. Individuals may lose their livelihood; they may experience profound impediments to their roles as husband, wife, parent, friend, and colleague. They may lose physical attractiveness, cognitive abilities, the freedom of spontaneity, and privacy. Limitations are always being negotiated. Since a chronic illness is unpredictable by nature and must be self-managed, it is also unrelenting, demanding constant adaptation and continuous flexibility.

Actual or potential losses are often associated with deterioration. These losses demand a continual revision of self-identity and adaptation to life circumstances. The life of an ill person demands trial-and-error learning and experimentation to discover what works and what does not work in controlling symptoms and suffering and allowing one to carry on with the activities and responsibilities of life.[15]

When viewed in terms of lived experience and meaning making, humans live in the world in a skilled and nonreflective way. In her article "Experiencing Chronic Illness: Cocreating New Understandings," Ironside explains that the body becomes habitual, in that it is experienced as an extension of concerns and activities that are embedded with meanings and significances. Humans involved in activities do not experience such involvement as a series of steps or tasks to be completed. For example, when we walk down the hall to the drinking fountain, we experience the activity of going to get a drink of water rather than the movement of the feet and legs, the swing of the arms, and the carriage of the torso for a defined distance on the way to getting a drink. However, in breakdown such as chronic illness, when the body is no longer able to function in the habitual way, activities are experienced differently in the nature of the lived or habitual body changes, requiring new understandings of living a life with a chronic illness. The experience of chronic illness can thus be understood only in the context of the lived world because it is the lived world that is made up of meanings and significances.[16]

Individuals with chronic illness know that they are functioning outside of our contemporary cultural norms. They cannot get on a bus quickly or gracefully, they provoke stares wherever they go, and they are torn between a sense of humiliation and their desire to participate in the world and be "normal." Because of fear, shame, grief, bitterness, and an overwhelming knowledge that they are not, and never will be, "like everyone else," people suffering from chronic illness may well isolate themselves from others at the same time that others are withdrawing from them. The urge to withdraw is particularly strong in the event of chronic pain—especially if the person "looks" healthy and hardy. It is not uncommon for a sufferer to be told that "it is all in their head" or they are "faking" the pain.

Chronic illness impacts not only an individual's ability to live like others but also the relationships that shape meaning and purpose in that individual's life.[17] A person's family suffers deeply when one of its members is diagnosed with a chronic illness. Everything we thought we knew about living in the world is shattered not only for ourselves but also for our families and our friends. As one man said about his wife, "She had it just as rough as I did, except she wasn't paralyzed, she wasn't in a wheelchair, but she went through the same thing I did. And she also took care of the kids."[18] It is our entire constellation of relationships that must adapt to the new reality. Despair, feelings of powerlessness, hopelessness, and fear are sure to ensue. Inevitably, the question of death comes to the fore either because of the proximity of death or because of the ongoing experience of loss and limitation.[19]

## *Chronic Illness and Suffering—Existential and Spiritual*

Perhaps an ill person's most profound suffering occurs in the realm of existential and spiritual well-being. Each of us creates an understanding of the world and our place in it as we live our lives and build our experiences. We use this assumptive view to create personal interpretations of our experiences.[20] This worldview may be healthy for us or it may not, but we live by the rules of our creation feeling secure and sure of a place relative to ourselves, our relationships, our spiritual selves, and the world we inhabit. Only a truly major upset can shake the structure we have built. A diagnosis of chronic illness and its attendant life changes are such an upset. The diagnosis begins a journey into disorientation and disruption. Because chronic illness affects every aspect of self simultaneously, and because uncertainty is pervasive and non-ending, those newly diagnosed with a chronic illness find that they no longer have a foothold on their beliefs about not only "who" they are, but also "why" they are. Life-changing events often lead to existential and spiritual suffering, raising questions of meaning and purpose in life: "I don't recognize myself anymore. Who am I now, and what can I offer? Is there a reason that I am still alive? Where will I find the strength to survive this?"

There is a slow erosion of prior identity. Until a new sense of self and world is built, one that can find the possibilities as well as the losses and that can find a way to accept uncertainty as part of a new rhythm of life and living, then those who suffer from a chronic illness will indeed suffer to their very core.[21] But reintegration and renewed coherence are, in fact, possible. Feelings of well-being and health may coexist with conditions of chronic disability.[22] It is possible to establish a new, and healthy, "normal."

How is this possible? In her book *A Time for Listening and Caring*, Christina Puchalski tells us that people have an instinctual drive to overcome adversity, while in their article "A Spirituality for the Long Haul: Response to Chronic Illness," Muldoon and King say that there is a drive to growth and wholeness in every individual.[23] But to regain a balance of body, mind, and spirit is hard and stressful work, requiring courage, strength, support, and hope.

Achieving integration is a dynamic and unpredictable process that is often thrown off kilter by the vagaries of chronic illness. Finding ways to cope is essential. Coping is defined as the person's constantly changing cognitive and behavioral efforts to manage specific internal and / or external demands appraised as taxing or exceeding the person's resources.[24] A person's ability to adjust is based upon the ability to mobilize those coping resources. Internal resources might include a person's faith and personal characteristics. (Clearly, some individuals are more resilient than others.) External resources may be a social support network and the nature of one's environment.

## *Spirituality as a Powerful Means of Coping and Growing*

Research into the efficacy of spiritual coping strategies within the context of chronic illness has shown that individuals who possess a strong sense of spiritual well-being fair better than those who do not.[25] As spiritual caregivers, we are often humbled by the power of the human spirit and its determination to thrive even in the most difficult of circumstances. But we also know that such triumph requires support and compassion to do so, as well as a faith in the meaning and purpose of one's life.

Spirituality is a quality that goes beyond religious affiliation, and it may or may not include a personal relationship with God. It is that which defines us and guides our everyday response to the world. It moves us past our "I" and connects us to the larger questions of what it means to be alive. Our spirit yearns for meaning and purpose, unity and wholeness. How we strive to achieve that is different for each person.

Although the literature on spirituality and chronic illness describes spirituality in diverse ways, it is united in some common themes, such as the experience of profound relationship, self-transcendence, and meaning making.

At the core of one's spirituality is profound relationship. For many persons, spirituality centers on a deep faith in God as defined by a specific religious tradition. This faithful relationship can give strength and comfort; it can empower and provide meaning and purpose. Others may believe in a higher transcendent power that they do not identify as God. For many, the spiritual dimension is possible through an interconnection with the self, family, others, community, nature, art, music, and the values that a person holds dear. Such relationships are dynamic and have the ability to enlarge a person's world and sense of self. Such an expansion allows a person to find a sense of personal value and purpose that transcends the present reality.

But it can be very difficult to maintain faith while a chronic illness is chipping away at a person's established identity and worldview. While some persons living with chronic illness find their religious faith strengthened, others may find a sense of faith for the first time, may falter in their faith, or may lose it entirely. For many, it is all these things and more.

Viktor Frankl, a psychiatrist and Nazi concentration camp survivor, wondered why some prisoners endured while others did not. He found a profound truth in Neitzche's words: "If you have a *why* to live for, you can bear with any *how*."[26] Frankl concluded that the most important driving life force for man was the search for meaning. Every human being has to have a task; it doesn't matter what it is, but it must be uniquely his or her own, and it comes with the responsibility to live up to the person's full potential as a human being.[27] Frankl insisted that an individual can find meaning in life even when challenged with immense suffering,[28] as suffering in itself does not annihilate the dignity of human beings or the meaning of life.[29] Forces beyond our control can take away everything we possess except one thing: our freedom to choose how we will respond to the situation. Rabbi Harold Kushner, in his introduction to the 2006 edition of Frankl's *Man's Search for Meaning*, sums up Frankl's message with the words, "We cannot control what happens to us in life, but we can control what we will do about what happens to us."[30] Finding and sustaining hope is the key. In his book *The Nature of Suffering and the Goals of Medicine*, Dr. Cassell posits that it is possible to transcend the suffering and to find an unselfish courage that leads to hope—the belief in a reality that transcends what is available as evidence.[31]

A woman crippled from birth, further disfigured by burns, and who successfully struggled to become a psychiatrist, summed up her situation in these words: "I am not what you see." She was affirming an inner wholeness and richness that was not reflected in how she looked or how others perceived her. She had found her task, transcended the limitations of her body, and chose to live her life and not her illness.[32]

As spiritual caregivers, it is our task and responsibility to accompany and encourage individuals on their journey toward spiritual, emotional, and existential integration and health.

## Notes

1. Centers for Disease Control and Prevention, www.cdc.gov/chronicdisease/overview/index.htm.
2. Partnership for Solutions, *Chronic Conditions: Making the Case for Ongoing Care* (Baltimore: Johns Hopkins University, 2004), 9, www.partnershipforsolutions.org/DMS/files/chronicbook2004.pdf.
3. 2002 U.S. Census Bureau.
4. Partnership for Solutions, *Chronic Conditions.*
5. Centers for Disease Control and Prevention.
6. Ibid.
7. Partnership for Solutions, *Chronic Conditions.*
8. Centers for Disease Control and Prevention, *Chronic Disease Overview: Costs of Chronic Disease* (Atlanta: CDC, 2005), www.cdc.gov/nccdphp/overview.htm.
9. KaiserEDU, *U.S. Health Care Costs*, citation from Centers for Medicare and Medicaid Services, Office of the Actuary, National Health Statistics Group, National Health Care Expenditures Data, January 2010, www.kaiseredu.org/Issue-Modules/US-Health-Care-Costs/Background-Brief.aspx?p=1.
10. M. Mishel, "Uncertainty in Chronic Illness," *Annual Review of Nursing Research* 17, no. 1 (1999): 269–94.
11. P. Ironside et al., "Experiencing Chronic Illness: Cocreating New Understandings," *Qualitative Health Research* 13, no. 2 (2003): 171–83.
12. Mishel, "Uncertainty in Chronic Illness."
13. Ibid.
14. E. Cassell, *The Nature of Suffering and the Goals of Medicine* (New York: Oxford University Press, 1991), 33.
15. C. Guzzetta, "Healing and Wholeness in Chronic Illness," *Journal of Holistic Nursing* 16, no. 2 (1998): 197–201.
16. Ironside et al., "Experiencing Chronic Illness."
17. W. Greenstreet, "From Spirituality to Coping Strategy: Making Sense of Chronic Illness," *British Journal of Nursing* 15, no. 17 (2006): 938–42.
18. R. Whittemore and J. Dion, "Chronic Illness: The Process of Integration," *Journal of Clinical Nursing* 17, no. 7B (2008): 177–87.
19. M. Muldoon and J. King, "A Spirituality for the Long Haul: Response to Chronic Illness," *Journal of Religion and Health* 30, no. 2 (1991): 99–108.
20. Greenstreet, "From Spirituality to Coping Strategy."
21. Mishel, "Uncertainty in Chronic Illness."

22. L. Rozario, "Spirituality in the Lives of People with Disability and Chronic Illness: A Creative Paradigm of Wholeness and Reconstitution," *Disability and Rehabilitation* 19, no. 10 (1997): 427–34.
23. C. Puchalski, *A Time for Listening and Caring: Spirituality and the Care of the Chronically Ill and Dying* (New York: Oxford University Press, 2006), ix; Muldoon and King, "A Spirituality for the Long Haul."
24. D. Baldacchino, "Spiritual Coping Strategies: A Review of the Nursing Research Literature," *Journal of Advanced Nursing* 34, no. 6 (2001): 833–41.
25. B. Landis, "Uncertainty, Spiritual Well-Being, and Psychosocial Adjustment to Chronic Illness," *Issues in Mental Health Nursing* 17, no. 3 (1996): 217–31; W. Breitbart, "Spirituality and Meaning in Supportive Care: Spirituality- and Meaning-Centered Group Psychotherapy Interventions in Advanced Cancer," *Supportive Care in Cancer* 10, no. 4 (2002): 272–80; K. Pargament, "Religious / Spiritual Coping," in *Multidimensional Measurement of Religiousness / Spirituality for Use in Health Research*, by Fetzer Institute / National Institute on Aging Working Group (Kalamazoo, MI: Fetzer Institute, 1999).
26. P. Krauss and M. Goldfischer, *Why Me? Coping with Grief, Loss, and Change* (New York: Bantam Books, 1988).
27. Breitbart, "Spirituality and Meaning in Supportive Care."
28. L. Agrimson and L. Taft, "Spiritual Crisis: A Concept Analysis," *Journal of Advanced Nursing* 65, no. 2 (2008): 454–61.
29. W. Noguchi et al., "Spiritual Needs in Cancer Patients and Spiritual Care Based on Logotherapy," *Supportive Care in Cancer* 14, no. 1 (2006): 65–70.
30. V. Frankl, *Man's Search for Meaning* (Boston: Beacon Press, 2006), x.
31. Cassell, *The Nature of Suffering and the Goals of Medicine*, 43.
32. Muldoon and King, "A Spirituality for the Long Haul."

## About the Contributor

**Rabbi Zahara Davidowitz-Farkas, MHL, BCJC, CPSP Diplomate Supervisor,** is a founder of the National Association of Jewish Chaplains (NAJC) and has served in a variety of elected and volunteer positions. In addition to being board certified by the NAJC, she is also a diplomate in the College of Pastoral Supervision and Psychotherapy. She currently teaches clinical pastoral education in Israel. She authored the chapter "Jewish Spiritual Assessment" in *Jewish Pastoral Care: A Practical Handbook from Traditional and Contemporary Sources*, and the LifeLight אורות החיים™ booklet *Facing and Recovering from Surgery* (both Jewish Lights Publishing).

# 25

## Complicated Grief

### Exploring Arresting Grief and Survival Grief in Spiritual / Pastoral Care

*Chaplain Timothy G. Serban, MA, BCC*

*The moment I realize just how little I know about a topic is usually immediately after I have just walked with someone who is actually living through it.*

### *Mary's Secret about "Why"*

Looking up from her bed, her smile sparkled and she motioned for me to sit down. Mary, in her mid-seventies, resembled actress Katharine Hepburn, powerful and deeply reflective. She had a secret about grief that she wanted to share with me, the hospice chaplain. She said, "In my life, I have faced a lot of grief. In just one day I lost my husband and two sons in a small plane accident over the Cascade Mountains in Oregon. It was a day I will never forget."

Now Mary had elected hospice care as she faced terminal cancer. She continued:

> For many years after the accident I asked the question, "Why? Why me? Just why?" I simply kept asking that question over and over and over. And you know what I learned about the question? It's an empty one! It echoes and echoes when you ask it and it doesn't help.
>
> I was able to see the word "WHY," and it just echoed forever. The question just pulls energy and strength out of you. And you end up back where you started again: hurting, alone, and empty. That is when I knew

> I had to change the question. I had to change from asking "Why?" to finding some way to learn about gratitude again. I had to start thinking about what I have to be grateful for today. And when I changed to gratitude, I began to remember moments of joy with my husband and my sons. I remembered their birth and the fact that they brought me two beautiful daughters-in-law and four grandchildren. When I began to look beyond the question "Why?" I began to find hope and strength again. So if you ever find yourself asking the question "Why?" go ahead and ask it for a while, but when you're ready, remember my secret about gratitude. Because I know it will help someday.

## *Introduction to Grief*

One of the many dangers in writing a chapter on grief is that the reader may try to apply the lessons as a recipe rather than as guidance on caring for those in need. Mary's story is but one of many powerful experiences that has helped shape my professional pastoral understanding about grief and complicated grief. Through this chapter we will explore the pastoral and spiritual nature of complicated grief, arresting grief, and survival grief. In addition, we will explore practical ways to walk with people experiencing grief.

There are many counseling experts in the field of grief, bereavement, and mourning. The expertise of these professionals is vast. The field of bereavement has been transformed since the early days when Elisabeth Kübler-Ross introduced the five stages of grief. Today the book by clinical psychologist Therese Rando, PhD, *Treatment of Complicated Mourning,* has become a cornerstone resource for many bereavement counselors. No matter how many definitions there are to describe grief, the bottom line is this: care of those who are grieving is integral to the nature of human beings and deeply present in the spiritual care of those who suffer.

Faith traditions are grounded in a profound call to care for the vulnerable. When most people experience loss, they become "vulnerable" for some period of time. Thus, there is a need for presence, support, and family. Rituals have been created to support these needs.

When a person faces grief, no matter how it is defined, one simply hurts. The mourner oftentimes feels out of control and overwhelmed. Like the *Peanuts* cartoon of Lucy pulling the football away from Charlie Brown at the last minute, grief can catch us off-guard, even when it's expected and we know it's going to happen. Sometimes even those we trust to hold the ball will unexpectedly pull it away.

## *Defining Grief*

The *Oxford Dictionary*'s definition of grief is as follows: "Deep sorrow, especially that which is caused by someone's death; the experience of deep loss especially of one with whom a deep bond is formed."[1]

Grief has many dimensions—spiritual, emotional, physical, and psychological. Often the experience of grief is best captured in art, music, or a movie, like the wood-carved image shown in Figure 25.1 called *Folk Grief*, which depicts a person sitting with the knees up, head resting in the folded arms alone, and the space from the back to the arms is empty and hollow. Carved out of wood, the torso appears to float above the lower half of the body. It is a powerful reflection of grief, loss, and aloneness.

**FOLK GRIEF**

*Figure 25.1*

Many authors and movies have depicted the experiences and images of grief. Some of the more notable authors and their works include C. S. Lewis's *A Grief Observed* and Rabbi Harold Kushner's *When Bad Things Happen to Good People*. Movies have a way of depicting the depths of emotions through the actors who portray those touching moments of grief and loss. One such movie, *Shadowlands* (1994), with Anthony Hopkins and Debra Winger, is about the life of author C. S. Lewis. In this movie, he faces two choices: "to love and lose" or "to not get close to the one you love for fear of losing them." Other great movies reflecting experiences of grief and hope are *Beaches* (1988), with Bette Midler and Barbara Hershey; *What Dreams May Come* (1998), with Robin Williams; *Wit* (2001), with Emma Thompson; and Disney's movie *Up* (2009), with Ed Asner. Throughout these films and many more works of art, the experience of grief and loss is explored in profound and ordinary ways.

Today, when one searches online bookstores for the topic "complicated grief," about fifty books are listed. However, there are fewer than five resources written on the topic of spiritual care and complicated grief. One such work is by Junietta Baker-McCall, DMin, *Bereavement Counseling: Pastoral Care for Complicated Grieving*.

## *Complicated Grief*

Harvard Medical School defines complicated grief as when

> normal grief responses and symptoms linger and become increasingly debilitating, the condition turns into what is now being called unresolved, protracted, traumatic, or complicated grief. It has features of both depression and post-traumatic stress disorder (PTSD).[2]

Complicated grief is often referred to when grief becomes paralyzing or delayed. Complicated grief can occur following traumatic or unexpected losses, such as the death of a child, including stillbirth or miscarriage; death by suicide; or death by murder. Sudden or traumatic deaths following a disaster or mass casualty event can have long-term debilitating effects that complicate one's ability to cope. Therese Rando, in her book *Treatment of Complicated Mourning*, defines complicated mourning as

> when there is compromise, distortion or failure to move through any one of the six "R" processes of mourning after a given amount of time since the death. The six "R" processes of mourning are when the grieving person can:[3]
>
> 1. Recognize the loss
> 2. React to the separation
> 3. Recollect and re-experience the deceased and the relationship
> 4. Relinquish old attachments to the deceased
> 5. Readjust to move adaptively into the new world without forgetting the old
> 6. Reinvest: "The emotional energy once invested in the relationship with the deceased must be reinvested where it can be returned to the mourner." Therefore, the emotional energy from the previous relationship with the loved one must be redirected toward rewarding new investments "in other people, objects, roles, hopes, beliefs, causes, ideals, goals pursuits, and so forth."[4]

In the American Psychiatric Association's publication *Focus*, the following criteria for diagnosing complicated grief were proposed in 2003 for addition in the fifth edition of the *Diagnostic and Statistical Manual of Mental Disorders* (*DSM-V*) when it is released:

> Criteria would include the current experience (more than a year after a loss) of intense intrusive thoughts, pangs of severe emotion, distressing yearnings, feeling excessively alone and empty, excessively avoiding tasks reminiscent of the deceased, unusual sleep disturbances, and maladaptive levels of loss of interest in personal activities.[5]

The Mental Health Academy in Fortitude Valley, Australia, is the largest provider of online education and professional development for counselors in Australia, and they have published an excellent graphic on the many aspects of complicated grief. Figure 25.2 shows how the varied types of unresolved / complicated grief overlap.[6]

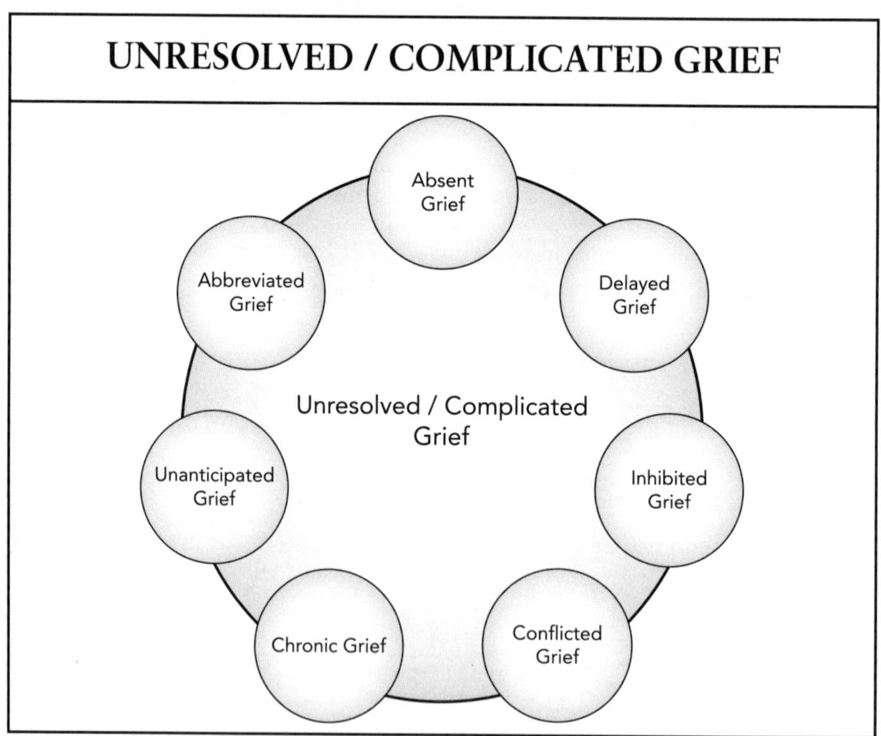




*Figure 25.2*

## Arresting Grief

Arresting grief is the type of grief that occurs when a person has been literally stunned by the impact of the disaster or loss. Rando addresses this type of complicated mourning in her work when she writes, "After a sudden unexpected death most mourners find it impossible to complete the fourth 'R' process (relinquish the old attachments to the deceased and the old assumptive world) within the first few months."[7]

Arresting grief may be observed as an overwhelming lament, causing one to simply shut down. In New York City, in the weeks and months after September 11, many of us who helped coordinate the provision of spiritual care through the Disaster Spiritual Care Response Team of the American Red Cross encountered this type of grief. We were part of teams that escorted families of the victims for their first up-close view of the devastation of the World Trade Center site. In such moments the grief was palpable. Arresting grief can be a paralyzing grief that may occur without significant physical traumatic impact to the mourner him- or herself. It is seen on a regular basis in hospitals with parents who lose a child in a tragic auto accident. Chaplains witnessed this repeatedly in both New York City with the fathers who hoped to find their sons in the midst of the 9/11 rubble if they were "just allowed to keep searching a little more" and in the faces of loved ones who lived while they had to say good-bye to their spouses / children / parents as the waters of Katrina rose above their heads. And this type of grief was experienced by the children who watched as family members were washed away by the tsunami waters in American Samoa.

Arresting grief may be lasting in its duration and is closely associated with another type of grief known as survival grief.

## Survival Grief

Survival grief is demonstrated when an individual is faced with the need to keep going for the sake of others. A parent raising three children who experiences the loss of a spouse may find that there is simply no time to grieve because the responsibilities at hand are so great. An individual may experience this type of grief when faced with a dangerous life-or-death situation. For example, soldiers in the midst of battle may experience survival grief as they remain engaged in the battle in the face of trauma, death, and sudden loss. To survive, they must push the grief below the surface until they are free from the danger. Survival grief in this situation may be observed when the soldier no longer feels the need to grieve and continues on "autopilot" well beyond the battle.

In a similar way, police and firefighters may experience survival grief in the midst of a disaster such as an earthquake, hurricane, or terrorist attack. Faced with the emotions that overwhelm the ability to cope, disasters where there are mass casualties will often cause survivors to go on "shutdown mode." Delayed grief can be healthy in such situations in order to continue to function in the capacity of saving lives. Care for individuals facing survival grief is best offered through simple reminders of the basics: eat, sleep, and breathe.

Rando describes certain factors that may delay mourning:

> A delay or relative delay in mourning may occur for any number of conscious or unconscious reasons. The mourner needs to put mourning on hold to attend to other pressing responsibilities. These responsibilities may concern herself (e.g., her own needs for survival after injury) or others' needs for comfort from her."[8]

Multiple losses can also be a trigger for survival grief. Losing multiple loved ones in an auto accident, air disaster, or natural disaster can complicate the ability to cope and grieve. Often survivors may feel that they have to grieve each loss in a certain order. Sometimes they do not know how to begin to grieve these losses and as a result they simply shut down, not grieving any. If a parent dies within months of a neighbor and best friend, sometimes the grieving person may feel the need to grieve the loss of the parent before the friend. However, the death of the friend may have been a totally unexpected or shocking loss that keeps coming to the surface for the grieving person. It may be helpful to simply give oneself permission to grieve the loss that surfaces first. Grief is not linear; it does not make sense and is not rational. There is more than one way to journey through grief.

Providing spiritual care in the midst of complicated grief is both a challenge and a gift. The spiritual caregiver need not have a road map for the grieving person. Grief is at times "out of control." It does not make sense. It can render us helpless and cause us at times to replay scenes of the loss in microscopic detail. Like trying to rationalize the irrational, trying to unpack one's grief involves concentric circles—circling the airport of the loss over and over, exploring every detail from many levels, trying to consider what could have been done to change the outcome.

In some situations, another aspect that complicates grief is when an action of the griever may have been instrumental or significant in the death, such as the driver of a vehicle who loses control of the car that kills the passenger. Accidents or disasters happen, and one person lives and others die. All of these situations may play back in our minds over and over. Before we can begin to unpack the grief, we must first get to safety.

Grief is very much like a river. The river is a symbol of grief; it will flow and it will rise and fall with some regularity on the anniversaries and special occasions in one's life. Like grief, the river can also be wild and unpredictable. We need not try to push the river; it will seek its own level and will flow at its own pace.

Complicated grief is like the river that gets shifted by a disaster. In a disaster, our river is pushed in a direction that is unlike any common direction. When this happens, it forever changes our life. I recently worked with a parent whose child was murdered several years ago. In the midst of the grief the parent wondered out loud whether she really processed the grief in the proper way. She wondered whether there was something she should have done to fully grieve her child's death. We explored the image of the river and how the death of a loved one can shift our river dramatically. And I suggested that in the bend of the river is a treasure chest full of memories—the love, the stories, and the life that they shared together. All of it is so priceless that we could never fully unpack it all. And on the journey of grief there are times when we are pulled back to this treasure chest and sit in front of it on the anniversaries and holidays or unexpected days. When we are ready, little by little, we may begin to unpack each memory. These moments of laughter are both a treasure and a time of healing.

We can come back to it whenever we want. Through the years as we unpack and relive the moments of the loss, we are able to simply be with the experience, without judgment or fear. We are safe to unpack its contents in such a way that enables us to experience the healing of the water at our feet. When these moments lift us up and carry us downstream, we need not fight against the current, but allow the memories and gifts of the relationship to heal and comfort us through our grief.

Survival grief, when attended to, can serve as a path to discovery and hope. It can be transformed into a renewed sense of gratitude for the gifts that remain behind. These gifts may be the people who have provided support through the storm, for the unexpected caregiver who asked, "How are you really doing today?" When we reflect on the memories of a lifetime and struggle to unpack the grief of many losses either as a chaplain providing spiritual / pastoral care, a hospice caregiver, or a pastor / rabbi / priest / imam in the congregation, we may encounter individuals whose grief is delayed. In such cases, the pastor / rabbi / priest / imam and pastoral caregiver must always ask, "Whose need am I trying to meet?" Pastoral caregivers are there to support the needs of the grieving person and his or her family, not our own need to change the grieving person or share our own experience of grief, hoping that it may relate to another's loss.

## *Spirituality and Grief Guide for Caregivers*

Through the years in my ministry I have heard it said that every grieving person needs to tell his or her story at least 150 times before he or she can begin to heal. If this is true, it may explain why our family and friends are burned-out after the first 50 times.

The role of the professional chaplain is to explore with patients their source of strength, their hopes and fears, and their journey. To this end I have created a tool to better help family and friends know how to support people in grief. "Spirituality & Grief: A Caregiver Guide," also known as the "Faith & Fear Factors" caregiver checklist, is one practical resource (see Figures 25.3 and 25.4). The more you know yourself and your fears, the better you are able to be present with the person who is grieving. This guide is designed as a tool to help prepare and slow down the caregiver prior to visiting the grieving person. When you are offering support, it is helpful to know your own faith factors. What types of assumptions are you possibly bringing to the visit? If you were raised in a faith tradition, what are some of the things that you recall being said in your tradition about suffering? What do you recall your tradition saying about the cause of suffering and death? All of these questions will help you know yourself better. Next, you explore your personal "fear factors." What makes you fearful about death or dying?

Finally, explore what you think you might know about the grieving person before you visit him or her. What do you know of the person's "faith factors?" What types of reflections and insights has he or she shared with you in the past about what the person's faith tradition says about suffering and death? Then continue on to think about what the griever might identify as his or her fear factors as it relates to suffering or dying. When you have filled in what you know about yourself and what you think you know about the other person, take a look at how the two columns of answers compare. Are there a lot of blank areas for you or for the person who is grieving? If so, perhaps this is an indication of how important it is for you to simply listen and learn the grieving person's story. If you have filled in both columns, look at them and see whether there are differences in your answers. Here you may learn that your assumptions about suffering and death may not be consistent with those of the person who is grieving. Once again, it can serve as a helpful reminder not to rush to give answers about the person's questions of faith and suffering. Rather, in the midst of the visit, together you can find possible common places where you honor the journey of grief and explore the memories and gifts that are discovered in the treasure chest.

## *Final Words*

If I were to boil this entire chapter down to a few words, I would say, "Show up, sit down, listen twice, and speak less." Grief can become too complicated when we try to rationalize it. What I have learned through walking with individuals in the face of overwhelming and complicated grief is that grief is not rational. It is not linear and does not often follow a specific path or stage. It hurts and simply doesn't make sense.

## *Wisdom Sayings on Grief*

- Grief is a "journey through," not around.
- We can deny its existence, but grief is patient and waits as long as we have the energy to ignore it.
- Grief is like a mountain that blocks our path; the only way through it is with the hand shovel we hold.
- Counseling is not a mysterious, scary thing; it just gives us a steam shovel to get through the mountain faster.

| SPIRITUALITY & GRIEF: A CAREGIVER GUIDE<br>FINDING COMMON GROUND FOR CAREGIVERS | | |
|---|---|---|
| INSTRUCTIONS: Prior to providing support to a person experiencing spiritual grief, review the following key FAITH FACTORS that apply to you and to the grieving person. The more you know about yourself and the grieving process, the better you will be able to provide a supportive presence to others in grief. | | |
| **FAITH FACTORS** | **MINE** | **OF THE GRIEVING PERSON** |
| 1. **Formal faith tradition practiced** (Orthodox Jewish, Roman Catholic, Sunni / Shi'ite Muslim, ELCA / Missouri Synod Lutheran, multiple faiths, no formal faith tradition) | | |
| 2. **Length of time (years)** (Entire life, a few years, recent faith conversion) | | |
| 3. **Formal religious education** (Theology, Hebrew, Islamic school, other) | | |
| 4. **Role of family in faith development** (Not involved 0–10 Strongly involved) | | |
| 5. **Role of authority** (Respect, fear, contempt for, challenge) | | |
| 6. **Image of God / Divine** (Distant, vindictive, personally involved) | | |
| 7. **What do you tell others about suffering?** (Be strong, it's okay, one step at a time) | | |
| 8. **Belief about the cause of suffering** (Lesson to learn, a test, a punishment, redemptive, karma, mystery) | | |
| 9. **Personal belief about death** (A beginning, an end, heaven, hell, reincarnation) | | |



*Figure 25.3*

## SPIRITUALITY & GRIEF: A CAREGIVER GUIDE FINDING COMMON GROUND FOR CAREGIVERS

INSTRUCTIONS: Prior to providing support to a person experiencing spiritual grief, review the following key FEAR FACTORS that apply to you and to the grieving person. The more you know about yourself and the grieving process, the better you will be able to provide a supportive presence to others in grief.

| FEAR FACTORS | IN ME | IN THE GRIEVING PERSON |
|---|---|---|
| 1. Loss of control | | |
| 2. Being a burden | | |
| 3. Pain / suffering | | |
| 4. The dying process | | |
| 5. Losing one's faith (doubt) | | |
| 6. The unknown | | |
| 7. God's *gonna getcha* | | |
| 8. The past | | |
| 9. The future | | |
| 10. Being alone | | |
| 11. Rejection | | |
| 12. Not knowing what to say | | |
| 13. Causing more pain | | |
| 14. Religion | | |
| 15. Anger / emotion | | |
| 16. Losing hope | | |



*Figure 25.4*

- Complicated grief shifts our river and leaves behind a treasure chest to unpack.
- There is no timetable with grief; when it brings you back to the treasure chest, sit and unpack it more.
- The calmest waters in a storm are just beneath the surface; go deeper.
- If you are getting pounded by the waves, stop running along the shore; get wet and move to the eye of the storm.
- Fear is never in the present moment; it is always in the future.
- If a tornado is destroying the room of your "present moment," you can't stop it with your hands; just open a window and breathe.
- To find the present moment, check your heartbeat and your breath; they are anchors to bring you back to "now."
- "The pain I feel today is the love we shared yesterday; it is worth the risk to love."[9]

Each of these wisdom sayings on grief has deep meaning and can be unpacked for years. As professional chaplains and caregivers, we are called to show up with people in grief and hold on as they share their story of loss again and again.

## Notes

1. *Oxford Dictionary*, www.oxforddictionaries.com.
2. Harvard Medical School, "Complicated Grief," *Family Health Guide*, www.health.harvard.edu/fhg/updates/Complicated-grief.shtml.
3. Therese A. Rando, *Treatment of Complicated Mourning* (Champaign, IL: Research Press, 1993), 149.
4. Ibid., 60.
5. M. J. Horowitz et al., "Diagnostic Criteria for Complicated Grief Disorder," *Focus* 1 (2003): 290–98.
6. Mental Health Academy, "Complicated Grief" (online course), www.mentalhealthacademy.com.au/courses_details.php?catid=6&courseid=76.
7. Rando, *Treatment of Complicated Mourning*, 149.
8. Ibid., 160.
9. Hopkins, Anthony and Debra Winger. *Shadowlands*. Directed by Richard Attenborough. Price Entertainment, 1994.

## Further Reading


Baker-McCall, J. *Bereavement Counseling: Pastoral Care for Complicated Grieving.* Binghamton, NY: Haworth Pastoral Press, 2004.

Kushner, H. S. *When Bad Things Happen to Good People.* New York: Avon Books, 1981.

Lewis, C. S. *A Grief Observed.* New York: Bantam Seabury Press, 1976.

Serban, T. "Spirituality & Grief: A Caregiver Guide," 2004, www.nacc.org/docs/conference/S5%20Theology%20of%20Disaster%203.pdf.


## About the Contributor

**Chaplain Timothy G. Serban, MA, BCC,** is vice president of mission integration and spiritual care at Providence Regional Medical Center, Everett, Washington, supporting a team of twenty-one board certified chaplains and music thanatologists. He has been in the field of spiritual care, mission, and ethics for more than twenty-two years. He holds his master's degree in theology and pastoral ministry in health care from Duquesne University in Pittsburgh, Pennsylvania. He is a board certified chaplain with the National Association of Catholic Chaplains. He serves as national volunteer lead for the Spiritual Care Response Team of the American Red Cross in Washington, DC, and liaison of the National Association of Catholic Chaplains to the American Red Cross. Chaplain Serban has taught and spoken abroad on disaster response, ethics, and spiritual care. He is a contributor to *Disaster Spiritual Care: Practical Clergy Responses to Community, Regional and National Tragedy* (SkyLight Paths Publishing), and *The Red Guide to Recovery: A Resource Handbook for Disaster Survivors.*

# PART IV

# *The Infrastructure of Spiritual / Pastoral Care*

# 26

## *Strategic Planning*

### A Basis for All Infrastructure Development and Growth within Spiritual / Pastoral Care

*Rev. W. L. (Bill) Bross, MDiv, BCC, and*
*Paula DeAngelo, MS, Senior OD Consultant*

It has been said that the "definition of insanity is to continue to do the same things over and over again, while expecting different results." Spiritual / pastoral care / chaplaincy departments that wish to be in the forefront of their facility's strategic thinking and involved in the foundational shaping of their culture need to begin by assessing their view of chaplaincy, and considering ways in which their department can become the basis for their hospital / hospice / long-term care facility's spiritual environment of caring.

## *A Definition of Strategic Planning*

An effective tool to help in facilitating this process is strategic planning. Phillip Blackerby, a business consultant and executive coach, defines strategic planning as "a continuous and systematic process where people make decisions about intended future outcomes, how outcomes are to be accomplished, and how success is measured and evaluated."[1] Implied in this process is a consideration of efficient use of resources, as well as an intentional direction of resources toward the desired goals.

To fully appreciate the value of strategic planning, let's take a closer look at some of the key ideas presented in the definition: Strategic planning is ongoing; it does not end with the publication of a plan; its success depends on it purposefully becoming an uninterrupted and never-ending cycle. Any effective strategic planning process has a deliberate and specific methodology and a sequence of events; it is never haphazard.[2]

The value of strategic planning lies more in the journey than in the destination. While strategic planning must indeed produce a product, a strategic plan document, the primary value comes from the teamwork, vision, and commitment to and ownership of departmental success the planners gain through the process of making the decisions the document contains.[3]

A strategic planning process must involve all the right people, and those people must be ready and willing to contribute to the process. Strategic planning is a decision making process. Spiritual / pastoral care / chaplaincy departments (SPCDs) that are ready to plan strategically have leaders who are ready to make decisions.

Strategic-level planning addresses external results, or the SPCD's effects on the organization and community, particularly how it affects its customers. An old adage states, "If you don't know where you're going, any road will take you there." Strategic planning is primarily about defining where "there" is, a type of road map outlining the outcomes and results designed to be achieved throughout the journey.

Strategic planners don't quit just because they have defined the future target; they go ahead and select the roads that will get them there. And, strategic planning is all about succeeding. A well-written strategic plan will describe clearly how anyone can tell whether the SPCD is successful. The plan may measure intended future outcomes either quantitatively or qualitatively, but it always defines threshold criteria for achieving success.

## *The Need for Strategic Planning within Spiritual / Pastoral Care*

As health care providers, we are concerned with the healing of the whole person—physical, emotional, and spiritual. If we are interested in engaging our health care facilities and communities at every level, then strategic planning is a tool that will benefit not only our departments but also the patients, facilities, and communities that we serve.

Increasingly, health care is calling upon all disciplines to exhibit evidenced-based outcomes. Spiritual / pastoral care is no exception. Even though our role in the health care setting is unique, in that we are often thought of as "the keepers of the mystery," it is no longer sufficient for us to settle for that role alone. As chaplains, we contribute significantly to the well-being of the whole person, and it is appropriate that we are accountable to that role. Strategic planning identifies, facilitates, and quantifies that process for our discipline, while making it possible for us to achieve measurable results.

An important component of strategic planning is the intentional involvement of key stakeholders from both the facility and the community. In short, we should be intentional about including representatives from every group that our department touches with its sacred work. Strategic planning is not a one-person process, nor is it a one-session event. At its best, it is a facilitated process where a large number of participants comprising a diverse cross-section of stakeholders come together to work on real issues of strategic importance.

This spirit of inclusivity produces several benefits for both the SPCD and the hospital as a whole:

- Systems theory teaches us that when any part of the system experiences change, the other components of the system cannot help but be affected. Strategic planning within the SPCD has the potential to facilitate change throughout the organization through participation by all stakeholder groups.
- Strategic planning, when approached in this way, finds and builds common ground, which is the only practical way to define, implement, and manage change.
- It can also create an alignment toward a shared vision.
- In strategic planning, participants take ownership of their problems and find their own ways forward.
- The efficiency of the process facilitates quick results. Time is saved because the whole system is in the room.
- Since the planning is done by the people who will carry it out, people are motivated and committed to action.
- The process also builds a team culture without doing "team building."

Through strategic planning, the SPCD is positioned to build community not only within the department but also throughout the health care facility as a whole. This is crucial to the SPCD being viewed as the foundation of the facility's spiritual environment of caring. The process also allows the SPCD to align itself with the larger goals of the organization and gives members of the department the information and impetus needed to match their personal and professional goals with those of the health care facility.

Rev. George Handzo writes in chapter 3 of this book, "Most chaplaincy departments that are not able to grow their service or, worse, lose jobs for their staff, fail because neither they nor the individual chaplains within the department have aligned what they do with the mission, goals, and strategic objectives of the institution in which they work." Without ongoing strategic planning, our SPCDs and the work we do are at risk of continued marginalization or, worse, elimination.

## *Strategic Planning*

As we begin, let's take a look at some important strategic planning terms:

- **Vision:** A challenging and imaginative picture of the future role and objectives of an organization or a department, significantly going beyond its current environment and competitive position.
- **Mission statement:** Defines the business that the organization is in (or the role of a department) or what it should be in considering the values and expectations of the stakeholders.
- **Objectives (or goals):** These state more precisely than a mission statement what must be achieved for the organization to achieve its vision and success and by what time. These are measurable by results and are usually established for from three to five years.
- **Strategies:** These are the means by which the objectives will be achieved over a definite period of time.
- **Tactics:** Specific actions (projects, programs, and the daily work) that support and activate the strategies.

- **Alignment:** The linking of individual, team, departmental, and a division's work (vision, mission, objectives, strategies, tactics) with the facility's vision, mission, and objectives.
- **Systems thinking:** This is the discipline of viewing causes and effects in other than a straight-line sequence of "this happened because of that" or seeking single causes for any event. Systems thinking is seeing all the elements influencing an outcome, seeking the many connections between various components in a system.

## *Environmental Analysis: Planning to Plan*

Strategic environmental analysis is the first step in strategic planning (see Figure 26.1, "Strategic Planning Process") and asks the question "Where are we now?" Its purpose is to gather data to prepare your group for visioning and planning. With a rich collection of analysis information, visions and plans will stand on a solid foundation. With this information, you will have a better understanding of your community and the internal conditions of your facility. This will also give you insight into the gaps, challenges, and opportunities that need your attention as you plan for success.

Four areas need to be considered when conducting an environment analysis:

- **Strengths:** Discuss and list the strengths of your department. Consider the unique gifts of your staff and the contributions that you make to the health care facility environment. Consider your patient satisfaction scores in relation to spiritual / pastoral care. Look at the strengths of your facility and how your daily work as a department informs that picture.
- **Weaknesses:** Every department has growing edges, areas where we can stretch and grow. Some weaknesses are inherent within the organizational structure or are reflective of leadership or staff attitudes. Whatever the weaknesses are, it is important to identify them. These could represent real opportunities for your department as you embark on strategic planning.

## STRATEGIC PLANNING PROCESS

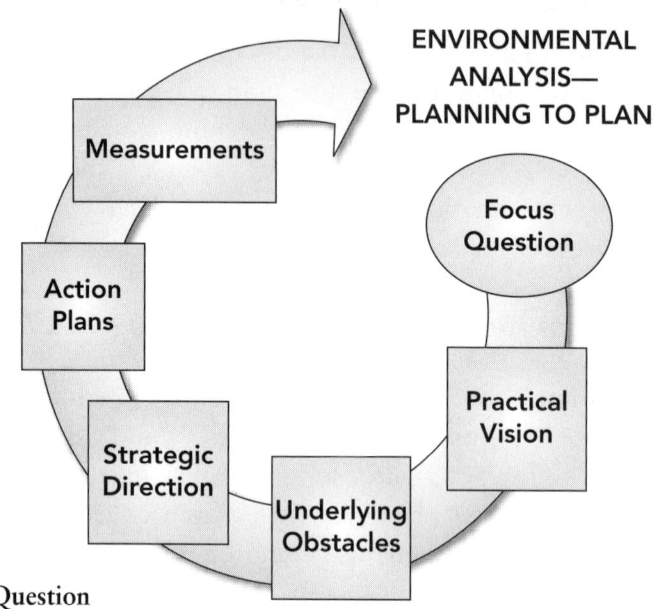


**Focus Question**

A question that focuses attention of the group on a specific subject while allowing creative responses—e.g., What do we want to see going on in the Spiritual Care Department in five years?

**Practical Vision**

Purpose: Identify what we want to see happening in three to six years

**Underlying Obstacles**

Purpose: Identify what is blocking us from realizing our hopes and dreams (vision)

**Strategic Direction**

Purpose: Identify what we can do to deal with obstacles and release our vision. Create a chart of strategic direction. Prioritize

**Action Plans**

Purpose: Create an action plan for each new direction (tactics and accountability)

Identify tasks, costs, and deliverables for each

**Measurements**

What measures will we put into place that will indicate achievement of the objective?

*Figure 26.1*

- **Opportunities:** Opportunities are also identified through listening to your stakeholders and customers. What needs are being expressed by patients, families, staff, and the community that are not currently being met? One of the biggest mistakes a SPCD can make is to assume that it knows what is needed by those it serves. Environmental analysis involves listening carefully and being open to entrepreneurial opportunities that present themselves.
- **Challenges:** We would be remiss in our planning if we didn't take seriously the challenges or threats that we may be up against. In fact, through clearly identifying our obstacles, we set in motion the foundational basis of our strategic plan.

It is important to keep in mind that environmental analysis represents the foundational work of your strategic plan. The stronger your foundation is, the stronger your plan will be. Inasmuch as strategic planning is an ongoing process, so is environmental analysis an ongoing process.

## *The Strategic Planning Process*

### Visioning

Meaningful strategic planning involves purposeful thinking about the future. This involves giving some intentional thought to the collective vision for your department. Where would you like your department to fit within the health care facility structure? What perception would you like the health care facility to have of the SPCD? How would you like the community to view your department? In order to map a viable strategy, you need to know where you're going. If you believe that your department could make a greater impact within the facility or the community, then this is where you begin. Create a picture of what that vision looks like. Here are some suggested questions to begin the visioning process:

- What will be happening in the world five years from now? What will the headlines be?
- What will your community / geographic areas look like within the next five years?

- What will be happening in spiritual / pastoral care at your health care facility five years from now? What will the headlines be?
- How will spiritual / pastoral care impact the various houses of worship in your community five years from now? What will the headlines be?
- What will your health care facility look like in five years? What will spiritual / pastoral care look like?

Other important considerations when developing your vision are as follows:

- Does your vision give your staff and your department the confidence you need?
- Does your vision give your staff and your department the challenge you need?
- Can the vision help you formulate your personal goals in a satisfactory manner?
- Do you feel that your vision is meaningful and that it is yours?

A vision statement for your department can be generated from this discussion. For example: "The SPCD of this health care facility is committed to providing the highest quality spiritual care for our facility and the community. We promise to be available, to seek and promote balance in all of our activities, to open ourselves to the wonder and amazement of each life encounter, and to respect and honor the gift of diversity. We are called to offer direction in the formation of our facility's culture, to demonstrate God's love in all of our interactions, and to invite each member of our staff to take their place within our spiritual environment of caring."

## Identifing Obstacles

It is important to identify the obstacles that are keeping you from moving forward with your vision. Brainstorm the blocks and then perform a root cause analysis. Ask, "What is going on that causes or sustains these blocks or obstacles?" It is important at this point in the process to ask, "Is this block real? Does it actually exist? Can we do something about it?" If the answer to any of these questions is "no," then don't focus on these during the strategic direction phase. Remove these blocks from discussion if they don't pass "the test." Once you've identified obstacles that are real and that you can do something about, then you are ready to move forward with strategic direction. Next, identify the strategies to remove the obstacles. Ask, "What can we do to deal with the obstacles and realize our vision?"

## Seizing Opportunities

As mentioned earlier in this chapter, there are many opportunities for spiritual / pastoral care in today's health care environment. At the authors' work location, Methodist Sugar Land Hospital, we are intentional in addressing two questions: (1) "How can the SPCD further engage the hospital, at every level, today?" and (2) "How can the SPCD further engage the Sugar Land community today?" Invariably, the discussions that result from asking those questions lead to the identification of opportunities for our department to serve. In relation to the first question, opportunities abound in the area of service to hospital physicians and staff. As we have moved toward living out our hospital and departmental visions, hospital administration and management have come to rely on the SPCD in providing support and growth opportunities for staff. In relation to the second question, our department has entered into productive discussions with area houses of worship and organizations around matters that relate to the spiritual health and well-being of our community.

## Designing Goals (Objectives)

Review your vision, mission, and environmental analysis. Then, write several strategic goals that answer the question "What must we do to fulfill our mission and translate our vision into reality?" One thing to remember is that there are no priorities among strategic goals. By definition, all objectives are something your organization or department must do (see Figure 26.2, "Implementation Plans").

One of the goals of the SPCD at Methodist Sugar Land Hospital over the past three years has been the development of a "Compassionate Care Initiative." It is our belief that the success of this initiative is critical to the realization of our departmental vision of "inviting each member of our staff to take their place within our spiritual environment of caring."

| IMPLEMENTATION PLANS | | | | |
|---|---|---|---|---|
| Goal / Objective:<br>Measures: | | | | |
| | **Strategy** | **Tactics** | **Accountability** | **Status** |
| **A** | | | | |
| **B** | | | | |
| **C** | | | | |
| **D** | | | | |
| **E** | | | | |
| **F** | | | | |

*Figure 26.2*

## Designing Strategies: "How We Accomplish Our Goals"

The next step is to design strategies, which are specific actions and specific innovations that will guide the achievement of your goals or objectives (see Figure 26.2). At Methodist Sugar Land Hospital, some of the specific strategies we devised that have supported our goal of developing a Compassionate Care Initiative are Compassionate Care Film Rounds, Living Compassion Staff Stories, Compassionate Thoughts (via e-mail), and the development of Compassionate Care in-services for staff.

## Assigning Tactics and Action: "Who Must Do What?"

Strategic planning truly moves your departmental thinking beyond the publication of mission, objectives, and strategies. The members of your department must embrace the planning process, for they are the ones who will make things happen. Beyond the work of the planning team, these are the people that you want to create the tactics and make the departmental vision a reality. Here are some suggested next steps (see Figure 26.2):

- Assign responsibilities for managing strategies.
- Take a hard look at what it will take to implement the strategies. This leads to the development of your tactical plan.
- Ask your staff and project teams to design tactics to help make the strategies a reality.
- Establish an accountability schedule—develop a timeline.
- Schedule periodic review of goals, strategies, and progress.

## Defining Targets and Measures: "How You Will Recognize Success"

Each objective must have a measure of success. This is how you will know you've achieved your objective. By this measure, you will also focus your strategies and communicate the value of the objective. The following are suggested criteria for developing meaningful measurement:

- **Validity:** Does the measure really measure the intended concept?
- **Reliability:** Does the measure exhibit a minimum amount of error?
- **Ease of understanding:** Can the measure be easily explained and understood?
- **Breadth:** Are the measures broad enough so that everyone in the organization can understand their individual contribution?
- **Unifying:** Do the measures unify the organization—its culture, systems, processes, and output?
- **Future oriented:** Are the measures future oriented so that they will still be effective as the hospital grows?

## *Final Words*

As the discipline of spiritual / pastoral care continues to grow within the health care environment as a whole, it is important that we bring meaningful planning and measurement to the table, demonstrating our participation in and strategic support of the facility's vision and mission. As we involve ourselves in intentional strategic planning, we ensure that our work engages both the health care facility and the community we serve.

### Notes

1. Phillip Blackerby, "Definition of Strategic Planning," Blackerby Associates, 2003, www.blackerbyassoc.com/spdefine.html.
2. Ibid.
3. Ibid.

### Further Reading

Bradford, Robert W., et al. *Simplified Strategic Planning: The No-Nonsense Guide for Busy People*. Worcester, MA: Chandler House Press, 2000.

Burns, Michael, et al. "Effective Strategic Planning: Getting Your Organization Focused and Directed." www.practitionerresources.org/cache/documents/36796.pdf.

Fogg, C. Davis. *Team-Based Strategic Planning*. New York: AMACOM, 1994.

Goodstein, Leonard David, et al. *Applied Strategic Planning: How to Develop a Plan That Really Works*. New York: McGraw-Hill, 1993.

McNamara, Carter. "Basic Overview of Various Strategic Planning Models." www.managementhelp.org/plan_dec/str_plan/models.htm.

Napier, Rod, et al. *High Impact Tools and Activities for Strategic Planning*. New York: McGraw-Hill, 1998.

### About the Contributors

**Rev. W. L. (Bill) Bross, MDiv, BCC,** is the director of spiritual care and values integration at Methodist Sugar Land Hospital, Sugar Land, Texas. He has been the recipient of several grants awarded to study the effectiveness of bereavement interventions and has been involved in hospice, palliative care, and oncology chaplaincy for twenty-two years. He is currently involved in studying factors that inform hospital and organizational culture.

**Paula DeAngelo, MS, Senior OD Consultant,** is an organizational development consultant for Methodist Sugar Land Hospital, Sugar Land, Texas. She received her master's degree in training and development and has worked supporting clients in the areas of training design and development, needs analysis, curriculum design, change management, strategic planning, communication strategy development and implementation, competency modeling, and team building interventions.

# 27

# *Outcome Oriented Chaplaincy*

## Intentional Caring

*Rev. Brent Peery, DMin, BCC*

The term "outcome oriented chaplaincy" seems to have been introduced by Larry VandeCreek and Art Lucas in their book *The Discipline for Pastoral Care Giving: Foundations for Outcome Oriented Chaplaincy*,[1] though, as they acknowledge, there were certainly those writing about and doing research on the subject for at least two decades before their book was released in 2001.[2] Their work has been so formative in the movement that some professional chaplains use "The Discipline" as a label for this approach to chaplaincy care; however, "outcome oriented chaplaincy" generally communicates the concept more clearly. Also, the specific model of outcome oriented chaplaincy articulated by Lucas and his colleagues is not the only approach available. It may not even be the best approach for every context.

My interest in the subject began as a group of chaplains employed by our large health care system were brainstorming ways we could more meaningfully engage the company's mandated quality improvement program. This eventually led to the discovery of VandeCreek and Lucas's work. A few months later we invited Art Lucas and Sue Wintz, who had been trained by Art and his staff, to come spend a full day training us. For over five years outcome oriented chaplaincy has been a strong and fruitful emphasis among the chaplains within the Memorial Hermann Healthcare System.

How does one define outcome oriented chaplaincy (OOC)? It is a method of chaplaincy care that emphasizes achieving, describing, measuring, and improving outcomes that result from a chaplain's work. Its primary components include chaplaincy assessment, chaplaincy interventions, and chaplaincy outcomes.

Many chaplains initially recoil at the notion of associating terms like "achieving, describing, measuring, and improving outcomes" with their care. These are objective concepts. They protest, "How can one quantify the sacred?" "Who can compute what occurs between a professional chaplain and another when spirit touches spirit?" "Can one measure meaning?"[3]

The reality is that there *are* aspects of chaplaincy care that will remain subjective. They cannot be adequately observed, described, or measured. They remain part of the complex beautiful art and mystery of the profession. However, this truth does not negate the fact that much of chaplaincy care is objective. OOC intentionally concerns itself with these aspects. It does so for a variety of reasons discussed later in this chapter. Above all, its aim is to improve the care chaplains give to others. It is about intentional caring.

In this chapter we will first discuss how OOC came to be. Then we will examine the foundational ideas of OOC and its components.

## *How Did OOC Come to Be?*

Very often when chaplains discuss OOC or one of its component parts, they make the error of focusing on one impetus for its evolution to the exclusion of all others. The most frequent of these is health care reform.[4] However, OOC has its origins in a variety of sources. At this time in the history of professional chaplaincy, there are numerous influences—personal, contextual, and historical—coming together to contribute to its emergence. These are like streams flowing together from a variety of directions but headed toward the same end. It is a confluence. A confluence is "a flowing or meeting together; a joining."[5]

### Personal Influences

Chaplaincy is intensely personal work. The chaplain's primary instrument of care is his or her self. So certainly among the strong influences affecting OOC is the individual person working as a chaplain. His or her personal spirituality and sense of vocation impact practice. Other aspects of the chaplain's individuality, including character, temperament, personality, culture, ethnicity, gender, and sexual orientation, could be potential personal influences on his or her care. The chaplain's competency is another personal factor. In 2004 the Spiritual Care Collaborative defined minimum competencies needed to be a professional chaplain.[6] Nonetheless, there remains great variety of education, training, skills, and experiences among professional chaplains beyond the minimum needed to be board certified. These also affect practice.

Although the relative neglect of OOC in the training of professional chaplains needs to be addressed in the future, it certainly should not be at the expense of focus on traditional issues of clinical pastoral education (CPE) like self-awareness and pastoral authority. Again, OOC's emphasis on the objective aspects of chaplaincy care does not negate the influences of the personal and subjective. It seeks to understand these and their potential impact—for good or for ill—on the care provided to others.

In sum, who we *are* as chaplains is as essential to our efficacy as what we *do* and the *context* in which we do it.[7] There may be health care disciplines in which there is little correlation between the type of person doing the work and the outcomes achieved by that work. Chaplaincy is not one of them.

## Contextual Influences

That said, context has a powerful and justifiable influence on how any professional does his or her work. Chaplaincy is no exception. Most professional chaplains work in the context of health care organizations, a complex and dynamic milieu in which to serve. Let's examine a few of the many cultural influences that shape both the context of health care and the work of chaplains.

Professional chaplains are generally clergy. As such we are influenced by the ministry culture of our particular faith tradition. We are also influenced by the broader cultural expectations—from within and without—of how a clergyperson should carry out his or her work. In an earlier, more homogeneous, era of chaplaincy, there was greater consensus regarding these expectations. Today chaplains work in an environment of cultural and spiritual diversity. However, there remains relatively broad agreement that clergy should be persons of integrity and faith who care about others. These values shape OOC. For almost all chaplains who engage in it, OOC will never be primarily about data. That is not what motivates us. It will be about caring for people.

Health care is shaped by the culture of science. Science can be defined as "the observation, identification, description, experimental investigation, and theoretical explanation of phenomena."[8] These are also the endeavors of OOC. The specific phenomena of interest to chaplains is the struggling and coping of persons—patients / residents, their families, and the professionals who care for them—in a health care setting. Since the mid-1970s there has been a growing emphasis on the practice of evidence-based medicine within health care. OOC is in part chaplaincy's response to this focus on choosing health care interventions based on their demonstrable potential for producing desirable outcomes. Some erroneously contend medicine is a purely scientific enterprise. Medicine, like chaplaincy, is both art and science. Both commingle the subjective and mysterious and soft with the objective and known and hard.

Health care is shaped by business culture. More specifically, health care organizations are concerned with generating at least enough income to keep the organization operating. While most chaplains do not bill for their services, there are aspects of OOC that have in the past and can in the future demonstrate the value of chaplaincy care to the business of health care.[9] Another feature of business culture is quality improvement programs. The principles of OOC have enabled the chaplains with whom I work to participate in these in meaningful ways. It has been rewarding to both meet an organizational obligation and improve our chaplaincy care.

Health care is shaped by academic culture. This is true even when the institution is not an academic medical center. Those who work in health care are frequently well educated. This includes professional chaplains, who must complete an accredited graduate theological degree to be board certified. Most have spent at least nineteen years in school before obtaining their first chaplain position. Academic culture places a high value on publishing articles and books that advance thinking and practice. OOC includes values that facilitate research and publishing.

OOC reflects many influences from the complex context of health care. It is a contextually appropriate method for chaplaincy in that setting. It also remains true to the personal influences that have formed the chaplains who serve in that context. All of these features make

OOC a timely emphasis for professional chaplains. That has never been truer than now.

## Historical Chaplaincy Paradigms

To appreciate the timeliness of OOC, it is helpful to broadly and briefly examine the past century of professional chaplaincy. John Gleason has been a chaplaincy educator, researcher, and author for several decades. Borrowing from the concepts of the late philosopher of science Thomas Kuhn, he contended there have been three succeeding prominent paradigms under which chaplains have approached their work in the past hundred years.[10] As professional chaplaincy emerged in the early twentieth century, it operated primarily from a paradigm of "a response to individual sin." Chaplains helped persons heal from the effects of their sin within the mutually agreed upon theological constructs of a shared faith tradition. The three dominant American faith traditions of this era were Judaism and Catholic and Protestant Christianity.

In the 1960s, as societal norms and institutions enjoyed far less consensus, there arose a new paradigm for professional chaplaincy. It was based upon the client-centered therapy of Humanist psychologist Carl Rogers. Chaplains embraced a method of caregiving built primarily on the three principles of congruence / genuineness by the helper paired with empathic understanding of and unconditional positive regard for the client. Prominent among chaplains during this era has been a strong emphasis on the "ministry of presence." It stressed the healing sufficiency of a calm and caring chaplain. Gleason called this the "Rogerian paradigm," which he explained dominated through the later part of the twentieth century.

As Gleason wrote in 1998 he observed a new paradigm for chaplaincy care was on the ascent. "The emerging paradigm appears to have as its defining aim and coherent principle *a response to individual need.* It is arising—uneasily, conflictually, but irresistibly—within the increasing inadequacy and breakdown of the current paradigm."[11] Among the signs of paradigm shift he cited are new models of chaplaincy assessment, interventions, and outcomes accompanied by increasing attention to research in chaplaincy care.[12] Though Gleason reflected on chaplaincy primarily in the United Sates, Meg Orton noted similar changes in the United Kingdom and Australia.[13] In other words, OOC is the operant paradigm for professional chaplaincy for the twenty-first century.

## *Contemporary Evidence of the OOC Paradigm*

In the fall of 2004, six major North American professional pastoral care organizations developed and affirmed *Common Standards for Professional Chaplaincy*.[14] This document defined the minimum required competencies for someone to be board certified as a professional chaplain. Among these are several that support the practice of OOC:

- Formulate and utilize spiritual assessments in order to contribute to plans of care.
- Provide effective pastoral support that contributes to well-being of patients, their families, and staff.
- Document one's contribution of care effectively in the appropriate records.
- Establish and maintain professional and interdisciplinary relationships.[15]

In the spring of 2010, the Association of Professional Chaplains (APC) completed *Standards of Practice for Professional Chaplains in Acute Care Settings*.[16] "Standards of practice are authoritative statements that describe broad responsibilities for which practitioners are accountable."[17] This document articulated expectations regarding the ongoing work of a professional chaplain in an acute care hospital setting. Of the thirteen standards, six strongly and specifically reiterate principles of OOC:

> Standard 1, Assessment: The chaplain gathers and evaluates relevant data pertinent to the patient's situation and / or bio-psycho-social-spiritual / religious health.
>
> Standard 2, Delivery of Care: The chaplain develops and implements a plan of care to promote patient well-being and continuity of care.
>
> Standard 3, Documentation of Care: The chaplain enters information into the patient's medical record that is relevant to the patient's medical, psycho-social, and spiritual / religious goals of care.
>
> Standard 4, Teamwork and Collaboration: The chaplain collaborates with the organization's interdisciplinary care team....
>
> Standard 11, Continuous Quality Improvement: The chaplain seeks and creates opportunities to enhance the quality of chaplaincy care practice.

> Standard 12, Research: The chaplain practices evidence-based care including ongoing evaluation of new practices and, when appropriate, contributes to or conducts research.[18]

Together these two relatively recent documents represented important landmarks in the advancement of chaplaincy as a profession. The priority they placed on the principles of OOC illustrates the growing value within the profession for chaplains to be knowledgeable and skilled in the application of OOC in their daily practice. Let us now examine more thoroughly the substance of OOC.

## *The Substance of OOC*

Having examined the confluence of factors that have given rise to OOC, we turn our attention to the matter of understanding the substance of OOC in more detail. As a reminder, our definition of OOC is *a method of chaplaincy care that emphasizes achieving, describing, measuring, and improving outcomes that result from a chaplain's work*. Below you will find the commitments upon which OOC is built and a discussion of its component parts.

### Foundational Commitments

OOC is built upon three foundational commitments. These can be called the ABCs of OOC. The first is the commitment to *accountability*. It is a commitment we make to our employers. Health care institutions that employ chaplains have a right to evidence that the chaplain's work is making a positive difference in the lives of the patients / residents and their families the organization serves and the health care professionals it employs. As administrators make difficult budgetary decisions about staffing, they should do so with information about the unique and valuable contributions professional chaplains can make to quality health care. Through the practice of OOC, chaplains demonstrate accountability for their work.

The second foundational commitment of OOC is *best practice*. It is a commitment we make to those we serve. "Best practice refers to a technique, method, or process that is more effective at delivering a particular outcome or a better outcome than another technique, method, or process. Best practices are demonstrated by becoming more efficient or more effective. They reflect a means of exceeding the minimal standard of practice."[19] OOC reflects the commitment of a chaplain to discover and practice the most helpful chaplaincy interventions known to the profession. The motive for such a pursuit is for others to benefit from the best possible chaplaincy care.

The third foundational commitment of OOC is *collaboration*. It is a commitment we make to our fellow health care professionals. Patients / residents and families in a health care setting receive optimal care when they are able to access all the needed resources of a well-functioning interdisciplinary care team. In part, OOC is an attempt to demystify chaplaincy as much as possible. It is rooted in the idea that the better other members of the health care team understand our work, the better equipped they will be to partner with us in caring for others. We are committed to that partnership.

## Primary Components

The primary components of OOC are *assessment*, *interventions*, and *outcomes*. The whole infrastructure of OOC is built on just these three. This is an important realization for those who find the notions of OOC foreign or confusing. It all comes together around assessment, interventions, and outcomes.

According to the *Standards of Practice for Professional Chaplains in Acute Care Settings*, "Assessment is a fundamental process of chaplaincy practice. Provision of effective care requires that chaplains assess and reassess patient needs and modify plans of care accordingly."[20] Note that chaplaincy assessment is a dynamic and ongoing process. It occurs before, during, and after intervention. An assessment is more involved than a screening or a history. (See chapter 4 for a more extensive treatment of these subjects.)

There are numerous models for chaplaincy assessment available for use. OOC can appropriately utilize a variety of those plans. George Fitchett, a contributor to this book, is one of the most widely-known and respected chaplaincy researchers in the profession. He provides thoughtful and helpful guidelines for evaluating the alternatives.[21] For the purposes of this chapter, I will offer some broad reflections on chaplaincy assessment.

Lucas noted the importance of identifying a person's needs, hopes, and resources in his model of assessment:

> The traditional approach starts with patient needs. The caregiver finds out the patient's needs based on their diagnosis and various

> assessments, and then, as a caring professional, takes care of those needs. That traditional approach casts the patient as a big bag of needs, and each caregiver, including the chaplain, as big bags of resources involved in a one-way repair and reclamation process. Starting with Needs, Hopes *and* Resources acknowledges that the patient has needs. It also acknowledges they have *hopes* that provide energy, direction, impetus, and motivation for the future. Hopes draw the individual forward. The illness is part of that life. This means that the question becomes, "How can the chaplain help this patient cope with, integrate, or overcome this illness in a way that taps the extant energy present in the hopefulness?" Additionally, starting with Needs / Hopes / Resources acknowledges that patients have *resources* available. Patients typically possess a wide variety of spiritual resources that were helpful to them up to the present moment. Ignoring those resources demeans the person, makes ministry more difficult (and our lives poorer), and lessens the availability of healing for patients and families.[22]

This approach is important because it respects the strength and dignity of the person being helped along with the expertise of the chaplain as a helper.[23] The two work together to seek the well-being of the chaplaincy care recipient.

Fundamentally, chaplains provide spiritual, emotional, and relational support to patients / residents, their families, and the health care team. Consequently, chaplaincy assessments are primarily concerned with these areas. It should be noted that these spheres of concern are not completely distinct from one another. They are deeply intertwined with each other and with the biomedical status of the person. A chaplain must keep all of these in mind during the process of assessment. So, as a chaplain approaches a chaplaincy care situation, he or she seeks answers to the following questions:

- What are the spiritual needs, hopes, and resources?
- What are the emotional needs, hopes, and resources?
- What are the relational needs, hopes, and resources?
- What are the biomedical needs, hopes, and resources?

Some answers to those questions will come from recipients of chaplaincy care. Others will derive from the experience and observations of the chaplain or other members of the health care team. All of the answers—

or lack thereof—will inform the desired chaplaincy outcomes and the chaplaincy interventions employed to achieve those goals of care.

Lucas writes:

> The things we intentionally do in the name of movement toward … outcomes constitute interventions. Interventions include being with the patient in ways we believe will be helpful. Interventions include doing what we planned, in the way we assessed would be helpful and with an eye toward the contributions to care we intended to make.... They are, at base, relational, intentional and something for which we own responsibility.[24]

Interventions are the means through which those for whom we care benefit from all of our knowledge, skill, and experience. Interventions are paired with the resources of the others to address their needs and / or move toward their hopes. My observation in teaching and consulting with chaplains on the subject of OOC is that frequently their skill at offering chaplaincy interventions exceeds their ability to articulate them. See Figure 27.1 for an alphabetical sampling of potential chaplaincy interventions. On a related note, Gleason has worked on research called the "Ideal Intervention Project." Through it he is gathering data from chaplains and CPE students about the efficacy of various chaplaincy interventions in addressing needs.[25]

Outcomes are simply the observable results of our care. There are no doubt important non-observable subjective results of our care. However, OOC is concerned with the objective. Lucas stressed that outcomes should be sensory based. They can be recognized through what we see, hear, or feel. He additionally emphasized that they should be communicable. Chaplaincy outcomes can be clearly and briefly described in a manner other members of the health care team can comprehend. Clarity and brevity are related. Lucas suggested outcomes requiring more than one sentence to describe are not yet clear. The language of outcomes can initially feel too clinical or manipulative to chaplains. He reframed them thusly: "After we have gotten to know the patient, what are we hoping for? What is our prayer for the patient?"[26] Examples of chaplaincy outcomes are:

- Patient / resident is able to express gratitude
- Patient / resident is able to articulate a hopeful story about the future that incorporates the sequela of his or her injury

## CHAPLAINCY INTERVENTIONS

- Advocated for patient / family
- Arranged, upon death, expedited death notice and body release so funeral can take place within 24 hours to meet family's religious needs
- Celebrated with patient / family
- Clarified, confirmed, or reviewed information
- Consulted with interdisciplinary team
- Encouraged focus on present
- Encouraged self-care
- Explored issues of faith & belief
- Facilitated decision making
- Facilitated exploration of ethical considerations
- Facilitated exploration of meaning
- Facilitated identification of emotions
- Facilitated religious needs / rituals after death
- Facilitated respect for religious practice during hospitalization
- Facilitated story telling
- Heard confession
- Helped alert staff to upcoming religious fasting
- Helped with advance directive
- Helped with waiting
- Identified & evaluated alternatives
- Identified & evaluated coping strategies
- Identified & evaluated spiritual resources
- Identified & evaluated support system
- Initiated a relationship of care and support
- Listened empathically
- Mediated conflict
- Normalized patient's / family's experience
- Provided anxiety containment
- Provided baptism
- Provided chaplaincy education
- Provided grief counseling
- Provided guilt counseling
- Provided hospitality
- Provided information
- Provided prayer
- Provided relationship counseling
- Provided religious material needed for prayer such as Sabbath candles, rosary, etc.
- Provided religious reading matter
- Provided religious resources
- Provided ritual
- Provided silent and supportive presence
- Read sacred text
- Reinforced appropriate coping strategies

*Figure 27.1*

- Patient / resident achieved calm as evidenced by the reduction of visible signs of distress and verbal report
- Patient / resident is engaging effective coping strategies
- Patient / resident is able to identify and effectively utilize their support system

## Secondary Components

The secondary components of OOC are no less important than the primary components of assessment, interventions, and outcomes. They are secondary because they are derivative of or consequential to chaplaincy care focused on the primary components. We will discuss six: documentation, chaplaincy care pathways, chaplaincy education, quality improvement, research, and publication.

I taught an eight-hour professional development intensive at the annual APC conference in 2010. At the beginning of our day together, I asked the participants to tell me why they came. By far the most frequently cited reason was related to chaplaincy documentation. These chaplains wanted to improve their ability to document their care in the patient's medical record. This interest in charting seems to be linked to the increasing number of health care organizations converting from paper to electronic medical records. However, OOC documentation can be implemented through either medium.

For an expanded treatment of the subject of documentation, I refer the reader to chapter 6 of this work. For the purpose of illustration I share here the chaplaincy charting model developed by the chaplains of the Memorial Hermann Healthcare System.[27] I helped develop it, and it is the one I use in my daily practice. The Memorial Hermann model consists of five parts:

- **Reason:** Why is the chaplain making the visit?
- **Interventions:** What did the chaplain do to help the person?
- **Outcomes:** What difference did the chaplain's interventions make?
- **Assessment:** How would the chaplain summarize this person's current spiritual / emotional / relational state to the rest of the interdisciplinary health care team?
- **Plan:** What does the chaplain intend to do further or recommend to the interdisciplinary health care team?

Some chaplains using this model have found the mnemonic phrase "run in on a prayer" to be helpful. See Figure 27.2 for a sample chart note using this model.

One of the benefits to OOC experienced by the chaplains at Barnes-Jewish Hospital was they began to notice patterns of struggling and coping among different patient populations.[28] This has led some chaplains to develop chaplaincy care pathways as a tool for describing these patterns. A chaplaincy care pathway has been defined as "a descriptive series of indicators of what may be happening to a person spiritually in the midst of a particular life predicament and some suggested ways of optimally assisting that person."[29] See Figure 27.3 for a sample of a chaplaincy care pathway.

Chaplaincy care pathways have informed and improved the care chaplains provide to specific groups. They use the collective past experiences of others in similar circumstances to guide the care of a person in the present. This knowledge should be balanced with the recognition of the uniqueness of any one person's needs, hopes, and resources. We are cautioned not to assume all the characteristics of the general population are true for every individual.

Chaplaincy care pathways have also been a valuable tool for educating the interdisciplinary team. Sharing them with other members of the health care team has increased their knowledge of the spiritual, emotional, and relational needs of patients and families. It has additionally increased their knowledge of how chaplains can partner with them to address those needs.

Chaplaincy education involves both training professional chaplains and helping others understand the capabilities of chaplains. The principles of OOC have been beneficially used as a part of some CPE programs.[30] Expanding this would increase the readiness of CPE graduates for work as professional chaplains.

As for the latter part of chaplaincy education, very few health care professionals finish their training with a thorough understanding of professional chaplaincy. Most, however, have a good understanding of patient care based upon assessment, interventions, and outcomes. OOC provides an easily understood conceptual framework for describing our work to them. Their awareness of our work benefits patient and family care because it leads to more appropriate partnership with chaplains toward that end. It also benefits chaplains because our fellow

## SAMPLE CHART NOTE USING MNEMONIC "RUN IN ON A PRAYER"

**Reason for Visit:**

- Visit per referral from RN because of spiritual and emotional distress

**Interventions:**

- Consulted with RN regarding observations of patient's needs / hopes / resources
- Initiated a relationship of care and support with patient
- Provided chaplaincy education
- Facilitated story telling
- Listened empathically
- Explored issues of faith & belief
- Facilitated identification of emotions
- Identified & evaluated coping strategies
- Reinforced appropriate coping strategies
- Identified & evaluated spiritual resources
- Identified & evaluated support system
- Encouraged focus on present
- Provided prayer

**Outcomes:**

- Patient shared his medical narrative
- Patient verbally and tearfully processed anxiety regarding prognosis
- Patient articulated questions of theodicy
- Patient identified both intermediate and ultimate hopes
- Patient distinguished between matters within and beyond his control
- Patient expressed gratitude for life experiences and important relationships
- Patient and chaplain identified ways to utilize support system
- Patient appeared less agitated and more calm as visit progressed

**Assessment:**

- Patient expressed moderately elevated anxiety normal to circumstance, which visibly decreased after chaplaincy interventions
- Patient cites his Roman Catholic faith as a significant source of support
- Patient reports no one from his faith community is aware of his hospitalization
- Patient reports supportive relationships with wife and three adult children, but geographic distance and employment responsibilities limit their availability
- Patient could benefit from follow-up chaplaincy support

**Plan:**

- Per patient's request, will contact his faith community (St. Mary's) and request sacramental visit by priest
- Chaplain will follow for spiritual, emotional, and relational support
- Chaplain recommends bedside caregivers page chaplain on duty if patient shows signs of acute spiritual or emotional distress

*Figure 27.2*

# CHAPLAINCY CARE PATHWAY

## Pediatric Traumatic Brain Injury

Division of Spiritual Care—Memorial Hermann Healthcare System

| Possible Spiritual, Emotional, and / or Relational Issues | Possible Chaplain Actions / Interventions | Desired Outcomes |
|---|---|---|
| • Shock / denial<br>• Helplessness; powerlessness<br>• Loss of control<br>• Impatience regarding uncertain prognosis<br>• Grief<br>• Guilt<br>• Anxiety<br>• Fear<br>• Anger<br>• Gratitude<br>• Family conflict<br>• Disrupted cultural & spiritual beliefs / practices<br>• Theodicy questions<br>• Providence questions<br>• Ethical concerns<br>• Hopelessness<br>• Emotional or physical fatigue | • Establish and maintain relationship of empathy, trust, and caring<br>• Elicit and listen carefully to story of patient's injury<br>• Discover family cultural and spiritual beliefs / practices<br>• Access relational support system<br>• Identify desired outcomes of chaplaincy support<br>• Help family process experience and reactions through questions, listening, clarifying, and summarizing<br>• Facilitate ritual, scripture, or prayer needs<br>• Normalize family's spiritual, emotional, & relational issues<br>• Provide education or referral resources available from chaplaincy and interdisciplinary team<br>• Encourage self-care<br>• Document assessment, goals, interventions, and outcomes<br>• Participate professionally with interdisciplinary team | • Family talks openly about experience of injury, hospitalization, and rehabilitation, including thoughts, emotions, and beliefs<br>• Family identifies and accesses spiritual, emotional & relational resources<br>• Family demonstrates increasingly healthy spiritual, emotional & relational coping with injury, hospitalization, and rehabilitation<br><br>Family is able to:<br>• participate appropriately in their child's care<br>• remain focused on concerns of present, rather than past or future<br>• understand the difference between functional and dysfunctional guilt and able to respond accordingly<br>• articulate losses and begin grief process<br>• envision a hopeful future that incorporates effects of patient's injury |

*Figure 27.3*

| CHAPLAINCY CARE PATHWAY (continued) | |
|---|---|
| **Pathway Triggers for Chaplain Referral** | **General Triggers for Chaplain Referral to Patients and / or Families** |
| 1. Admission to PICU<br>2. Sustained intracranial pressure (ICP) above 20 | 1. Anxiety / fear / ineffective coping<br>2. Spiritual / emotional distress<br>3. Significant change in diagnosis / prognosis / condition<br>4. Spiritual / religious needs (Communion, prayer, etc.)<br>5. Diverse spiritual / cultural needs<br>6. End-of-life concerns<br>7. Ethical issues |

Developed by Chaplain Brent Peery, DMin, BCC, Memorial Hermann Healthcare System—Division Approval / Revision 12/10/2007. (Editor's note: Research articles cited in the development of this pathway omitted because of space limitations.)

*Figure 27.3 (continued)*

health care professionals are able to have a deeper appreciation for the value of our contributions.

Another of the benefits to OOC noted by the chaplains at Barnes-Jewish Hospital was evaluating and improving their care.[31] This relates to the quality improvement component of OOC. Providing spiritual, emotional, and relational support to persons in the midst of illness and injury is important work. Most chaplains want to do that work well. OOC provides us with some tools to evaluate and advance the quality of our work. Those we serve deserve our commitment to do all we can to provide them with the best possible care. As alluded to earlier, the business culture of health care is increasingly interested in improving the quality of patient-centered care and customer satisfaction. Chaplains bring valuable expertise to those organizational quality improvement efforts.[32] Memorial Hermann chaplains have built quality improvement initiatives around researching and writing chaplaincy care pathways, improving customer and employee satisfaction, and improving chaplaincy documentation through chart audits. (See chapter 29 for a more extensive examination of the subject.)

Research and publication are the last components of OOC to be addressed in this chapter. I have paired them together because they so readily complement each other. OOC provides a vocabulary and framework for chaplaincy research design. As the findings from these research studies are published, they serve to improve chaplaincy care across the profession.

One example of chaplaincy research comes from one of my colleagues. Chaplain Hazel Thomas developed an assessment tool to be used with new spinal cord injury patients at the rehabilitation hospital where she serves. She assessed patients upon admission and again as they neared discharge. Between the assessments she provided chaplaincy interventions. Her research demonstrated marked improvement in spiritual wellness among the patients in the study. She was able to present her findings at two different national spinal cord injury conferences.[33] (See chapter 30 for more on chaplaincy research.)

## *Final Words*

I have subtitled this chapter "Intentional Caring." A simple definition of intention is "a determination to act in a certain way."[34] Intentional caring, therefore, is a determination to act in a caring manner. OOC is intentional caring. It is a timely method for chaplains within the context of health care to deliberately deliver the best care possible to patients, their families, and our fellow health care professionals.

## Notes

1. L. VandeCreek and A. Lucas, eds., *The Discipline for Pastoral Care Giving: Foundations for Outcome Oriented Chaplaincy* (Binghamton, NY: Haworth Press, 2001).
2. Ibid., xiii–xx.
3. Gleason writes, "The majority of U.S. professional chaplains today say directly or act out silently the following: 'Our work is too holy, too special for us to submit to much analysis. The mystery out of which divine caring and healing comes refuses to be deconstructed into systematic spiritual assessment, predetermined pastoral care responses, or measurable outcomes. We will do the reports required to keep us on the payroll, but begrudgingly.'" See J. Gleason, "An Emerging Paradigm in Professional Chaplaincy," *Chaplaincy Today* 14, no. 2 (Autumn / Winter 1998): 10.

4. See, e.g., L. VandeCreek, *Professional Chaplaincy and Clinical Pastoral Education Should Become More Scientific: Yes and No* (Binghamton, NY: Haworth Press, 2001), xv–xviii. It should be noted that health care reform in the United States has been a matter of debate and action for at least three decades.
5. *Dictionary.com*, http://dictionary.reference.com/browse/confluence.
6. See Association of Professional Chaplains, *Common Standards for Professional Chaplaincy*, www.professionalchaplains.org/uploadedFiles/pdf/common-standards-professional-chaplaincy.pdf.
7. Mark LaRocca-Pitts contended professional chaplains choose their context because of who they are. See "The Chaplain's Motive," *PlainViews* 4, no. 7 (May 2, 2007), www.plainviews.org. This is no doubt true for some.
8. *Dictionary.com*, http://dictionary.reference.com/browse/science.
9. The coming changes that link Medicare reimbursement rates to patient satisfaction scores is one area among many where chaplaincy can be revenue enhancing, if not revenue producing.
10. Gleason, "Emerging Paradigm," 9–14.
11. Ibid., 10.
12. Ibid., 11.
13. M. Orton, "Emerging Best Practice Pastoral Care in the UK, USA and Australia," *Australian Journal of Pastoral Care and Health* 2, no. 2 (December 2008): 1–28.
14. The organizations were the Association of Professional Chaplains, the American Association of Pastoral Counselors, the Association for Clinical Pastoral Education, the Canadian Association for Pastoral Practice and Education, the National Association of Catholic Chaplains, and the National Association of Jewish Chaplains. See *Common Standards for Professional Chaplaincy*, www.spiritualcarecollaborative.org/docs/common-standards-professional-chaplaincy.pdf.
15. Association for Clinical Pastoral Education, "Objectives and Outcomes of ACPE Accredited Programs," *Standards & Manuals: 2010 Standards*, 29–30, www.acpe.edu/NewPDF/2010%20Manuals/2010%20Standards.pdf.
16. See Association of Professional Chaplains, *Standards of Practice for Professional Chaplains in Acute Care Settings*, www.professionalchaplains.org/uploadedFiles/pdf/Standards%20of%20Practice%20Draft%20Document%20021109.pdf#Project_Update. See also Association of Professional Chaplains, *Standards of Practice for Professional Chaplains in Long-Term Care Settings*, www.professionalchaplains.org/uploadedFiles/pdf/Standards_of_Practice_LTC_Document02162011.pdf.
17. *Standards of Practice for Professional Chaplains in Acute Care Settings*, 3.
18. Ibid., 1.
19. Ibid., 3.
20. Ibid., 5.
21. G. Fitchett, *Assessing Spiritual Needs: A Guide for Caregivers* (Lima, OH: Academic Renewal Press, 2002), 90–104.

22. Arthur Lucas, "Introduction to *The Discipline* for Pastoral Care Giving," in *The Discipline for Pastoral Care Giving: Foundations for Outcome Oriented Chaplaincy*, ed. Larry VandeCreek and Arthur Lucas (Binghamton, NY: Haworth Press, 2001), 8.
23. Fitchett wrote of balance on this topic: "The question is whether it is possible for caregivers to locate themselves and their power and authority somewhere between the coercive extreme of authoritarian, moralistic pastoral care and the vagueness and indistinct perspective of modern value-neutral pastoral care. Can curious or troubled souls find counselors who will neither burn them at the stake nor leave them at a loss for guidance?" (*Assessing Spiritual Needs*, 96).
24. Lucas, "Introduction to *The Discipline*," 23–24.
25. John Gleason, www.acperesearch.net/IIP.html.
26. Lucas, "Introduction to *The Discipline*," 19–20.
27. B. Peery, "Chaplaincy Charting: One Healthcare System's Model," *PlainViews* 5, no. 8 (May 21, 2008), www.plainviews.org.
28. Lucas, "Introduction to *The Discipline*," 3.
29. G. Hillsman, "A Spiritual Pathway for Prior Grief," *Chaplaincy Today* 14, no. 2 (Autumn / Winter 1998): 38. This issue of *Chaplaincy Today* contains several other articles on chaplaincy pathways.
30. VandeCreek and Lucas, *Discipline for Pastoral Care Giving*, 133–41, 149–58. See also S. Nance, K. Ramsey, and J. Leachman, "Chaplaincy Care Pathways and Clinical Pastoral Education," *Journal of Pastoral Care and Counseling* 63, nos. 1–2 (Spring–Summer 2009): 12.1–4; and A. Van Hise and P. Derrickson, "Curriculum for a Spiritual Pathway Project: Integrating Research Methodology into Pastoral Care Training," *Journal of Health Care Chaplaincy* 16, nos. 1–2 (January–June 2010): 3–12.
31. Lucas, "Introduction to *The Discipline*," 2.
32. N. Berlinger, "The Nature of Chaplaincy and the Goals of QI: Patient-Centered Care as Professional Responsibility," *Hastings Center Report* 38, no. 6 (2008): 30–33.
33. H. Thomas, "Creating and Using a Spiritual Wellness Assessment at a Rehabilitation Facility," *PlainViews* 7, no. 16 (September 15, 2010), www.plainviews.org.
34. *Dictionary.com*, http://dictionary.reference.com/browse/intention.

## Further Reading

Berlinger, Nancy. "The Nature of Chaplaincy and the Goals of QI: Patient-Centered Care as Professional Responsibility." *Hastings Center Report* 38, no. 6 (2008): 30–33.

Fitchett, George. *Assessing Spiritual Needs: A Guide for Caregivers*. Rev ed. Lima, OH: Academic Renewal Press, 2002.

Gleason, John. "An Emerging Paradigm in Professional Chaplaincy." *Chaplaincy Today* 14, no. 2 (Autumn / Winter 1998): 9–14.

Hillsman, Gordon. "A Spiritual Pathway for Prior Grief." *Chaplaincy Today* 14, no. 2 (Autumn / Winter 1998): 38–41.

LaRocca-Pitts, Mark. "The Chaplain's Motive." *PlainViews* 4, no. 7 (May 2, 2007).

Nance, Susan, Kenneth Ramsey, and Joseph Leachman. "Chaplaincy Care Pathways and Clinical Pastoral Education." *Journal of Pastoral Care and Counseling* 63, nos. 1–2 (Spring–Summer 2009): 12.1–4.

Orton, Meg. "Emerging Best Practice Pastoral Care in the UK, USA and Australia." *Australian Journal of Pastoral Care and Health* 2, no. 2 (December 2008): 1–28.

Peery, Brent. "Chaplaincy Charting: One Healthcare System's Model." *PlainViews* 5, no. 8 (May 21, 2008).

Thomas, Hazel. "Creating and Using a Spiritual Wellness Assessment at a Rehabilitation Facility." *PlainViews* 7, no. 16 (September 15, 2010).

VandeCreek, Larry, ed. *Professional Chaplaincy and Clinical Pastoral Education Should Become More Scientific: Yes and No*. Binghamton, NY: Haworth Press, 2002.

VandeCreek, Larry, and Arthur Lucas, eds. *The Discipline for Pastoral Care Giving: Foundations for Outcome Oriented Chaplaincy*. Binghamton, NY: Haworth Press, 2001.

Van Hise, Angelina, and Paul Derrickson. "Curriculum for a Spiritual Pathway Project: Integrating Research Methodology into Pastoral Care Training." *Journal of Health Care Chaplaincy* 16, nos. 1–2 (January–June 2010): 3–12.

## About the Contributor

**Rev. Brent Peery, DMin, BCC,** is director of the Chaplaincy Services Department for Memorial Hermann–Texas Medical Center in Houston, Texas. He previously served as a congregational clergyperson and as a pediatric chaplain. In addition to serving as chair of the OOC task force for Memorial Hermann Healthcare System, he has taught, consulted, and written on the subject for several years.

# 28

## *Referral Plans*

### Developing and Implementing Tactical Plans Regarding Who Chaplains Should Visit

*Rabbi Stephen B. Roberts, MBA, MHL, BCJC; Rev. Sue Wintz, MDiv, BCC; and Rev. George Handzo, MDiv, BCC, CSSBB*

*Consensus is developing in the field of professional pastoral care around several best practices. The discipline is becoming a multifaith, referral service. Generally, it is no longer the case that particular clergy come in and visit all of the patients of their faith tradition. This model does not make efficient use of pastoral care resources and does not promote integration into the health care team, which is so essential to the continuity of care and quality practice. In current best practice, chaplains are assigned to specific locations, generally selected for their strategic importance to the institution, and visit patients of all faiths selected according to specific protocols.*[1]

It is a rare pastoral / spiritual care department that has the staffing levels to provide an in-depth professional chaplaincy visit to every single patient / resident on a daily or even a weekly basis. Further, not all patients / residents need, or even desire, extensive professional chaplaincy care. Often those in most need, such as patients (and their families) on intensive care or high acuity oncology units, are least able to request the services they need.

## *Length of a Chaplaincy Visit*

Chaplains have a limited amount of time each day to provide direct care. Assuming a chaplain can provide a full six hours of direct patient care time on an average day,[2] how many visits could she or he make? It is essential to be able to answer this question for planning purposes.

Very little research exists on the lengths of chaplaincy visits. One of the few published peer review studies ever conducted was by the HealthCare Chaplaincy in New York City.[3] The results of the 1994–96 study are important to discuss and to be familiar with. At the same time, the changes in health care and professional chaplaincy point to the need for chaplaincy departments to be proactive in creating tactical plans regarding who can benefit from chaplaincy care.

According to the published results, the mean length of a 1994–96 chaplaincy visit in an acute care setting was fifteen minutes. Thus, the maximum number of visits a professional chaplain might make in an acute care setting on an average day is only twenty-four. Of import to note is that the median length of a visit when responding to a referral was almost twenty minutes, in contrast to the length of visit without a referral being around twelve minutes. Thus, professional chaplains who respond primarily based upon referrals, such as those from screenings or protocol triggers, on an average day were most likely in 1994–96 to visit eighteen patients and their families.

While this data provides important information for guidance in determining maximum number of visits that may be accomplished on a daily average, it is not intended to be a final measuring stick. For example, if the intent of the chaplain contact is only to introduce the patient and family to the services of the department, as it was in 1994, it may be possible to complete a high number of contacts each day.

However, the current context of health care requires more expertise and focus, which in turn requires more time for chaplain assessment and intervention. Current chaplains report that the number of referrals they receive has risen by 25 percent or more since this cited study was done and also that the complexity of situations in which they are consulted has increased.

As professional chaplains have become more recognized for their expertise and integrated into the interdisciplinary team, the role of the chaplain has expanded. Chaplains who complete spiritual assessments and / or participate in family / team meetings as part of a palliative care or unit-specific multidisciplinary team will likely spend more time per contact, resulting in fewer contacts with more in-depth outcomes.

It is also important to recognize that chaplains are often part of the trauma and code team responses in their organization, both of which often take significantly more of the chaplain's time. An increasing number of chaplaincy departments are responsible for education and completion of advance directives. These and other calls are unpredictable and may either increase or decrease the length and number of chaplaincy contacts.

What are the expectations of the organization in terms of chaplains providing care to employees? How are those contacts, whether they be through unit rounding, one-on-one conversations, or leading a debriefing after a crisis event, reported? Are chaplains to round each shift on every unit of the hospital? Are they expected to teach in medical programs, for nursing in-services, or patient / family education?

The key issue continues to be determining what the focus of the chaplaincy department is to be to support the service lines, mission, and focus of the employing organization. This should be done in consultation with the clinical, administrative, and senior leadership of the organization. Determining what length a chaplaincy intervention should be or how many visits should be accomplished in a day, month, or year is a quantity focus, whereas a thought-out, measured, outcome-based plan is focused on and measured by quality.

Given the numbers gleaned from the HealthCare Chaplaincy 1994–96 study and the various demands upon the chaplain's time, it is extremely important to proactively and consciously make departmental management decisions about who in your health care facility will not only receive pastoral care but also how in-depth that care will be.

## *Process of Developing and Implementing Tactical Plans Regarding Who Chaplains Should Visit*

### Institutional Assessment

The first step in developing a department tactical plan is assessing your institution's goals and objectives. Your department's plans then need to be fully integrated within the larger institution's plans and approved by upper management. If this sounds like strategic planning, you are right. As Rev. George Handzo writes in chapter 3:

> Chaplaincy care services are based on a plan agreed to by institutional management and other stakeholders. This plan, which is keyed to the mission and strategic plan of the organization, lays out specific objectives and goals and is consistent with institutional culture. For example, if the institution has a trauma center, the chaplaincy care plan will likely have a focus on 24/7 availability and swift response to crises.

As Rev. Bill Bross and Paula DeAngelo write in chapter 26:

> Through strategic planning, the SPCD [spiritual / pastoral care / chaplaincy department] is positioned to build community not only within the department but also throughout the health care facility as a whole. This is crucial to the SPCD being viewed as the foundation of the facility's spiritual environment of caring. The process also allows the SPCD to align itself with the larger goals of the organization and gives members of the department the information and impetus needed to match their personal and professional goals with those of the health care facility.

You must be able to answer the following questions before moving on:

- What is the organization's mission and vision?
- What are the organization's internal and external strategic goals?
- What are the organization's financial priorities currently and in the future (e.g., renovating the emergency department's physical facilities to increase percentage of local market share; recruiting and building up the oncology service line; moving more surgery from inpatient to same day)?
- What is the culture / nature of the organization, including how the organization serves its local and regional community?

## Creating Departmental Priorities

The next step, after assessment, is setting departmental priorities. In a patient care plan, we would call these goals (see chapter 5). As with a care plan, they need to be specific and measurable. It is worth rereading the following from chapter 3:

> Chaplaincy care resources are targeted to particular services or patient populations chosen for their strategic importance to the institution and / or the demonstrated impact of chaplaincy care on those patients and staff. This is preferred to having chaplains cover all parts of the hospital equally. Generally, the clinical service lines chosen reflect high volume and / or high acuity. Intensive care units often receive priority coverage along with cardiac and cancer units, where spiritual issues related to mortality and the meaning of life are common. Emerging standards of practice suggest a dedicated chaplain on palliative care teams.

The following are some examples of how departmental priorities might read:

- In-person coverage 24/7 of the emergency department, by either a professional chaplain or a CPE [clinical pastoral education] student, with particular focus on trauma cases. (*Example*: acute care hospital with a level-1 trauma center)
- Every nonemergency referral that goes through the on-call paging system and is received prior to noon will be responded to by 4 p.m. Those received between noon and 3 p.m. will be responded to by 6 p.m. Those received after 3 p.m. will be responded to by noon of the following day, if not the same day. All responders will have at least one unit of CPE. (*Example*: community hospital)
- Each patient will have access to a chaplain at least twice a week via groups facilitated by a chaplain. (*Example*: behavioral health hospital)
- Department will prioritize that each resident is visited weekly by a fully trained, screened, and supervised volunteer from the resident's own faith community. (*Example*: long-term care facility)

Each priority listed above is both specific and measureable. With a proper system built, both the department and upper management should be able to determine how close they are to meeting the agreed-upon priorities.

## Determining Resources Needed to Meet These Priorities

Now comes the "fun" part of this whole process. It is only now that you begin to look at implementing the priorities. Having upper management as part of the process up to now is essential. It is only after everyone has agreed upon clear and measurable priorities that the next step of determining necessary resources to meet the priorities can be started. Depending on what is determined, priorities might then change. Let us look at one example from above: "In-person coverage 24/7 of the emergency department, by either a professional chaplain or a CPE student, with particular focus on trauma cases."

Resources to meet this priority include the following: 24/7 staffing 365 days a year; on-call room for overnights; possible flex time for those providing night and weekend coverage; coverage when there are no students present; appropriate supervision when students are covering the emergency department; training emergency department staff, on an ongoing basis, when to page the on-call chaplain regarding a trauma case; time for chaplain to write appropriate chart notes and to create referrals for appropriate and timely follow-up by members of the department.

Once both the priority and the necessary resources are determined, management has to be involved and approve moving forward.

## The Business Plan

The best way to present the information to management for approval is in a business plan. The business plan should include the steps taken up to now to come to this priority, what is involved in implementing the priority, and a discussion of opportunity costs for this priority (e.g., a focus on the emergency department might mean that the remaining staff time available would only allow intensive care unit coverage and that only on a referral basis).

It is important that the plan discuss how the proposed priorities align with Joint Commission expectations and standards and also with the organization's current systems. Further, the business plan needs to discuss the priorities with outcome-oriented and evidence-based language. What outcomes can management see from fully implementing this priority now that the resources have been determined? What systems will need to be built to produce the evidence to determine the proposed outcomes? What cost will be involved in setting up these systems? All of this and more need to be addressed in the business plan.

In-person staffing 24/7 for an emergency department is a significant financial commitment. Once management sees the specific costs and benefits, properly presented in a business plan, they may decide to work with the department and set other priorities. Or they may decide to find the financial resources to allow the department to move forward with this priority.

## *Building Protocols*

Protocols are essential in an outcome oriented chaplaincy department intending to meet agreed-upon priorities. Protocols are systems that are used in a particular area with each patient / resident who enters or who becomes involved in certain types of situations, such as a "code."

Building effective protocols helps reach the department's priorities. Here are some examples of protocols to help you better understand how they function:

- Protocol developed for non-intensive care units: Nursing staff do a patient spiritual screen upon each patient's admission to a new unit, after each seven days on a unit, and prior to any surgical procedure. As part of such protocol, chaplains are permanently assigned to different units to train new nursing staff on a monthly basis, one-on-one, how to use the screening tool. Further, to build ongoing relationships with the nursing staff, the same assigned chaplain will meet once a quarter with the nurse manager and at least two nurses from each shift to discuss issues and concerns about implementing the spiritual screen.
- Protocol for codes: A chaplain will always be part of the response team to any code within the facility.
- Protocol for natural disaster impacting the hospital's catchment area (e.g., tornado, flood, hurricane): Upon impact of the disaster, all chaplains on staff will be contacted and requested to report for service. During times of disasters, chaplains will be expected to work twelve-hour

shifts, like all other hospital staff, and there will be at least one chaplain on-site at all times.

- Protocol for referrals to the chaplain based on diagnostic trigger: As part of the protocol of care for new spinal cord injuries, a consult will be placed for the chaplain to complete a spiritual and cultural assessment. As part of this protocol, the opportunity is present for the chaplain to participate in team meetings to communicate and address the specific spiritual, religious, and cultural issues, beliefs, and values of the patient.
- Protocol for risk issues and responses to family concerns: Chaplains provide a unique contribution to organizations when there is a risk issue, including medical error, compromised communication, or responding to an angry family. A multidisciplinary protocol for identifying spiritual and psychosocial issues that may be contributing to the situation, as well as the chaplain providing a neutral source of support, can assist organizations in providing patient-centered care.

## *Religion or Line of Care Focus?*

A key discussion that is occurring more and more as the field continues to professionalize is, should chaplains be assigned by religion or to a specific service area, such as oncology, pediatrics, neurology, and so on?

In a keynote presentation to the National Association of Jewish Chaplains in 2011, Chaplain Sue Wintz, a past president of the Association of Professional Chaplains, presented the following: "In terms of spiritual dimension dynamics—more commonality was found among people of different faiths facing the same health care challenge than among people of the same faith facing different health care challenges." Other forward-thinking leaders in our field have also written similarly and published evidence supporting this position.

Chaplains will only become integrated fully into health care systems when they fully integrate into the teams / cultures of the different units within the systems. Integration is essential for both quality practice and continuity of care. At the same time, there is important work that can be done to contribute to the overall care of specific service teams. Chaplains can develop spiritual pathways that recognize and address the unique spiritual needs of patients receiving certain services, such as adolescent pediatric patients, neuro rehabilitation patients, or geriatric patients recovering from a stroke. More work within the profession remains to be done in this area.

## *Documentation and Statistics*

The final area to discuss regarding tactical plans is quantitative measurement. Who are the chaplains actually visiting? How do they get there (e.g., referral, rounding, pages)? How much time do they spend? Does the visit time spent differ based upon location, presenting issues, source of referral, acuity, and so on? Is there a congruence between agreed-upon departmental priorities and actual visit times spent with patients / family / staff / residents? If not, what is the cause of the difference?

Equally important are qualitative questions: What outcomes result from the different visits? Are the outcomes expected / unexpected? Do the outcomes help meet the stated priorities? What growing edges, either with the whole system or with individual parts of the system, are preventing the priority from being met? How can the chaplaincy department contribute to the overall goals of the organization, and how much time will that take?

## Notes

1. G. Handzo, "Best Practices in Professional Pastoral Care," *Southern Medical Journal* 99, no. 6 (June 2006): 663.
2. The assumption of a full six hours of direct patient care tries to take into account and acknowledge up front the various other responsibilities that professional chaplains have in their facilities, such as being involved on ethics and other health care committees, attending rounding, participating in research / writing, leading worship services, and more.
3. G. Handzo et. al., "What Do Chaplains Really Do? Visitation in the New York Chaplaincy Study," *Journal of Health Care Chaplaincy* 14, no. 1 (2008): 20–38; the author of this chapter was associated with this organization during the period in which the research took place. He was an active participant in the research first as a CPE student and then as a professional chaplain employed by the organization.

## About the Contributors

**Rabbi Stephen B. Roberts, MBA, MHL, BCJC,** is the editor of this book and coeditor of *Disaster Spiritual Care: Practical Clergy Response to Community, Regional and National Tragedy* (SkyLight Paths Publishing). He is a past president of the National Association of Jewish Chaplains. Most recently he served as the associate executive vice president of the New York Board of Rabbis, directing their chaplaincy program, providing services in more than fifty locations throughout New York, plus serving as the endorser for both New York State's and New York City's Jewish chaplains. Prior to this he served as the director of chaplaincy of the Beth Israel Medical System (New York), overseeing chaplains and CPE programs at three acute care hospitals, one behavioral health hospital, plus various outpatient facilities served by chaplains.

**Rev. Sue Wintz, MDiv, BCC,** is board certified by the Association of Professional Chaplains and is a past president of that organization. She is the managing editor of HealthCare Chaplaincy's professional publication *PlainViews,* which translates knowledge and skills into effective and palliative care. Her work in teaching, research, writing, and consulting has contributed to organizations such as the Joint Commission and the U.S. Navy Bureau of Medicine and Surgery. She is a staff chaplain at St. Joseph's Hospital and Medical Center, Phoenix, Arizona, where she is assigned to the intensive care units of the Barrow Neurological Institute.

**Rev. George Handzo, MDiv, BCC, CSSBB,** is the vice president of Chaplaincy Care Leadership and Practice at HealthCare Chaplaincy. Rev. Handzo directs the only consulting service devoted to the strategic assessment, planning, and management of chaplaincy services. HealthCare Chaplaincy employs best practices in strategic planning and clinical practice to maximize the effectiveness of an organization's pastoral care and to align it with the institution's overall objectives. Prior to his current position, Rev. Handzo was the director of Chaplaincy Services at Memorial Sloan-Kettering Cancer Center for more than twenty years and is a past president of the Association of Professional Chaplains. He serves on the Distress Guidelines Panel of the National Comprehensive Cancer Network. Rev. Handzo has authored or coauthored more than fifty chapters and articles on the practice of pastoral care.

# 29

## *Quality Improvement*

### A Chaplaincy Priority

*Rev. Jon Overvold, MDiv, BCC*

Chaplains who work in health care perform their duties in an environment that is permeated by the practice of quality improvement. Every monthly leadership meeting asks the question "How are we doing as an organization?" Financial performance is measured by factors such as income, volume of patients, payer case-mix, expense management, and other measures. Positive results of quality improvement projects are celebrated. Problem areas are identified to make all leaders aware of what needs improvement. Patient satisfaction survey results are reviewed and compared to previous months. One could argue that all the answers to the question "How are we doing as an organization?" have to do with some measure of quality.

Where does the chaplain fit into this macro view of quality in the health care organization? At first look it may be hard to see where the chaplain addresses or contributes to overall quality. Chaplains do not generate income for the organization (unless they are a part of hospice). Generally, the chaplain's department is a fixed expense for the organization. Chaplains don't require a lot of equipment or consumables, since the work is with the patient, family, and even staff. So chaplains may be tempted to view their work as on the sidelines of the organization's quality agenda. This chapter looks closely at the field of quality improvement and makes the case that chaplains need to make quality improvement a priority in the delivery of chaplaincy care and embrace the practice of quality on an ongoing basis. Chaplains can make significant contributions to an organization's quality program, if they understand how to interpret their work in terms of quality.

## *Background: Quality Improvement in the Context of Health Care*

The science of quality improvement developed in the manufacturing industry as it invented and developed processes to improve the quality of manufactured goods. To ensure the uniform quality of the item that was made, every step of the manufacturing process would be analyzed to eliminate variation and produce items that conform to standards. Whatever did not meet those standards could be pulled from the inventory before being sent out to the consumer. Tools were developed to break down a process into its individual parts in order to understand what might cause inefficiencies, waste, or defective parts and so improve the manufacturing process.

In the early 1990s, health care leaders began to consider whether the tools of quality improvement from industry could be used in the health care setting. The National Demonstration Project in Quality Improvement in Health Care was the first attempt to apply quality improvement in health care.[1] It concluded that quality improvement tools could work in health care. One recommendation coming out of this project was that health care would need to develop its own definition of quality, recognizing that the delivery of health care is not the same as manufacturing a widget. Some processes in the health system may be very similar to a manufacturing process—for example, processing test results in a laboratory or processing linen in the laundry. Other processes, like diagnosis and treatment, are based on more complex human interaction, with greater variability, and any measure of quality must account for this. It is important for chaplains to note this broadening view of quality as it is applied in health care, a view that accounts for the human experience of care. As the quality movement develops in health care, greater emphasis is placed on this human dimension, as will be seen in the definitions of quality in health care.

## *Definitions of Quality*

In 1988 the U.S. Office of Technology Assessment defined quality of care as "the degree to which the process of care increases the probability of outcomes desired by the patient, and reduces the probability of undesired outcomes, given the state of medical knowledge."[2] It is striking to notice how even this early definition of quality defines quality in terms of the patient. The provider, be that the doctor or the chaplain, needs to have an understanding of what outcome the patient desires and support the process that ensures it to come about as far as is possible. Additionally, the providers must ensure that an undesired outcome is avoided as much as is possible. In this definition of quality, chaplains are asked to consider what part of their care contributes to the patient's desired outcome. As my mentor in chaplaincy, Rev. Paul Steinke, always said, "Patients don't check into the hospital to get chaplaincy care." In other words, they come for a desired health outcome, and the chaplain's interventions should contribute toward the desired outcome. (For more on this, see chapter 27.)

The Institute of Medicine published two significant reports—*To Err Is Human* (2000)[3] and *Crossing the Quality Chasm* (2001)[4]—that have become the operative definition of quality in health care. "All health care organizations, professional groups, and private and public purchasers should pursue six major aims: specifically health care should be safe, effective, patient-centered, timely, efficient, and equitable."[5] These six qualities—*safe, effective, patient-centered, timely, efficient, and equitable*—provide the framework for how quality is to be understood and measured. If chaplains can speak to the way their work aligns with these six dimensions of quality, they will be better able to demonstrate how chaplaincy care improves the overall care of patients in the organization.

## *Where Does Chaplaincy Fit In?*

With some creative imagination it is not hard to see where chaplains can contribute to all six dimensions of quality. However, it will become obvious that some are more readily applicable to the work that chaplains do. Here are some ways to think about each of the dimensions of quality.

## Safe

How does a chaplain contribute to the safety of patients? One of the greatest skill sets of the chaplain is what is sometimes called "cultural broker."[6] Chaplains assess the religious and cultural needs of patients and their families and help the health care team understand the special needs of patients. This enhances the communication between patient and staff and directly contributes to improved safety outcomes. This is evidenced by the Joint Commission making effective communication a national patient safety goal for 2011. But are there other ways that chaplains ensure patient safety? Perhaps providing spiritual / emotional support that contributes to greater medication compliance; ensuring that Eucharistic ministers and other religious volunteers practice appropriate infection control; protecting vulnerable patients from inappropriate religious intrusions; responding to emotionally explosive situations and helping to de-escalate potentially violent outcomes. There are many ways to view the work of chaplains with respect to patient safety.

## Effective

This dimension of quality in health care is more often associated with effectiveness of medications or surgeries. Rigorous drug trials demonstrate whether a new medication is more effective than other therapeutic treatments. But there is room for the chaplain's contributions here as well. How effective is the response of other staff to the patient's grief and loss? Can the chaplain contribute to more effective emotional response to patients' needs through education of staff? How would a chaplain demonstrate that the grief support group produces a desired outcome (appropriate grief) and avoids an unwanted outcome (complicated grief, which may have an associated increased cost factor)?

## Patient-Centered

This dimension of quality would seem to have the most natural fit with what chaplains do. In direct patient care, chaplains establish relationships with patients; attend to them by listening on a deep level; identify their unique needs, hopes, and resources; and develop a plan to accomplish the goals of care. By focusing on the patients with the greatest needs and fewest resources, chaplains bring forward the unique needs of these patients to the health care team so that care can be individualized and by so doing enhance the quality of care to the patient. Almost everything the chaplain does with respect to patient care can be described in terms of patient-centered care.

## Timely

What aspect of chaplaincy can be explored in terms of timeliness? Certainly there are internal processes within a chaplaincy program that can be monitored for timeliness. For example, are responses to referrals addressed in a timely fashion? Are follow-up visits made according to the documented plan of care? But thinking more broadly, are there types of patients for whom chaplain interventions result in a more timely discharge? Are there cases where the chaplain enlists community religious resources on behalf of the patient that allow for a more timely discharge, resulting in both improved timeliness and efficiency? An example of the chaplain's contributions toward reducing length of stay is provided later in this chapter.

## Efficient

Talk of efficiency around chaplains often means doing more with less. As staff members of a non-revenue-generating department in health care, chaplains may be particularly sensitive to this subject. Health care organizations that maintain robust chaplaincy care tend to view their chaplains as an investment in quality, recognizing that chaplaincy care makes great contributions to other dimensions of quality care. However, it is still important for chaplains to consider the efficiency of the service they provide. As health care directs more and more of its care to the outpatient and community setting because it is just as effective and more efficient, will traditionally hospital-based chaplain departments be able to demonstrate in terms of efficiency and effectiveness the need for chaplains to move to those settings as well?

## Equitable

Quality is concerned about whether a health care organization provides the same level of care to all patients based on their assessed need. That is not only a concern for quality, but it is also the right thing to do. Chaplains may be particularly well suited to help health care organizations with this dimension of quality. The chaplain functioning as a liaison to community religious and cultural centers can be a point of contact between the health care organization and the community it serves. These community leaders can be helpful to health care organizations in identifying the underserved in the community and other health care disparities within the community. This view of quality looks at both the individual receiving care and the larger perspective of the health of the community as a whole.

## *Resistance*

Before moving ahead with next steps for how a chaplain might implement a quality improvement program, it is important to address the resistance among chaplains to quality improvement. A number of factors could contribute to a chaplain's hesitation to embrace the quality movement in health care. First, chaplains receive little if any formal training in quality improvement methods or theory. For board certified chaplains, there is not yet any requirement to demonstrate any competency having to do with quality improvement. Chaplains with respect to quality are largely self-taught and may have stumbled upon a special project that entailed quality measures while doing clinical pastoral education (CPE) training. Some chaplains may be welcomed onto a quality improvement team that is multidisciplinary and learn a basic methodology from the project leader. So if quality is never addressed in a chaplain's training, how can it be considered important and valuable in professional practice? These gaps in the chaplain's formal training can largely be addressed through ongoing continued education at professional conferences or training offered by the quality department in the health care organization.

A more difficult resistance to deal with is the chaplain who avoids any use of measurement or scientific analysis in the practice of chaplaincy care. Chaplains may be quite comfortable using the insights of the behavioral sciences to better understand their patients, but when it comes to better understanding the effectiveness or appropriateness of certain chaplaincy care interventions, resistance goes way up. It is as if the chaplain presumes what happens in a pastoral visit is so mysterious it defies description, as though it takes place in a black box. They think to themselves, perhaps another chaplain could understand what happened in the visit, but I know it is not understandable to another health care provider. This description of the problem may be a bit exaggerated but not totally inaccurate. Some chaplains will make the point that quantitative data cannot begin to describe the benefit of chaplaincy care and fear that any quantifying will lead to a reductionist practice with little or no benefit to the patient. Can you imagine chaplaincy only concerned with measuring? "On a scale of one to ten, with ten being the highest, how spiritual do you feel today?"

I believe the caution against reductionism has merit but it, too, is exaggerated. Can't we do both? Certainly we can never forget that our practice is based on human relationships and these relationships are the context of our care. But can we also join in with our colleagues who are involved in diagnosis and treatment (doctors, nurses, social workers, therapists), whose practice is also based on a human relationship, and seek to better understand what is safer, more effective, efficient, patient-centered, timely, and equitable? Perhaps in trying to better understand our practice, by struggling to better define what may be imprecise but is still totally relevant, we will in fact support our colleagues who also struggle and try to better define and understand what is imprecise in their professional practice.

## *Getting Started*

Chaplains who intend to integrate quality improvement into their professional practice should begin by determining what resources are available in their practice setting. An institution that is accredited by the Joint Commission will definitely have an organization-wide program in place, since continuous quality improvement is a requirement for accreditation. Many health care organizations have extensive quality management departments that are staffed by professionals who are used to helping frontline staff implement performance improvement projects. Quality management professionals provide expertise in terms of methodology and help define the scope of the project. They recognize that the clinician is an invaluable part of the quality process because clinicians know from their direct experience what processes may be working well and what areas have room for improvement in the care of patients. So chaplains are encouraged to spend the time to get a good understanding of how quality management is done in their particular setting. The chaplain will find the quality management staff more than happy for the opportunity to teach about quality improvement and perhaps to learn from the chaplain's perspective of an opportunity for a quality improvement project.

Other resources the chaplain should consider have to do with the collection of data. Most health care settings are awash in all kinds of systems that collect data. The chaplain must remember that quality improvement is based upon collecting objective data but only certain data may be relevant to the scope of the project. Again, the quality management staff can be extremely helpful to the chaplain in identifying the essential data that needs to be collected for the project. Either the quality management department or the administration may even make a data analyst available from time to time for use on a chaplain's project. And finally, one can never be too friendly with the information technology team. They possess invaluable information about the resources that may be available in the organization.

There is an important difference between knowing what resources are available in your practice setting and knowing how to use each of these resources. Quality improvement is not limited to the technically savvy chaplain. Further, it is not necessary for the chaplain to master all aspects of a quality project. The chaplain can always make use of the expertise of others within the organization. Some projects might entail a simple paper-based data collection tool completed by the chaplain that is later entered into a database by someone else.

*Keep it simple and keep it focused.* "Mission creep" is a term used to describe a project that starts with one objective and gradually creeps into other areas and ends up stuck in a quagmire. Consult with your quality management team. They will help you define a manageable and effective project that doesn't get lost, like a child wandering off at the fair.

With respect to knowing what resources are available in the wider organization, the chaplain needs to have a clear understanding of where the resources within the department of chaplaincy care are deployed in the organization. Before you can even begin to consider an improvement in quality, you have to know what is actually in place and what the existing level of service is. In other words, you have to have some baseline with which to compare. The important point for the discussion now is that the chaplain needs to be able to accurately represent the breadth and scope of services that the chaplains provide within the organization.

An example of this comes out of my experience establishing a new department of pastoral care and education at North Shore University Hospital in Manhasset, New York. Despite being a major teaching hospital with 830 beds that was fifty years old, there had never been a formal department of pastoral care. The hospital relied on the community clergy for religious care until a few strong advocates for professional chaplaincy care were able to convince administration to invest in a department. A basic database was developed to capture information about patient visits, and despite not using a formal methodology, the database proved quite useful in tracking the growth of the department. This database collected date of the visit, patient's name and medical record number, chaplain, whether it was a referral or not, source of the referral, location of the patient, visit theme, intervention, number of patients in this visit, number of family members, and a free text note.

Because of this database I was able to quantitatively present the department's growth from the first chaplain placed in oncology, to the addition of a second chaplain placed in cardiology, and through the eventual establishment of a CPE program to reach out into other areas of the hospital. Tracking referrals was particularly helpful in identifying who was asking for chaplaincy care services and which units were asking for chaplaincy services.

This experiment with a database proved to be an important learning experience that would later support the department's quality initiatives. First, it gave a fairly objective picture of where the chaplains were spending their time with patients. It demonstrated that the chaplains followed administration's priorities in utilizing chaplaincy resources in the acute units, oncology, and cardiology. Chaplaincy students were able to extend the provision of service in less acute areas that matched the skill level of the student. Studying the source of referrals also proved interesting. As we suspected, in the beginning more referrals came from nurses or family members. Over time as the department became more integrated into the hospital, the number of referrals from social work and doctors grew. The chaplains could begin to formulate hypotheses that could later be tested out with quality improvement tools. What effect, if any, would in-service training with the social workers have on the number of referrals to chaplains? Would there be a measurable effect in the number of referrals because the chaplain started rounding with the palliative care physicians?

## *Choosing a Methodology*

There are many methods for quality improvement. Many share similar tools, with some variation in how they are applied. Examples of quality improvement methods used in health care are Total Quality Management, Six Sigma, and PDCA (Plan Do Check Act), among others. Health care organizations have already made considerable investment in quality improvement strategies and have been using them over time. For that reason, it makes no sense for the chaplain to choose his or her own methodology. The chaplain should use the most prevalent methodology found in his or her institution. This helps align the goals of the chaplain's quality initiatives with the wider institution, allows for team members from other disciplines to use a common methodology, and communicates the results of the project with concepts understood throughout the organization. As noted earlier, the chaplain should become familiar with the resources already in use within the organization. In the North Shore–Long Island Jewish Health System, for example, a combination of methodologies are used, primarily Six Sigma and PDCA.

## *Selecting a Project*

How does the chaplain decide on where to begin with quality improvement? The project needs to be based upon some kind of objective data that helps define what might be opportunities for improvement in a process. A good source of information can be the direct feedback from patients found in patient surveys such as Press Ganey or NRC Picker. Again, use whatever is available in your organization. Press Ganey transcribes all the written comments into a report called "Hot Comments," and the chaplain can search for key words to identity comments about the religious or cultural aspects of care.

These patient surveys gather information over long periods of time and can be broken down to particular care units within the organization. This is particularly helpful to the chaplain in helping define the scope of a particular improvement project. If the project has a hypothesis that certain interventions will positively impact the patient experience, it can be tested on a smaller scale where variables can be better managed and if proved effective can be implemented in other areas of the hospital. If the problem is not clearly defined and the scope not focused, the chaplain may expend great effort for little or no meaningful results.

There is one final consideration with respect to selection of a project. In addition to aligning with one or more of the six dimensions of quality (safe, effective, patient-centered, timely, efficient, and equitable), the project should align with the quality priorities of the health care organization. If the chaplain is choosing between two different projects, greater consideration should be given to the one that is more likely to positively impact the organization's goals.

## *An Example of Quality Improvement Using PDCA*

In the fall of 2006, a number of factors came together resulting in identifying the needs of the Orthodox Jewish patients as an area for quality improvement at my institution. Largely because of Press Ganey comments, it became increasingly clear that the religious needs of Orthodox Jews were not being adequately addressed. Attention to the religious needs would have a direct impact on quality in terms of care that is patient-centered and responsive to the individual needs of the patient. Demographic studies showed this was a large and growing constituency in the hospital's service area.

With the assistance of a new staff chaplain who is himself an Orthodox Jew, a project team was assembled to begin the plan. The team included community rabbis, chaplains, and dietary, engineering, nursing, and senior administration leadership. An initial assessment determined that some attempts to meet the needs of the Orthodox had been made in the maternity department, including cultural education of staff with respect to a number of different populations. But throughout the hospital as a whole, there were gaps that created obstacles for our Orthodox families to be fully involved in the care of their loved one. This planning stage included a survey of the practices of other hospitals in the New York City metropolitan area with respect to accommodating the needs of Orthodox Jews.

Having arrived at a plan, the next step was to implement it by doing the following: A new kosher vendor was contracted for patient food and food for staff and families in the cafeteria; a public sink was added near the cafeteria; a limited number of guest rooms were made available for families to stay overnight on the Sabbath; a Sabbath elevator provided for access to all floors of the hospital; nursing postmortem patient care procedures were reviewed and edited, with special attention to religious needs; a hospitality room was created with kosher foods provided by the community; and a team of *bikkur cholim* volunteers (Hebrew for "visiting the sick"; a common term used by those within this community in reference to those who volunteer to visit the sick and infirm) was recruited and developed. In order to communicate information about the new services that were available, a new brochure was created and the staff in-serviced.

The data used to check the impact of the intervention was basically anecdotal and qualitative, based on the comments in Press Ganey and letters from patients and families. A dramatic increase in comments of surprise, appreciation, and gratitude were evident in the Press Ganey comments. Further, when the planning committee met again to review the project, the community rabbis provided more positive feedback on the favorable impact of this project on their communities. One outcome that we did not anticipate was the response of the hospital staff, who expressed great appreciation for the improved selection of kosher foods, the cafeteria sink, and other services. Senior administration recognized the positive impact of this quality initiative and held it up as a model of how to do quality improvement with respect to the cultural needs for the ever-increasing culturally diverse population served. The project was presented at the Service Excellence Committee of the entire North Shore–Long Island Jewish Health System of fifteen hospitals.

Monitoring of the Press Ganey comments and patient letters continues on a regular basis to ensure that the quality gains in this aspect of patient-centered care do not slip. And the project has been extended with respect to the cultural needs of other groups served by the hospital. Needs of Islamic patients and staff are served with halal foods, a place to pray, and contacts with our community clergy.

## *Multidisciplinary Quality Improvement Projects*

Chaplains are often welcome participants in unit-based, multidisciplinary quality improvement projects or projects focused on specific populations. Especially one-person chaplain departments may find joining a unit-based project as a way to demonstrate the chaplain's contributions to the team on a specific quality initiative. For example, the respiratory care unit (RCU) has identified managing patient and family expectations with respect to extubation, recovery, and discharge home as a problem area. The plan for this project entails adapting the interventions of a successful, patient-centered quality project from another unit in the hospital to the RCU. Particular attention will be given to the patients' and families' experience of communication from the team, and all team disciplines will be evaluated by survey. Depending on the survey findings, there may be opportunities for improvement among any and all disciplines. More important, in this plan the chaplain is integrated into the process and recognized as contributing to the overall quality improvement initiative.

Quality improvement projects that cover populations organization-wide but with a clear focus can be important demonstrations of the chaplain's contributions to enhance the quality of care. An example of this is another project I am currently involved in at my hospital. Administration has an initiative to monitor the number of patients in the hospital for greater than twenty days. A number of factors could contribute to extended stays, including treatment complications, social needs, limited community-based care, and communications breakdown. With respect to the dimensions of quality, one could frame the problem as a great opportunity for quality improvement in terms of timeliness, effectiveness, efficiency, and patient-centered care. One of the early interventions of this project was to increase social work staffing to assist with social issues and complicated discharge plans. The increased monitoring of this population also had the effect of motivating those involved in the care to address problems sooner. Within a year, the number of patients in the hospital for longer than twenty days decreased from the 120s to the low 70s.

A second project has now been implemented to address the quality of care for patients in the hospital for greater than forty-five days. A team made up of a hospitalist, palliative care physician, care coordinator, social worker, and chaplain make weekly complex care rounds to the ten to fifteen patients on the list. The team's approach is to provide consultation to the care providers about other resources that may help in the complicated situation. Early examination of the data seems to indicate a decrease in the number of patients with stays greater than forty-five days.

The chaplain's participation is important for a number of reasons. For many of the patients with forty-five-day length of stay, there is a high probability that there is a component of spiritual distress. The rounds deploy the resources of a chaplain to take a fresh look at these patients, reassess their needs, and develop a plan of care to address their issues of suffering. The project has impacted the way our chaplains work because it is now an expectation that the chaplain will ensure that any patient in the hospital longer than twenty days will be visited and an appropriate plan of care developed. This approach not only aligns the department with the priorities of the organization's quality initiatives, but it has also resulted in identifying a population of the hospital that is at high risk for spiritual distress and should be a priority for the chaplain's attention.

## *Final Words*

Quality improvement is an essential part of the chaplain's practice. It is a tool that helps chaplains tell the story of their work in language that is understood by colleagues and senior leadership. Most important of all, our patients deserve the best of spiritual care—care that is patient-centered, efficient, effective, safe, timely, and equitable.

## Notes

1. Curtis P. McLaughlin and Kit N. Simpson, "Does TQM / QI Work in Health Care?" in *Continuous Quality Improvement in Healthcare: Theory, Implementations, and Applications*, 3rd ed., ed. Curtis P. McLaughlin and Arnold D. Kaluzny (Sudbury, MA: Jones and Bartlett Publishers, 2006), 42; Susan I. DesHarnais and Curtis P. McLaughlin, "The Outcome Model of Quality," in *Continuous Quality Improvement in Healthcare: Theory, Implementations, and Applications*, 3rd ed., ed. Curtis P. McLaughlin and Arnold D. Kaluzny (Sudbury, MA: Jones and Bartlett Publishers, 2006), 68.
2. *The Quality of Medical Care: Information for Consumers* (Washington, DC: Congress of the U.S., Office of Technology Assessment, 1988).
3. Linda T. Kohn, Janet Corrigan, and Molla S. Donaldson, *To Err Is Human: Building a Safer Health System* (Washington, DC: National Academies Press, 2000).
4. Institute of Medicine, *Crossing the Quality Chasm: A New Health System for the 21st Century* (Washington, DC: National Academies Press, 2001).
5. DesHarnais and McLaughlin, "The Outcome Model of Quality," 69.
6. Joint Commission Resources, *Providing Culturally and Linguistically Competent Health Care*, ed. Lisa Tinoco (Oakbrook Terrace, IL: Joint Commission on

Accreditation of Healthcare Organizations, 2006), 45—definition of "cultural broker": "The emerging, prominent role of clinically trained, professional board certified chaplains working with health care organizations in completing spiritual assessments functions as the 'cultural broker,' and leading cultural and spiritual sensitivity assessments for staff and physicians can be of great value."

## Further Reading

Berwick, Donald M., A. Blanton Godfrey, and Jane Roessner. *Curing Health Care: New Strategies for Quality Improvement: A Report on the National Demonstration Project on Quality Improvement in Health Care*. San Francisco: Jossey-Bass, 1990.

Committee on Quality of Health Care in America, Institute of Medicine. *Crossing the Quality Chasm: A New Health System for the 21st Century*. Washington, DC: National Academies Press, 2001.

Dlugacz, Yosef D., Andrea Restifo, and Alice Greenwood. *The Quality Handbook for Health Care Organizations: A Manager's Guide to Tools and Programs*. San Francisco: Jossey-Bass, 2004.

## About the Contributor

**Rev. Jon Overvold, MDiv, BCC,** is on the staff of HealthCare Chaplaincy, New York City, and since 2002 has served as the founding director of pastoral care and education at North Shore University Hospital, Manhasset, New York. Rev. Overvold is an ordained minister in the Lutheran Church (ELCA). He is a board certified chaplain in the Association of Professional Chaplains and since November 2006 has been elected to its board of directors, serving as chair of the Commission on Quality in Pastoral Services. He was the cochair of the work group that developed *Standards of Practice for Professional Chaplains in Acute Care Settings* in January 2010.

# 30

## Health Care Chaplaincy as a Research-Informed Profession

*Dr. George Fitchett, DMin, PhD, BCC, ACPE Supervisor, and Chaplain Dr. Daniel Grossoehme, DMin, BCC*

There is a growing consensus that health care chaplaincy should become a research-informed profession. We begin this chapter with a brief description of theological foundations for this position. We continue by describing some of the existing research about chaplaincy and next steps for chaplaincy research. We end the chapter with a description of three levels of chaplain involvement in research.

### A Research-Informed Profession: Vision and Rationale

Professional chaplains should be "research-literate"—clinicians whose practice of chaplaincy is informed (and open to change) by the available evidence. This doesn't mean every chaplain should begin carrying out research projects. All chaplains need to be consumers of research to continuously refine their clinical practice, while a minority design and collaborate in research studies. Pastoral counselors Thomas O'Connor and Elizabeth Meakes state that to do otherwise may lead to care "that is ineffective or possibly even harmful."[1] In most contemporary health care settings, chaplains are a limited resource and should not waste their time with ineffective clinical practices.

The Association of Professional Chaplains (APC), the largest multi-faith association of professional chaplains in the United States, recently developed *Standards of Practice for Professional Chaplains in Acute Care Settings*, which reflects this growing consensus for research-informed chaplaincy. Standard 12 reads, "The chaplain practices evidence-based care including ongoing evaluation of new practices and, when appropriate, contributes to or conducts research."[2] Chaplaincy within the United Kingdom has made similar steps, culminating in *A Standard for Research in Health Care Chaplaincy*.[3] Contemporary health care in the United States and the United Kingdom (at least) has moved to evidence-based practices, and chaplaincy needs to make the same transition.

Chaplains traditionally enjoy significant discretion over how their time is managed. The current health care climate, in which chaplains are a limited resource, means they must decide how to ration their time. This is not simply a time-management issue, but a theological issue of stewardship: what is the best use of the gift of time the chaplain has to offer? Research in chaplaincy is theologically grounded.

Theology and science have a long relationship, ranging from well integrated to antagonistic. Theologian Ian Barbour outlines four ways in which science and religion relate to one another.[4] The first way is conflict. In this light, rationality and logic are prized above faith—or equally, the infallibility of scripture is prized above data. Both sides claim to be the sole means of arriving at knowledge and truth, and it is necessary to choose between them. The second way is independence. Without disparaging the other, science and religion move along different paths, exerting no influence upon the other field. Each field uses a different language to pursue answers to different questions, "how?" and "why?" respectively. Dialogue is the third way by which science and religion may relate to each other. The means of gaining knowledge by science and religion are distinct but have points of contact. Experiences of physical reality are a means of encountering the holy, which is done most fully through scriptures. Finally, Barbour describes the fourth way, integration. The essential point is a "coherent vision of reality can still allow for the distinctiveness of different types of experience."[5] Chaplains making use of research do not abdicate their faith and trust in the holy, but instead seek knowledge wherever and however it may be found.

Faith-based acquisition of knowledge also has roots in the three monotheistic, Abrahamic faith traditions. Judaism has the tenet of *tikkun olam* (to repair the world). Efforts to repair the world are *mitzvot* (acts of human kindness rooted in commandments). Just as we may repair the world by prescribing an antibiotic to treat a bacterial infection, research studies leading to improved care repair the world. Repairing the world is not a choice but an obligation of faith. *Tikkun olam* was the motivation for engaging in research (instead of or in addition to clinical care of the sick) in a discussion among contemporary Jewish health service researchers and clinicians.[6] Among Christians, research follows from the theology of creation. Creation was given into the hands of humanity to care for; stewardship, including time, is a Christian responsibility. Research literacy can help chaplains be good stewards of their time. Christians are called to participate in the healing of brokenness by participating in the ongoing creation of the world according to God's plan by discovering and implementing new means of healing the world's brokenness. Islam has a long tradition of science.[7] Narratives of the Prophet Muhammad's words and actions (known as *hadith*) speak directly to the relationship between science and faithfulness in Islam. Surgeon and scholar M. Bucaille records the *hadith*, "Seek for science, even in China," and "The seeking of knowledge is obligatory for every Muslim."[8] It is not simply that knowledge acquisition is important, but it must be coupled with making it available to the wider community: "Acquire knowledge and impart it to the people." Adherents of each of the three monotheistic Abrahamic faith traditions stand firmly rooted in their own faith community when they make use of the knowledge gained by others through research and when they seek to gain knowledge themselves and make what they learn available to others.

## *Research about Health Care Chaplaincy: What Do We Know?*

While chaplains have a long way to go to become a research-informed profession, there already is a sizable body of research about what we do. Unfortunately, that research is scattered in many publications, making it difficult to get a good perspective on it. An important exception is a thorough, critical review of research about chaplaincy in the United Kingdom.[9] This survey organized the existing U.K. research into eight categories (see Figure 30.1). Scottish social scientist Harriet Mowat found many articles with opinions about chaplaincy (65 percent of the U.K. articles), some research about what chaplains do, and no research about the effects of the spiritual care provided by chaplains. "The research

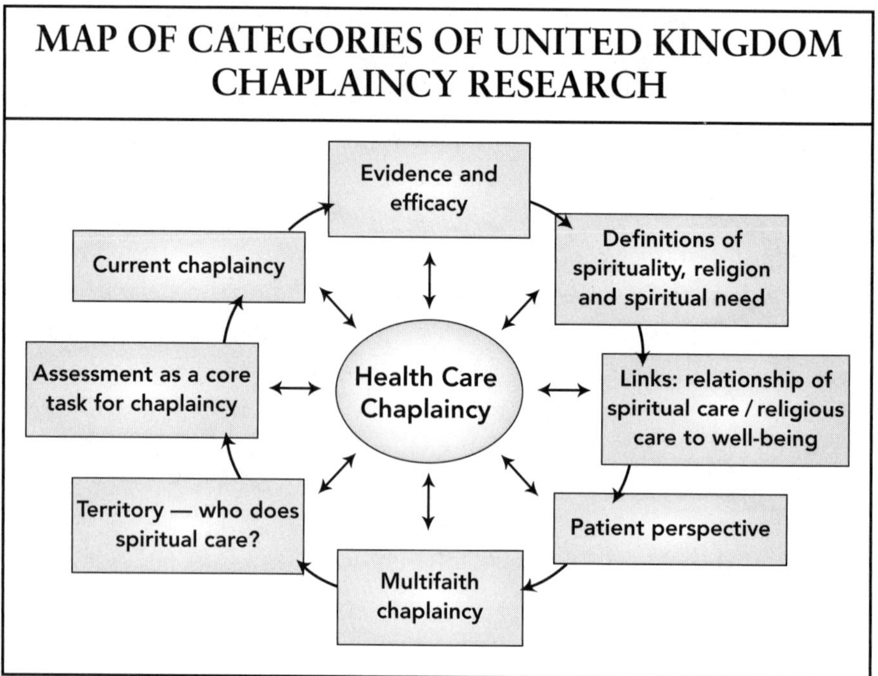


Reprinted with permission from H. Mowat, *The Potential for Efficacy of Healthcare Chaplaincy and Spiritual Care Provision in the NHS (UK): A Scoping Review of Recent Research* (Aberdeen, Scotland: Mowat Research Ltd., January 2008), 70.

*Figure 30.1*

literature ... as it stands does not directly or substantially address the issue of efficacy in health care chaplaincy."[10]

While we do not have a comparable review, our assessment of the U.S. chaplaincy literature is similar to what Mowat reported for the U.K, with a few notable exceptions. We have many articles with opinions about chaplaincy, a modest and interesting body of research about what chaplains do, a few studies of the effects of chaplains' spiritual care, and two frequently quoted studies that on closer look do not provide evidence about the spiritual care chaplains provide.

Research about what chaplains do includes studies of the number and types of chaplain visits[11] and studies of who makes referrals to chaplains,[12] including patient self-referrals.[13] There also is research about chaplains' different roles and health care colleagues' perceptions of them.[14] An interesting study asked 535 discharged Mayo Clinic patients to rate different reasons they might want to see a chaplain.[15]

Eighty-four percent of the patients indicated the chaplain's visits were important or very important because they were reminders "of God's care and presence"; 76 percent said having the chaplain visit at "times of particular anxiety or uncertainty" was important or very important.

Research about patient / family or staff satisfaction with chaplains is one type of research about the effects of chaplains' care. Larry VandeCreek and colleagues have done important work in this area, developing an instrument to measure patient / family satisfaction with chaplains and reporting their results.[16] Other studies of patient / family satisfaction with chaplains' care have also been reported.[17] A large national study of 1,102 physicians found that 90 percent had worked with chaplains, and among them, 90 percent were satisfied or very satisfied with that experience.[18]

Some research reports the impact of care provided by chaplains in the context of a multidisciplinary intervention. Chaplains at the Mayo Clinic led four sessions in a multidisciplinary quality of life intervention for radiation oncology patients.[19] Compared to those in the control group, quality of life improved for the participants in the intervention. Another study of oncology patients near the end of their lives found that those who reported spiritual care from a chaplain or the medical team had better quality of life.[20]

Two randomized studies of the effects of chaplains' care have been reported in peer-reviewed journals. In one study, led by Chaplain William Iler, fifty patients with chronic obstructive pulmonary disease (COPD) were randomized to a daily chaplain visit or to usual care, which in this hospital was no chaplain visit.[21] Compared to those who did not receive chaplain visits, patients who did receive visits had a greater decrease in anxiety, shorter length of stay (average 9.0 versus 5.6 days, $p < 0.05$), and higher ratings of satisfaction.

In the second study, led by Chaplain Paul Bay, 170 patients who received coronary artery bypass graft (CABG) surgery were randomized to receive chaplain visits or not.[22] Outcomes were assessed one month and six months post-surgery. There were no differences between the two groups for changes in depression or anxiety. At six month follow-up, the patients who received chaplain visits had higher scores on positive religious coping and lower scores on negative religious coping.

Why did the COPD study find beneficial effects on anxiety for the chaplains' visits when the CABG study found no such effects for either anxiety or depression? One possible explanation is the difference in baseline levels of anxiety, which were generally low for the CABG patients but moderately high for the COPD patients. The important point here is that it may be difficult to find measurable benefits of chaplains' care among patients who are in minimal distress or coping well. It is very challenging to organize and conduct clinical trials, but they yield very convincing evidence. The chaplains who conducted these studies have made a major contribution by demonstrating that they can be done.

A study of orthopedic patients[23] is one of two frequently cited studies that we would argue do not provide evidence of the beneficial effects of chaplains' care. This study examined whether it would lower their anxiety to provide patients with information about what to expect leading up to and after their surgery. The patients were assigned to receive one of three types of care: (a) a supportive preoperative visit, (b) a supportive visit with information about what to expect, and (c) neither support nor information. The support and information interventions were provided by chaplains, but the first concern with this study is that the chaplains were not there to provide spiritual care.

The second concern is that results are reported for 150 patients, but only 60 of them were randomly assigned to the support or support plus information groups. The overall results include 90 other patients who were not randomly assigned. The study reports that all the patients were relatively similar on background factors such as age, previous hospitalizations, and anxiety, and thus it could be assumed that any differences in the outcomes were due to the differences in the interventions they received. The key fact that is overlooked here is that random assignment matches groups on all background factors, including those that were not assessed. Thus, for this study we have no assurance that the results were not confounded by a difference between the groups in an unmeasured factor. This study is widely cited as providing evidence that chaplains' visits reduced patients' length of stay, need for pain medication, and calls for the nurse. Because of the issues we have described, we do not believe this study provides evidence for these beneficial effects of chaplains' care.

The main claim in the second investigation is that "studies of the effect of chaplains' interventions in orthopedic, cardiac bypass surgery, CCU, and other relatively homogeneous groups, have already shown statistically significant savings of from 19.6 to 29.9 percent per case."[24] The Florell orthopedic patient study described above is one of the references for this claim. Another is a study that reports, "Patients who rated themselves as moderately to highly religious left the hospital 19.5% earlier than those rating themselves uninterested or little interested in religion."[25] This statement confuses the beneficial effects of patients' religiousness, for which there is good evidence,[26] with the effects of chaplains' care, for which no evidence is given. For understandable reasons, including their uncritical presentation in the well-respected *Handbook of Religion and Health*,[27] chaplains have taken these claims at face value. However, if we are to have credibility as research-informed professionals, we cannot perpetuate claims about our effectiveness that are not well supported by the evidence.

## *Research about Health Care Chaplaincy: Next Steps*

Several helpful discussions about next steps for chaplaincy research have been published.[28] The following five-step outline is based on a description by pediatrician and researcher Chris Feudtner and colleagues.[29] The first step is to understand the religious and spiritual needs and resources of patients and families. Just as effective spiritual care is built on a sound spiritual assessment, research about chaplains' spiritual care should be built on knowledge about patients' and families' spiritual needs and resources. We have a head start here because a number of studies of patients' spiritual needs and resources have been published, in fact many more than can be cited in this brief overview. For example, each of us has published some work in this area.[30] Illustrative studies by colleagues in other professions include investigations about cancer patients,[31] older adults in long-term care,[32] and parents of children who died in the intensive care unit.[33]

However, many of these existing studies are based on small, unrepresentative samples, so further investigation is important. In addition, few studies have followed patients or their families over time to describe the trajectory of religious / spiritual coping with illness. Examining these trajectories may disclose points of vulnerability where chaplains' spiritual care may be especially important. This initial step in the chaplain research process is a place where good case studies can play an important role in building a base of knowledge. This is also a place to remember the lesson from the randomized trials with the COPD and CABG patients and focus on patients with high levels of distress and / or spiritual struggle. Perhaps most important, we need critical reviews of this existing research to bring into focus what has been well established based on high-quality research and where additional research is needed.

The next step is to synthesize this descriptive research into theories about the role of religion and spirituality in coping with illness. Again, it makes sense to build on existing theoretical models such as the excellent work of psychologist Kenneth Pargament on religious coping.[34] This theory has informed the research one of us (DG) has conducted about the role of religion in the lives of parents of children newly diagnosed with cystic fibrosis. Based on interviews with fifteen parents, this team developed a theoretical model of the role of religion in coping with this difficult event (see Figure 30.2).[35] Along with two colleagues, the other of us (GF) used Pargament's work to develop a theory of religious coping with chronic illness, and we then used that theory to review the evidence about religious coping with mental illness and with cancer.[36]

The third step in a program of research for health care chaplaincy is to test the theories we use or develop. For example, one of us (GF) used Pargament's model to describe positive and negative religious coping among patients with diabetes, congestive heart failure, and cancer.[37] Many other investigators, including Pargament and his colleagues, have also conducted studies of patients' religious coping.[38] The team that interviewed the parents of children with cystic fibrosis also used these interviews to test which elements of Pargament's model of religious coping were most salient for these parents.[39]

A critical fourth step in chaplaincy research is to develop or select measures of key outcomes associated with effective spiritual care. Since Florell's work,[40] chaplains have been interested in the impact of their care on patients' length of stay, and Iler and his colleagues found that daily chaplain visits did shorten COPD patients' length of stay.[41] But for many groups of patients there is small variation and little excess in length of stay, and chaplains' care will have little influence on this outcome. In contrast, anxiety is a common and distressing symptom for COPD and other patients. Chaplains' care could reduce anxiety through reinforcing reassuring religious beliefs, repeating familiar religious rituals, and empathic listening. All these things made anxiety a

## PARENTAL USE OF RELIGION TO CONSTRUCT MEANING AFTER THEIR CHILD'S CYSTIC FIBROSIS DIAGNOSIS

**Constructed meaning: "We can handle this devastating diagnosis."**

"At least if *N.* had to be sick, He gave us something that we can cope with and we can feel, even if it's not something that He's going to take away from us quickly...." We can "handle this devastating diagnosis."

**God is active, benevolent, and interventionist**

"I didn't want to be pregnant but God said, 'No, you're gonna have another one.' Obviously, He had His plan and I had mine and He just overruled my plan."

"When I feel hopeless and when I pray for strength ... I think He grants it in His own way. He helps us get the medications that she needs to help her feel better ... He helps in ways I can't explain but I give all the credit to Him."

**Religion is a source of hope**

"I know God doesn't give me more than I can handle."

"If God takes her home early, I hope she's old enough at that time ... that she has accepted Christ and I'll meet her in heaven someday ... So at that point, we have hope ... it's wonderful to be in that situation."

"God has more confidence in me than I have in myself."

**Parents feel supported by God**

"Everything we've been through, we haven't gone through alone; God has been there. He has given us strength. It's not Him that's doing this to her, it's through Him that we're getting *through* this."

"Prayer is definitely a help. It's the peace of mind knowing that you're not going through this alone ... that God is with us."

**Religion can be associated with adherence intentions**

"He puts things in place for me to make decisions for her and do things ... and if it's what I feel the right thing is for her, God gives me peace."

"Faith helps me do things I need to do that aren't easy, like wound care ... it's hard to hurt her, but God gives me the strength to go through with it."

"We used prayer instead."



*Figure 30.2*

smart choice of outcome for the COPD study. Chaplains' care may also have beneficial effects on patients' quality of life.[42]

What about the choice of negative religious coping for the CABG study? A growing body of research points to the harmful effects, for many groups of patients, of negative religious coping (also known as religious struggle), which includes feeling abandoned or punished by God or feeling angry with God. These harmful effects include poorer quality of life, greater depression, greater functional limitations, and possibly increased risk of death.[43] This evidence supports the choice of negative religious coping as an important outcome for the CABG study. Selecting good outcomes for studies about chaplains' care requires a good understanding of important outcomes for the patients being studied. Developing new, reliable outcome measures should generally not be attempted unless colleagues with measurement expertise are available to collaborate.

Before we can implement the fifth and final step in chaplaincy research, testing the effects of chaplains' care, we need to develop a sound theoretical understanding of how what we do affects our patients. Iler's intervention with the COPD patients was a daily visit with them.[44] Beyond that, we do not know much about what occurred in those visits or why Iler thought they would have an impact on the patients' anxiety. But as we noted above, there are several ways in which we might specify the beneficial impact of a chaplain's visit for an anxious patient.

In contrast, Bay's ministry with the CABG patients included structured visits that were based on an earlier model of spiritual care with CABG patients developed by Chaplains Robert Yim and Larry VandeCreek.[45] Key themes in the Yim-VandeCreek model included grief, hope, and meaning. The extent to which the Yim and VandeCreek model was grounded in research about the emotional or spiritual issues faced by CABG patients is not clear, and this weakness may have affected the results of this study.

Case studies can be a helpful approach for developing descriptions and theories about the elements of chaplains' care that make it effective.[46] It is striking and sad to realize that there are almost no published case studies about chaplains' care that include the kind of detail about what happened in the chaplain-patient relationship that is needed to build future research. Presenting case studies at our conferences and publishing them in our journals will provide an essential base for research about the effects of our care.

Conducting further research about the effects of chaplains' interventions is the fifth and final step in building a body of research about chaplaincy. The studies by Iler and Bay and their colleagues provide evidence that we can do this kind of research. We can learn from the strengths and the limitations of their studies, as well as the work by Florell. The level of patient distress is important to keep in mind when planning studies of chaplains' care. As noted earlier, one of the reasons the CABG study may have found no effects of the chaplains' visits on patients' anxiety and depression was the overall low levels of anxiety and depression in the study participants. Repeating that study, but limiting it to patients with moderate or high levels of anxiety or depression, or to patients who showed evidence of religious struggle, might produce very different results.

## *A Research-Informed Profession: How We Get There*

In the opening section, we described how chaplains in the United States and United Kingdom have been called to adopt evidence-based practices. Both have encouraged a tiered approach to research. The U.S. standard contains three levels of expertise, ranging from the research informed to major studies. We describe how chaplains might live into the fullness of this standard's spirit.

### Research-Informed Chaplains: Basic Level

The distinguishing features of chaplains at this level is that they read and discuss research articles in professional journals, consider the practice implications, and use published material to educate administrators and others about chaplaincy's role, value, and impact. Research literacy implies a familiarity with current writings. There are two excellent journals in our own discipline, the *Journal of Pastoral Care and Counseling* and the *Journal of Health Care Chaplaincy*, and individuals and departments may strongly consider subscriptions. However, other disciplines have extensive literature about religion and health that they publish in their journals. Accessing those articles can be arranged in some cases through the medical library in a health care institution. A "table of contents" service may be available, in which journals' tables of contents are photocopied and sent to you. Many publishers have an electronic subscription option on their journals' web page, providing e-mails with the table of contents of each new issue.

Not everything written is meaningful or of equal worth. To determine what is meaningful to you, don't read articles straight through. Read the abstract first. If the abstract suggests this article may be helpful, skip to the references. Are relatively current works cited, or only older, well-known reference works? Is there a balance of viewpoints, or is one person cited multiple times? The narrower (or newer) the topic, the fewer works there may be to cite. Next, look at the methods section, which should be clear enough that you could repeat the study if you had the same resources. Keep in mind how the data was collected. Data is easy to collect in a laboratory setting. How does the study strike the balance between what is practical and feasible (laboratory) and what will be meaningful ("real world"). All authors want to think they have written an "important work." However, authors need to make sure they do not overstate the importance of their results. Does the results section make explicit linkages between their findings and the study's hypotheses? To what extent do the authors generalize their findings? Are the findings "meaningful" or merely "significant"? Achieving statistical significance, in which two things are found to be different from one another, is much easier than showing that this difference matters. Why change your practice unless you can potentially make a meaningful difference? In the discussion, the questions are "So what?" and "Who cares?" Authors should discuss their findings in light of the material cited in the introduction. Where does this fit in terms of what was already known or believed? If you believe the study has implications for how you practice chaplaincy, how might you integrate the findings into your practice?

Some chaplains may process such questions individually. Others find it helpful to reflect with a group of peers. Electronic chaplains' discussion lists are forums where reflections might be posted with an invitation to discuss an article's implications. This is particularly helpful for chaplains in one-person departments. Multi-staff departments or settings where there are multiple institutions in the same geographic area might have a "journal club" meeting regularly (perhaps quarterly) to discuss an article during a staff meeting or at an off-site location such as a coffee house. A good source for interesting articles is the "Article-of-the-Month" feature on the ACPE Research Network website.[47]

The other avenue for discussion about research called for by the APC *Standards of Practice* is with health care administrators. Many administrators seek to be financially responsible with the limited assets they manage and won't reallocate assets unless someone presents evidence that a different allocation will change outcomes for patients, families, or staff. The "White Paper" summarizes a number of research studies that may be useful.[48] Most chaplains have narratives about times when their care made a difference to a patient or a loved one. Stories rarely change attitudes toward spiritual care. For some, that is because stories cannot be quantified. For others, stories represent a different language. Christian scriptures tell how the apostle Paul began his defense by speaking to the people of Athens in language they already understood (Acts 17). In contemporary health care, the language is evidence-based practice. Chaplains need to be able to speak that language to be understood and professionally valued by our peers.

## Research-Informed Chaplains: Intermediate and Advanced Levels

What can one chaplain do? The answer may be, more than you think. Case studies provided by individual chaplains make an important contribution to our new knowledge. In some settings, individual chaplains may be able to carry out studies with a small or moderate number of participants. Iler's study of patient outcomes following regular chaplain visits is an example of just how much one chaplain working with just a few others can contribute.[49] Some chaplains may already be devoting effort to research without realizing it, through participation in quality improvement projects. Although these two areas have differences, there is significant overlap with implications for our discussion. Research is usually considered to be the pursuit of new knowledge and involves testing hypotheses. Quality improvement applies knowledge and / or demonstrates changes of outcome due to evidence-based process changes. Quality improvement studies may be within the reach of many chaplains, especially those in larger institutions or health care systems.

Because most research questions are too complex and multidimensional for a single person, collaboration is essential to good research. In general, collaboration with investigators from other disciplines will provide expertise that is essential to the successful completion of chaplains' research. Chaplains can also collaborate on others' research studies. Just as we offer a unique perspective to care at the bedside, we can offer a theological perspective to a study.

Chaplaincy departments with multiple staff, health care systems with large chaplaincy departments, and chaplaincy departments situated in academic health care settings are likely to play a key role in the future of chaplaincy research. These departments typically have the resources, including time and finances, to devote to research efforts, as well as the research "culture" in which chaplains' efforts may flourish. It may be possible in these settings to develop "academic research chaplains" whose main task is to design and carry out studies, mentor chaplains in other settings, and build collaborations between chaplains and health care researchers. These chaplains will hold faculty appointments in the medical schools with which their institution is affiliated. The resources necessary to carry out good research may exist outside of the chaplains' department, typically coming from large, private foundations and the National Institutes of Health.

Just as large chaplaincy departments will likely play a key role in the future of chaplaincy research, professional chaplaincy organizations have a significant role in the development of research-informed professional chaplains by providing educational opportunities for their membership. The inclusion of research among the *Standards of Practice* for professional chaplains is a laudable and needed step, but it represents a step on the journey and not the destination. Opportunities for developing research literacy and even research skills can be effectively provided by such organizations in the context of national and regional meetings and workshops and increasingly through online media such as webinars. Initial steps have already been taken in this direction and need to be ongoing.[50]

## *Final Words*

As chaplains embrace the goal of becoming a research-informed profession, it is helpful to remember the work of Anton Boisen. Boisen is widely remembered as one of the founders of clinical pastoral education (CPE), but he should also be remembered as someone who practiced an evidence-based approach to pastoral care.[51] Much of Boisen's research involved collecting and categorizing case studies of the psychiatric patients with whom he worked. One aim of his research was to identify patients whose psychiatric symptoms represented a religious crisis and to provide appropriate pastoral care for them.[52] Contemporary chaplains have embraced Boisen's view of patients as "living human documents." We encourage chaplains to also embrace Boisen as a model for research-informed chaplaincy.

## Notes

1. T. S. O'Connor and E. Meakes, "Hope in the Midst of Challenge: Evidence-Based Pastoral Care," *Journal of Pastoral Care* 52, no. 4 (1998): 367.
2. Association of Professional Chaplains, *Standards of Practice for Professional Chaplains in Acute Care Settings* (2009), www.professionalchaplains.org/index.aspx?id=1210.
3. Peter W. Speck, *A Standard for Research in Health Care Chaplaincy* (2005), www.mfghc.com/researchstandards_speck.pdf.
4. I. Barbour, *Religion in an Age of Science* (San Francisco: Harper & Row, 1990).
5. Ibid., 30.
6. E. Lipstein, personal communication, October 29, 2010; M. Seid, personal communication, October 29, 2010.
7. See Barbour, *Religion in an Age of Science.*
8. M. Bucaille, *The Bible, the Qur'an and Science* (Indianapolis: North American Trust Publications, 1979).
9. H. Mowat, *The Potential for Efficacy of Healthcare Chaplaincy and Spiritual Care Provision in the NHS (UK): A Scoping Review of Recent Research* (Aberdeen, Scotland: Mowat Research Ltd., 2008), www.nhs-chaplaincy-collaboratives.com/efficacy0801.pdf.
10. Ibid., 7.
11. G. F. Handzo et al., "What Do Chaplains Really Do? I. Visitation in the New York Chaplaincy Study," *Journal of Health Care Chaplaincy* 14, no. 1 (2008): 20–38; G. F. Handzo, et al., "What Do Chaplains Really Do? II. Interventions in the New York Chaplaincy Study," *Journal of Health Care Chaplaincy* 14, no. 1 (2008): 39–56; M. Montonye and S. Calderone, "Pastoral Interventions and the Influence of Self-reporting: A Preliminary Analysis," *Journal of Health Care Chaplaincy* 16, nos. 1–2 (2010): 65–73. Due to space limitations we only give selected references here and later.
12. K. Galek et al., "Referrals to Chaplains: The Role of Religion and Spirituality in Healthcare Settings," *Mental Health, Religion & Culture* 10, no. 4 (2007): 363–77.
13. T. R. Chapman and D. H. Grossoehme, "Adolescent Patient and Nurse Referrals for Pastoral Care: A Comparison of Psychiatric vs. Medical-surgical Populations," *Journal of Child and Adolescent Psychiatric Nursing* 15, no. 3 (2002): 118–23; G. Fitchett, P. Meyer, and L. A. Burton, "Spiritual Care: Who Requests It? Who Needs It?" *Journal of Pastoral Care* 54, no. 2 (2000): 173–86.
14. K. J. Flannelly et al., "A National Survey of Hospital Directors' Views about the Importance of Various Chaplain Roles: Differences Among Disciplines and Types of Hospitals," *Journal of Pastoral Care and Counseling* 60, no. 3 (2006): 213–25.

15. K. M. Piderman et al., "Patients' Expectations of Hospital Chaplains," *Mayo Clinic Proceedings* 83, no. 1 (2008): 58–65.
16. L. VandeCreek and M. A. Lyons, *Ministry of Hospital Chaplains: Patient Satisfaction* (Binghamton, NY: Haworth Pastoral Press, 1997); L. VandeCreek, "How Satisfied Are Patients with the Ministry of Chaplains?" *Journal of Pastoral Care and Counseling* 58, no. 4 (2004): 335–42.
17. J. L. Gibbons et al., "The Value of Hospital Chaplains: Patient Perspectives," *Journal of Pastoral Care* 45, no. 2 (1973): 117–25; K. J. Flannelly et al., "The Correlates of Chaplains' Effectiveness in Meeting the Spiritual / Religious and Emotional Needs of Patients," *Journal of Pastoral Care and Counseling* 63, nos. 1–2 (2009): 9.1-15.
18. G. Fitchett et al., "Physicians' Experience and Satisfaction with Chaplains: A National Survey," *Archives of Internal Medicine* 169, no. 19 (2009): 1808–10.
19. K. M. Piderman and M. E. Johnson, "Hospital Chaplains' Involvement in a Randomized Controlled Multidisciplinary Trial: Implications for Spiritual Care and Research," *Journal of Pastoral Care and Counseling* 63, nos. 3–4 (2009): 8.1-6.
20. T. A. Balboni et al., "Religiousness and Spiritual Support among Advanced Cancer Patients and Associations with End-of-Life Treatment Preferences and Quality of Life," *Journal of Clinical Oncology* 25, no. 5 (2007): 555–60.
21. W. L. Iler, D. Obenshain, and M. Camac, "The Impact of Daily Visits from Chaplains on Patients with Chronic Obstructive Pulmonary Disease (COPD): A Pilot Study," *Chaplaincy Today* 17, no. 1 (2001): 5–11.
22. P. S. Bay et al., "The Effect of Pastoral Care Services on Anxiety, Depression, Hope, Religious Coping, and Religious Problem Solving Styles: A Randomized Controlled Study," *Journal of Religion and Health* 47, no. 1 (2008): 57–69.
23. J. L. Florell, "Crisis Intervention in Orthopedic Surgery: Empirical Evidence of the Effectiveness of a Chaplain Working with Surgery Patients," *Bulletin of the American Protestant Hospital Association* (March 1973): 29–36, reprinted in L. VandeCreek, ed., *Spiritual Needs and Pastoral Services: Readings in Research* (Decatur, GA: Journal of Pastoral Care Publications, 1995), 23–32.
24. E. McSherry, M. Cuilla, and L. A. Burton, "Continuous Quality Improvement for Chaplaincy," in *Chaplaincy Services in Contemporary Health Care*, ed. L. A. Burton (Schaumburg, IL: College of Chaplains, 1992), 36.
25. E. McSherry et al., "Spiritual Resources in Older Hospitalized Men," *Social Compass* 34, no. 4 (1987): 519.
26. M. J. Brady et al., "A Case for Including Spirituality in Quality of Life Measurement in Oncology," *Psychooncology* 8, no. 5 (1999): 417–28; Y. Chida, A. Steptoe, and L. H. Powell, "Religiosity / Spirituality and Mortality: A Systematic Quantitative Review," *Psychotherapy and Psychosomatics* 78, no. 2 (2009): 81–90.
27. H. G. Koenig, M. E. McCullough, and D. B. Larson, *Handbook of Religion and Health* (New York: Oxford University Press, 2001), 420–21.

28. Mowat, *Potential for Efficacy*; A. J. Weaver, K. J. Flannelly, and C. Liu, "Chaplaincy Research: Its Value, Its Quality, and Its Future," *Journal of Health Care Chaplaincy* 14, no. 1 (2008): 3–19.
29. C. Feudtner, J. Haney, and M. A. Dimmers, "Spiritual Care Needs of Hospitalized Children and Their Families: A National Survey of Pastoral Care Providers' Perceptions," *Pediatrics* 111, no. 1 (2003): e67–e72.
30. G. Fitchett, L. A. Burton, and A. B. Sivan, "The Religious Needs and Resources of Psychiatric In-Patients," *Journal of Nervous and Mental Disease* 185, no. 5 (1997): 320–26; G. Fitchett et al., "Religious Struggle: Prevalence, Correlates and Mental Health Risks in Diabetic, Congestive Heart Failure, and Oncology Patients," *International Journal of Psychiatry in Medicine* 34, no. 20 (2004): 179–96; D. H. Grossoehme, S. Cotton, and A. Leonard, "Spiritual and Religious Experiences of Adolescent Psychiatric Inpatients Versus Healthy Peers," *Journal of Pastoral Care and Counseling* 61, no. 3 (2007): 197–204; D. H. Grossoehme and L. Gerbetz, "Adolescent Perceptions of Meaningfulness of Inpatient Psychiatric Hospitalization," *Clinical Child Psychology and Psychiatry* 9, no. 4 (2004): 589–96.
31. S. R. Alcorn et al., "'If God Wanted Me Yesterday, I Wouldn't Be Here Today': Religious and Spiritual Themes in Patients' Experiences of Advanced Cancer," *Journal of Palliative Medicine* 13, no. 5 (2010): 581–88.
32. T. P. Daaleman et al., "Spiritual Care at the End of Life in Long-Term Care," *Medical Care* 46, no. 1 (2008): 85–91.
33. K. L. Meert, C. S. Thurston, and S. H. Briller, "The Spiritual Needs of Parents at the Time of Their Child's Death in the Pediatric Intensive Care Unit and During Bereavement: A Qualitative Study," *Pediatric Critical Care Medicine* 6, no. 4 (2005): 420–27.
34. K. I. Pargament, *The Psychology of Religion and Coping: Theory, Research, Practice* (New York: Guilford Press, 1997); K. I. Pargament, *Spiritually Integrated Psychotherapy: Understanding and Addressing the Sacred* (New York: Guilford Press, 2007).
35. D. H. Grossoehme et al., "We Can Handle This: Parents' Use of Religion in the First Year Following Their Child's Diagnosis with Cystic Fibrosis," *Journal of Health Care Chaplaincy* 16, nos. 3–4 (2010): 95–108.
36. P. E. Murphy, G. Fitchett, and A. L. Canada, "Adult Spirituality for Persons with Chronic Illness," in V. B. Carson and H. G. Koenig, eds. *Spiritual Dimensions of Nursing Practice*, rev. ed., (West Conshohocken, PA: Templeton Foundation Press, 2008), 193–235.
37. Fitchett et al., "Religious Struggle."
38. K. I. Pargament et al., "Religious Coping Methods as Predictors of Psychological, Physical and Spiritual Outcomes among Medically Ill Elderly Patients: A Two-Year Longitudinal Study," *Journal of Health Psychology* 9, no. 6 (2004): 713–30; N. Tarakeshwar et al., "Religious Coping Is Associated with Quality of Life of Patients with Advanced Cancer," *Journal of Palliative Medicine* 9, no. 3 (2006): 646–57.

39. D. H. Grossoehme et al., "Parents' Religious Coping Styles in the First Year after Their Child's Cystic Fibrosis Diagnosis," *Journal of Health Care Chaplaincy* 16, nos. 3–4 (2010): 109–22.
40. Florell, "Crisis Intervention in Orthopedic Surgery."
41. Iler, Obenshain, and Camac, "Impact of Daily Visits."
42. Balboni et al., "Religiousness and Spiritual Support."
43. Fitchett et al., "Religious Struggle"; Pargament et al., "Religious Coping Methods"; K. I. Pargament et al., "Religious Struggle as a Predictor of Mortality among Medically Ill Elderly Patients: A Two-Year Longitudinal Study," *Archives of Internal Medicine* 161, no. 15 (2001): 1881–85; A. C. Sherman et al., "Prospective Study of Religious Coping among Patients Undergoing Autologous Stem Cell Transplantation," *Journal of Behavioral Medicine* 32, no. 1 (2009): 118–28.
44. Iler, Obenshain, and Camac, "Impact of Daily Visits."
45. P. Bay and S. S. Ivy, "Chaplaincy Research: A Case Study," *Journal of Pastoral Care and Counseling* 60, no. 4 (2006): 343–52; R. J. R. Yim and L. VandeCreek, "Unbinding Grief and Life's Losses for Thriving Recovery after Open Heart Surgery," *The Caregiver Journal* 12, no. 2 (1996): 8–11.
46. G. Fitchett, "Making Our Case(s)," *Journal of Health Care Chaplaincy* 17, no. 1 (2011): 3–18.
47. See Resources at the end of this chapter for the ACPE Research Network website and other helpful research resources.
48. L. VandeCreek and L. Burton, "Professional Chaplaincy: Its Role and Importance in Healthcare," *Journal of Pastoral Care* 55, no. 1 (2001): 81–97, www.professionalchaplains.org/index.aspx?id=229.
49. Iler, Obenshain, and Camac, "Impact of Daily Visits."
50. P. E. Murphy and G. Fitchett, "Introducing Chaplains to Research: 'This Could Help Me,'" *Journal of Health Care Chaplaincy* 16, no. 3 (2010): 79–94.
51. G. H. Asquith, Jr., ed., *Vision from a Little Known Country: A Boisen Reader* (Decatur, GA: Journal of Pastoral Care Publications, 1992).
52. A. T. Boisen, *Exploration of the Inner World: A Study of Mental Disorder and Religious Experience* (Philadelphia: University of Pennsylvania Press, 1971 / 1936).

## Further Reading

Carson, V. B., D. E. King, and H. G. Koenig. *Handbook of Religion and Health*. 2nd ed. New York: Oxford University Press, 2012.

Koenig, H. G., ed. *Handbook of Religion and Mental Health*. San Diego: Academic Press, 1998.

Levin, J. *God, Faith and Health: Exploring the Spirituality-Healing Connection*. New York: John Wiley and Sons, 2001.

Paloutzian, R. F., and C. L. Park, eds. *Handbook of the Psychology of Religion and Spirituality*. New York: Guilford Press, 2005.

Pargament, K. I. *The Psychology of Religion and Coping*. New York: Guilford Press, 1997.

Plante, T. G., and A. C. Sherman, eds. *Faith and Health: Psychological Perspectives*. New York: Guilford Press, 2001.

VandeCreek, L. ed. *Professional Chaplaincy and Clinical Pastoral Education Should Become More Scientific: Yes and No*. Binghamton, NY: Haworth Pastoral Press, 2002.

______, ed. *Spiritual Needs and Pastoral Resources: Readings in Research*. Decatur, GA: Journal of Pastoral Care Publications, 1995. www.jpcp.org.

## Resources

### MEASURES OF RELIGION

Fetzer Institute / National Institute on Aging Working Group. *Multidimensional Measurement of Religiousness / Spirituality for Use in Health Research*. Kalamazoo, MI: Fetzer Institute, 1999. www.fetzer.org/images/stories/pdf/MultidimensionalBooklet.pdf.

### ABSTRACTS

Pastoral Research Abstracts, Noel Brown, ed. (oreresource@rocketmail.com). For many years, Noel Brown has provided informative abstracts of important research in each issue of the *Journal of Pastoral Care and Counseling* and APC's *Chaplaincy Today*.

### JOURNALS

*Journal of Health Care Chaplaincy*. www.informaworld.com/smpp/title~db=all~content=t792322384~tab=issueslist.

*Journal of Pastoral Care and Counseling*. www.jpcp.org. (Subscription with membership in ACPE and other groups.)

*Journal of Religion and Health*. www.springer.com/public+health/journal/10943.

*Journal for the Scientific Study of Religion*. www.sssrweb.org. (Subscription with membership in Society for the Scientific Study of Religion.)

### WEBSITES

ACPE Research Network: www.acperesearch.net. The existence of this website and its excellent resources is not widely known or appreciated, but it should be. It is sponsored by the Research Network in ACPE, but it is open to everyone. It includes more than eight years of the Article-of-the-Month feature in which a research article relevant to the work of chaplains and chaplaincy educators is reviewed. In addition to a brief summary of the article, the reviews include helpful suggestions for using the article in CPE programs and regularly updated lists of research by the same authors or on related topics. Frequently there are links to free downloads of the articles. We all owe a big debt of gratitude to Chaplain John Ehman, who is the network convener and author of almost all of these excellent reviews.

George Washington Institute for Spirituality and Health, Christina Puchalski, MD, executive director: www.gwish.org.

Pastoral Care Department, University of Pennsylvania Heath System: www.uphs.upenn.edu/pastoral/resed/index.html, Spirituality and Health Bibliographies. Check here for free copies of an annual annotated bibliography of research, begun in 1999, about issues of interest to chaplains. Another excellent resource from John Ehman.

## About the Contributors

**Dr. George Fitchett, DMin, PhD, BCC, ACPE Supervisor,** is an associate professor and the director of research in the Department of Religion, Health, and Human Values, Rush University Medical Center, Chicago, Illinois. He has been a certified chaplain (Association of Professional Chaplains) and pastoral supervisor (Association for Clinical Pastoral Education) for more than thirty years. Since 1990 he has been involved in research examining the relationship between religion and health in a variety of community and clinical populations. His research has been funded by the National Institutes of Health and published in chaplaincy, medical, and psychological journals.

**Chaplain Dr. Daniel Grossoehme, DMin, BCC,** is an assistant professor of pediatrics at the University of Cincinnati College of Medicine and staff chaplain III in the Department of Pastoral Care at Cincinnati Children's Hospital Medical Center, serving the Cystic Fibrosis Center. He is a board certified chaplain (Association of Professional Chaplains). His research, funded by a National Institutes of Health Career Development Award (K23 HD062642), focuses on the role of religion in adherence to home treatment routines by parents of children with cystic fibrosis. He is the author of several works on adolescent mental health and religion, prayer and meaning, and pediatric pastoral care.

# 31

## *Cultural Competencies*

*Sr. Norma Gutierrez, BA, BCC*

The emergence of cultural competency erupted in the last twenty years for several reasons. The United States has become more diverse. It is now a place where there is an expectation that all cultures are respected and acknowledged. This diversity is directly seen in hospitals, clinics, state institutions, prisons—everywhere a certified chaplain is found providing spiritual care. That is why it is important for us to include this material at this time.

This diversity comes with social and cultural aspects. I have especially found this when applying for positions. There are needs in many environments for bilingual chaplains, but it is not simply bilingual needs but also bicultural understanding. I hear from many who have learned to speak Spanish that it is not enough to simply know the language. Rather, they must also understand the "experience." What does that experience mean?

The experience is that of being an immigrant—even if they are one or even two generations away from the moment they or their family immigrated. That experience is of being separated from a place and people one called home. It can, at times, feel like a "pillage / plunder," something taken away without your permission, that feeling of always looking behind you. It is the experience of losing something, at times the feeling of losing one's own blood. It is a feeling of losing total control of a situation. People live in fear of being "caught." It is an experience of feeling cheated, of having to do without, of not having enough. Let me give you an example.

I was born in Texas. I am an American citizen. Yet, I still remember as a teen, while working the fields, people scattering because immigration officers arrived on the scene. I too ran to hide even though I am an American citizen and have always been one. That stays as an experience in my blood, not only for me but also for so many others who come from immigrant situations.

Being an immigrant is not necessarily a natural choice, but it is a choice for life, for security, for education, for freedom of religion, for possibilities not offered in one's home country. It is this understanding, this "experience," that can assist us in being well-prepared and understanding chaplains.

Some patients are coming to health care facilities with limited English, and it is difficult for nursing, medical, and other staff to treat them as needed. Also, recent immigrants are arriving with symptoms at times not found in any medical / nursing / social work textbooks. Slowly some of these, such as cupping and *mal de ojo*, are being addressed in professional textbooks.

## Why Care about Cultural Competency?

First and foremost, as shown above, cultural competency has become a quality issue. Second, understanding a patient and his or her needs might cut costs of unnecessary testing. Third, providing culturally competent care will raise patient satisfaction scores. And of most importance, providing culturally competent care will address the values of many of our institutions.

In this chapter we will look at what cultural competency means, why it is important, what compliance means, and how some systems are addressing this critical issue.

## Understanding and Assessing a Person's Cultural Identity

We, as chaplains, are called by our profession to meet the needs of those before us. Many times we are the advocates who speak for people who cannot speak for themselves. At times, we are the ones to remind people we are a nation who has from the beginning been made up of immigrants. Once there were Italian ghettos and Polish neighborhoods; today there are neighborhoods where Puerto Ricans and East African and Columbian families live together. Today my grandnephews are speaking English because of school, Spanish because of *Dora the Explorer*, and Chinese because of *Kai-Lan*. The media is doing so much to incorporate cultural awareness into society. Thus, this new generation will not have the issues we were faced with because their experience is totally inclusive.

A person's *cultural identity* is made up of things such as country of origin, language, education, spiritual traditions, family traditions, diet and nutrition, traditional medical practices, attitudes about illness and death, and migration experiences.

*Cultural competency* is the ability to interact successfully with people from various ethnic and / or cultural groups. As health care providers, we must gather information from the patient and / or family that could be useful in the plan of care. The Association of Professional Chaplains' (APC) *Standards of Practice for Professional Chaplains in Acute Care Settings* emphasizes this principle directly with Standard 1: "Assessment: The chaplain gathers and evaluates relevant data pertinent to the patient's situation and / or bio-psycho-social-spiritual / religious health."[1] Sometimes this "data" includes traditional spiritual rituals that may impede health. Maybe it is using certain herbs that do not mix well with medication someone is on. Sometimes, it is using remedies that have been handed down but that today are not as effective because things have changed.

I remember as a child that while we were running around, one of my friends fell and cut himself pretty intensely on the stomach from a broken glass. His parents could not afford going to the hospital. We all scattered to collect all the spider webs we could find to put on him. It worked then, but I don't think it would be the best treatment today.

Understanding someone's cultural background helps create a comprehensive plan of care. All of my nieces and nephews are professionals, but even today when their children are fussy and have a temperature, they will go straight for the egg and the ritual for *el mal de ojo*. Becoming culturally competent is an ongoing process. There are many more people of different languages and dialects yet to arrive in the United States.

Awareness is consciousness of one's personal reactions to people who are different. A nurse who recognizes that he profiles people who look like they are from Mexico as "illegal aliens" has cultural awareness of his reactions to this group of people. Attitude emphasizes the difference between training that increases awareness of cultural biases and beliefs in general and training that has participants carefully examining their own beliefs and values about cultural differences.

Be aware of stereotyping. No one should assume that a patient from a specific racial or cultural background will necessarily have the same traditions or beliefs often associated with that race or culture. Today, the number of Hispanics / Latinos who are other than Catholic has doubled in the past few years. Now there are Latinos who are Baha'i, Mormon, and everything else.

"Culturally competent health care requires a commitment from doctors and other caregivers to understand and be responsive to the different attitudes, values, verbal cues, and body language that people look for in a health care setting by virtue of their heritage."[2] Recently, I was with a patient and her family who had just received notice of her cancer. The patient was very clear from the beginning that she did not want any other treatment; she was simply tired and was ready to go home with her family and die naturally in her home. The next day, I saw her daughters, who all shared that they had spoken and were ready to honor their mother's wishes. I spoke to them of hospice, a possible program that might help them. They loved the concept and wanted to speak to a hospice representative. I thought it was all taken care of until three days later when I saw the patient still in the intensive care unit. I asked the case manager why the patient was still there. It was then I heard that the doctor did not want to write the order for hospice. The patient and her daughters were all Spanish speaking. One grown granddaughter spoke English and was serving as the family translator, but the doctor refused to see her as the family spokesperson. Since the doctor is seen as the one who knows better, the family had not shared their problem with us, and the case manager simply thought the family had reconsidered going home with hospice. Needless to say, the patient and her family went home on hospice the following day. So, we need to pay extra attention to these and similar situations. We need to follow through with making sure patients' and family's needs are met.

## *Tools to Learn about Other Cultures*

There are a number of cultural competency tools that have been developed specifically to help health care providers learn about their own culture and about the cultures of others:

- *Kleinman's Eight Questions* help providers explore patients' understanding of their illness and listen to patients with empathy.[3]
- The *Learn* tool provides helpful guidelines for attending to issues in cross-cultural communication with patients.[4]
- The *Ethnic* tool approaches communication in a respectful manner while recognizing that other healers may also be involved in the patient's care.[5]
- The *Berg Cultural / Spiritual Assessment* tool helps providers seek to understand the impact of cultural and spiritual values and beliefs on their interactions with patients.[6]

## *Cultural Competency Standards*

So how do we make our places of chaplaincy more culturally competent? I found the following standards in a reference from the Office of Minority Health (OMH).[7] These are helpful to be aware of as our health care facilities continue to prepare to become culturally competent. Culturally and Linguistically Appropriate Services (CLAS) has fourteen standards[8] and are organized by themes: Culturally Competent Care (Standards 1–3), Language Access Services (Standards 4–7), and Organizational Supports for Cultural Competence (Standards 8–14). Within this framework, there are three types of standards of varying stringency: mandates, guidelines, and recommendations, as follows:

- CLAS **mandates** are current federal requirements for all recipients of federal funds (Standards 4–7).
- CLAS **guidelines** are activities recommended by OMH for adoption as mandates by federal, state, and national accrediting agencies (Standards 1–3, 8–13).
- CLAS **recommendations** are suggested by OMH for voluntary adoption by health care organizations (Standard 14).

The following shows the CLAS standards and then a chaplaincy action idea, reminder, assessment idea, or sharing idea that I created. I encourage you to add items after each standard.

**Standard 1:** "Health care organizations should ensure that patients / consumers receive from all staff members effective, understandable, and respectful care that is provided in a manner compatible with their cultural health beliefs and practices and preferred language."

*Chaplaincy Reminder:* The Joint Commission looks at this type of standard very closely. Thus, in places where there are large concentrated areas of a specific culture, they will begin a patient tracer to make sure this is being met by each department / discipline that interacts with the patient.

**Standard 2:** "Health care organizations should implement strategies to recruit, retain, and promote at all levels of the organization a diverse staff and leadership that are representative of the demographic characteristics of the service area."

*Chaplaincy Action Idea:* Encourage your organization to publicize job openings by targeting language publications and / or media.

**Standard 3:** "Health care organizations should ensure that staff at all levels and across all disciplines receive ongoing education and training in culturally and linguistically appropriate service delivery."

*Chaplaincy Action Idea:* Identify staff concerns or suggested improvements for providing care that meets unique patient needs. One hospital went so far as to create a "diversity intranet" to educate its staff on how to provide culturally sensitive care to patients from diverse ethnic backgrounds. (See chapter 29, on quality improvement.)

*Chaplaincy Action Idea:* Promote staff discussions about the challenges of providing care to diverse cultures.

*Chaplaincy Action Idea:* Help train staff to address patient communication needs. Role-play, during clinical pastoral education (CPE) or staff training, to give the opportunity to experience the perspective of hearing or visually impaired patients. Help your health care facility by encouraging them to incorporate this type of activity for staff enrichment.

*Chaplaincy Reminder:* Notify management about competency issues of individuals providing language services.

**Standard 4:** "Health care organizations must offer and provide language assistance services, including bilingual staff and interpreter services, at no cost to each patient / consumer with limited English proficiency at all points of contact, in a timely manner during all hours of operation."

*Chaplaincy Assessment Idea:* Ask the question, "In what language do you prefer to discuss your health care?"

*Chaplaincy Reminder:* Hospitals may have the best programs, but there are times when even experienced staff members do not want to use "the blue phone" because it takes too much time to set up the language-speaking operator. Help explain to staff the value of this service to both the patient / resident and the staff member.

*Sharing Idea:* One hospital successfully eliminated "financial" barriers to units willingly providing interpreter services for limited-English-speaking patients. It centralized its budget so that interpreter service expenses were no longer charged to individual departments.

**Standard 5:** "Health care organizations must provide to patients / consumers in their preferred language both verbal offers and written notices informing them of their right to receive language assistance services."

*Sharing Idea:* Some hospitals use stickers or color-coded armbands to easily identify the languages spoken by different patients.

**Standard 6:** "Health care organizations must ensure the competence of language assistance provided to limited English proficient patients / consumers by interpreters and bilingual staff."

*Chaplaincy Reminder:* Family and friends should not be used to provide interpretation services.

**Standard 7:** "Health care organizations must make available easily understood patient-related materials and post signage in the languages of the commonly encountered groups and / or groups represented in the service area."

*Sharing Idea:* St. Mary's Hospital in Long Beach, California, has everything translated into Cham, English, Spanish, and Tagalog. St. Mary's Hospital in Athens, Georgia, has wonderful signage in Spanish even though there is only a small percentage of Hispanics in that area.

**Standard 8:** "Health care organizations should develop, implement, and promote a written strategic plan that outlines clear goals, policies, operational plans, and management accountability / oversight mechanisms to provide culturally and linguistically appropriate services."

*Chaplaincy Action Idea:* Collect feedback from patient, families, and the surrounding community. This could be part of a strategic planning process for the department. (See chapter 26, on strategic planning.)

*Chaplaincy Action Idea:* Share the information with the surrounding community about the hospital's efforts to meet unique patient needs. Remember, the Joint Commission will always ask to see the plan, how it was created, and how it is implemented.

**Standard 9:** "Health care organizations should conduct initial and ongoing organizational self-assessments of CLAS-related activities and are encouraged to integrate cultural and linguistic competence-related measures into their internal audits, performance improvement programs, patient satisfaction assessments, and outcomes-based evaluations."

*Chaplaincy Action Idea:* Help collect a baseline assessment of the hospital's efforts to meet the unique patient needs of the area. An organization's assessment can include standardized tools like the Joint Commission's "Tailoring Initiatives to Meet the Needs of Diverse Populations: A Self-Assessment Tool."[9] Planetree (www.planetree.org) also has a "Self-Assessment Tool"[10] in its Patient-Centered Care Improvement Guide.

**Standard 10:** "Health care organizations should ensure that data on the individual patient's / consumer's race, ethnicity, and spoken and written language are collected in health records, integrated into the organization's management information systems, and periodically updated."

*Chaplaincy Reminder:* Hospitals, hospices, and long-term care facilities can and should identify their own policies and procedures that support effective cultural competencies.

*Chaplaincy Action Idea:* Help be part of the staff to develop a system to collect patient-level race and ethnicity information if not already completed. Health care facilities can choose from standardized categories, such as those found in the Office of Management and Budget. They can also use the book from the Institute of Medicine, *Race, Ethnicity and Language Data and Resources.*[11]

**Standard 11:** "Health care organizations should maintain a current demographic, cultural and epidemiological profile of the community as well as a needs assessment to accurately plan for and implement services that respond to the cultural and linguistic characteristics of the service area."

*Chaplaincy Action Idea:* Neighborhoods change rapidly. Do not expect staff to understand everything about every culture. Instead, invite, encourage, and even help train other staff to engage patients to gather information about individual needs, beliefs, and preferences that can impact their care.

**Standard 12:** "Health care organizations should develop participatory, collaborative partnerships with communities and utilize a variety of formal and informal mechanisms to facilitate community and patient / consumer involvement in designing and implementing CLAS-related activities."

*Chaplaincy Action Idea:* Get to know your local League of United Latin American Citizens (LULAC), Thai community leadership, and other local neighborhood action groups and incorporate them into your plan of action.

**Standard 13:** "Health care organizations should ensure that conflict and grievance resolution processes are culturally and linguistically sensitive and capable of identifying, preventing, and resolving cross-cultural conflicts or complaints by patients / consumers."

*Chaplaincy Action Idea:* Complaints do not always need to be in written form. Someone may not feel comfortable putting a complaint in writing. Remember, some cultures are better at speaking their complaint than writing it out. Chaplains can help facilitate this process.

*Chaplaincy Reminder:* A word of caution—please pay special attention to this: People who have come from countries where their voices have not been heard, which are most of our immigrants, will be very careful as to who they complain to. I was recently with a patient who had a legitimate concern / complaint. When I said, "I will speak to the lead nurse," he quickly sat up and said, "No, don't say anything because then they will all treat me bad, because I complained." I tried at length to reassure him that this is a way for us to learn, yet he was so scared (since, of course, he was very vulnerable, with a leg that had just been cut off and the other one with skin grafts on it) of receiving less than the best care. And of course when the charge nurse did go in to make her regular rounds, he was not able to mention anything about the "less than 100 percent" care he had received.

**Standard 14:** "Health care organizations are encouraged to regularly make available to the public information about their progress and successful innovations in implementing the CLAS standards and to provide public notice in their communities about the availability of this information."

*Chaplaincy Action Idea:* Share your hospital plan and initiatives through public events, health fairs, faith-based organizational events, and cultural media outlets, and remember to post your plan on your hospital website.

## *The Joint Commission*

The Joint Commission does not endorse a specific plan, but they do evaluate systems that impact patient care. They use the tracer methodology. They will ask about policies for language access, how the plan was designed, and how they reached that specific decision. The Joint Commission will especially pose these questions to institutions serving highly diverse populations.

Using the tracer model, they will observe how it is implemented throughout the chart of a person who does not speak English. They will especially observe how individuals providing care access language services and how the language needs of the patient are met or not met. I suggest you look at the Joint Commission presentation, "Improving Patient-Provider Communication."[12]

## *Some Basic Guidelines for Delivering Culturally Competent Interventions*

Here are some basic guidelines for delivering culturally competent interventions:

1. Learn about the values, family norms, traditions, and so on.
2. Involve staff workers who are bilingual and bicultural.
3. Establish rapport.
4. Gain acceptance.
5. Be nonjudgmental, respectful, and credible.
6. Practice active listening skills.

We, chaplains who are trained in listening skills, can continue to teach other staff how best to be culturally sensitive.

## *One Organization's Initiatives for Cultural Competency*

Kaiser Permanente has developed initiatives in cultural competency. They have education monographs to full-fledged Centers of Excellence in Cultural Competencies, targeting specific populations. The Centers of Excellence include centers addressing African American health,

Armenian health, Latino health, persons with disabilities, and women's health. The principles include the following:

1. Contribute new knowledge through population-based research that provides compelling evidence about how culture, race, and ethnicity affect health outcomes in the clinical setting.
2. Disseminate, within and outside of Kaiser Permanente, advances in clinical practice, program expertise and innovations that offer contributions to the reduction and elimination of health care disparities.
3. Apply the principles and practices of cultural competence, cultural humility and cross-cultural communication in health care and health care delivery.[13]

Kaiser has one of the best programs for appreciating the different cultural groups within its staffing; it celebrates the cultures and strongly promotes future diversity leaders through its cultural scholarship programs.

Something Kaiser has trained its staff to do is to focus on those in the waiting room. This is something we could all do to become more familiar with ethno-cultural groups that we might be encountering in waiting areas or anywhere else in the health care system. Kaiser trains staff to pay attention in the waiting room to the following:

- What one hears and also what one sees
- How those waiting relate with each other
- Who is in charge and who does the family / group look to for help
- How they address staff or other family members

In my culture, the titles "Don" and "Doña" are terms of respect.

Pay attention to eye contact. Most especially notice whether children are being used as translators. Once I met a thirteen-year-old boy who in tears said, "I can't do what the doctor wants me to do." After listening to his story I was baffled to learn the doctors had asked him to translate to his mother that: (1) she had cancer, (2) it was inoperable, and (3) she had less than a year to live. Family members in general, and children in particular, should never be asked to translate. This action is the opposite of being culturally competent and aware.

## *Final Words*

May we continue to be role models of active listeners for those among us. May we share our values of welcoming all and being attentive to the needs of all. May we challenge those among us to make the necessary changes so that all who walk through our doors experience a true welcoming spirit and a place where their needs are met and honored.

### Notes

1. See Association of Professional Chaplains, *Standards of Practice for Professional Chaplains in Acute Care Settings*, www.professionalchaplains.org/uploadedFiles/pdf/Standards%20of%20Practice%20Draft%20Document%20021109.pdf#Project_Update. See also Association of Professional Chaplains, *Standards of Practice for Professional Chaplains in Long-Term Care Settings*, http://professionalchaplains.org/uploadedFiles/pdf/Standards_of_Practice_LTC_Document02162011.pdf.
2. Oliver Goldsmith, "Culturally Competent Healthcare," *Permanente Journal* 4, no. 1 (Winter 2000): 53–55.
3. A. Kleinman, *Patients and Healers in the Context of Culture* (Berkeley, CA: University of California Press, 1980).
4. Elois Ann Berlin and William C. Fowkes, "A Training Framework for Cross-Cultural Health Care: Application in Family Practice," *Western Journal of Medicine* 139, no. 6 (December 1983): 934–38.
5. Developed by Steven J. Levin, MD; Robert C. Like, MD, MS; and Jan E. Gottlieb, MPH, Center for Healthy Families and Cultural Diversity, Department of Family Medicine, UMDNJ–Robert Wood Johnson Medical School, New Brunswick, NJ.
6. David Berg, MA, MDiv, dberglfairview.org, Fairview Health Services, University of Minnesota, Office of Diversity, 2412 27th Ave., South Minneapolis, MN.
7. Office of Minority Health: www.omhrc.gov/clas.
8. The CLAS standards were published in the *Federal Register* in December 2000 (U.S. Department of Health and Human Services, Office of the Secretary, 2000). The standards have become the basis for subsequent government and private sector activities to define, implement, and evaluate cultural competence activities among health care providers. In particular, CLAS—the final report for the Cultural Competence Research Agenda project—was sponsored by the Office of Minority Health (OMH) and Agency for Healthcare Research and Quality (AHRQ) to examine how cultural competence affects health care delivery and health outcomes. Its publication completes a process begun in 1998 with the OMH-sponsored development of national standards for culturally and linguistically appropriate services (CLAS) in health care.
9. Amy Wilson-Stronks et al., *One Size Does Not Fit All: Meeting the Health Care Needs of Diverse Populations* (Oakbrook Terrace, IL: Joint Commission, 2008).

10. Planetree and Picker Institute, *Patient-Centered Core Improvement Guide*, www.patient-centeredcare.org/inside/chapter3_Form_Self-Assess_Tool1.pdf.
11. Cheryl Ulmer, Bernadette McFadden, and David R. Nerenz, eds., Subcommittee on Standardized Collection of Race / Ethnicity Data for Healthcare Quality Improvement, Institute of Medicine, *Race, Ethnicity, and Language Data: Standardization for Health Care Quality Improvement* (Washington, DC: The National Academies Press, 2009).
12. "Improving Patient-Provider Communication: Joint Commission Standards and Federal Laws (Part 1)," YouTube video, 7:56, posted by "TheJointCommission," November 10, 2009, www.youtube.com/watch?v=5mR0Vk2zHqs.
13. Melanie Tervalon, "At a Decade: Centers of Excellence in Culturally Competent Care," *Permanente Journal* 13, no. 1 (Winter 2009): 87–91.

## Further Reading

Matlins, Stuart M., and Arthur J. Magida, eds. *How to Be a Perfect Stranger: The Essential Religious Etiquette Handbook*. 5th ed. Woodstock, VT: SkyLight Paths Publishing, 2010. The indispensable guidebook to help the well-meaning guest when visiting other people's religious ceremonies. A straightforward guide to the rituals and celebrations of the major religions and denominations in the United States and Canada from the perspective of an interested guest of any other faith, based on information obtained from authorities of each religion. Belongs in every living room, library, and office.

## Resources

Department of Health and Human Services: www.hrsa.gov/culturalcompetence

Disparities Solutions Center: www.massgeneral.org/disparitiessolutions. Website focused on cultural competence and racial / ethnic disparities in health care

DiversityRx: www.diversityrx.org

National Resource Center for Family Centered Practice—University of Iowa School of Social Work: www.uiowa.edu/~nrcfcp

## About the Contributor

**Sr. Norma Gutierrez, BA, BCC,** is a member of the Missionary Catechists of Divine Providence of San Antonio, Texas, and currently serves on the Leadership Team. She is board certified with the National Association of Catholic Chaplains and also has served on the Board of Directors, on the Conference Planning Committee, and as a certification interviewer. She is a first-generation Hispanic and ministers primarily in hospitals with high concentrations of Hispanics. She is at this time a staff chaplain at Sharp Medical Center, Chula Vista, California.

# 32

## *Sacred Space*

*Rev. Curtis W. Hart, MDiv, BCC, CPSP Diplomate Supervisor*

### *A Meditation*

*The act of creating sacred space is one of courage, judgment, imagination, and intellect. The creation of sacred space partakes of an aesthetic vision sculpted out of prayer, conversation, study, and hospitality. The creation of sacred space is a venture encompassing a collection of voices, talents, and perspectives. It is a place where beauty and the holy embrace each other. Sacred space is in a temporal location. And yet it also exists outside the bounds of time and history. Sacred space opens out into the world while at the same time remains safe for the inner life and its secrets. Without audible words it says,* "Shantih," "Shalom Aleichem / Salem Alekem," *and "Come unto me all you who travail and are heavy laden and I will give you rest." Those who suffer and serve need this space more than words can express.*

This brief meditation suggests how I have experienced the nature and meaning of sacred space in thirty-seven years of ordained life. What follows is *not* a manual designed to rescue those engaged in the hurly-burly of meeting deadlines and the pressured writing of proposals for funding. It seeks to evoke more than prescribe. It pays attention to both means and ends. It is far from exhaustive. It is not going to provide ready answers or shortcuts to the hard but rewarding work that goes into the design of sacred space. It is, however, written as a resource for the builders and creators of sacred space. It provides a set of reference points for a journey in service to others. It is intended to have a generic character useful for adaptation to acute care, behavioral health, and long-term care settings.

## *The Preparation: The Planning Group*

There is necessarily going to be a small group engaged in the overall design and implementation of a plan for sacred space. There almost always must be a single individual, probably the spiritual care director, who is ultimately responsible for the project. That person should, like Harry Truman while president, keep a sign or plaque closely at hand stating, "The buck stops here." Someone has to be in charge, even though all those engaged in the execution of a plan share this call to service.

There is an abundance of willing and able persons in every institution capable of lending time, insight, and skill to this endeavor. It should include representatives from all stakeholders in the project, including but not limited to the following:

- Spiritual care staff
- Clinicians who have an interest in or who are known to be thoughtful about how sacred space might be utilized
- Volunteers and faith group representatives from the local community
- Institutional administrators
- Grants and development staff
- Public affairs officers
- A project manager
- A representative from the religious body with which the institution is historically or presently identified

In the case of a permanent location for sacred space, the services of an architect experienced in its design may be employed on a contract basis. Make certain to obtain a portfolio of the architect's work along with references ensuring competence and trustworthiness.

Avoid, if at all possible, the selection to the planning group of any difficult or refractory individuals known to require excessive attention. They will absorb far too much time and will likely be an impediment to what otherwise should be a fulfilling and joyful experience for those involved.

It is the responsibility of the members of this group to help create the mission statement and the aesthetic vision. The planning group is a resource of incalculable worth. Members of the planning group can be instrumental not only in the construction of formative ideas and statements but also in offering an array of good counsel and practical advice as the project develops. Trust them and use them well. Keep all meetings with this group moving along according to a clear agenda. Their time is valuable and a gift to the project.

## *The Aesthetic Vision*

The formulation of an aesthetic vision for sacred space sounds more daunting than, in fact, it is. Aesthetics has to do with the philosophical foundations of beauty, taste, and design. Everything a spiritual care provider has ever learned in professional training or as part of ministry in a congregation is of assistance here.

- Put simply, what will make the proposed sacred space beautiful?
- What is the location, permanent or temporary, for sacred space, and how can it become a place of beauty persons will want to enter? Lobbies are ideal but not always available.
- Are there other options for an alternative location that should be considered?
- Is the location accessible, and will its design and ambience encourage persons to remain in or return to this space for public events (e.g., worship) or help them feel secure for more private moments (e.g., meditation and prayer)?
- What in the environment will make it hospitable for families and children? This question is especially important for those who work in pediatrics or in some form of long-term or elder care.
- How can a proposed sacred space address the isolation and loneliness often found in being a patient?
- How will light be used?
- What is the imagined role of music in the environment for sacred space?
- What colors will be used?

- Will it feel safe for the community gathered there? This question is particularly important for behavioral health settings.

These and other related questions emerge in a period of preparation and discernment even as formal plans are laid down and spelled out. The refined and reflected-upon responses to these questions provide groundwork and direction for the creative process going forward. Their integration constitutes a new gestalt. Together they embody an aesthetic vision for sacred space.

## *Creating Sacred Space*

The following points are meant to be adapted to the needs of a particular setting for creating sacred space. They will be useful only when considered carefully and used in the context of the history, culture, and state of the institution where a project is intended to take place.

### The Mission Statement

The mission statement should be brief, to the point, and avoid as much as possible any jargon, religious or bureaucratic. The statement should be congruent with the institution's goals and mission statement and consistent with its overall philosophy and treatment aims. Institutional leadership must be made aware of this project from the outset. It should be given a draft of the project's mission statement and plans for sacred space once the planning group is on its way with the work. The institution's administrative and clinical leadership should have the opportunity to examine the mission statement and make recommendations as they see fit. The mission statement can be revised if the need arises. There should be little need for revision if the initial work is accomplished carefully and is in good order. A copy of the mission statement should be circulated to all members of the planning group. It should occupy a prominent place alongside the director's sign saying "The buck stops here."

### Preparing the Institution

Informing the institution regarding a new location for sacred space follows the principle "Think globally but act locally." Have the general purpose in mind, but shape the information sharing to the populations and locale where it needs to be communicated. Information sharing does not have to degenerate into bland, pale bureaucratic formalities. It can and should be lively, colorful, and expressive. And it needs to be repeated. Even with all the repetition there is bound to be at least a few calls or visits to the spiritual care office where something of the following will be asked: "What is happening to the chapel? *I* did not have any idea. No one ever informed *me* (or *us*). Why wasn't *I* included?" As is the case with other vexing occasions in ministerial life, it is best at these times to keep a clear head and a reserve of inner amusement. Avoid becoming reactive, and respond with diplomacy and tact.

Much of what constitutes preparation for sacred space will depend on the nature and character of the way information is typically handled within that institution. The following guidelines or suggestions are offered to assist in helping a planning group and pastoral care staff do its job effectively:

- If there is to be any temporary change or disruption in institutional life in relation to construction or traffic patterns, staff and patients need to be informed well in advance.
- Announcements need to be made at all appropriate administrative meetings. E-mails or other forms of suitable communication need to be sent to advise staff of the developments involved in impending change.
- Place flyers in locations where they are permitted along with announcements in institution-wide newsletters and other places where staff typically get their information. Make whatever announcements are circulated appear as attractive and colorful as possible. They should include an illustration of what the sacred space is expected to look like.

In the several acts of informing the institution, as with other informational bulletins regarding the use of sacred space, the emphasis should be on making clear that the space, when completed, will be open and welcoming to all.

The development of a new location (e.g., a chapel or space designated for meditation) is an ideal occasion to revise any policies and procedures governing conduct and use of sacred space. If for some reason none exist, this is the time to create them. They should include standards regarding usage of the space for specific liturgical or spiritual activities (e.g., weddings, baptisms, prayer groups, memorial services). By and large, preference should be given to already existing worship services and other activities. The spiritual care department and its director should be responsible for the scheduling of use of this space. Institutions should trust the spiritual care department to be responsible for optimal use and functioning in matters pertaining to sacred space. The writing of new or revised policies represents an opportunity to confirm that status.

## Funding and Formation of the Budget

This step includes budgeting expenses for both the construction of sacred space and its ongoing maintenance. These latter expenses include heat, light, ventilation, regular cleaning, and supplies. As to the new construction, special attention needs to be paid to the selection of furniture:

- Furniture should be tasteful, functional, and sturdy.
- Furniture needs to be easily shifted or moved to accommodate configurations for differing services and groups.
- If there is an altar or lectern, it, too, should be movable.
- Altars and other furniture cost money and need periodic repair.
- Musical instruments, especially an organ, can be expensive to install and maintain, as are sound and video systems designed to broadcast worship and other activities throughout the institution.
- There needs to be a careful assessment of the need for cabinets and other means for storage of literature, worship materials, and other necessities (e.g., musical instruments). The selection of storage cabinets and other furniture can be eased if someone, perhaps a member of the planning group, can take on this task. Empower him or her to do the research required, and ask him or her to make recommendations for purchase.

The most important ingredient for successful fund-raising is a belief in the project and a capacity to articulate this core belief multiple times in different settings. Funding streams vary but there needs to be organizational support from the institution itself. Ideally, this support should be separate from either operational or salary line expenses. It is important to know that support from individual benefactors and certain foundations can be "off-limits" for solicitation if they are spoken for by other interests or departments. Government grants are hard to come by for sacred space, given church and state issues. Religious bodies are, however, very much a potential resource. Family foundations with religious identities are likewise a possible source for support. Their grants are often not large, but their support has value not only for its dollar amount but also because their commitment may encourage other donors. If anyone involved in the sacred space project has a contact with a potential donor or other foundation, make use of that connection. In all cases, an initial contact is in order, followed, if possible, by a face-to-face meeting to outline the project's objectives. Have a figure for foundation or individual donor support in mind, and if appropriate, be prepared to state that amount plainly. Those doing the asking need to practice and refine their introductory thirty-second "elevator speech" and its two-, five-, and eight-minute versions. Always follow up any visit for solicitation of an individual or foundation with a carefully worded, personalized thank-you note. The same holds true for more general presentations to religious or community groups. Say thank you and indicate that there is an intention to stay in touch.

The budgets, for both construction and maintenance, must be accurate insofar as possible and complete. Do not ask or aim for any amount less than what is needed, whether it is to be provided by the institution or other donor sources. The institution's response to a request for funding is a clear indicator of how spiritual care is perceived and valued. Space in institutions will never be at anything less than a premium. Institutions may resist requests for support, particularly in hard times. Keep asking, insisting, lobbying, cajoling, soliciting, and pushing. In matters of sacred space, the spiritual care department is the community's advocate. Work to get the community what it deserves.

## Donors and Benefactors

Donors and benefactors are important people. They are, above all else, the friends of spiritual care. Their contributions are central to the creation of sacred space. They are, through their beneficence, friends to all throughout the institution. Identify them, contact them, cultivate them, keep them informed, and thank them in tasteful ways and in a timely manner. Donors include *everyone* who participates. Everyone who contributes has a stake in this new expression of care and compassion in their midst. Recognize them through names on a plaque, memory books, and letters of thanks. Individuals and families may wish to offer a memorial for a loved one. Unit staffs may want to give a gift as a group. Invite all of them to public celebrations dedicating the new space or a reception honoring their generosity. Let them know how much they are appreciated. These are core principles of conduct in stewardship or building drives in congregations. They conform to standards for civility and good manners. They also make good common sense.

### A Warning

Most everyone in the institution and community will be thrilled and happy for the presence of new or revitalized sacred space. At the very least, almost no one will seem to mind a new space or service innovation. Sadly, there are a few persons who are given to envy the good fortune and success of others. Success in the creation of sacred space, no matter how benign it is, may bring forth envy and veiled desires to wreak havoc, to get even. The reasons for these dynamics are complex. The philosopher Rene Girard has written extensively about the phenomenon that he identifies as "scapegoating." Some individuals and communities need a target for their often unconscious envy and desires for retribution. A new or successful department or leader figure for a project can become threatening and thus a target. What Girard says about scapegoating, and he uses biblical texts as examples, may well be relevant to those made vulnerable through their successful efforts in the creation of sacred space. This is an uncomfortable truth but one that should be kept in mind. Scapegoating is not deserved nor is it necessarily destined to happen. It does, however, remain a potential reality.

## *Implementation*

Creating sacred space requires asking continual questions having to do with the purpose and mission of the project. These questions serve as a "moral compass" that steers, directs, and keeps things on course. The following questions and brief elaborations suggest the phrase that animated the civil rights struggle: "Keep your eyes on the prize." The prize in this case encompasses both the end product in the creation of sacred space as well as the means or process through which it is accomplished.

Again, asking these questions should be contextualized according to the progress of a particular project. The list does not have to be followed serially but rather adapted to specific settings.

## Why Are We Doing This?

This question is, of course, addressed in the mission statement. It should be repeated or at least referred to as the process of creation of sacred space moves forward. The recitation of such hypothetical mission statement sentences as, for example, "Our sacred space is welcoming to all" is a reminder of both the charge and the purpose of the project in the first place. Often mission statements get lost as organizations or groups do their work. As an act of remembrance, this process functions like liturgy as "the work of the people." Reflection of this sort may be supplemented through study of sacred and other texts. These reflective acts provide a source for remembrance and renewal of spirit over the long haul of creating sacred space.

## Where Are We Doing It?

The process requires a careful reexamination of what sacred space means for the life of an institution. As the project evolves, are those creating sacred space remaining faithful to their institutional responsibilities? Is the location for sacred space utilizing light and other natural attributes effectively? Have things been learned thus far that can make this space even more inviting, more prayerful? Is the design working?

Important to note here is how sacred space is used in temporary settings where access to regular sacred (e.g., chapel) space is not tenable. Most often these services are conducted in places close to those who need them. This is often true for major religious holidays (e.g., High Holy Days, Passover, Easter, Christmas, Ramadan) where there are specific rituals or structures required for the occasion. The tent for Sukkot is an example. These events are valuable, first of all, for those most likely to use them. Structures and displays, such as those for

Kwanzaa, provide a learning opportunity about the ways and traditions of others. Worship or other spiritual observances on units or in dayrooms have a special role. These places temporarily become sacred space, and they need to be understood as such. They are an outreach from the department of spiritual care to those isolated by reason of illness or infirmity. These services, seasonal or otherwise, are central to the department and its calling.

## Who Are We Serving?

The response to this question is relatively simple though it requires careful and ongoing attention. Certainly it is for the patients, families, staff, and visitors who use sacred space. Creation of sacred space must recognize the variety of religious expression in contemporary culture. Those responsible for sacred space need to be aware of the existence and needs of these communities and populations. The discernment of needs and responding to them can be truly enlightening and rewarding. Avoid the temptation to act in paternalistic ways. Let the representatives of religious and cultural groups express to the planning group and the institution what *they* need in regard to sacred space. Simple, direct inquiry is effective here. Do not be afraid of the presumed "dumb question." People appreciate how those within the institution express an earnest concern for their interests. Moreover, this is an occasion to identify or enhance outreach to these groups. The creation of sacred space may be characterized as an act of servant ministry. And, as in the case in all such ministry, both sides become better informed and enriched in a sustained encounter with one another.

## When Are We Going to Finish?

Create a time line with benchmarks for completion of varying aspects of the project. Stick to this schedule as closely as possible. Revise this schedule if necessary. Keep all the original stakeholders and the institution informed of any change and the reasons for this change. Here, as in other dealings with those in authority, transparency is a key to maintaining and building trust. If there are difficulties or unimagined problems in construction, for example, institutional leadership, once informed, may be willing and able to help provide or search for alternative solutions. They may be able to find resources to help the project regain momentum and move forward.

## *Celebrate the Accomplishment!*

The dedication or rededication of sacred space is a unique and wonderful moment. Its celebration can use the full creative power and imagination of those who have planned and seen the project through to its conclusion. There can be music and indigenous artistic expression from the community. There can be prayers, music, and readings from all sorts of languages and traditions. Recognize those who have contributed their time, talent, and treasure. Lift them up for their stewardship. Bountiful refreshments are, of course, in order. This is one of those times when everyone has a right to feel good and proud about what has taken place, how things have turned out, and how they have changed life for the better. Enjoy.

## *Epilogue: The Eternal Now*

Once the celebration is over, it is time to step back into the quiet and reflect once more. Here intense thoughts and external pressure give way to a contemplative mood. The questions that shaped the project surface but are engaged from a now different perspective:

- *Is our sacred space beautiful and inviting?* Yes. As well as we could do it.
- *Have we been good stewards of the resources granted us?* Yes. We have behaved with decorum and honor in the disposition of human and material resources.
- *Have there been missteps along the way?* You bet. We owned up to them and corrected our mistakes and flaws.
- *Could we have done better?* Well, probably, but only time will provide the best answer for that.
- *Will our community feel well served by our efforts?* Yes, it will.

This valedictory touches the depths. It is as real as real can be. It is a signifier, a connection to the Ground of Being itself. Philosophers, poets, and theologians have described this experience, but none better than theologian and renowned preacher Paul Tillich. From the pulpit, six months before his own death, he grasped in words the eternal as it is known in the creation of sacred space:

> For we experience the eternal in us and in our world in the here and now. We experience it in moments of silence and creativity. We experience it in the conflicts of our conscience and in the hours of peace with ourselves, we experience it in the seriousness of the moral command and in the ecstasy of love.... We experience it in moments when we feel this is a holy place, a holy time; it transcends ordinary experience: It gives more, it demands more, it points to the mystery of my existence, of all existence.... Where this is experienced, there is awareness of the eternal.[1]

## *Brief Notes of Biographical Background*

A few brief notes of biographical background are included to describe the experiences informing this narrative. My journey through ordained life began as an assistant in an inner-city church in Brooklyn, New York, in 1973. It has included service as a hospital spiritual care department head for thirty-one years in both a state psychiatric hospital (Toledo Mental Health Center, Toledo, Ohio) and a major urban academic teaching hospital (NewYork-Presbyterian Hospital, Weill Cornell Center, New York) and its adjoining medical school. During this period, I simultaneously served as an interim clergyperson on seventeen different occasions, often in troubled and transitional parish situations. Thus, I am familiar with a wide range of sacred spaces and consecrated places. In institutional settings, I was involved with fashioning temporary or semipermanent sacred space in dayrooms, waiting areas, conference rooms, and several closet-sized nooks and corners designated for meditation. I had the pleasure of having among my responsibilities the maintenance and renovation of a chapel of exquisite design. I helped plan for the building of another chapel, for sacred space. I oversaw that project through to its conclusion. During that time I helped raise funds, was engaged in developing budgets, hired an architect, and was responsible for the dedication of the finished space for worship and meditation. I was also charged with overseeing the design and construction of two separate sets of office and educational space for department staff and clinical pastoral education residents.

I went into professional spiritual care in part to avoid the career pitfalls and potential nervous collapse that are the storied fate of anyone who runs a big church and oversees major building programs. In my case, quite the opposite took place. I ended up doing precisely what I, consciously at least, said I did not want to do. I was fortunate in having gifted and loyal spiritual care staff persons and inspired lay leadership to aid me along the way. Theologian and social ethicist Reinhold Niebuhr once said, "Nothing we do, however virtuous, can be accomplished alone; therefore we are saved by love."[2] My experience in the creation of sacred space provides abundant witness to the truth of Niebuhr's words. As I have said, elsewhere and often, without their help I would have sunk like a stone.

## Notes

1. M. K. Taylor, *Paul Tillich: Theologian of the Boundaries* (London: Collier, 1987), 330–31.
2. R. Niebuhr, *The Irony of American History* (New York: Scribners, 1952), 63.

## Further Reading

Bergman, E. F. *The Spiritual Traveler: New York City; The Guide to Sacred Spaces and Beautiful Places*. Mahwah, NJ: Hidden Spring / Paulist Press, 2001.

Girard, R. *Job: The Victim of His People*. Stanford, CA: Stanford University Press, 1987.

Golsan, R. J. *Rene Girard and Myth*. New York: Routledge, 1993.

## About the Contributor

**Rev. Curtis W. Hart, MDiv, BCC, CPSP Diplomate Supervisor,** is an Episcopal priest and lecturer in public health, medicine, and psychiatry, Division of Medical Ethics at Weill Cornell Medical College, Cornell, New York, and editor-in-chief of the *Journal of Religion and Health*. At Weill Cornell Medical College, he teaches medical students in the "Medicine, Patients, and Society" curriculum and is a member of the Institutional Review Board, Committee on Human Rights in Research. At Weill Cornell he is an active participant in the Richardson History of Psychiatry Research Seminar and its Working Group on Psychoanalysis and the Arts. He is a lecturer in the Program in Psychiatry and Religion at Union Theological Seminary and a contributor to the *Encyclopedia of Psychology and Religion*. His other professional associations include being a Fellow of the New York Academy of Medicine and a Fellow of the Society for Values in Higher Education.

# 33

# *Blessings of a Mixed Population*

## Institutional Prayer in Multifaith Communities

*Rabbi Dr. Shira Stern, MHL, DMin, BCJC*

## *Recognizing Pain and Need in Others*

A rabbi once asked his students how one knows when night has ended and the day has come.

One student said, "Is it when you can tell a palm tree from a fig tree?"

"No," said the rabbi.

Another ventured, "Could it be when you can tell a sheep from a goat?"

"No," replied the rabbi.

A third student said, "It's when you can tell a rabbit from a dog."

"No," said the rabbi.

The students were confused and demanded an answer.

So the rabbi said, "It is daylight when you can look into the face of another human being and recognize that he or she is your brother or sister. Until then," he said, "it is night."

Most chaplains function within multifaith communities in institutions of varying size. Though they are often attached to a unique community with singular needs, they must sometimes be the one spiritual coordinator for a diverse religious population in a variety of situations. That diversity can even be present together in a single room: patients, family members, and supportive friends who gather together each may have different though intersecting spiritual needs in response to a common crisis. The more flexible and aware the chaplain, the better the outcome of a pastoral encounter.

Because the focus of the institution is inherently not spiritual—it may be medical, residential, penitentiary, or disaster related—the chaplain must be aware of four distinct rubrics to provide good spiritual care: the chaplain needs to be able to create sanctified space and sanctified time, as well as honor special secular observances and multiple religious adherents with specific religious needs.

## *Sanctified Space*

The chaplain needs to create sanctified space in what is, by definition, "unholy ground." The sights, smells, sounds, and particular ambience of institutions do not set the stage for a normative religious experience. Thus, it is up to the chaplain to pull together all the elements that will allow a patient / resident / inmate to enter a sacred domain. Sometimes this can be achieved by setting aside an area that is separated from the area of focus: in a hospital, the visitors' lounge can become a chapel if there is none in the building; in a long-term care facility, a common room can be decorated to address a particular holiday or reflect a particular service. At other times, the chaplain must create a special atmosphere where the constraints are fixed: at a bedside with machines beeping, IVs dripping, and medicinal odors, the chaplain can close the curtains, clear a sidetable of items to display religious artifacts, and sing or provide music to establish the boundaries between the holy and the ordinary.

## *Sanctified Time*

The chaplain needs to create sanctified time. Some observances are fixed, like the Jewish Sabbath, which begins at sundown on Friday; Islamic daily prayers five times a day; or Christian rites for Sunday Mass. Honoring those time-bound religious needs as best as one can may alleviate anxiety for patients and families alike.

Other observances are less constricted, but fulfilling these religious needs—like confession before Mass, last rites for Jews (*Viddui*), or *Shahadah* for Muslims—will allow adherents the kind of spiritual comfort and peace most needed and least likely to be offered by other staff members.

## *Secular Time*

Ironically, chaplains can also be responsible for elevating secular holidays into "holy moments"—Veterans Day in a military institution, Memorial Day, and the Fourth of July can provide meaning and solace to the larger community and can help reinforce the commonality of a mixed population. Separating the "sacred secular" from "ordinary time" also provides meaningful guideposts; "I've made it through the summer—I never thought I'd be here to see another fall" are words I have often heard, prompting spontaneous words of gratitude so necessary for spiritual healing.

## *Religious Diversity*

Patients / residents / inmates can often feel isolated in their religious faiths; when a particular season emphasizes one or another holiday, some people feel even more alone in their illness, condition, or present circumstance, so it is particularly important for the chaplain to be aware of the different faiths represented in the institution's daily roster. In addition, there will be patients with no particular religious history or who are committed Atheists, and the chaplain must find ways to serve those individuals as well. The chaplain can determine what the person values and cherishes and then provide that individual with the opportunity to talk about his or her fears, dreams, and concerns, with no religious overtones. Instead of ending a visit with fixed or spontaneous prayer, the chaplain can "hope" that the patient is able to find healing in the near future. While the chaplain's own faith may be strong and central in his or her life, the patient's need to create a bond with another human being who will be a patient listener—pun intended—is paramount and can be the determinant in how willing a participant the person will be in his or her own recovery process.

## *Demographics*

It helps to know the entire cast of characters when the chaplain is responsible for the spiritual well-being of an institution. In particular, it is important for the chaplain to see both the obvious and the hidden recipients of spiritual care—the primary, secondary, and extended populations. Like concentric circles, the primary, secondary, and tertiary populations all have both common and unique needs that may fall under the purview of the chaplain.

## Primary Population

- **Patients.** The daily manifest can include people in emergency departments, acute care areas, and long-term and palliative care units. The most vulnerable ones are often those waiting in wheelchairs and stretchers in corridors who are "invisible" to staff members and separated from family. If the chaplain is immediately identifiable by name tag or religious garb, the patient may reach out to him or her. If not, the chaplain can approach the person and ask how she or he can be helpful. Regardless of whether the chaplain and the patient share the same religious faith, an ecumenical blessing may relieve the anxiety and fear for the patient.
- **Residents.** Long-term institutions often have populations who reflect a large continuum of cognitive and physical abilities. Some may exhibit signs of moderate and severe dementia; other may have a range of limitations that are organic but do not affect their mental acuity. Spiritual care in such cases needs to reflect the audience; music and simple rituals that the individuals or groups are familiar with provide the most accessible and cathartic care. The main obstacle for positive outcomes is when residents are all brought together without any sensitivity to individual needs or capacity, the "shotgun" approach to pastoral care. In those cases, the chaplain can provide a modified "buffet" of prayers, music, and meditations, to accommodate the greatest number of people present.

  Residents of psychiatric institutions may need individualized care or smaller groupings to benefit from good spiritual attention. (See chapter 21 for appropriate guidance and examples.)
- **Inmates.** Prison chaplains serve inmates, correctional staff, and their families. They may teach, counsel, and provide spiritual services to those mentioned above and provide appropriate religious articles required for both personal spiritual growth as well as set religious services. Finally, prison chaplains have a particular responsibility to ensure that all prisoners have access to some religious connection, within the realm of available resources and correctional structure.

The chaplain need not be fluent in all religious faiths represented by inmates but can coordinate the volunteer visits from area clergy who can fulfill their religious needs. It is particularly important for the chaplain to have a current list of spiritual leaders in the community who are willing to serve the institution.

## Secondary Populations

- **Families.** Families, whether fully present and supportive or more absent and tentative, tend to play out the dynamics that originated before the patient became ill. These dynamics are heightened in times of crisis when multiple faiths are represented. Should the patient receive the Sacrament of the Sick, or should a rabbi be called in? Can a Jehovah's Witness be the final arbiter of end-of-life decisions if a health proxy has not been named? Can drumming, bells, or incense be used in an intensive care unit for a dying patient from a Buddhist or Taoist tradition? The chaplain in these situations can serve as facilitator for family discussions and be present for staff and family interactions when there is divergence of opinion.

  Often chaplains serve in institutions where patients or residents are roomed together regardless of their own cultural sensibilities. In these cases, the chaplain should have a basic understanding of those differing traditions (see further reading) so that adjustments to décor, limited privacy, even food or drink, can be made to enhance the patient's or resident's well-being.

  Prayer by the bedside need not be curtailed but should be adjusted to accommodate a shared room. Should a chaplain be called on to visit a specific patient, it is particularly important to stop in at the neighboring bed's occupant after the first patient has been cared for and to offer spiritual care. Such considerations, even if they are politely declined, remind the roommate that he or she too is sacred and worthy of attention.

- **Friends.** Friends can often bring support to patients and their families, especially when the patient comes from a culture that encourages both multigenerational and communal interaction. While an institution may have a limit to the number of visits per person or per room, accommodating a larger group in a separate area retains the roommate's privacy and quiet while it allows the patient multiple visitors.

## Tertiary Populations

- **Staff.** The chaplain has the unique position of being both an extension of the staff and at the same time an advocate for the patient. The staff serving a mixed population of patients / residents / inmates has to ensure they function within the scope and limitations of their jobs; they cannot always anticipate the particular needs of one person or group. The chaplain, while functioning in a worship or counseling capacity, can be the conduit to the staff, identifying the needs of those they serve.

  A secondary but equally important role for the chaplain is to serve as a sounding board and support for individual staff members and for groups of staff when a problem occurs on a unit, as may happen in a multicultural community. Creating such a precedent for chaplain / staff interaction allows the chaplain to return to a unit for educational purposes or to bring healing after a particularly tragic death on the floor.

- **Volunteers.** Many institutions have volunteer departments, which may function through the spiritual / pastoral care / chaplaincy office or as a stand-alone department that coordinates visits of individual and groups. Churches, synagogues, and mosques may send regular teams of visitors before the Sabbath or to perform lay duties before a Mass is read. While these visits are beneficial to patients / residents and their families, the chaplain, if a paid staff person is not charged to do so, must ensure coordination to avoid multiple visits in a single day that would overwhelm individual floors and impede the routines of daily care necessary for healing.

Volunteers also benefit from basic training for performing pastoral visits. Chaplains can teach or oversee such training and provide laypeople with a basic understanding of major issues confronting them. As an example, Jewish pastoral visitors making rounds at the New Year's celebration in the fall may startle both staff and other patients if they blow the *shofar*, the ram's horn, for ceremonial purposes. If a particular faith group has a holiday celebration that will affect others on the floor, the chaplain can make prior arrangements in anticipation of such events.

- **Co-clergy / Pastoral caregivers.** Many smaller institutions, whether in health care, long-term care, or assisted-living facilities, employ a single clergy member to service the entirety of the institution. Such chaplains need to be both versatile and self-motivated to cover the variety of religious, spiritual, and cultural segments of the organization, as they will be an important resource for patients / residents and staff.

  Larger institutions may have a department with multiple chaplains from different denominations and faith groups. There may be more chaplains reflecting a particular denomination depending on the average census of the institution, and during the "high season"—major holidays or fast days—chaplains may need to coordinate use of public spaces and ritual objects in order to service all patients and their families. Given the need for additional funding to hospital departments deemed "noncritical" for the physical welfare of patients, chaplains can call upon local churches, mosques, synagogues, and so forth to supplement necessary supplies and to supply volunteers to deal with additional hospital traffic.

## Special Populations

- **Children.** Finding ways to connect to children who are in pain or are afraid is difficult enough, especially when they are hospitalized or undergoing treatments; trying to find a way to pray with them may seem an impossible task. Younger patients are remarkably open to simple spontaneous prayers: "I'm hoping you can be home for your birthday, but if not, I hope we can make it a very special day for you right here." Children will also respond to familiar songs from their own traditions or inclusive repertoire from popular TV shows, so spending time with them alone as well as with their families will inform the chaplain's choices for appropriate songs to sing (or play on CDs or on guitar, for example).

When children are forced by circumstance to be in a hospital or rehabilitation or long-term setting, normalizing the experience is very helpful. Sitting by the bedside and watching a favorite cartoon with the child may not qualify in seminary or clinical pastoral education programs as prayer per se, but it may break down barriers between the chaplain and the patient that will be beneficial to the spiritual well-being of the child and his or her family in the long run.

- **Short-term patients.** Short-stay patients / families (e.g., emergency department) may be most in need of proffered prayer, although may not be as receptive to a chaplain's visit because of the urgency of the medical situation or anxiety before a procedure. It may be helpful to offer a general prayer of well-being that can be applicable to all faith traditions, omitting the use of specific God language.

## *Services*

---

### Regularly Scheduled Worship Services

Institutional prayer—despite taking place in a large facility—has the power to transform moments of fear, anxiety, and isolation into feelings of quiet calm and hope. Ideally, these services should be available at appropriate times, though every chaplain knows that not every ritual object, sacred space, or appropriate officiant can be made available in every instance. The following is an extremely limited guide. Please seek out clerics of each faith tradition to provide full details.

- **Roman Catholic services:** Priests are needed to hear confession and to celebrate Mass, but there are other rituals that can be fulfilled by deacons or other lay volunteers. Chaplains can contact local Catholic parishes for such volunteers or contract for clerical services. A fully visible crucifix with the body of Jesus depicted—not simply a cross—prayer books, rosary, padded kneelers for genuflecting, incense, and holy water can be made available and stored when not in use in a multifaith chapel setting.
- **Protestant services:** Protestants encompassing a number of denominations (e.g., Anglican, Lutheran, Reformed Presbyterian, Southern Baptist) tend toward a plainer sacred space, a simple cross, and more austere surroundings than their Roman Catholic counterparts. Providing patients, families, and friends with appropriate hymnals and copies of the Bible will enhance both individual and group devotion.
- **Jewish daily and Sabbath observance:** Prayer books, ideally reflecting both liberal and Orthodox denominations, should be easily accessible. In addition, prayer shawls (*tallitot*) and head coverings (*kippot / yarmulkes*) must be made available in the room or chapel set aside for public prayers. Each spiritual / pastoral care / chaplaincy department should also have electric candlesticks and small bottles of wine or grape juice to deliver when patients / residents want to observe the Sabbath in their own rooms. No rabbis are needed to lead services, though it is preferable to have someone conversant with the liturgy.
- **Islam:** Observant Muslims are required to pray five times daily as well as for the Sabbath, which is on Friday morning. Muslims require an open space, without chairs or a podium. Additionally, individual prayer rugs and copies of their holy book, the Qur'an, should be readily available on request.

## Memorial Services

As difficult as it is to lose a loved one, the circle of pain and sadness can encompass family and staff as well. When a patient or resident is beloved by those who have cared for him or her, chaplains can offer brief memorial services or moments of personal reflection to doctors, nurses, and other caregivers to acknowledge the loss and allow them to move forward as they care for other patients.

Such losses are compounded when an infant or child dies, and memorial services that include both family and staff can be particularly comforting when the teamwork that had been established to heal the child is recognized.

## Religious Observances

- **Multifaith calendaring:** No single chaplain can be expected to know every major celebration or solemn day for every religion, so chaplains responsible for serving a multifaith community should use a multifaith website (e.g., www.interfaithcalendar.org) at the start of each calendar year.
- **Multifaith healing service:** While each faith tradition may have individual and unique types of healing services, asking members of the clergy from different faith traditions to participate in an ecumenical or multifaith service can benefit all the institution's population: administrative have staff, medical staff, support staff, patients, residents, and their families. See Figure 33.1 for a sample interfaith service.
- **Pastoral Care Week:** Chaplains are usually the quiet "go-to" people who are called to serve in regular, chronic, and emergency situations. During Pastoral Care Week, celebrated since 1985, chaplains and pastoral caregivers are provided the chance to "share their story and to celebrate various ministries" (http://pastoralcareweek.org/History.aspx). The purpose of establishing this week, usually at the beginning of October, was to promote professional chaplaincy, to encourage best practices for all chaplains, to show gratitude to professional chaplains, and to recognize the institutions that have supported professional chaplaincy. Creating a celebratory meal with a day of specialized learning for chaplains, displaying materials outlining the observance of Pastoral Care Week, and offering staff in-services to clarify the finer points of serving multifaith communities are all appropriate activities to acknowledge this festive time.

## SAMPLE INTERFAITH MEMORIAL SERVICE ORDER OF SERVICE

### The Light of Comfort

Chaplain: We have come here to share our grief and give strength and comfort to one another.

All: We come together as fellow travelers, each of us at different points along the pathway called grief.

Chaplain: We come to honor and remember all those whom we loved and who have died recently. We come seeking comfort and we come to celebrate life.

All: We come seeking courage, to survive this journey of grief, to find new ways of living and going forth.

Chaplain: God understands our feelings, this grief. God's unfailing love and mercy still continue, as fresh as the morning, as sure as the sunrise. We may not see the sun today, yet its rays will warm us again.

All: Guide us, O God, that today's pain, sorrow, and death will lead us to comfort, hope, and new life.

### Words for It

*By Julia Cameron*

I wish I could take language
And fold it like cool, moist rags.
I would lay words on your forehead.
I would wrap words on your wrist.
"There, there," my words would say—
Or something better.
I would ask them to murmur,
"Hush" and "Shh, shhh, it's all right."
I would ask them to hold you all night.
I wish I could take language
And daub and soothe and cool
Where fever blisters and burns,
Where fever turns yourself against you.
I wish I could take language
And heal the words that were the wounds
You have no names for.



*Figure 33.1*

## SAMPLE INTERFAITH MEMORIAL SERVICE
(continued)

**Gathered Prayer**

*By Rev. Joan Hemenway*

God, Maker of mystery and miracle, settle our souls down
into Your abiding light as we pray together.
Make us each aware of ourselves:
the intricate weave of our lives,
the loose strands of forgotten loves,
the soft texture of forgiven sins,
the bright colors of shared joy,
the winding and unwinding of time and the stars.
Yes, You are the Mystery and the Miracle and the Maker.
Bless our life's fabric
and make it flexible and iridescent and strong.

O God, Healer of hurts and hates,
hold us close to Your forgiving heart,
Make us each aware of the troubles of others:
stiff lips protecting a broken heart,
eyes glazed by the pain of loneliness,
hands made cold by the fear of rejection,
bodies muted by too much sadness.
Help us to venture beyond the comfortable and familiar,
to welcome strangers,
to abandon old people-prejudices
for the joy of new people-discoveries …
Yes, You are the Healer and the Forgiver.
Bless our brokenness and make of it a new wholeness
and a new holiness.

*Figure 33.1 (continued)*

## SAMPLE INTERFAITH MEMORIAL SERVICE
(continued)

Today, we remember those we love who have died:

________________________________________

### A Litany of Remembrance

*By Rabbi Sylvan Kamens and Rabbi Jack Riemer*

Reader: In the rising of the sun and in its going down, we remember them.

All: In the blowing of the wind and chill of winter, we remember them.

Reader: In the opening of buds and in the rebirth of spring, we remember them.

All: In the blue sky and the warmth of summer, we remember them.

Reader: In the rustling of leaves and in the beauty of autumn, we remember them.

All: At the beginning of the year and when it ends, we remember them.

Reader: When we are weary and in need of strength, we remember them.

All: When we are lost and sick at heart, we remember them.

Reader: When we have joys we yearn to share, we remember them.

All: As long as we live our memories will live on, as we will remember them!

### Benediction

*By Father Arnoldo Pangrazzi*

Receive, O God, our prayers together with our tears, our broken plans, and our fears. Remind us again that sorrow is a part of life and loving with all its risks. Help us to understand that You did not promise a life without pain or challenge, but You did promise to be with us, to be light in times of darkness, a caring and steady support as we walk through our valleys. Help us gain wisdom through our suffering, and give us patience and time to work through our feelings. Help us discover the inner resources that are there deep within us. Guide us into the future, as our grief is transformed into compassion, and our hurt into help and hope for others, that in the dawn of memory we will find peace.



*Figure 33.1 (continued)*

## Secular Observances

- **Memorial Day:** In an institution, a prayerful Memorial Day can have deeper meaning than in the general community, where parades and memorials are interspersed with consumerism. This day can be recognized with a candle-lighting service, with appropriate quiet music, that would include individuals who have lost loved ones to illness as well as to military interventions.
- **Veterans Day:** Such remembrances and tributes can be expected in a Veterans Administration institution, but every institution can mark the day with a ceremony including flags, a moment of quiet, and patriotic music. Readings can be interspersed with names (see Figure 33.2).
- **Martin Luther King Day:** As Reverend King was dedicated to nonviolent activism in the civil rights movement, planning activities that include opportunities for volunteering in the community, marking the day as a celebration of King's vision, promoting a short essay contest among staff members and publishing them in-house, and inviting prominent civil rights activists to speak during a short multifaith prayer service can bring new meaning to the day. Chaplains might also invite area schools to participate with a children's choir or by displaying pictures depicting their perspectives of King's ideals.
- **Thanksgiving:** Thanksgiving, because it is most associated with home celebrations, can be the most difficult to promote in an institution but can be achieved if the chaplain or pastoral care director is willing to include participation from many demographics within its walls. The chaplain also needs to be sensitive to those for whom giving thanks may be difficult due to circumstance: a current health crisis, a patient isolated from family or bereft of family, or staff who would rather be home with their own loved ones than working on the fourth Thursday in November. Acknowledging those issues rather than dismissing them can transform an otherwise miserable holiday into one that provides meaning.

## A PRAYER FOR VETERANS DAY

*By Rabbi Dr. Shira Stern, MHL, DMin, BCJC*

Dear God, Support and Strength of those who serve
And of those who await their return,
Remind us to acknowledge their sacrifices:
  Of time
    Of risk
      Of hardship
        Of devotion
          Of courage
Above all, encourage us to recognize their pride.

Help those who fight and protect and serve,
Hold close those whose lives are made empty by their absence.
Watch over the men and women who have been touched by war
  Who become leaders on the field
  Who become patients in the wards
  Who become veterans in times of peace
And help us honor those who lie in quiet, green places for eternity.

Grant wisdom and courage to those in command,
In our government and on front lines,
And may their efforts lead us to peace once more.

For those who are now in service
  *We offer our prayers*
For those who have served and returned
  *We offer our gratitude*
For those who have given their all
  *We offer our tears*
For all of us who gather to remember
  *We offer our voices together*

*Figure 33.2*

While Thanksgiving has particular religious origins, it also lends itself to community-wide prayer in an interfaith setting. A chaplain might invite members of his or her own pastoral care department or volunteer clergy who provide services to patients or residents to participate in a prayer service in conjunction with a food collection to be donated to a local food bank.

## *Disaster or Trauma Response*

Within the middle of every disaster, survivors and families seek emotional, psychological, and spiritual comfort at the same time, but not in the same fashion. Even in largely homogeneous communities, such as a localized disaster in a relatively isolated area, chaplains can be faced with a variety of spiritual needs that defy a cookie-cutter response. Being prepared in advance for such an eventuality will ensure that the spiritual care offered is the most effective and deliverable.

Local disasters (e.g., flood, earthquake, hurricane) may affect a more homogeneous population, especially in isolated areas, but no assumptions should be made. In a multicultural setting, the chaplain should connect immediately with local clergy to help determine liturgical needs—memorial services, masses, daily prayers, or healing services—that the chaplain's institution can provide.

National disasters require greater coordination with the major institution in charge of emergency response; doing so eliminates duplication of services or any one faith group dominating spiritual care offered to survivors and / or their families. Having adequate representation of clergy from as many faith groups as possible may reduce the feelings of isolation and disorientation that prevail in the immediate aftermath of a larger disaster.

## *Final Words*

Prayer in multifaith institutions can be daunting. Not only is the chaplain faced with multiple needs reflected by the population of the institution, but she or he must also recognize the particular culture of that institution:

- Does the administration encourage community expressions of holidays?

- Is there a commitment to facilitating individual worship or only major community observances?
- Does the institution have a tradition that cannot be changed even if it is broken?
- Does the institution reward creativity among its departments, including its pastoral care department?

Chaplains working to provide good spiritual care need not do so alone. There are ample resources, in libraries, seminaries, professional chaplaincy organizations, and on the Internet, to enhance and inform the chaplain's work.

## Further Reading

Evans, Abigail Rian. *Healing Liturgies for the Seasons of Life*. Louisville, KY: Westminster John Knox Press, 2004.

Moen, Larry. *Meditations for Healing*. Lithia Springs, GA: World Tree Press, 1998.

Weintraub, Simkha Y. *Healing of Soul, Healing of Body*. Woodstock, VT: Jewish Lights Publishing, 1994.

Weintraub, Simkha Y., and Aaron Lever. *Guide Me Along the Way: A Jewish Spiritual Companion for Surgery*. New York: National Center for Jewish Healing, 2001.

## Resources

Sample interfaith service: www.nami.org/MSTemplate.cfm?Section=Interfaith_Worship_Service&Site=FaithNet_NAMI&Template=/ContentManagement/HTMLDisplay.cfm&ContentID=32398

Interfaith Calendar: www.interfaithcalendar.org

## About the Contributor

**Rabbi Dr. Shira Stern, MHL, DMin, BCJC,** is a past president of and certified through the National Association of Jewish Chaplains and currently chairs the Ethics Committee. She has served on the CCAR Board of Trustees as the vice president for member services. She currently has a private pastoral counseling practice in Marlboro, New Jersey, and serves Temple Rodeph Torah of Marlboro, New Jersey, as its educator. Previously, she was the director of community chaplaincy of Middlesex County, New Jersey, and director of the Jewish Institute for Pastoral Care, part of the HealthCare Chaplaincy, providing programs for rabbinic and cantorial students, chaplains, and clergy in the field. She was trained by the Red Cross to serve on the SAIR team—Spiritual Air

Incident Response Team (now the Critical Incident Response Team)—and worked for four months at the Liberty State Park Family Assistance Center in the aftermath of 9/11. Her selected works include "Visions of an Alternative Rabbinate," *CCAR Journal*, and "Healing Muses: Music as Spiritual Therapy," *Jewish Relational Care A to Z.*

# Index

# AVAILABLE FROM BETTER BOOKSTORES. TRY YOUR BOOKSTORE FIRST.

## *Inspiration*

**The Rebirthing of God**
Christianity's Struggle for New Beginnings
*By John Philip Newell*
Drawing on modern prophets from East and West, and using the holy island of Iona as an icon of new beginnings, Celtic poet, peacemaker and scholar John Philip Newell dares us to imagine a new birth from deep within Christianity, a fresh stirring of the Spirit.
6 x 9, 160 pp, HC, 978-1-59473-542-4 **$19.99**

**Finding God Beyond Religion:** A Guide for Skeptics, Agnostics & Unorthodox Believers Inside & Outside the Church
*By Tom Stella; Foreword by The Rev. Canon Marianne Wells Borg*
Reinterprets traditional religious teachings central to the Christian faith for people who have outgrown the beliefs and devotional practices that once made sense to them.
6 x 9, 160 pp, Quality PB, 978-1-59473-485-4 **$16.99**

**Fully Awake and Truly Alive:** Spiritual Practices to Nurture Your Soul
*By Rev. Jane E. Vennard; Foreword by Rami Shapiro*
Illustrates the joys and frustrations of spiritual practice, offers insights from various religious traditions and provides exercises and meditations to help us become more fully alive.
6 x 9, 208 pp, Quality PB, 978-1-59473-473-1 **$16.99**

**Journeys of Simplicity:** Traveling Light with Thomas Merton, Bashō, Edward Abbey, Annie Dillard & Others *By Philip Harnden*
Invites you to consider a more graceful way of traveling through life. PB includes journal pages to help you get started on your own spiritual journey.
5 x 7¼, 144 pp, Quality PB, 978-1-59473-181-5 **$12.99**
5 x 7¼, 128 pp, HC, 978-1-893361-76-8 **$16.95**

**Perennial Wisdom for the Spiritually Independent**
Sacred Teachings—Annotated & Explained
*Annotation by Rami Shapiro; Foreword by Richard Rohr*
Weaves sacred texts and teachings from the world's major religions into a coherent exploration of the five core questions at the heart of every religion's search.
5½ x 8½, 336 pp, Quality PB Original, 978-1-59473-515-8 **$16.99**

**Saving Civility:** 52 Ways to Tame Rude, Crude & Attitude for a Polite Planet
*By Sara Hacala*
Provides fifty-two practical ways you can reverse the course of incivility and make the world a more enriching, pleasant place to live.
6 x 9, 240 pp, Quality PB, 978-1-59473-314-7 **$16.99**

**Spiritually Healthy Divorce:** Navigating Disruption with Insight & Hope
*By Carolyne Call*
A spiritual map to help you move through the twists and turns of divorce.
6 x 9, 224 pp, Quality PB, 978-1-59473-288-1 **$16.99**

*Or phone, fax, mail or email to:* SKYLIGHT PATHS **Publishing**
Sunset Farm Offices, Route 4 • P.O. Box 237 • Woodstock, Vermont 05091
Tel: (802) 457-4000 • Fax: (802) 457-4004 • www.skylightpaths.com
***Credit card orders:*** (800) 962-4544 (8:30AM–5:30PM EST Monday–Friday)
*Generous discounts on quantity orders. SATISFACTION GUARANTEED. Prices subject to change.*

# *Resources for Prayer & Healing*

**The Sacred Art of Listening**
Forty Reflections for Cultivating a Spiritual Practice
*by Kay Lindahl; Illus. by Amy Schnapper*
8 x 8, 160 pp, b/w illus., Quality PB, 978-1-893361-44-7 **$16.99**

**Practicing the Sacred Art of Listening**
A Guide to Enrich Your Relationships and Kindle Your Spiritual Life
*by Kay Lindahl* 8 x 8, 176 pp, Quality PB, 978-1-893361-85-0 **$18.99**

**The Sacred Art of Forgiveness**
Forgiving Ourselves and Others through God's Grace
*by Marcia Ford* 8 x 8, 176 pp, Quality PB, 978-1-59473-175-4 **$18.99**

**The Sacred Art of Lovingkindness:** Preparing to Practice
*by Rabbi Rami Shapiro; Foreword by Marcia Ford*
5½ x 8½, 176 pp, Quality PB, 978-1-59473-151-8 **$16.99**

**Recovery—The Sacred Art:** The Twelve Steps as Spiritual Practice
*by Rami Shapiro; Foreword by Joan Borysenko, PhD*
Deepen your capacity to live free from addiction—and from self and selfishness.
5½ x 8½, 240 pp, Quality PB, 978-1-59473-259-1 **$16.99**

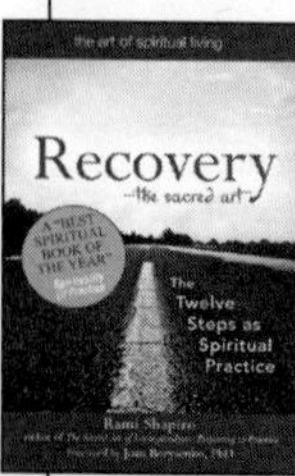


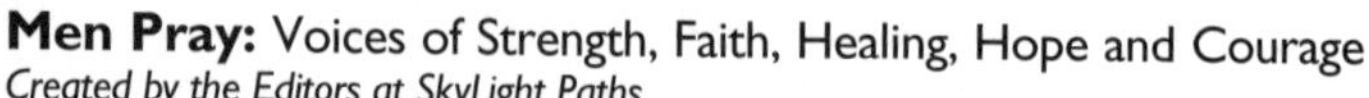
**Men Pray:** Voices of Strength, Faith, Healing, Hope and Courage
*Created by the Editors at SkyLight Paths*
Celebrates the rich variety of ways men around the world have called out to the divine—with words of joy, praise, gratitude, wonder, petition and even anger—from the ancient world up to our own day.
5 x 7¼, 192 pp, HC, 978-1-59473-395-6 **$16.99**

**Women of Color Pray:** Voices of Strength, Faith, Healing, Hope and Courage
*Edited and with Introductions by Christal M. Jackson*
Through these prayers, poetry, lyrics, meditations and affirmations, you will share in the strong and undeniable connection women of color share with God.
5 x 7¼, 208 pp, Quality PB, 978-1-59473-077-1 **$15.99**

**Secrets of Prayer:** A Multifaith Guide to Creating Personal Prayer in Your Life *by Nancy Corcoran, CSJ*
This compelling, multifaith guidebook offers you companionship and encouragement on the journey to a healthy prayer life. 6 x 9, 160 pp, Quality PB, 978-1-59473-215-7 **$16.99**

**Finding Grace at the Center, 3rd Edition**
The Beginning of Centering Prayer
*by M. Basil Pennington, OCSO, with Thomas Keating, OCSO, and Thomas E. Clarke, SJ; Foreword by Rev. Cynthia Bourgeault, PhD*
A practical guide to a simple and beautiful form of meditative prayer.
5 x 7¼,128 pp, Quality PB, 978-1-59473-182-2 **$12.99**

## *(Books from Jewish Lights Publishing, SkyLight Paths' sister imprint)*

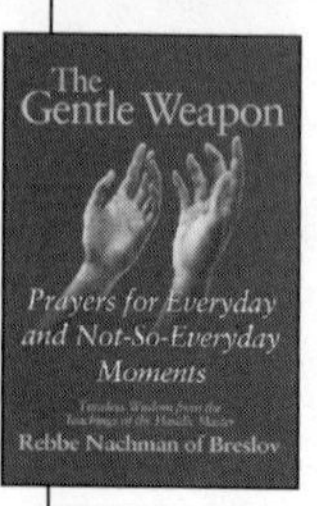


**The Gentle Weapon:** Prayers for Everyday and Not-So-Everyday Moments—Timeless Wisdom from the Teachings of the Hasidic Master, Rebbe Nachman of Breslov
*Adapted by Moshe Mykoff and S. C. Mizrahi, together with the Breslov Research Institute*
4 x 6, 144 pp, Deluxe PB w/ flaps, 978-1-58023-022-3 **$9.99**

**Healing of Soul, Healing of Body:** Spiritual Leaders Unfold the Strength & Solace in Psalms *Edited by Rabbi Simkha Y. Weintraub, LCSW*
6 x 9, 128 pp, 2-color illus. text, Quality PB, 978-1-879045-31-6 **$16.99**

**Facing Illness, Finding God:** How Judaism Can Help You and Caregivers Cope When Body or Spirit Fails *By Rabbi Joseph B. Meszler*
Will help you find spiritual strength for healing amid the fear, pain and chaos of illness. 6 x 9, 208 pp, Quality PB, 978-1-58023-423-8 **$16.99**

# Professional Spiritual & Pastoral Care Resources

**College & University Chaplaincy in the 21st Century**
A Multifaith Look at the Practice of Ministry on Campuses across America
*Edited by The Rev. Dr. Lucy Forster-Smith*
Examines experiences and perspectives that arise at the intersection of religious practice, distinct campus culture, student counseling, and the challenges of the secular context of today's college or university campus.
6 x 9, 368 pp, HC, 978-1-59473-516-5 **$40.00**

**Spiritual Guidance across Religions:** A Sourcebook for Spiritual Directors and Other Professionals Providing Counsel to People of Differing Faith Traditions *Edited by Rabbi Stephen B. Roberts, MBA, MHL, BCJC*
This comprehensive professional resource offers valuable information for providing spiritual guidance to people from a wide variety of faith traditions. Covers the world's major faith traditions as well as interfaith, blended and independent approaches to spirituality.
6 x 9, 400 pp, HC, 978-1-59473-546-2 **$50.00**

**Disaster Spiritual Care**
Practical Clergy Responses to Community, Regional and National Tragedy
*Edited by Rabbi Stephen B. Roberts, BCJC, and Rev. Willard W.C. Ashley, Sr., DMin, DH*
The definitive guidebook for counseling not only the victims of disaster but also the clergy and caregivers who are called to service in the wake of crisis.
6 x 9, 384 pp, HC, 978-1-59473-240-9 **$50.00**

**Learning to Lead:** Lessons in Leadership for People of Faith
*Edited by Rev. Williard W.C. Ashley Sr., MDiv, DMin, DH*
In this multifaith, cross-cultural and comprehensive resource for both clergy and lay persons, contributors who are experts in the field explore how to engage spiritual leaders and teach them how to bring healing, faith, justice and support to communities and congregations.
6 x 9, 384 pp, HC, 978-1-59473-432-8 **$40.00**

**How to Be a Perfect Stranger, 5th Edition**
The Essential Religious Etiquette Handbook
*Edited by Stuart M. Matlins and Arthur J. Magida*
The indispensable guidebook to help the well-meaning guest when visiting other people's religious ceremonies. Covers: **African American Methodist Churches • Assemblies of God • Bahá'í Faith • Baptist • Buddhist • Christian Church (Disciples of Christ) • Christian Science (Church of Christ, Scientist) • Churches of Christ • Episcopalian and Anglican • Hindu • Islam • Jehovah's Witnesses • Jewish • Lutheran • Mennonite/Amish • Methodist • Mormon (Church of Jesus Christ of Latter-day Saints) • Native American/First Nations • Orthodox Churches • Pentecostal Church of God • Presbyterian • Quaker (Religious Society of Friends) • Reformed Church in America/Canada • Roman Catholic • Seventh-day Adventist • Sikh • Unitarian Universalist • United Church of Canada • United Church of Christ**
6 x 9, 432 pp, Quality PB, 978-1-59473-294-2 **$19.99**
"The things Miss Manners forgot to tell us about religion."
—*Los Angeles Times*

**The Perfect Stranger's Guide to Funerals and Grieving Practices**
A Guide to Etiquette in Other People's Religious Ceremonies
*Edited by Stuart M. Matlins* 6 x 9, 240 pp, Quality PB, 978-1-893361-20-1 **$16.95**

**Jewish Pastoral Care, 2nd Edition:** A Practical Handbook from Traditional & Contemporary Sources *Edited by Rabbi Dayle A. Friedman, MSW, MAJCS, BCC*
6 x 9, 528 pp, Quality PB, 978-1-58023-427-6 **$35.00**
*(A book from Jewish Lights, SkyLight Paths' sister imprint)*

**Caresharing:** A Reciprocal Approach to Caregiving and Care Receiving in the Complexities of Aging, Illness or Disability *By Marty Richards*
6 x 9, 256 pp, Quality PB, 978-1-59473-286-7 **$16.99**; HC, 978-1-59473-247-8 **$24.99**

**InterActive Faith:** The Essential Interreligious Community-Building Handbook
*Edited by Rev. Bud Heckman with Rori Picker Neiss*
6 x 9, 304 pp, Quality PB, 978-1-59473-273-7 **$16.99**; HC, 978-1-59473-237-9 **$29.99**